The Myths of Narasiṁha and Vāmana

SUNY Series in Hindu Studies

Wendy Doniger

The Myths of Narasiṁha and Vāmana

Two Avatars in Cosmological Perspective

Deborah A. Soifer

STATE UNIVERSITY OF NEW YORK PRESS

Production by Ruth East
Marketing by Dana E. Yanulavich

Published by
State University of New York Press, Albany

Printed in the United States of America

For information, address the State University of New York Press,
State University Plaza, Albany, NY 12246

Library of Congress Cataloging-in-Publication Data

Soifer, Deborah A., 1950-
The myths of Narasiṁha and Vāmana : two avatars in cosmological
perspective / Deborah A. Soifer.
p. cm. — (SUNY series in Hinduism)
Includes bibliographical references and index.
ISBN 0-7914-0799-3 (hard : alk. paper). — ISBN 0-7914-0800-0
(pbk. : alk. paper)
1. Narasiṁha (Hindu deity) 2. Vāmana (Hindu
deity) 3. Cosmology.
Hindu. I. Title. II. Series.
BL1225.N35S65 1991
294.5′2113—dc20 90-21260
CIP

10 9 8 7 6 5 4 3 2 1

To

Alf Hiltebeitel, Mircea Eliade, and Hans van Buitenen—
for their precious guidance and inspiration

Contents

List of Figures

Acknowledgments

Because this project has a long history, it benefitted from the counsel and support of many. In some sense, its beginning coincided with the birth of my interest in Asian religions, to which Alf Hiltebeitel was seminal. His influence and inspiration have remained strong since that beginning. During the years of research and translation in Chicago, Frank Reynolds provided invaluable insight and guidance; and Tony Yu, sustained support and interest. The late Hans van Buitenen spent countless hours patiently working with me on the myth translations.

In Washington, D.C., Saudamini Deshmukh oversaw the completion of the translations with competence and grace. My colleague Randy Kloetzli shared his understanding of Buddhist cosmology in many stimulating discussions, as well as lending me moral support.

In the final phase of preparing this work for publication, Bowdoin College has aided me by providing secretarial and student assistant services. I am indebted to Louise Caron for her capable and good-humored handling of the manuscript and to my delightful student Tina Rodfong for proofreading the translations. Jane Moss of Colby College helped with French translation, as did Peter Nutting of China for German.

In the final stage of revision, Paul Courtright offered helpful suggestions, and inspiration through his beautiful book on Gaṇeśa. In all phases of creating this book, the works of Wendy Doniger have been an unending source of detailed information, common sense, and wisdom.

The continued interest in religion and especially myth I have found in my students over the years has helped to sustain my sometimes fragile belief that research such as this is worthwhile. The sustained enthusiasm for and fascination with myth on the part of my own children, Dakota and Tyler, confirms my strong conviction that myth is still a vital and necessary expression of life.

To my father, who was sure I would shave my head and dance in the street, and my late mother, who knew I wouldn't, I express gratitude for the unique incentive their concerns provided.

And foremost, from the beginning of this project to its completion, my husband, Johnny, has maintained unbroken support and unwavering faith in my ability to carry out the task. I cannot imagine having brought this work to completion without his patience with and confidence in me.

A Note on Translations and Abbreviations

The Narasiṁha and Vāmana myths found in the *Brahmāṇḍa Purāṇa, Brahmā Purāṇa, Viṣṇudharmottara Purāṇa, Matsya Purāṇa, Padma Purāṇa, Skanda Purāṇa, Bhaviṣya Purāṇa, Nārada Purāṇa*, and *Vāyu Purāṇa* are translated by the author and appear as apprendices to this book. Translations of all other Narasiṁha and Vāmana myths, as well as other Sanskrit sources, are as noted in the bibliography.

List of Abbreviations

AB	Aitareya Brāhmaṇa
JB	Jaiminīya Brāhmaṇa
Kaus.B.	Kauśītaki Brāḥmaṇa
MS	Maitrāyanī Saṁhitā
PB	Pañcaviṁśa Brāhmaṇa
RV	ṚgVeda
ŚB	Śatapatha Brāhmaṇa
Tait.A.	Taittirīya Āraṇyaka
TB	Taittirīya Brāhmaṇa
TS	Taittirīya Saṁhitā
VS	Vājaseneyi Saṁhitā
Mbh.	Mahābhārata
Ram.	Rāmāyaṇa
HV	Harivaṁśa
A.P.	Agni Purāṇa
Br.P.	Brahmā Purāṇa
Brmḍa.P.	Brahmāṇḍa Purāna
Bhg.P.	Bhāgavata Purāṇa

Bh.P.	Bhaviṣya Purāṇa
L.P.	Liṅga Purāṇa
K.P.	Kūrma Purāṇa
M.P.	Matsya Purāṇa
N.P.	Nārada Purāṇa
P.P.	Padma Purāṇa
S.P.	Śiva Purāṇa
Sk.P.	Skanda Purāṇa
V.P.	Vāyu Purāṇa
Vi.P.	Viṣṇu Purāṇa
Vām.P.	Vāmana Purāṇa
Vdh.P.	Viṣṇudharmottara Purāṇa
ABORI	Annals of the Bhandarkar Oriental Research Institute
BEFEO	Bulletin d'École Française d'Extrême Orient
EMH	"Études de mythologie hindoue"
EPHE	École Pratique des hautes études
ERE	Encyclopedia of Religion and Ethics
ESS	Encyclopedia of Social Sciences
HRJ	History of Religions Journal
IHQ	Indian Historical Quarterly
JAOS	Journal of the American Oriental Society
JRAS	Journal of the Royal Asiatic Society
SBE	Sacred Books of the East
WZKSO	Weiner Zeitschrift für die Kunde Sud-und Ostasiens

①

Introduction

Myth creates an often paradoxical world of meaning through its unique use of language, through a combination of familiar themes yoked to inventive metaphor, of uncommon fantasy clothed in ordinary words; it is the junction of the familiar and strange, the "cosmic map of the intersecting territories of reality and fantasy."[1] Yet as much as it reveals to us, even more is eclipsed by what myth suggests but conceals; the diverse and innumerable ideas and issues it gives rise to attest to myth's wellspring nature as well as its ultimate value.

Our study of Vāmana and Narasiṁha is foremost an exploration into the world of myth; into the ways in which it uses language, into its interconnection with other forms of conceptualization and expression, into the questions it raises as it unravels a vision of life.

> Long ago, in the Kṛta Yuga, the mighty demon Hiraṇyakaśipu performed severe austerities. After 11,000 years of fasting head down and observing a vow of silence, he became tranquil. Brahmā, pleased with the demon's tapas, arrived at his side and granted Hiraṇyakaśipu a boon. "Whatever you desire, that you shall have." Hiraṇyakaśipu replied, "Inviolability from all beings, and immortality. Neither gods nor men nor beasts may kill me. Neither by arrows nor missiles, nor by wet nor dry, neither

by night nor by day may I be slain. I will become the sun and moon, wind, fire, and rain, the god of all." Brahmā said, "So be it," and returned to Vairāja, his own abode.

Having heard the granting of that boon, all the gods, celestials, and sages approached Grandfather Brahmā. "Because of that boon the demon will kill us! Please find a way to bring about his death." Brahmā replied, "The fruit of tapas must be obtained. At the end of the demon's tapas, Viṣṇu shall become his conqueror."

Meanwhile Hiraṇyakaśipu, arrogant from the granting of the boon, oppressed the triple world. He harassed illustrious sages in their hermitages, he vanquished the gods in heaven and made the demons recipients of the sacrificial shares. The gods sought shelter with Lord Viṣṇu, and he promised them a swift end to Hiraṇyakaśipu's reign.

Having given his word, the Blessed One went to the abode of the demon Hiraṇyakaśipu at dusk. Having made his form half man and half lion, he shone like a golden mountain adorned by a mass of flames. His powerful body looked like burning coals, and his tongue quivered like the lightning of the cloud at the destruction of the world.

Shattering the assembly hall and slaying the demon army, Viṣṇu himself, raging man-lion, seized Hiraṇyakaśipu and, swiftly placing him upon his lap, tore open the demon's chest with his claws, leaving him lifeless.

Having worshiped Viṣṇu Narasiṁha, the gods together with Indra returned to heaven, and that man-lion form of the god vanished.

The son of Hiraṇyakaśipu was Prahlāda, and his son, Virocana. Mighty Bali, son of Virocana, endowed with great strength, conquered all the earth and set his sights on heaven. That righteous ruler, having vanquished Indra, gained sovereignty over the triple world. Under his reign, the earth produced crops without cultivation. People, following their caste duties, were happy and long-lived, and there was no war between the gods and demons.

However, ousted from heaven and deprived of the shares of the sacrifice, Indra and the gods sought refuge in Viṣṇu. Out of concern for their welfare, the Blessed One told the gods this. "After some time, I shall be born from Aditi, mother of the gods, to deceive Bali and win back the triple world. Now calm yourselves."

In time, and after performing severe austerities, Aditi gave birth to Viṣṇu in the form of Vāmana, the dwarf. The gods conferred on him all the accoutrements of a brahmin; staff, water jar, sacred thread, and so on. All these were given to Vāmana in his upanáyana ceremony.

At this time, Bali was preparing for the great horse sacrifice, to ensure his universal sovereignty. Vāmana, arriving at that sacrifice, was duly greeted and honored. Despite the warnings of his priest, Śukra, who suspected foul play, Bali offered this brahmin dwarf a gift. "I am fortunate! This lord of sacrifice visits my sacrifice. Pray, choose a gift. Whatever you desire, I will grant it to you." To this generous offer the dwarf modestly replied," I have no need of wealth. Please give me three steps of land for my own sacrificial ground."

Bali readily consented, and as he poured the water into Vāmana's hands, the dwarf grew to cosmic proportions, like Puruṣa himself. Striding thrice, he covered earth, atmosphere, and heaven with his steps, reclaiming the triple world on behalf of the gods. Thus vanquished, Bali was sent back to the netherworlds, and Viṣṇu placed Indra on the throne of heaven once again.

These myths of Viṣṇu as Narasiṁha and Vāmana present two strikingly different visions of one deity. Narasiṁha, half man and half lion, storms the palace of the demon Hiranyakaśipu and, surrounded by images and omens of cataclysmic destruction, rips the demon apart with his claws. Vāmana, the dwarf priest, respectfully approaches the demon Bali at his sacrifice, modestly requests three steps of land so that he, too, may have sacrificial ground, and strides over the universe instead, displaying his all-encompassing, beneficent form.

As dissimilar as these figures appear, at the same time we sense something similar about them and their myths. Both descend to confront similar crises—a demon threatening the welfare and stability of the world—and both resolve the crisis through means that are not exactly straightforward. Although Narasiṁha *acts* directly, his nature is circumventive; he slips through the loopholes in the conditions of Hiraṇyakaśipu's boon by creating a form, coming at a time, and employing a "weapon"—all of which do not violate the conditions of the pact. Vāmana is cunning and deceptive, concealing his pervasive, cosmic size within a diminutive form while he begs a boon from the unsuspecting demon. How are we to understand these forms of one deity, markedly dissimilar but somehow alike? And how do multiple forms relate to the unity of the god as Viṣṇu, one of Hinduism's most popular deities, as evidenced in mythology, iconography, and temple and festival worship for over a millennium?

Let us draw this circle of inquiry wider. The man-lion and dwarf are but two of Viṣṇu's manifestations. The myths tell of his appearances in the theriomorphic forms of a fish, tortoise, and boar. He appears on earth as the cowherding lord Kṛṣṇa and the genocidal Paraśurāma, annihilator of the kṣatriya caste. He becomes noble Rāma, beloved hero of the Indian epic *Rāmāyaṇa*, he descends as the Buddha, and as Kalkin, herald of the apocalypse, he will usher in the eschaton atop a white steed.

These ten manifestations of Viṣṇu, known primarily (but not exclusively) through their myths, are the avatāras of the deity. This term (from the Sanskrit root tṛ, "cross over," and prefix ava, "downward"), meaning to cross downward or descend, refers both to the literal descent of Viṣṇu from the highest celestial abode to the earthly domain and to the metaphysical descent from Viṣṇu's complete and transcendent form to a partial, material manifestation.

The corpus of myths of Viṣṇu's avatāras raises many questions. Why, out of the limitless range of possibilities, are the ten figures just enumerated accepted by tradition as the "classical list?" Why does Viṣṇu appear as a tortoise, but not an elephant? What is the intentionality of choice behind a man-lion avatāra? Is there a significance to the *order* in which the avatāras appear? As a deity with multiple forms, is Viṣṇu in his avatāric forms a mythological expression of a unity-in-diversity theology, or is this just another example of what one Indologist wryly called "Vaiṣṇava imperialism"[2]; that is, the taking over of any religious expression or mythological manifestation to view it as derivative of or related to Viṣṇu?

These issues, among others, claimed the attention of scholars who have examined the avatāras from a variety of perspectives. The quasi-evolutionary progression of the avatāras from fish to anthropomorphic deity has been noted[3] and understood as an allegory for the "psychophysical evolution"[4] of moral and spiritual growth.[5] The use of the loaded term *incarnation* as the English equivalent of *avatāra* prompted several scholars to look comparatively at the two forms in Hindu and Western religious traditions.[6] Such an approach demonstrates the danger of translating Hindu (or any non-Eurocentric) concepts into Christian terminology and highlights the differences and incomparability of the two traditions on this point, rather than uphold any valid similarities.

By default, studies such as Parrinder's *Avatar and Incarnation* indicate that the avatāra is most deeply rooted in mythology and exhibits little significance as a theological construct. This has been substantiated by those who have linked the avatāra with the propensity toward ideas of divine multiplicity or cosmic repetition within Indian traditions of thought,[7] and more particularly by the work of Jan Gonda[8] as well as those who have contributed valuable studies of single avatāras or avatāra myths.[9]

Although the relationship between a theology of multiple forms and the stories of Viṣṇu's avatāras appears to have been of little concern to the mythographers themselves, questions of why, for example, a boar avatāra but not a horse avatāra, of intentionality of choice, are in some sense answered by the myths themselves, by the resonances these ten figures have with the whole of Hindu culture, with the "world" these figures evoke, both on universally symbolic and culturally specific levels. The relationship *between* avatāras has been examined only summarily on a general level[10] but not specifically, as we will do in looking at Narasiṁha and Vāmana as a pair as well as individually.

It will be our purpose, in the ensuing chapters, to address some of the questions raised here, by way of observing these two avatāras within their mythic milieu; not just the avatāras in their own stories, but their relationship to the cosmos as it is understood and delineated within the mythological corpus; the universe that Viṣṇu, as avatāra, descends through and, as supreme deity, that he pervades.

The Literary Context

Although we have presented summaries of both myths by way of introduction, in actuality the myths examined here are found in many versions, scattered chronologically and geographically throughout India. The myths under consideration are found in the two Sanskrit epics, *Mahābhārata* and *Rāmāyaṇa*, and in the eighteen Purāṇas; in total, eighteen versions of the Narasiṁha myth, and thirty of the Vāmana.

To understand the differences between the versions of each myth, the unique and problematic nature of the Purāṇas as a genre should be briefly noted. As the written retellings of fluid oral traditions, the Purāṇas are stratified by interpolations that reflect sectarian allegiances, temple and pilgrimage site-related data, as well as caste-specific concerns. These interpolations further complicate an already difficult situation for attempting to delineate a chronology for these texts. As our approach to the myths is thematic and motific rather than historical, it can suffice to outline broadly the chronological boundaries of our texts.[11] The dates for the composition of the *Mahābhārata,* also a highly interpolated text, are commonly accepted as 400 BC–400 AD, and the *Rāmāyaṇa,* 200 BC–200 AD. The earliest Purāṇas[12] can be dated at approximately 300–500 AD, and the latest[13] at roughly 500–1300 AD.

More than any historical, geographical, or sociological factor, the development of bhakti, the ideology of sacred love between deity and devotee, seems to account for much of the variation in the versions of the two myths. Thus the myth versions reflect a progression that appears to have a *loose* relationship to chronological progression from a myth free from the theme of bhakti to one where saving grace bestowed by the avatāra on the demon devotee becomes a leitmotif. We find this line of development more meaningful to our study than a strictly historical one.

The Religious Context

Understanding the myths of Narasiṁha and Vāmana as sacred stories about descents of a deity puts them squarely in a religious context. And although we might pursue their study further along the lines of the avatāras as deities (how they are like or unlike other Hindu gods; if they fit or challenge concepts of deity formulated by scholars of religion) or their relationship to structures of soteriology (if their mission is to confer salvation, as earthly manifestations of deities in other religious traditions often do), our most productive approach has been to follow the direction pointed to by the avatāras themselves, in what might be seen as their own "statement of purpose," Kṛṣṇa's words to his friend Arjuna in the *Bhagavad Gītā*: "Whenever the dharma withers away and adharma[14] arises, then do I send myself forth. For the protection of good, for the destruction of evil-doers, for the establishment of the dharma do I come into being age after age"[15] (*Bhagavad Gītā* 4.7–8). Kṛṣṇa, the eighth avatāra, relates the periodic descent of Viṣṇu to the nature of dharma, the cosmic "glue," to its deterioration and the complementary rise of its inverse, adharma or disorder.

As the predictable fall and rise of dharma are inextricably related to the cosmological structures of time in Hinduism, specifically the yuga system, Kṛṣṇa's words beckon us to examine this relationship more carefully. Further, if we adopt Courtright's understanding of religion as "a world of its own,"[16] taking this definition in a literal sense, we can seek to understand this world in its sense as a cosmos, constructed in the Purāṇic myths with intricate conceptions of time and space, creation and destruction, and the movement of all beings through this universe.

The relationship of the avatāras and dharma to the cosmology is made explicit through the system of the yugas, four successive ages in which dharma and all that it governs deteriorate progressively from a golden age of perfection to a world of chaos in need of annihilation and renewal. The pursuit of Narasiṁha and Vāmana along these lines of explicit interrelation leads into a web of subtle and intricate associations in which these avatāra myths find, to our mind, their most significant context of meaning.

Methodology

As myths reveal their multivalent nature to us, so they demand a multifaceted approach to understanding them; as O'Flaherty aptly puts it, "the toolbox approach of pluralism."[17] O'Flaherty sees the pluralistic approach as the necessary complement to the multiple levels of meaning simultaneously present in myth.[18] Our use of the toolbox approach is based to some degree on a concurrence with her notion of levels, which we have termed *contexts*, but also is a serial use of methods, as will be seen.

Our approach evolved from the simple observation, made from reading a sampling of avatāra myths, that several points seemed to present themselves in the myths over and over again, appearing as threads that might hold together the mythological fabric. This observation had to be turned into a "methodology" to become a valuable tool, enabling us to systematically check the material for these traits, as well as guard against turning our observations into assumptions, mangling the material.

One technique used most successfully on material like our myths, the bulk of which often makes it unwieldy, is that of motif-checking or motific analysis. Our familiarity with this method comes first from folklorists. However, there is considerable lack of clarity as to what exactly is meant by motif on their part. Stith Thompson defines motif initially as "any one of the parts into which an item of folklore can be analyzed,"[19] but goes on to specify that motifs exist independent of or without regard for context. Vladimir Propp[20] defines motif as a function of the character, having a fixed place in an order of motifs, but independent of the character performing it. Problematic explanations. We have modified our understanding of motif to be less structurally and more contextually oriented, taking a cue from the extremely successful and sophisticated use of the method on Purāṇic myth by Wendy O'Flaherty in her exhaustive work, *Asceticism and Eroticism in the Mythology of Śiva*. However, we perceived the motif as a tool to uncover basic elements in the myth, not to discern the structure of each one. In other words, the group of motifs used in our analysis were thought to be central but by no means exhaustive of those that could be found in each myth, representing a group of traits which were thought at the outset to be present in most of the avatāra myths. Thus, motif checking became a *preliminary* methodology to guard against pursuing and maintaining a thesis not borne out by the data.

Those characteristics appearing over and over in the sample readings of the avatāra myths (which extended beyond Narisiṁha and Vāmana myths) became the five motifs used in the preliminary analysis, and represent a diverse group of statements of relationship, context, action, and position. They were these:

1. *A special relationship with Indra:* The avatāra continues an alliance with Indra that began as early as the Vedic literature, which often united the two gods in battle against demons, portraying Indra as a kṣatriya par excellence, possessor of physical strength, and Viṣṇu as his aid, his subordinate, who nevertheless possessed a higher, superior power.
2. *Invocation of a cosmogonic scenario:* The avatāra invokes the quality of the interstitial period of pralaya (destruction) and recreation through the use of cosmological language describing his appearance and the events surrounding it.

Motifs 3, 4, and 5 are basically variations on the theme of liminality and should be understood as a cluster:

3. *Mediating power and activity:* The avatāra amasses power by positioning himself "betwixt and between" two opposing groups, gaining the role of mediator.
4. *Action through trickery:* The avatāra often employs deceit, guile, or trickery to win a victory for the gods (or protagonists) over the demons (or antagonists).
5. *The loophole in the law:* Faced with what appears to be an airtight situation that threatens to imperil the gods (or protagonists), the avatāra finds a chink, a loophole that provides

> a solution to the conflict without direct violation of the pact or law.[21]

These motifs were seen not as independent entities, but in relation to each other.

The overriding emphasis in the development of these motifs was the concept of liminality. Through an understanding of such a highly pregnant concept, enriched foremost by the works of Victor Turner,[22] what appeared to be at the heart of the avatāras at the outset, generating four out of five motifs (excluding motif 1), was what Turner might have called a *liminal* character. That is, the avatāra brought with him, clothed himself in, an "interstructural" period, via the pralaya imagery, appearing as a figure of pure potency, oftentimes an unlikely hero, the "underling made uppermost," an amoral trickster, the very principle of ambivalence. It seemed, at the outset, that the avatāra, through his liminal properties, caused the collapse of a temporal structure and created a "betwixt and between" through his own power to do so; he even transgressed the cosmology: "He is believed to break through the progressive decay, arrest its course, and even reverse it."[23] So it appeared going into the motif checking.

The motif analysis was applied to all versions of the Narasiṁha and Vāmana myths found in the epics and Purāṇas. We have insisted on the use of the word *version* rather than *variant,* as the latter seems to imply variation from something—an ur myth, a favorite, one that fits the methodology best, and so on—and we were looking at the totality of the myths, ideally as equal texts. O'Flaherty concurs with such an approach: "There is no way to begin with any 'basic' myth or any 'basic' theme, for the entire corpus interlocks and feeds back so that the total fabric resembles a piece of chain-mail rather than the brachiated, family-tree structure sought by the text-historical analysis and some structuralists."[24]

At the conclusion of the motific analysis it was evident that, although motifs had headed us down the right track, the cart was before the horse. A poverty of check marks in the triad of liminal motifs (3, 4, and 5) and an overwhelming number in the cosmogonic scenario column brought the realization that the avatāra was not the *creator* of this liminality, but relied on that quality inherent in the cosmological structures to *appear* liminal. The cosmology contained within it that liminal, unstructured period of chaos and potency, a time in which the *sacra* is communicated (via the avatāra), a period whose gnosis brings a change in being (furthermore, the liminality of the cosmology during the avatāra's appearance reinforces on a mythical level the communitas characteristic of the bhakti movement). This is not to imply that the avatāra is a mere instrument of cosmological structure; he becomes not the creator, but the manipulator, of liminal "structures" already existent in the Purāṇic cosmology.

This perception brings us back to the importance of language, especially cosmological language; and basically an awareness of this vocabulary and its conceptual ramifications, as well as the multi-leveled nature of all mythical language, governs our efforts beyond the preliminary motif checking. This approach is couched in an awareness that the Purāṇas stand at the end of a long Sanskritic tradition of mythology, and in many ways are the culmination and storehouse of that tradition. A living dialogue is carried to it and the entire mythological milieu in which it exists. This dialogue is often expressed in subtleties of phrase or image or even in a single word, and the meaning of the myth is multiplied by how well versed the reader is in its heritage.

Thus, to study these myths, it would be unwise to employ a method that searches only for the structure of the myth, and sees the words of the myth as meaningful only by way of their arrangement in a larger structure. As Mary Douglas has stated: "The best words are ambiguous, and the more richly ambiguous the more suitable for the poet's or the mythmaker's job. Hence there is no end to the number of meanings which can be read into a good myth."[25] Therefore, dealing with the myths that stand near the end of a long mythological corpus, one must constantly be aware of the multivalency of a word or phrase, which may evoke images from several strata of myth. One must seek to understand the unspoken "givens" or multiple entendres in the language of myth. Through this process of understanding all the "reference points" of the myth, we hope to uncover the wider intent and significance of these avatāra myths.

Thus we are brought back, as we will be over and over in this study, to the significance of language, especially cosmological language, and the need to understand it as context for theophany and soteriology, indeed for every mythic drama played out on its stage. Our work on the avatāras attempts to show the need to understand deity in an ongoing cosmological context; not simply as one who begins the cosmos or one who arrives to obliterate it.

In the following chapters, we will examine the development of Viṣṇu in pre-Purāṇic literature, highlighting antecedents to his avatāric form in general and with specific reference to Narasiṁha and Vāmana. After acquainting the reader with the Purāṇic cosmology, we turn to the specific analysis of the myths of the two avatāras. In concluding, we hope that Viṣṇu's epithet of *Pervader* of the cosmos will be revalued in light of an understanding of these two avatāras, and that the tangle of Narasiṁha's and Vāmana's myths, which weaves itself through the Purāṇas and in and out of Hindu life, will unfold as a tapestry of meaning.

Notes

1. Wendy D. O'Flaherty, "Inside and Outside the Mouth of God: The Boundary between Myth and Reality," *Daedalus* 109, no. 2 (1980):93–125.

2. The late J. A. B. van Buitenen, in private conversation.

3. Ronald Huntington, "A Study of Purāṇic Myth from the Viewpoint of Depth Psychology," (unpublished dissertation, University of Southern California, 1960).

4. Bhagavan Das, *Krishna: A Study in the Theory of Avatāras* (Bombay: Bharatiya Vidya Bhavan, 1962), p. 9.

5. Jean Herbert, *Narada: précédé d'une étude sur Les Avatars de Vishnou* (Lyon: Author, 1949).

6. Geoffrey Parrinder, *Avatar and Incarnation* (London: Faber & Faber, 1970) and G. Parrinder and H. Jacobi, "Incarnation (Indian)," *ERE* 7:193ff.

7. R. G. Bhandarkar, *Vaiṣṇavism Śaivism and Minor Religious Systems* (Varanasi: Indological Book House, 1965), p. 2; Sukumari Bhattacharji, *The Indian Theogony* (Cambridge: Cambridge University Press, 1970), p. 308.

8. Jan Gonda, *Viṣṇuism and Śivaism* (London: Athlone Press, 1970), pp. 49–50; B. Badshah, *Aryan Theory of Divine Incarnations* (Lisbon: Geographical Society of Lisbon, 1892); Oswald Joseph Grainger, "The Rise of the Incarnation Idea in Indian Religion," (dissertation, University of Chicago, 1927); Paul Hacker, "Zur Entwicklung der Avatāralehre," *Weiner-Zeitschrift für die Kunde Sud-und Ostasiens* 4 (1960):47–70.

9. K. S. S. Janaki, "Paraśurāma," *Purāṇa* 8, no. 1 (1966); V. M. Bedekar, "The Legend of the Churning of the Ocean in the Epics and Purāṇas: A Comparative Study," *Purāṇa* 9, no. 1 (1967); A. P. Karmarkar, "The Matsyāvatāra of Viṣṇu," *A Volume of Studies in Indology* (Poona: Oriental Book Agency, 1941); J. B. Long, "Life Out of Death: A Structural Analysis of the Myth of the 'Churning of the Ocean of Milk,'" *Hinduism: New Essays in the History of Religions* (Leiden: E. J. Brill, 1976); Adam Hohenberger, *Die Indische Flutsage und das Matsya Purāṇa* (Leipzig, 1930); M. Biardeau, "Narasiṁha: mythe et culte," *Puruṣārtha: Récherches de Sciences Sociales sur l''Asie du Sud* (Paris: Centre d'Études de L'Inde et de l'Asie du Sud, 1975); A. C. Swain, *A Study of the Man-Lion Myth in the Epics and Purāṇa-Texts*, Publications of the

Centre of Advanced Study in Sanskrit, Class A, No. 3 (Poona: University of Poona, 1970); G. C. Tripathi, *Die Ursprung und Entwicklung der Vāmanalegende in der Indischeliteratur* (Weisbaden: Otto Harrassowitz, 1968). Interestingly, two excellent studies focus not on the avatāra but on demon figures in the two avatāra myths under discussion: Paul Hacker, *Prahlāda: Werden und Wandlungen einer Idealgestalt* (Weisbaden: Akademie der Wissenschaften und der Literatur No. 9, 1959) and Clifford Hospital, *The Righteous Demon* (Vancouver: University of Columbia Press, 1984).

10. David C. Pocock, "The Anthropology of Time-Reckoning," in *Myth and Cosmos* (Garden City: Natural History Press, 1967); M. Biardeau, "Études de mythologie hindoue IV: Bhakti et Avatāra," *BEFEO* 63 (1976).

11. See Paul Courtright, *Gaṇeśa* (London: Oxford University Press, 1985), pp. 17–18 for corroboration on this view.

12. That is, the *Harivaṁśa, Brahmāṇḍa, Matsya,* and Sṛṣṭikhanda of the *Padma Purāṇa*. It would be interesting to pursue a comparative and historical study of these texts, as there is a marked similarity and identity between some of their versions of the Narasiṁha and Vāmana myths.

13. That is, the *Bhāgavata, Liṅga, Śiva, Skanda, Vāmana,* and *Varāha Purāṇas.*

14. Adharma, literally "not dharma" (Sanskrit utilizes the alpha privitif, like English), might be translated as disorder, chaos, unrighteousness, lawlessness. Its opposition to dharma is seen most clearly in its untranslated form.

15. yadā yadā hi dharmasya glānir hi bhārata
abhyutthānam adharmasya tadā 'tmānam sṛjāmyaham
paritrāṇāya sādhūnāṁ vināśāya ca duṣkṛtām
dharmasaṁsthāpan 'ārthāya saṁbhavāmi *yuge yuge*

16. P. Courtright, *Gaṇeśa,* p. 14; he provides a "provisional definition of religion as a world of its own."

17. Wendy D. O'Flaherty, *Women, Androgynes, and other Mythical Beasts* (Chicago: The University of Chicago Press, 1980), p. 5.

18. That is, the narrative, divine, cosmic, and human. See Wendy D. O'Flaherty, *Asceticism and Eroticism in the Mythology of Śiva* (London: Oxford University Press, 1973), p. 2. Courtright adopts this schema but adds a fifth level, the etiological; see *Gaṇeśa,* pp. 18–19.

19. Stith Thompson, "Motif," *ESS* 2:711.

20. Valdimir Propp, *The Morphology of the Folktale* (Austin: University of Texas Press, 1968), pp. 20ff.

21. I am indebted to A. K. Ramanujan for highlighting this trait and coining the term, *loophole in the law* with reference to it.

22. Victor Turner, *The Ritual Process* (England: Routledge & Kegan Paul, 1969); *The Forest of Symbols* (Ithaca: Cornell University Press, 1967); "Liminal to Liminoid in Play, Flow, and Ritual: An Essay in Comparative Symbology," *Rice University Studies* 60, no. 3.

23. Pocock, "The Anthropology of Time Reckoning," p. 313.

24. O'Flaherty, *Asceticism and Eroticism in the Mythology of Śiva*, p. 21.

25. Mary Douglas, "The Meaning of Myth, with Special Reference to 'La Geste d'Asdiwal,'" in *The Structural Study of Myth and Totemism*, A.S.A. Monographs 5 (England: Tavistock Publications, 1957), p. 63.

2

Vedic Antecedents to the Avatāric Nature of Viṣṇu

The rise in status of the god Viṣṇu from his Vedic beginnings to his Purāṇic glory might well be considered the Horatio Alger story of Indian mythology. Faced with the profoundly pervasive and varied role Viṣṇu plays in later Hinduism and the rather meagre amount of praise and description given him in the *ṚgVeda*, scholars have labored nonetheless, at minimum, to define who the Vedic Viṣṇu was, if not to accord him some weighty mythological function that did not receive proper amplification due to the nature of ṚgVedic literature.[1] Given the situation, by working with the Vedic materials scholars managed to easily produce more theories about Viṣṇu's Vedic character than there are mentions of the god in that literature:[2]

> Besides, he has been held to represent the Moon,[3] or the Fire-god,[4] Soma,[5] or a mountain god associated with vegetation,[6] a god of fertility,[7] or a deity connected with Vṛtrahan.[8] He has been stated to be an awakener of life,[9] or the sacrifice,[10] a popular personification of the brahman- or ātman-,[11] or a god of veneration or propitiation.[12] It has further been suggested that "the original character of Viṣṇu" was a non-Aryan[13] or proto-

> Indian[14] religious concept. He has been considered a philosopher's[15] as well as a "late popular" god,[16] a striding giant,[17] no less than an anima, the essence of the pitaras and, at the same time, the solar bird,[18] the god of evolution,[19] of movement,[20] or of immanence.[21]

Added to this list is the most predominant theory, that Viṣṇu is a solar deity,[22] a difficult hypothesis to swallow, when faced with Müller's concept of the primacy of solar mythology based on his research in the *ṚgVeda,* and the pitifully few stanzas of praise to the "solar deity," Viṣṇu.

Other scholars have begun to move away from this urge toward functional pinpointing and, instead, toward a proposition that the character of Vedic Viṣṇu was in a sense undefinable; such an approach is taken by Sukumari Bhattacharji. Deeming Viṣṇu (and Rudra) a "minor" god in the Veda, she states:

> Only those whose characters were not explicitly known, and who, at the same time, offered one or two significant traits which could be developed into a rich and complex mythology, survived. Only Viṣṇu and Rudra fulfilled these conditions: they were suitably vague and indistinct with few or no definite achievements to their credit so as to allow new feats to be ascribed to them . . .[23]

Bhattacharji has a feel for the situation, yet she errs in seeing Viṣṇu's features as vague and indistinct; as we shall shortly see, the hymns are anything but vague in eliciting a sense of Viṣṇu's traits; the point is, those traits have a broad and overarching nature that remains, in the *Veda,* for the most part simply stated and not elaborated in mythological detail. Viṣṇu is benevolent, bountiful, a guardian, and willing to help mankind; all traits that could and would develop mythologically, given the proper circumstances. Even the two feats of Viṣṇu described in the *Veda,* the taking of three steps and aiding Indra in his battle with Vṛtra, have at their basis, as we contend, a cosmogonic and hence far-reaching and pervasive tone.

Thus, we would argue that avatāric Viṣṇu, whose mythology is one pinnacle of expression for bhakti, shows a clear congruity with Vedic Viṣṇu and further, that the traits basic to Viṣṇu in the *Veda* remain central to Viṣṇu in his avatāras. This is not to say that the avatāras reflect nothing more than a mythological fattening of the Vedic character, but that with few exceptions, one can see the development of the general avatāric character as being natural and understandable given Viṣṇu's Vedic roots.

You two have conquered, and never have been conquered:
never have either of the two been vanquished.
You, Indra-Viṣṇu, when you fought the battle,
produced this infinite with three divisions.

These two gods together fought a battle and, striding, produced living space with three divisions for humanity. As Indra and Viṣṇu are allied frequently in combat against demons (cf. RV V.5, "Indra and Viṣṇu, ye have broken open the nine and ninety firm forts of Śambara, and have overwhelmingly beaten the hundred and thousand warriors of the Asura Varcin altogether"; RV VII.99.4, "Ye procure free scope for the sacrifice, by making sun, dawn, and fire shine out; ye have brought to naught the wiles of the demon Vṛṣaśipra, O, Ye Heroes"), the most important task for which they combine forces is unquestionably the act to which RV VI.69 alludes, the slaying of Vṛtra. This is attested to in RV VI.20.2: "To you the gods yielded as it were the whole dominion over the sky, when you, O Indra, allied with Viṣṇu, slayed the dragon Vṛtra, who enveloped the waters." RV IV.18.11b is more explicit with regard to Viṣṇu's part in the deed: "Then Indra, about to slaughter Vṛtra, said: O Friend Viṣṇu, stride out farther." As in RV VIII.100.12:

Step forth with wider stride, Friend Viṣṇu;
Make room, Dyaus, for the leaping of the thunderbolt.
Let us slay Vṛtra, let us free the rivers:
let them flow loosed at the command of Indra.

and RV VIII.12.26–27 couples Indra's and Viṣṇu's foremost deeds:

When you slay Vṛtra, stayer of the floods,
Thunderer with Might,
Then your two beautiful horses carried you on.

When Viṣṇu, through your energy, strode
wide those three great steps of his,
Then your two beautiful horses carried you on.

Although early scholars belittled the significance of this Vṛtra myth as being of highest cosmic import, as well as Viṣṇu's role in the Vṛtra-Indra combat,[34] after the work of Benveniste and Renou,[35] Luders,[36] and W. Norman Brown,[37] even Gonda is ready to admit that

> it seems clear that this central myth refers to a cosmic drama of paramount importance. . . . In the Vedic Vṛtra combat the release of the waters was considered the central feature, and this occurrence meant the transformation of an inhabitable chaotic universe into a cosmos . . . [and] It was the assistance of the hero-god, to wit Viṣṇu who played the important role in this drama.[38]

Thus it is clear through Viṣṇu's participation in this battle that he has a strong alliance with Indra and an integral part in another "secondary" type of creation through a characteristically nonmartial act; opening space through a striding activity. We cannot agree with Tripathi who feels that, at first, Viṣṇu's role in the Vṛtra combat was negligible: "It is clear that the mention of Viṣṇu in these verses (RV VIII.100.12) makes little sense and actually serves no important purpose in the cosmic Vṛtra-struggle. Indra and not Viṣṇu asks for space and also the heavens."[39] It seems unlikely that, with Viṣṇu present, the god whose sole activity in the *Veda* is striding thrice to open up space, to make room, Indra's request for him to step forth or stride widely could be seen as inconsequential at any point. One must agree with Hermann Oldenberg, who states that, in the *ṚgVeda,* the three strides of Viṣṇu serve to create for Indra, "'the vast field which will be the theatre of their victory' " over Vṛtra.[40] That this role as a nonmartial aid in battle remains a significant one for Viṣṇu throughout the literature is obvious; as Kṛṣṇa, he is noncombatant counselor to Indra's son, Arjuna, in the *Mahābhārata,* and as Kūrmāvatāra, mediating support between the warring Devas and Asuras, but as Mohinī ultimately throwing the victory to the gods with Indra at their head, in the myth of the Churning of the Ocean.

Because Indra is the only other god, in hymns in praise of Viṣṇu, who is "incidentally associated with him either explicitly (VII.99.5–6; I.155.2) or implicitly (VII.99.4; I.154.6; 155.1)"[41] and whose mythological legacy Viṣṇu is chief heir to in post-Vedic literature, we should look further at the two for other common features that may have foreshadowed the basic nature of the avatāras.

Besides this common demon-slaying activity, it should be noted that both Indra and Viṣṇu are gods who can change form, or who have another form, a characteristic not very common within the Vedic pantheon. That Indra possesses this ability is attested to in RV VI.47.18:

> For every form he was the model:
> this is his only form for us to look on.

Indra moves multiform through his powers,
for his thousand horses are yoked together.

In RV I.51.5 and VIII.97.12 he is said to take the shape of a sheep to usurp Medhātīthī's Soma, in RV X.119 the shape of a quail, and in RV VIII.97.12 that of a ram. That Vedic Viṣṇu had this ability too, or at least had another form is a less known, but surely no less significant fact, revealed to us in RV VII.100.6:

What was there to despise in you, O Viṣṇu, when you declared,
'I am Śipiviṣṭa?'
Do not hide this form from us, or keep it secret,
Since you wore another form [*anyarūpaḥ*] in battle.

To identify this as the germ of the avatāra concept would be an overstatement, as Tripathi concurs.[42] But we should nevertheless keep in mind that Viṣṇu is said to have two forms: one seen, one unseen. And, significantly, that he takes on another form when in battle. This is of obvious importance with respect to the large part the daivāsura conflict plays in avatāra mythology, it often being the immediate raison d'être for the descent of another form of Viṣṇu. Further, faced with a god with more than one form, and his intimate ally who changes form through *māyā* and several of whose attributes are taken on by the former as the latter's abilities (and popularity) decline, it does not seem foolish to state that, considering these facts, the notion of different forms for Viṣṇu would not be incongruous with his Vedic roots. One last, puzzling verse can be added with regard to this statement, RV I.155.3:

These offerings increase his mighty manly strength; he brings
down both Parents to share the genial flow.
He lowers, though a son, the Father's name;
the third is that which is high in the light of heaven.

Although Griffith, in his notes to this hymn, explains the verse as such, "the meaning appears to be that Viṣṇu takes rank in the sacrifice above his own father Dyaus, and that Agni has the third place,"[43] several ideas are called to mind by the passage: that as Viṣṇu is the son of Dyaus in the Vedas, so as Vāmana is he the son of Kaśyapa and Aditi, progenitors of the gods; that 'the third' here seems more understandable as a reference to Viṣṇu's third and highest step, which reaches the highest heavens. With such a difficult but pregnant verse, we can only raise possibilities, but make no claims.

With all the evidence thus far discussed, we can summarize by way of several statements:

1. In terms of an avatāra doctrine, a philosophical concept involving a definite notion of descent and an underlying structure of transmigration or reincarnation, the Vedic material supplies us with no antecedents.
2. In terms of the specific mythological *figures* described as avatāras in the epic and Purāṇic literature, the Vedic hymns are again devoid of any association of these figures with Viṣṇu.
3. There is, as demonstrated, a clear-cut congruity between the major characteristics of Vedic Viṣṇu and those common to his avatāras:
   a. A benevolence toward and active concern for man and his world.
   b. A cosmogonic nature inherent in his activity alone and with Indra.
   c. An intimate connection with Indra linking the two in
      i. demon-slaying activity
      ii. cosmogonic activity
      iii. the ability to have more than one form.
   d. An association, through the act of taking three steps, with the highest abode, the *paramaṁ padaṁ*, which is most highly praised and aspired to by humanity; that is, the place of highest "soteriological" import, if such a term can be applied with reference to the *Vedas*.

Vedic Antecedents with Specific Reference to the Vāmana and Narasiṁha Avatāras

The obvious need not be stressed with regard to Vedic Viṣṇu and the Vāmana avatāra myth. Nearly every important structural element of the Vāmana myth is already present in the *Veda:* the taking of three steps to recapture or recreate the world for humankind; the vertical course of the steps; the taking of the steps in conquest of a demon; the taking of the steps to aid Indra (e.g., RV Val.4.3.b: "He [Indra] for whom Viṣṇu came striding his three wide steps, as Mitra's statutes ordered it"). What *is* missing is the element of deception, provided by the avatāra form of the dwarf and the conquering theophany. But even this element, absent in the *Ṛg Veda*, will be introduced very early on, in the *Śatapatha Brāhmaṇa*.

If the Vāmana avatāra provides a classic case of lucid (almost too lucid for an Indian text) development through nearly 2,000 years of literature, the Narasiṁha avatāra balances as its opposite. We have virtually no precursors in the Vedic material for the figure of a man-lion, and only one phrase that simply does not rule out the possibility of a savage side to the benign Viṣṇu; that is his epithet as "like some wild beast, dread, prowling, mountain-roaming" (RV I.154.2a), a phrase used to describe Indra as well (RV X.180.2a, "Like a dread wild beast roaming on the mountain").[44] Interestingly, within the context of praise of the three steps and the slaying of Vṛtra, Viṣṇu and Indra are described, respectively, in such a manner. There is one tiny clue, however, to the beginnings of the Narasiṁha myth, which is developed more fully in the Brāhmaṇa material: an allusion to knowledge of the Namuci myth in RV VIII.14.13: "With waters' foam you tore off, Indra, the head of Namuci, subduing all contending hosts."[45] This short reference is the beginning of that slender thread of myth which culminates in the full-blown Purāṇic mythology of the highly popular Narasiṁha avatāra. To follow that thread, we turn to the Brāhmaṇa literature.

Notes

1. Jan Gonda, *Aspects of Early Viṣṇuism* (Delhi: Motilal Banarsidass, 1969), on the fact that the ṚgVedic collection represents a narrow range of interests, and "the comparative prominence of the gods is not necessarily fully brought out in that collection" (p. 3); F. B. J. Kuiper, "Indeed, we are confronted here with the fundamental difficulty of Vedic mythology, viz., the impossibility of understanding a single mythological figure isolated from the context of the mythological system" ("The Three Strides of Viṣṇu," p. 139); Andrew Lang, "Nothing in all mythology is more difficult than the attempt to get a clear view of the gods of Vedic India" (2:148); cf. also A. B. Keith, *The Religion and Philosophy of the Veda and Upaniṣads*.

2. Kuiper, "The Three Strides of Viṣṇu," pp. 137–138: Kuiper's footnotes are important.

3. H. Kunike, "Viṣṇu, ein Mondgott," *Mythologische Bibliothek* 8, no. 4 (1916):5–17; von Schroeder, *Arische Religion* II, p. 669. Cf. Hardy, *Die Vedischbramanische Periode*, pp. 33f.

4. Bergaigne, *Religion vedique* II, pp. 416, 418 ("l'identité primitive de Vishnu avec Agni et Soma, prototypes de tous les sacrificateurs"); Sarkar, *The Folkelements of Hindu Culture,* p. 12.

5. Kasten Rönnow, *Trita Aptya* I, pp. 93f.: "der vedische Soma-gott par preference."

6. Havell, *The History of Aryan Rule in India* (1918), pp. 28, 111, 182f. (but at the same time a solar god).

7. H. Guntert, *Der arische Weltkonig und Heiland* (1923), p. 292 (an ithyphallic god, similarly Haggerty Krappe, *Mythologie universelle,* 1930, pp. 141ff.). Cf. Neisser, *JAOS* 45 (1925):288.

8. G. Dumezil, *Revue de l'histoire des religions* 117 (1938):167.

9. Paul Mus, *L'Inde vue de l'est,* p. 22: "doué . . . du pouvoir d'éveiller la vie dans le monde qu'ouvraient ses trois pas mythiques."

10. L. D. Barnett, *Hindu Gods and Heroes* (1922), pp. 37ff.; J. Charpentier, *Festgabe Jacobi* (1927), p. 277 n. 2 (but according to H. Oldenberg, *Die Lehre der Upanishaden,* p. 17, a later interpretation).

11. Deussen, *Der Gesang des Heiligen,* Introduction, p. iv.

12. B. Faddegon, in Van der Leeuw (e.a.), *De godsdiensten der wereld* I[1] (1940), pp. 296f., 303.

13. For example, Przyluski, *Archiv Orientální* 4 (1932):261ff.; R. Otto *Zeitschrift fur Missionsmunde und Religionswissenschaft* (1936):16 (reprint); von Eiokstedt, *Hirt-Festschrift* I, p. 362. Cf. Paul Mus, *L'Inde vue de l'est,* p. 22 (concerning Kṛṣṇa); W. Ruben, *Eisenschmiede und Dämonen ind Indien,* p. 284.

14. *Census Report* 1931, I, 1, pp. 394ff. (p. 396: "the fruit of reaction of . . . proto-Hinduism to the Rigvedic invaders"); Hrozný, *Archiv Orientální* 13 (1942):48.

15. L. von Schroeder, *Mysterium und Mimus* (1908), p. 56 (cf. Lassen, *Indische Altertumskunde* 1, no. 2 [1867]:919), contested by Oldenberg, *Religion des Veda* 3–4, (1923):228 n. 2; Wust, *Vergleichendes und etymologisches Wörterbuch des Alt-Indo-Arischen* I (1934), p. 92.

16. See Lassen, ibid., 1.c.

17. Oldenberg, *Religion des Veda* 3–4 (1923):233; cf. *Nachrichten der Gottinger Gesellschaft der Wissenschaften* (1915):374f.

18. K. F. Johansson, *Solfageln i Indien* (1910), pp. 9, 14, 28, 70. Cf. also idem., "Uber die altindische Gottin Dhiṣanā und Verwandtes" (1917), pp. 47 n. 2, 49; J. Charpentier, *Die Suparṇasage* (1921), pp. 329ff. (originally a bird, either the solar bird or a bird with a bough of the tree of Life [Soma], or the

primodial father of the living, conceived of as a bird. Bur [sic] in the Veda a solar god). See also *Festgabe Jacobi,* p. 277 n. 2.

19. G. J. Held, "The Mahābhārata, An Ethnological Study" (thesis, Leiden, 1935), p. 222: "Śiva is the god of saṁhāra, Viṣṇu the god of the sṛṣhṭi". Cf. p. 221: "Vishnu is the All-god, viewed from the side of life, Śiva the same, but viewed from the side of death"; p. 224: "Síva especially is the god of involution, Vishnu of evolution" (but see also pp. 145, 194!). Cf. Hopkins, *Religions of India,* p. 388: "Vishnu and Çiva are different gods. But each in turn represents the All-god, and consequently each represents the other."

20. Hopkins, *JAOS* 36 (1916):264.

21. R. Otto, *Gottheit und Gottheiten der Arier* (1932), pp. 833ff.; *Zeitschrift für Missionskunde und Religionswissenschaft* 49 (1936):296ff. Cf. *Gefühl des Überweltlichen,* p. 111: "Einschlüpfer, a haunting something."

22. Cf. A. A. Macdonnell, *Vedic Mythology* (Delhi: Motilal Banarsidass, 1974), p. 38; Gonda, *Aspects of Early Viṣṇuism,* p. 172.

23. Bhattacharji, *The Indian Theogony,* p. 13.

24. Ibid., p. 284.

25. Gaya Charan Tripathi, *Die Ursprung und Entwicklung der Vāmana-legende in der Indische-literatur* (Wiesbaden: Otto Harrassowitz, 1968) p. 4.

26. Gonda, *Aspects of Early Viṣṇuism,* p. 22.

27. RV I.22.17a: "Through all the world strode Viṣṇu: thrice his foot he planted." RV I.154.3b: "Him who alone with triple step hath measured this common dwelling place, long, far extended." RV I.155.4b: "Him who strode, widely pacing, with three steppings forth over the realms of the earth, for freedom and for life."

28. RV VI.49.13a: "He who for man's behoof in his affliction thrice measured out the earthly regions, Viṣṇu." RV VII.100.3a: "Three times strode forth this god in all his grandeur over this earth bright with one hundred splendours."

29. RV I.155.5: "A mortal man, when he beholds two steps of him who looks upon the light, is restless with amaze. But his third step doth no one venture to approach nor the feathered birds of air who fly with wings." RV VIII.29.7: "Another, with his mighty stride hath made his three steps thither where the gods rejoice." Tripathi, pp. 8–12; see also Kuiper's account of Macdonnell's classification of the steps, "The Three Strides of Viṣṇu," pp. 139–140.

30. Cf. RV I.22.20; I.154.5.

31. Kuiper, p. 140.

32. Note the multivalent meaning of the verb root *mā* in the *ṚgVeda*, according to M. Monier-Williams, *A Sanskrit-English Dictionary* (Oxford: Clarendon Press, 1899), "to measure, mete out, RV & etc. . . . to prepare, arrange, fashion, *form, build, make*, RV" (italics mine), p. 804.

33. Kuiper, p. 141.

34. Cf. Hillebrand, "The three steps which he, for example, in IV.18.11; VIII.12.27:52.3, took for Indra, are completely superfluous, and here, in the fight with Vṛtra, are taken over from the Viṣṇuistic legend-cycle in order to bind the two for whatever reason was important for the worshipers." *Vedische Mythologie* 2:313; see also Hermann Oldenberg, *La Religion du Veda* (Paris: Felix Alcan, 1903), p. 231.

35. Emil Benveniste and Louis Renou, *Vṛtra and Vṛthragna* (Paris, 1932).

36. H. Luders, *Varuṇa I* (Gottingen, 1951), pp. 167ff.

37. W. Norman Brown, "The Creation Myth in the Rig Veda," *JAOS* 62, no. 2 (1942).

38. Gonda, *Aspects of Early Viṣṇuism*, p. 30.

39. Tripathi, p. 23.

40. Oldenberg, *La Religion du Veda*, p. 193, as quoted by G. Dumézil, "Études et memoires I, Remarques sur le 'ius fetiale,'" *Revue des Études Latines* 34 (1956); as noted in A. Hiltebeitel, *The Ritual of Battle* (Ithaca: Cornell University Press, 1976), p. 136, n. 46.

41. Macdonell, p. 39.

42. "One cannot indeed speak here of an 'avatāra'," p. 6.

43. Ralph T. H. Griffith, *The Hymns of the ṚgVeda* (Delhi: Motilal Banarsidass, 1973), p. 103.

44. Gonda, *Aspects of Early Viṣṇuism*, p. 31.

45. Sayana's commentary on RV VIII.14.13 gives a myth telling that Indra had to kill Namuci at the juncture of day and night with foam because the demon had been granted immunity from death during day and night and by wet and dry missiles.

3

Brāhmaṇic Antecedents to the Avatāric Nature of Viṣṇu

Although there may be little consensus among scholars about the relative "worth" of the Brāhmaṇas, all concur that the Brāhmaṇas are books overwhelmingly, even obsessively, concerned with the sacrifice.[1] Written roughly around 900 BC, the Brāhmaṇas were composed by priests to explain, in great detail, "the meaning and purpose of the Vedic ritual. That is their ostensible and ever-present agenda; every line is permeated with explicit references to the sacrifice."[2] So inextricably bound up with the sacrifice are these texts, that those folkloric elements present in the *Jaiminīya Brāhmaṇa*, for example, were until recently believed to be interpolations. Now, through O'Flaherty's work in *Tales of Sex and Violence*, we can understand those folktales not only as integral parts of the Brāhmaṇa, but connected firmly to the sacrifice by addressing the same dangers and fears in a dramatic mode as the sacrifice did in its ritual setting.

Thus, we must understand, in examining the Brāhmaṇic context, that sacrifice was the controlling element in the development of deities and mythologies in these texts. That Viṣṇu becomes associated and even identified with the sacrifice in the Brāhmaṇas does not surprise us; we need to pay close attention, however, to the images, epithets, and mythemes that are drawn into this web of associations as Viṣṇu's avatāric nature continues to form.

The developments that occur in the general character of Viṣṇu in the Brāhmaṇa literature have far-reaching influence on the growth and molding of avatāric Viṣṇu in general and with specific reference to the two avatāras under examination, as well as to several others. These areas of development, which we shall attempt to discuss separately for clarity's sake, continually flow into each other in a multidirectional way, as shall be seen.

Probably the single most important development, which is first found in the Brāhmaṇas and exerts the most influence over all other factors, is the identification of Viṣṇu with the sacrifice. Although he is not the only god identified in this manner, given the primacy of the sacrifice in the Brāhmaṇas, the importance of such an equation should not be underrated. Acknowledgment and understanding of this can correct the often-expressed view that Viṣṇu was a relatively unimportant deity until the epic and especially the advent of bhakti. We would not, however, as Tripathi verges on doing, accord Viṣṇu the highest place of prominence in the Brāhmaṇa literature.[3]

These identifications of Viṣṇu with the sacrifice, which are many, come in several different contexts. The following occur in a strictly ritualistic (sacrificial) setting, devoid of any immediate mythological surroundings. In *Kauśītaki Brāhmaṇa* 4.2, "[He offers] to Viṣṇu Śipiviṣṭa a pap in milk milked in the morning; Viṣṇu is the sacrifice [*yajño vai viṣṇuḥ*]. In that he sacrifices to these deities, [it is because he thinks], 'Let me not wander from the path of the sacrifice.' The sacrificial fee is a bow with three arrows; that is the symbol of a safe journey."[4] In Kauś.B. 18.8, "With a verse to Viṣṇu [RV VII.36.9] they pour them down [Soma plants]; Viṣṇu is the sacrifice [*yajño vai viṣṇuḥ*]."[5] In Kauś.B. 18.14, "He concludes facing north, for north is the world of the living. Having concluded facing north, he offers a full libation with a verse to Viṣṇu. Viṣṇu is the sacrifice [*yajño vai viṣṇuḥ*]; verily thus he grasps the sacrifice."[6] In *Śatapatha Brāhmaṇa* I.7.4.20, praise of Viṣṇu takes on the power of an expiatory mantra, to rid the brahmin priest of the offence of a breach of silence: "If he should utter any human sound before that time, let him there and then mutter some Rik or Yagus-text addressed to Vishnu; for Vishnu is the sacrifice [*yajño vai viṣṇuḥ*], so that he thereby again obtains a hold on the sacrifice: and this is the expiation of that."[7] And in *Aitareya Brāhmaṇa* 3.4, during the guest reception of Soma in the Agniṣṭoma sacrifice, "It [oblation of guest reception] is for Viṣṇu: the sacrifice is Viṣṇu [*yajño vai viṣṇuḥ*]."

The same identification of Viṣṇu with the sacrifice is made again in several variants of a peculiar myth about the beheading of Viṣṇu, which provides an etiological explanation for several objects of sacrificial paraphernalia. In ŚB XIV.1.1.1ff., Viṣṇu is said to have become preeminent among the gods because he comprehended the sacrifice. "He who is this Viṣṇu is the sacrifice (*sa yaḥ sa viṣṇur yajñaḥ sa*]." (This is a pun on the words *sa yaḥ sa* and the word *yaśas*, "fame.") But Viṣṇu, unable to support his fame, his *yaśas*, as the sacrifice, leaves with bow and three arrows.[8] The gods, unable to overcome him, make a deal with the ants to gnaw at Viṣṇu's bowstring so it snaps, cutting off his head. From this decapitation are created several sacrificial implements; from the sound of the bowstring—*ghṛn*—comes the sacrificial kettle, *gharma;* from the wiping—*sammamṛjuḥ*—of the gods' hands in the blood that flowed came the title *samrāṭ* (a name for the Pravargya sacrifice); from the honorific given to Viṣṇu by the gods at this time—*mahān vīraḥ*—came the name *mahāvīra* for the sacrificial vessel; and finally, because Indra rushed forward first (significantly) and embraced Viṣṇu, becoming possessed with his glory, so is Indra named *Makhavan*, which the text strains to designate as an alternate for the "mystical" title, *Maghavan*.

Thus Viṣṇu, as sacrifice, is sacrificed by the gods to create the sacrifice, not unlike the fate of Puruṣa in RV X.90.

Tait.A. V.1.1–7 provides a variant of the ŚB myth, with more etiological explanations; as Viṣṇu's head is severed, it travels through heaven and earth: "From its so travelling [*prāvarttata*], the *pravargya* got its name. From its falling with the sound of *ghrāṁ*, *gharma* obtained his name. Virile energy [or seed, *vīryam*] fell from the mighty one [*mahātaḥ*]: hence the *mahāvīra* [sacrificial kettle] got its name" (Tait.A. V.1.5). And the *Pañcaviṁśa Brāhmaṇa* offers a collapsed version of the former two, calling Viṣṇu *makha* at all times. The identification of Viṣṇu is here affirmed rather redundantly, in the statement that "*Makha* is the sacrifice [*yajñaṁ*]."[9]

The third setting for the identification of Viṣṇu with the sacrifice is the most familiar one, that of ŚB I.2.5.1ff., the so-called germ myth of the Vāmanāvatāra, in which the gods sacrifice Viṣṇu, the sacrifice, to win back the entire earth from the Asuras. Again an etiology accompanies the myth: "By it [Viṣṇu, the sacrifice] they [the gods] obtained [*samavindanta*, from *sam*√*vid*] this entire earth; and because they obtained by it this entire [earth], therefore it [the sacrificial ground] is called *vedi* [altar]" (ŚB I.2.5.7).

The implications of the identification of Viṣṇu with the sacrifice, which seems to be widely accepted in the Brāhmaṇas, as witnessed by the variety of texts and contexts in which it appears, are manifold. First of all, as Biardeau points out, the identification of the sacrifice with Viṣṇu establishes for the god a close rapport with dharma. As the sacrifice, he not only maintains order in the universe, but "the primacy of the brahmins and the good royal government on earth" as well.[10] With the identity of Viṣṇu and the sacrifice is more easily understood Viṣṇu's concern for the triple world, and especially the earth, the sphere of dharma: a concern *not* superseded cosmologically in avatāric Viṣṇu, even though the three worlds themselves and Viṣṇu's spatial relation to them are.

Importantly, what follows almost immediately after the identification of the sacrifice with Viṣṇu is that of Viṣṇu with the Puruṣa of RV X.90 (cf. ŚB I.3.2.1; ŚB XIII.6.1.1).[11] In this significant identity, several basic characteristics of avatāric Viṣṇu may have had their roots, or at least become more understandable in a developmental sense. One of these traits is a cosmogonic function like that of the primeval Puruṣa and, tied to this, the *viśvarūpa,* the all-encompassing form, from which emanates all of creation, be it through an act of sacrifice (Vedic Puruṣa, Brāhmaṇic Viṣṇu) or through power and cosmological knowledge (avatāric Viṣṇu).

Through his identification with the sacrifice and Puruṣa, Viṣṇu is seen to have a close association with another deity identified with these two, Prajāpati. This link is of special significance for the development of specific avatāras; notably the tortoise and boar. For Prajāpati becomes a boar and strokes the earth in TB I.1.3.5f., TS VII.1.5.1, and ŚB XIV.1.2.11: "spreading her out so that she became extended." Further, this idea of expanding was easily connected with the expanding and pervading aspects of Viṣṇu.[12] The tortoise also is said to be Prajāpati in ŚB VII.5.15; significantly this tortoise encompasses the three worlds with its shell; and Prajāpati, in this form, creates living beings. The raison d'être of the tortoise avatāra, whose myth is not one of strict cosmogony and expansion, hence is more understandable in light of the Brāhmaṇa myth.

This series of identifications of Viṣṇu with sacrifice, Puruṣa, and Prajāpati leads us into a further discussion of the development of the cosmogonic nature of Viṣṇu. The creative function develops in Brāhmaṇic Viṣṇu not only from this new set of associations, but also from a continued and now expanded role as the strider of three steps. Viṣṇu's identity as both the sacrifice and strider of three steps forms a link to the human sacrificer or *yajamāna,* the measure of whose height, by measuring stick or possibly by stride, became the unit of measure for marking the parameters of sacrificial ground. This draws the deity and man, sacrifice and sacrificer, acts of creation, striding, and sacrifice into a tightly woven web of associations, all of significant import from the Brāhmaṇic world view.

The association of Viṣṇu's three steps with the three worlds, only tentative in the *ṚgVeda*, is made explicit in the Brāhmaṇa literature, as Tripathi notes.[13] Such is the case in TB III.1.2.6: "Wide-striding Viṣṇu strode three times [over] the great earth, the atmosphere, and heaven." And in ŚB I.9.3.9:

> Vishnu, truly, is the sacrifice, by striding (*vi* √*kram*) he obtained for the gods that all pervading power (*vikrānti*) which now belongs to them. By his first step he gained this same [earth], by the second this aerial expanse, and by his last [step] the sky. And this same pervading power Vishnu, as the sacrifice, obtains by his strides for him [the sacrificer]: for this reason he strides the Vishnu strides.[14]

In VS 2.25 the strides, taken through the medium of the three meters, are also associated with the three worlds:

> By Jagati metre in the sky [heaven] [*divi*] strode Viṣṇu. Therefrom excluded is the man who hates us and whom we detest. By Triṣṭūp metre in the air strode Viṣṇu. Therefrom excluded is the man who hates us and whom we detest. By Gayatrī upon this earth strode Viṣṇu. Therefrom excluded is the man who hates us and whom we detest.

This verse circles back to the identification of the power of the three strides with the power of the sacrifice: the three meters of sacrificial verse are equated with or give "power" to the three strides. Further, in AB 28.7, the strides encompass not only the three worlds, but basic components of the sacrificial universe: the Vedas and Vāc. "Indra and Viṣṇu fought with the Asuras: having conquered them they said, 'Let us make an arrangement.' The Asuras said, 'Be it so.' Indra said, 'So much as Viṣṇu three times traverses, so much be ours; let the rest be yours.' He traversed these worlds, then the Vedas, then speech."[15] The final extension of this comes in the "germ myth" of the Vāmanāvatāra, ŚB I.2.5.1ff., in which Viṣṇu is identified with the sacrifice and the three strides are replaced completely by the three meters that, encompassing Viṣṇu, win the entire earth back from the Asuras. In this myth, several elements join together to express a lasting cosmological statement: the creative power of Viṣṇu as sacrifice, as strider of the three steps (or translated into the sacrificial terms of the three meters), and as obtainer of the earth. As O'Flaherty succinctly points out, "The cosmology implicit in the Brāhmaṇa myth [of the dwarf] is stated explicitly in the Purāṇa version: the whole universe is in Viṣṇu's body."[16]

Further, the sacrificer can associate himself with Viṣṇu and assimilate the power of his three strides by his own striding thrice, as in TS I.7.5.4:

> He goes to the bath along with the creatures which attend him as he performs the vow. Headed by Viṣṇu the gods won these worlds by the metres so as to be irrecoverable; in that he takes the steps of Viṣṇu, the sacrificer becoming Viṣṇu wins these worlds by the metres so as to be irrecoverable. "Thou art the step of Viṣṇu, smiting imprecations," he says; the earth is the Gayatrī, the atmosphere is connected with the Triṣṭūbh, the sky is the Jagati, the quarters are connected with the Anuṣṭūbh; verily by the metres he wins these worlds in order.[17]

And in TS V.2.1.1: "Headed by Viṣṇu the gods won finally these worlds by the metres; in that he strides the strides of Viṣṇu, the sacrificer becoming Viṣṇu wins finally these worlds."[18] Thus in the Brāhmaṇas, the three strides, now firmly equated with the three worlds, have grounded their own nature of cosmogony and cosmological totality in the creative milieu of the sacrifice.

In looking now to the development of Viṣṇu's relationship with Indra in the Brāhmaṇas, we must disagree with Biardeau, who claims that the relationship is an extension of Viṣṇu's sacrificial nature: "It is, moreover, his sacrificial nature which determines the habitual association of Viṣṇu with Indra, king of the gods, beginning with the Vedic hymns."[19] The sacrificial nature of Viṣṇu gives their relationship more depth, but we must see it basically as an extension of the ṚgVedic alliance, the *urgrund* of which lies in their demon slaying, particularly the conquest of Vṛtra.

In the Brāhmaṇas, Viṣṇu's role as aid to Indra in demon vanquishing continues, but becomes more active and explicit. In TS VI.5.1 Viṣṇu's part is still somewhat vague: Indra, when raising his bolt at Vṛtra, was "supported" by Viṣṇu. In AB 28.7, as Indra and Viṣṇu fight the Asuras and conquer them, Indra arranges for Viṣṇu to win back the worlds.[20]

The association of Viṣṇu's three strides (or a variation on them) with the Indra-Vṛtra fight is extended and made more explicit in TS II.4.12.3, in which Indra says:

> "Viṣṇu, come hither: we will grasp that by which he is this world." Viṣṇu deposited himself in three places, a third on the earth, a third in the atmosphere, a third in the sky, for he was afraid of his growth. By means of the third on earth Indra raised his bolt, aided by Viṣṇu. He said, "Hurl it not at me; there is this

> strength in me; I will give it to you." He gave it to him, he accepted it, and [saying], "Thou didst further me," gave it to Viṣṇu. Viṣṇu accepted it [saying], "Let Indra place power (*indriya*) in us." By means of the third in the atmosphere Indra raised his bolt, aided by Viṣṇu. He said, "Hurl it not at me; there is this strength in me; I will give it to you." He gave it to him; he accepted it, and [saying], "Twice hast thou furthered me," gave it to Viṣṇu. Viṣṇu accepted it [saying], "Let Indra place power in us." By means of the third in the sky Indra raised his bolt, aided by Viṣṇu . . .

Then, in the Brāhmaṇas, the Vedic alliance is clarified, and Viṣṇu's role as Indra's aid in Asura battle becomes more pronounced and certainly, with regard to the Vṛtra episode, essential. Whereas in the *ṚgVeda* the cosmogonic consequences of the slaying of Vṛtra are seen chiefly as Indra's feat, in the Brāhmaṇas that aspect of the fight is often given over to Viṣṇu, especially in AB 28.7. How far are we from the Purāṇic myth of the Vāmanāvatāra?

One Brāhmaṇa myth belonging to Indra has importance for all the elements discussed so far (with respect to Indra and Viṣṇu) and cements the commonality of the two as well as Viṣṇu's tendency to absorb traits of Indra. Tripathi refers to this little gem as "a dead branch of the Trivikrama-myth"[21] but we find, rather, that it is extremely important; hence the myth is presented in its entirety:

> The Asuras indeed at first owned the earth, the gods had so much as one seated can espy. The gods said, "May we also have a share in the earth?" "How much shall we give you?" "Give us as much as this Salāvṛkī can thrice run around." Indra taking the form of a Salāvṛkī thrice ran round on all sides the earth. So they won the earth, and in that they won it therefore is the Vedi so called. (TS VI.2.4.4)

The significant elements, for our purposes, are packed into this short myth. First, we see that even for Indra, warrior par excellence, cunning replaces force in this confrontation with the Asuras; next, Indra here takes on another form, that of a Salāvṛkī (hyena) to deceive the enemy; in complement to Viṣṇu's three strides, Indra runs round the earth three times to win it back, and the cosmogony inherent in such an act creates an integral sacrificial element, the Vedi. One feels confident in asserting that what we have here is nothing short of a "twin" to the Vāmana germ myth, ŚB I.2.5.1ff., in that all the important structural elements are present, complete with the etiological explanation at the end.[22] No greater case for a deep and lasting alliance between these two *sakhāyau* could be made than with this "dead branch" of a myth.

As we move toward a more particularized study of the Brāhmaṇa material, with specific reference to the Vāmana and Narasiṁha avatāras, we must first look at the development of Viṣṇu as the dwarf, which has relevance beyond the confines of the Vāmanāvatāra, chiefly with respect to another, more specific identification, that of Viṣṇu as dwarf with the sacrifice. Again we return to ŚB I.2.5.1ff, which contains, if not the first mention of Viṣṇu as a dwarf, at least the first of Viṣṇu as dwarf in the context of a sacrifice and involving the three strides and conquest of the Asuras. This dwarf form of Viṣṇu appears with no warning and, alas, no explanation: ŚB I.2.5.5 begins, "Now Viṣṇu was a dwarf [*vāmano ha viṣṇur āsa*]," preceded in ŚB I.2.5.3 by an identification of Viṣṇu with the sacrifice. MS 3.7.9 involves nearly all the same elements, lacking the sacrificial identification and milieu. In the context of a daivāsura conflict, the gods, having made Viṣṇu a dwarf [*viṣṇuṁ vai deva ānayam vāmanaṁ kṛtvā*] asked for as much land as he could cover in three steps. Viṣṇu then strides over the three worlds, winning them for the gods.

A variation, or perhaps a precursor to Vāmanaviṣṇu comes in TS II.1.3.1, again in the context of a daivāsura struggle, in which Viṣṇu gains the power of the three strides from the sacrifice of a dwarf beast: "The gods and the Asuras strove for these worlds; Viṣṇu saw this dwarf, he offered it to its own deity; then he conquered these worlds. One who is engaged in a struggle should offer a dwarf [beast] to Viṣṇu; then he becomes Viṣṇu and conquers these worlds." The idea of sacrificing the dwarf of a species to Viṣṇu is preceded by a mythological reference in TS II.1.5.2 and without one in TS II.1.8.3, respectively:

> The humpbacked cow is said to be worth 1,000 cows, for when Indra opened the "hole of Vṛtra," the first cow he pulled out was humpbacked, followed by 1,000 cows. "When one obtains a thousand cattle, he should offer a dwarf [beast] to Viṣṇu; upon it the thousand rested; therefore the dwarf, stretched out, affords support to cattle when born."

> He to whom the sacrifice does not come should offer a dwarf [beast] to Viṣṇu; the sacrifice is Viṣṇu; verily he has recourse to Viṣṇu with his own share; verily he gives him the sacrifice, the

sacrifice comes to him. It is a dwarf [beast], for it has Viṣṇu for its deity; [verily it serves] for prosperity.

The series of connections inherent in all this seems to be as follows: Viṣṇu's three steps regain the worlds—Viṣṇu as dwarf takes the three steps—a dwarf animal is sacrificed to Viṣṇu to gain the power of his three steps.

That the dwarf form of Viṣṇu takes hold of the Brāhmaṇas is easily established; the reason for or meaning of the dwarf character is certainly more difficult to ascertain. The only "explanation" that the texts themselves offer, found in JB III.354, is problematical: "Once the gods slept, the demons stole their strength, Viṣṇu saw it and consoled the gods. They offered the Vyāhṛtis [mystical names of the seven lokas] to Viṣṇu, hence he is short."[23] Bhattacharji concludes from this that "Viṣṇu's shortness is thus due to spiritual greatness,"[24] itself a hypothesis even more problematic than the text.

Other scholars have sought the raison d'être of the Vāmana form as well. Adalbert Kuhn, drawing from ŚB I.2.5.1ff., remarks, "He represents (though I cannot prove it in this place) [!!] the sunlight, which, on shrinking into dwarf's size in the evening, is the only means of preservation that is left to the gods . . ."[25] Kuhn's theory is unsatisfactory and untenable, for as Tripathi points out,[26] no natural phenomena is linked to the dwarf in the Brāhmaṇas; Viṣṇu there is the sacrifice and not the sun.

The reason for the dwarf form has also been seen as a necessary movement backward in setting for Viṣṇu's subsequent growth through his strides. Tripathi offers us this rather flat explanation: "for a rather strong dramatic effect—giant against dwarf."[27] Macdonell highlights the cunning element and sees the dwarf form as a clever strategy on the part of the gods: "The introduction of the dwarf as a disguise for Viṣṇu is naturally to be accounted for as a strategem to avert the suspicion of the Asuras."[28]

Attempting to see a more sophisticated meaning in this rather ignominious figure, several scholars have looked to metaphor and analogy. O'Flaherty points in particular to the potentiality for a philosophical allegory: "Here [ŚB I.2.5.1ff.] he actually changes from a dwarf to a giant, but in more philosophical texts he is viewed as the microcosmic soul [*ātman*] who is simultaneously the macrocosmic godhead [*brahman*]."[29]

The dwarf form is also linked to Viṣṇu's association with the sacrifice, as an analogy; one can associate the great form of Viṣṇu with the great power of the sacrifice, "which is apparently small and meaningless, but in reality possesses a transcendent, effective power,"[30] an analogy Tripathi goes on to describe as "colorless and vague," but the veracity of which Biardeau maintains: "The idea is always that of a modest, limited appearance—which is that of the space as it is that of the sacrificial rite—opposed to the real power of the sacrifice."[31]

At this point, we hesitate to offer another hypothesis. We can point out only that, in the Brāhmaṇas, the relationship between the identification of Viṣṇu with the sacrifice and Viṣṇu as dwarf is definitely a close one, and probably coterminous.

As we move now to pick up the thread of the developing Narasiṁhāvatāra myth, our examination of the Brāhmaṇa literature yields what must be considered as the prototype of that myth, the Indra-Namuci myth. As Devasthali concurs, "The story of the man-lion incarnation also appears to have its root in the Namuci legend of the *Śatapatha Brāhmaṇa*."[32] As pointed out before, the *ṚgVedic* poets seemed to have knowledge of this myth, although they did nothing more than allude to it. The Brāhmaṇas recall this allusion, expanding or recounting it into a full-fledged myth. "It may further be noted that the author of this legend himself points to RV VIII.14.13 as its original source."[33]

Although segments are scattered throughout the Brāhmaṇa literature (cf. VS 10.34; PB 12.6.8; MS IV.34; TB I.7.1.6), the fullest version of the Namuci myth is the one Devasthali refers to, ŚB XII.7.3.1–4:

> By means of the Sura-liquor Namuci, the Asura, carried off Indra's [source of] strength, the essence of food, the Soma-drink. He [Indra] hastened up to the Aśvins and Sarasvatī, crying "I have sworn to Namuci, saying, 'I will slay thee neither with the palm of my hand nor with the fist, neither with the dry nor with the moist!' and yet has he taken these things from me: seek ye to bring me back these things!"
>
> They spake, "Let us have a share therein, and we will bring them back to thee."—"These things [shall be] in common to us," he said, "bring them back, then!"
>
> The Aśvins and Sarasvatī then poured out foam of water [to serve] as a thunderbolt, saying, "It is neither dry nor moist;" and, when the night was clearing up, and the sun had not yet risen, Indra, thinking, "It is neither by day nor by night," therewith struck off the head of Namuci, the Asura.
>
> Wherefore it has been said by the rishi [RigVeda S. VIII.14.13], "With foam of water, Indra, didst thou sever the

> head of Namuci, when thou wert subduing all thine enemies." Now, Namuci is evil: having thus, indeed, slain that evil, his hateful enemy, Indra wrested from him his energy, or vital power. In his [Namuci's] severed head there was the soma-juice mixed with blood. They loathed it. They perceived that [means of] drinking separately [one of] the two liquids,—"King Soma, the drink of immortality, is pressed;"—and having thereby made that [Soma] palatable, they took it in [as food].

The following points have significant parallel for the later Narasiṁha myths: first, Namuci is an *Asura,* like his Purāṇic counterpart, Hiraṇyakaśipu; second, Namuci steals Indra's source of strength, the Soma, which may be seen as structurally analogous to Hiraṇyakaśipu's power from the boon granted by Brahmā and by his usurpation of Indra's sovereignty or, in the more bhaktic variants, of Hiraṇyakaśipu's attempts to put an end to Prahlāda's devotion, itself a source of "power" for Viṣṇu; third, and most strikingly similar are the neither-nor conditions of the pact made between Namuci and Indra. That this myth prefigures the Narasiṁha myth is dramatically evident in the presence of one condition of the pact, "neither with the palm of my hand nor with the fist," in the Brāhmaṇas and its absence in the Purāṇic variants, but in its stead the heretofore unexplained action that Narasiṁha takes just before he destroys Hiraṇyakaśipu—that is, he clasps his hands together, striking neither with the palm of the hand nor the first;[34] this motion [*pāṇiṁ saṁspṛśya pāṇinā*] is present in many of the Purāṇic variants (the *Brahmāṇḍa, Vāyu, Brahmā, Viṣṇudharmottara, Padma, Matsya,* and *Harivaṁśa*). And last, the element of trickiness or cunning is present here as well, but is carried out through the agents of the Aśvins and Sarasvatī.

Through this myth, we again are faced with an incomparable affinity between Indra and Viṣṇu. Perhaps due to its concern with sacrificial materials (e.g., the Soma), the myth is even more easily taken over by Viṣṇu later. Facilitating the Vaiṣṇava absorption further, we find that Namuci is later identified with Vṛtra; hence we might overstep our Brāhmaṇic boundaries here and close with a *Mahābhārata* myth that seems to form the link between the Namuci and Narasiṁha myths. In Mbh. V.10.23ff. (CE), Vṛtra pervades the whole universe; Indra goes to Viṣṇu for help, who advises the making of a pact, delineating Vṛtra's conditions of inviolability: "Let me not be killed by Śakra and the gods by anything dry or wet, by stone or by wood, by a weapon or a thunderbolt, by day or by night." With the conditions agreed upon, however, Indra knows he somehow must slay Vṛtra:

"If I do not kill Vṛtra now by deceiving the great demon, whose body and strength are great, I shall not prosper." Thinking in this way, Śakra remembered Viṣṇu, and then saw a mass of foam like a mountain in the ocean. "This is neither dry nor wet, nor is it a weapon. I will throw this at Vṛtra and kill him in a moment." And he hurled at Vṛtra that foam with a thunderbolt in it, and Viṣṇu entered into the foam and destroyed Vṛtra.[35]

When we turn to the figure of Narasiṁha itself, we are faced with the same enigma we encountered with Vāmana, only to a much greater degree: there seems to be no adequate explanation for either the dwarf *form* or man-lion form, save as a strategem;[36] the man-lion is obviously not even the only strategic figure associated with the myth, as its basic structural elements are present in the Brāhmaṇas but the man-lion does not appear until the Purāṇas, at least in the context of the myth.[37]

Thus, in sum, the Brāhmaṇas reflect highly important developments for the general avatāric nature of Viṣṇu, especially the identification of Viṣṇu with the sacrifice and its particularly cosmological repercussions for the Vāmanāvatāra myth and figure, particularly in ŚB I.2.5.1ff. and its partial variants, and for the structure of the Narasiṁhāvatāra myth, in its predecessor, ŚB XII.7.3.1–4. We can see, as has been recently shown in other studies of the Brāhmaṇas,[38] that these texts, long viewed as dominantly ritualistic, are, indeed, a wellspring of budding mythology.

Notes

1. Max Müller called them "theological twaddle"; W. D. Whitney, "absolutely puerile and inane"; A. A. MacDonell "an aggregate of shallow and pedantic discussions;" see O'Flaherty, *Tales of Sex and Violence* (Chicago: University of Chicago Press, 1985), pp. 3–6, for an expanded account of these comments and others.

2. O'Flaherty, ibid., p. 10.

3. "That Viṣṇu had not become one of the most important gods—if not the most important god—first in the Epics, but rather already in the Brāhmaṇas, results from the fact that he is always identified with the sacrifice, *yajña*, the all-encompassing and all-powerful being of the world." (Gaya Charan Tripathi, *Die Ursprung und Entwicklung der Vamanalegende in der Indische-lituratur* (Wiesbaden: Otto Harrossowitz, 1968), p. 39.

4. This occurs in the specific context of the Abhyuditā sacrifice.

5. In the specific context of the conclusion of the Jyotiṣṭoma section of the Agniṣṭoma.

6. In the specific context of the Anūbandhya section of the Agniṣṭoma.

7. In the specific context of new and full moon offerings.

8. Hence the bow and three arrows in Kauś.B.4.2 may be an oblique reference to this myth.

9. Cf. also *Taṇḍya Mahābrāhmaṇa* IX.7.5.8.

10. M. Biardeau, "Le Sacrifice dans l'Hindouisme classique," in *Le Sacrifice dans l'Inde ancienne,* ed. M. Biardeau and Charles Malamoud (Paris: Presses Universitaries de France, 1976), p. 90.

11. Ibid., pp. 91, 97.

12. W. O'Flaherty, *Hindu Myths* (Hammondsworth, England: Penguin Books, 1975), p. 185; further, the central motif of the Brāhmaṇa fish myth, ŚB I.8.1–6, is one of expansion, from small to giantesque fish. "Once the fish had become a god, his expansion frightened Manu just as Viṣṇu's cosmic form frightened Arjuna in the *Bhagavad Gītā* and Kṛṣṇa's cosmic form frightened his mother in the *Bhāgavata Purāṇa.*" *HM,* p. 181.

13. "These three steps are now quite expressly connected with the three worlds—earth, atmosphere, and heaven," p. 27.

14. In the context of the new and full moon offerings, during concluding ceremonies; cf. also ŚB I.1.2.13.

15. In the context of recitations for Hotrakas, to be recited at the third pressing of the Soma at the Agniṣṭoma.

16. O'Flaherty, *Hindu Myths,* p. 178.

17. In the context of new and full moon sacrifices, the reverence of the fires.

18. In the context of the Aśvamedha, preparation of the ground for the fire.

19. Biardeau, "Le Sacrifice dans l'Hindouisme classique," p. 90.

20. Perhaps this is an extension of Viṣṇu's Vedic role as retriever of goods stolen by an Asura after his defeat at the hands of Indra; cf. RV I.61.7; VIII.77.10.

21. Tripathi, *Die Ursprung und Entwicklung der Vamanalegende in der Indische-literatur,* p. 42.

22. Cf. ŚB I.2.5.7, cited on p. 31.

23. One is prompted by such a statement, to investigate the etymology of vyāhṛti: from vy-ā√hṛ, "to utter or pronounce a sound"; the closest one can come to an etymological connection with shortness is through √hṛ, which can mean "to cut off, remove, withhold." One must conclude, given the scanty evidence, that there is little etymological connection between Viṣṇu's shortness and the vyāhṛtis. See Biardeau, EMH III:32ff. on vyāhṛtis.

24. S. Bhattacharji, *The Indian Theogony* (Cambridge: Cambridge University Press, 1980), p. 286.

25. A. Kuhn, as quoted in "Ueber Entwicklungsstufen der Mythenbildung."

26. Tripathi, *Die Ursprung und Entwicklung der Vāmanalegende in der Indische-lituratur,* p. 37.

27. Ibid., p. 39.

28. A. A. Macdonnell, *Vedic Mythology* (Delhi: Motilal Banarsidass, 1974 [1898]), p. 41.

29. O'Flaherty, *Hindu Myths,* p. 177; this certainly raises the wider issue of the relationship between the mythological and philosophical or doctrinal representations of the avatāra concept.

30. Tripathi, *Die Ursprung und Entwicklung der Vāmanalegende in die Indische-lituratur,* p. 40.

31. Biardeau, "Le Sacrifice dans l'Hindouisme classique," p. 91, 1.

32. G. V. Devasthali, *Mythology of the Brāhmaṇas* (Poona: University of Poona, 1965), p. 10.

33. Ibid.

34. This condition is further adhered to in Narasiṁha's subsequent tearing apart of the Asura with his nails or claws, said to be neither wet nor dry.

35. O'Flaherty, *Hindu Myths.*

36. For discussions on the origin and development of the iconography of Narasiṁha, especially as it relates to the figure of Jagannatha, see "The Vaiṣṇava Typology of Hinduization and the Origin of Jagannatha," by A. Eschmann, and "The Formation of the Jagannatha Triad," by A. Eschmann, H. Kulke, and G. C. Tripathi, in *The Cult of Jagannath and the Regional Tradition of Orissa,* ed. A. Eschmann, H. Kulke, and G. C. Tripathi (New Delhi, 1986).

37. Although the man-lion is known as a form of Viṣṇu in the *Nṛsiṁhatapinī-Upaniṣad,* one of the Vaiṣṇava Upaniṣads, whose origin, date,

milieu, and so on remain a mystery to us at present, it is certainly possible that this text is coterminous with or even antedates the first Purāṇic Narasiṁha.

38. See W. D. O'Flaherty's *Tales of Sex and Violence* (Chicago: University of Chicago Press, 1985); and Charles Malamoud's *Cuire le monde* (Paris: Editions La Decouverte, 1989).

④

The Blink of an Unblinking Eye

To understand any text, one must understand its context. Analogously, to comprehend a certain myth or mythological character, the context, the terrain, the universe created *within* the text in which that myth is set, in which that character operates, must be well understood. It is not only a question of "exterior" context, that is, the date and place in which the text was written or gathered, its authorship, its sectarian bent, but also, and perhaps more importantly for our purposes, the "interior" context of the myth, the world constructed by the web of myths within the larger text or corpus of texts that becomes the field of action and interpretation for any myth singled out for study. For our purposes, it would be futile to attempt to know Viṣṇu, a god who, since the *Ṛg Veda*, has been associated with a cosmogonic act and a cosmological locale, without knowing his territory. The complexities of this territory make its comprehension not only a prerequisite, but a task unto itself. The Purāṇas themselves indicate a serious concern for cosmological speculation by designating three of their five defining characteristics as cosmological in nature. Of the *pañcalakṣaṇa* (five characteristics) of which the Purāṇas purport to be composed, one is creation [*sarga*], another recreation (*pratisarga*), and a third the description of a unit of time measurement [*manvantara*],[1] the other two being divine genealogies [*vaṁśa*] and genealogies of kings [*vaṁśānucarita*].

The variety of accounts of creation, time, space, and destruction make the cosmology a veritable jungle, and its comprehension indeed a revelation. It behooves us then, at this point, to take the time to lay out the Purāṇic cosmology in light of the significance it will be seen to have in relation to Viṣṇu and his avatāras. For, without a deep appreciation of the complexity and intricacy of the universe of the Purāṇas, one could never comprehend the full meaning of that epithet of Viṣṇu, "the pervader."

Cosmogony

"A cosmogonic tale is the form by which a culture expresses itself in myths, responds to the most essential questions which are posed by the human mind in the context of that culture."[2] The answer offered by the Purāṇas in the form of cosmogonic myth is specifically Hindu in its persistence to present various visions of reality rather than press toward a specific "ultimate."

> There is no single creation myth to be found in the Purāṇas, but rather a blending of several alternative views of the origins of the cosmos as the composers believed it to be. From the superimposition of various themes, or metaphors for creative process, emerges a complex and not wholly integrated vision of the primal emergence of phenomenal forms from formless potential . . . the blending of these different metaphors for creation has been ingeniously and creatively if not always consistently accomplished. And the attempt so to reconcile apparently different views of the creative process reveals here a distinguishing feature of Purāṇic style as a whole: the writer's refusal to choose between alternative versions of reality, a preference for synthesizing disparate views into a larger whole rather than rejecting apparently dissident elements in favor of one single view considered to be exclusively true.[3]

Despite this great variety, several cosmogonic viewpoints are meaningfully structured to initiate a complementarity with most of the following cosmological structures, while at the same time offering a variety of cosmogonic images that can be and are employed suggestively by the mythographers in other contexts.

Creation is said to be primarily of two types: original [*prākṛtasarga* or *sarga*] and continued [*pratisarga*]. Within this framework the various cosmogonic images are spelled out. The *prākṛtasarga* is that creation which occurs at the beginning of Brahmā's life, the starting point of recorded time. It involves the interaction of Brahmā as the *Puruṣa* or *kṣetrajña* ("knower of the field") with *Pradhāna* or *Prakṛti*, the original chaotic state of the cosmos, causing *Pradhāna* to generate several primary principles of creation in a manner quite similar to that explained in Sāṁkhyan philosophy (see Fig. 1).

Having emerged, these primary constituents of creation form an egg, each enveloping the next as layers of the shell, and holding within the egg the continents, seas, mountains, planets, divisions of the universe, gods, demons, and humankind. Resting on the primal waters the egg develops, and within it grows Brahmā. Thus, the primary creation is really one of making ready the basic structures and materials of the universe (cf. *Vi.P* I.2; *V.P.* I.4; *Br.P.* I.3; *Mark.P.* 42.32ff.; *K.P.* I.4).

The *pratisarga* is the "re-creation" of the cosmos that occurs at the beginning of each kalpa or day of Brahmā, throughout the lifetime of that god. The myth of this *pratisarga*, which seems to have two distinctly different parts, begins not exactly where the *prākṛtasarga* left off, but instead with a sleeping Nārāyaṇa, resting on the waters at the close of the cosmic night (that is, the night between two of Brahmā's days). He awakens to become Brahmā, who in turn becomes a boar (some variants relate this; others simply state that Nārāyaṇa himself became the boar directly; cf. *Mark.P.* 47.8) who dives down into the waters to lift up the earth on his tusks. He constructs the (three or) four lower worlds—earth [*bhūḥ*], atmosphere [*bhuvar*], heaven [*svarga*], and the Maharloka—and divides the earth itself into seven continents.

At this point a rupture occurs in the continuity of the recitation, and we move from the very mythic cosmogony of the boar back to the more abstract aspects of the creation, and to Brahmā himself. Said to be desirous of creating diverse creatures, Brahmā begins a secondary cosmogony that appears to be a harmonious continuation of the *prākṛtasarga*. Through meditation, Brahmā gives birth to six successive creations:

1. Creation beginning with ignorance and consisting of darkness and immovable objects (e.g., plants).
2. *Tiryaksrotas*, creation of animals.

PRADHĀNA primary germ — PURUṢA supreme being or spirit

MAHĀN the great principle, intellect

(SATTVA — RAJAS — TAMAS) GUṆAS strands

(purity, goodness — passion — heaviness)

AHAṀKĀRA I-maker, ego, individuality

VAIKĀRIKA — TAIJASA — BHŪTĀDI

5 BUDDHĪNDRIYA
organs of sense
or perception

\+

5 KARMENDRIYA
organs of action

\+

MANAS mind

ŚABDA TANMĀTRA sound
↓
ĀKĀŚA* ether
↓
SPARŚA TANMĀTRA touch
↓
VĀYU* air
↓
RŪPAN TANMĀTRA color
↓
JYOTIS* fire
↓
RASA TANMĀTRA taste
↓
ĀPAḤ* water
↓
GANDHA TANMĀTRA smell
↓
SAṄGHĀTA* earth

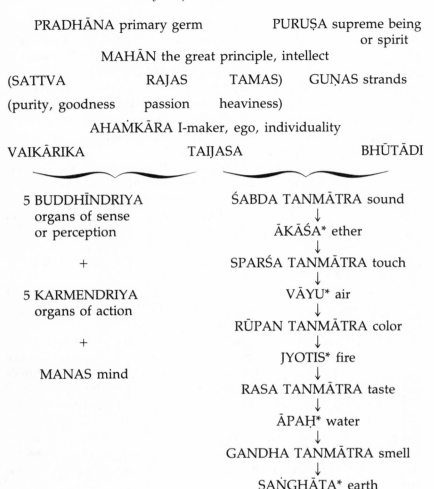

TANMĀTRA: subtle or rudimentary element

*: gross element

Figure 1 Prākṛtasarga (after Biardeau, *EMH* 1:27)

The inhabitants of the Tapaloka (lit., "sphere of austerities") are deities called *Vairājas*, about whom almost nothing is said, except that they are not consumable by fire.[10]

The highest world is the Brahmaloka or Satyaloka, of which the soteriological significance is great: "At six times the distance is situated the Satyaloka, the sphere of truth, the inhabitants of which never again know death" (*Vi.P.* II.7, p. 175). This sphere is the goal of those ascending to liberation at the end of a kalpa.

Two alterations take place in the Purāṇic conceptions of the highest sphere as sectarianism becomes more and more intrusive into the cosmological speculations. In some accounts, the Brahmaloka is said to also be the residence of Viṣṇu or Śiva; hence a devotee aspiring to Viṣṇu or Śiva's abode expects to gain liberation, freedom from rebirth upon attaining that abode, that is, the traditional soteriology of that highest sphere is kept when it is also made the residence of the sectarian deity:

> From Prajāpati loka is the Satya loka removed above by 60,000,000 leagues, the inhabitants where of never again know death; and it is also known as Brahmaloka. It is here that the universe-souled and world-observer Brahmā, the preceptor of the world, dwells perpetually in company with the yogins, by drinking the excellent nectar of yoga. It is the sole door for the yogins attaining to the highest goal, reaching which one is freed from all grief, verily it is Viṣṇu, it is also Śaṁkara. . . . There, in the abode of Brahmā, is also situated a reside of Nārāyaṇa, where the great deluder, the graceful yogin Hari sleeps. It is called the sphere of Viṣṇu, exempt from repeated births and can be attained only by those noble-souled men who are attached to Janārdana. (*K.P.* I.42.4, 5, 7, 9, 10)

In other accounts, the abode of Viṣṇu or Śiva is said to be above the Brahmaloka. For example, later in the *Kūrma Purāṇa*, the Rudraloka is placed above the Brahmā-Viṣṇu loka; the *Śiva Purāṇa* places the Viṣṇuloka above the Brahmaloka and the Rudraloka above that. The *Liṅga Purāṇa* states, "There are eight worlds, Bhuḥ, Bhuvaḥ, Svar, Mahar, Janar, Tapas, Satya, and Viṣṇu" (*L.P.* I.23.31–32). However, the significance of the Brahmaloka and those worlds of Śiva or Viṣṇu above it remains essentially the same; it is the abode of those who are free from the cycle of rebirth.

The Purāṇas also enumerate seven worlds below the earth, variously called *atalas* or regions of *Pātāla*. These nether regions, not to be confused with the more numerous hells or *narakas*, are the dwelling places of the Asuras, the demonic elder brothers of the gods. In beauty and luxury these residences rival the cities and palaces of the gods. Unlike the seven upper worlds, however, the nether regions have no place in the scheme of liberation and play no part in the movement of the *pralaya* or dissolution. For all intents and purposes, they appear to remain static.

The Saptadvīpa System

In addition to the enumeration of the saptaloka system, all the Purāṇas contain accounts of the geography of the earth, usually entitled *Bhuvanakośa* (lit., "the globe or sphere of the earth").[11]

It appears that there were two conceptions of the geography of the earth, one revolving around four islands, the other around seven islands, and to some extent, the texts have attempted to integrate them. Of the two, the *caturdvīpa* (four-island) scheme is probably more ancient and is found by itself only in the *Vāyu Purāṇa,* the cosmological section of which appears to be more ancient and more complete than those of the other Purāṇas. The *caturdvīpa* scheme also bears similarity to part of the Buddhist *cakravala* cosmology.[12] However, "The Purāṇas in their present form lay emphasis on the Saptadvīpa conception, and the more ancient Chaturdvīpa notion is somehow dove-tailed in the new Saptadvīpa frame."[13]

The *caturdvīpa* scheme envisioned the earth like a lotus floating in four oceans, the petals of which surrounded Mount Meru (see Fig. 2). The *saptadvīpa* (seven-island) system radically differed from this in its arrangement of insular continents separated by circular oceans. All that survives from the *caturdvīpa* system *in terms of the continents* is Jambudvīpa, the land in which lies India. A sample description of this ringed-continent conception comes from the *Vāmana Purāṇa:*

> In the middle he placed the well-known Jambudvīpa, which is said to be one lac yojanas in extent. Then stood the Fearful ocean which was its double in extent and then stood Plakṣa dvīpa which was its double externally. And its double was the Ocean of Cane Juice, round in external shape and Śalmalidvīpa was the double of the great Ocean. Its double was the Ocean of Wine and its twice in extent was the Kuśa continent. The Ocean of Clarified Butter is known to be the double of the Kuśa continent. O demon, the Krauñca continent is the double of the Ocean of Clarified Butter. The Ocean known as the Ocean of Curd is the double of it. The Śaka continent is the double of the Ocean of

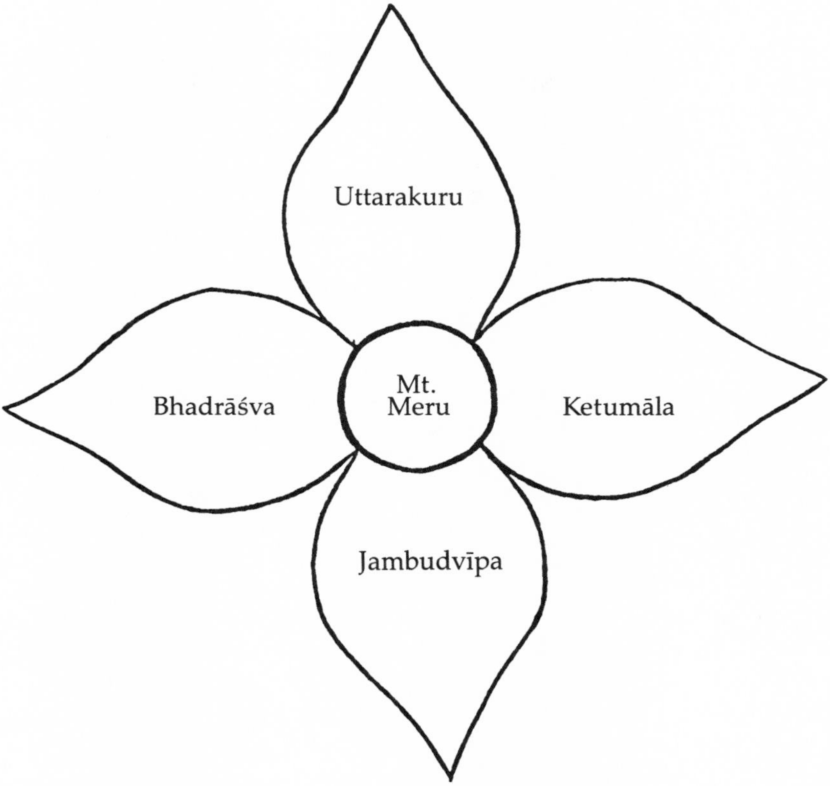

Figure 2 The *Caturdvīpa* Cosmology

> Curd and the great Milk Ocean the double of the Śaka continent. Herein reclines Hari on Śeṣa on his couch. O King of demons, beginning with Jambudvīpa and ending with the milk ocean, all these, double of each other, are known to be forty crores and ninety-five lacs of yojanas in extent. After it is Puṣkaradvīpa, and Svāduda comes after it, with a space of four crores and fifty two lacs of yojanas in extent between them. (*Vām.P.* 11.34–41)

It is much more easily understood when represented diagrammatically (see Fig. 3).

In several versions (e.g., *L.P.* I.53.31–35; *M.P.* 48.12–14; *Bhg.P.* V.20.33–45), the clearwater ocean is said to be surrounded by a kind of boundary called the Lokāloka Mountain (lit., "that which is the world and that which is not the world"), which is described most vividly in the *Bhāgavata Purāṇa:*

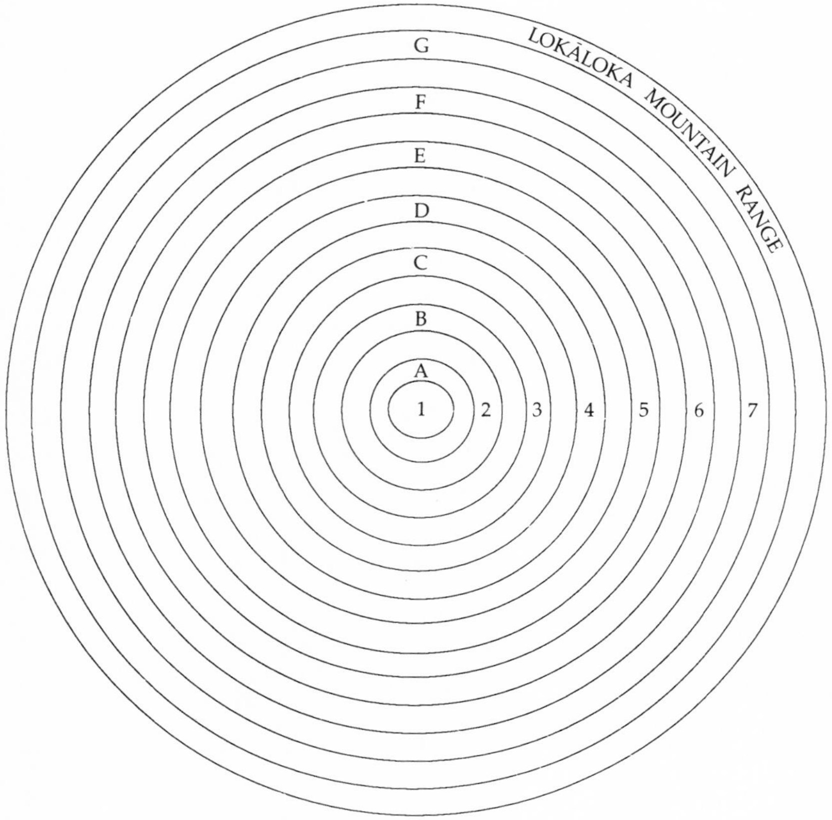

Continents

1. Jambudvīpa—Rose-apple tree island
2. Plakṣadvīpa—Fig tree island
3. Śalmalidvīpa—Silk-cotton tree island
4. Kuśadvīpa—Grass island
5. Krauñcadvīpa—Curlew island
6. Śakadvīpa—Teak tree island
7. Puṣkaradvīpa—Blue lotus island

Oceans

A. Kṣāra—Salt ocean
B. Ikṣurasa—Sugarcane Juice oce
C. Surā—Wine ocean
D. Ghṛta—Ghee ocean
E. Dadhi—Curds ocean
F. Kṣīrodha—Milk ocean
G. Svādu—Clear water ocean

Figure 3 The *Saptadvīpa* Cosmology

> Beyond the sea of fresh water is the mountain belt, called Lokāloka, the circular boundary between the world and void space. The interval between Meru and Manasottara is the land of the living beings. Beyond the fresh water sea is the region of gold, which shines like the bright surface of a mirror, but from which no sensible object presented to it is ever reflected, and consequently it is avoided by living creatures.[14]

Further elaboration on the geography of Jambudvīpa, the innermost continent, is given in all accounts. In this description of the nine *varṣas* or territories we find the most obvious modification of the earlier *caturdvīpa* system. Jambudvīpa, which in the *caturdvīpa* system referred to India, has in one sense become inflated to include within it the three other *dvīpas* (i.e., Uttarakuru, Bhadrāśva, and Ketumāla), but on the other hand refers to an area of which India, now called *Bharatavarṣa,* is only one-ninth.

Jambudvīpa refers to a continent composed of nine varṣas or territories divided by nine different mountain ranges, in the very center of which lies Mount Meru, the *axis mundi* of the terrestrial sphere. Diagrammatically, Jambudvīpa appears as in Fig. 4. Thus, in the horizontal cosmography, India is represented as the southernmost territory of the innermost continent of seven, and vertically as in the middle of fourteen regions (seven upper lokas and seven nether worlds); that is, just slightly south of dead center.

Time

The description of the divisions of time is found in the majority of the Purāṇas[15] and is usually integrated into the cosmogony, in that all the divisions of time are in some way measurements of Brahmā, the creator's, life. A typical description is found in the *Viṣṇu Purāṇa:*

> Oh, best of sages, fifteen twinklings of the eye make a Kashtha; thirty Kashthas, one Kala, and thirty Kalas, one Muhurtta. Thirty Muhurttas constitute a day and night of mortals: thirty such days make a month, divided into two half-months: six months form an Ayana: and two Ayanas compose a year. The southern Ayana is a night, and the northern a day, of the gods. Twelve thousand divine years, each composed of [three hundred and sixty] such days, constitute the period of the four Yugas, or ages. They are thus distributed: the Krita age has four thousand divine years, the Treta three thousand; the Dwapara two thou-

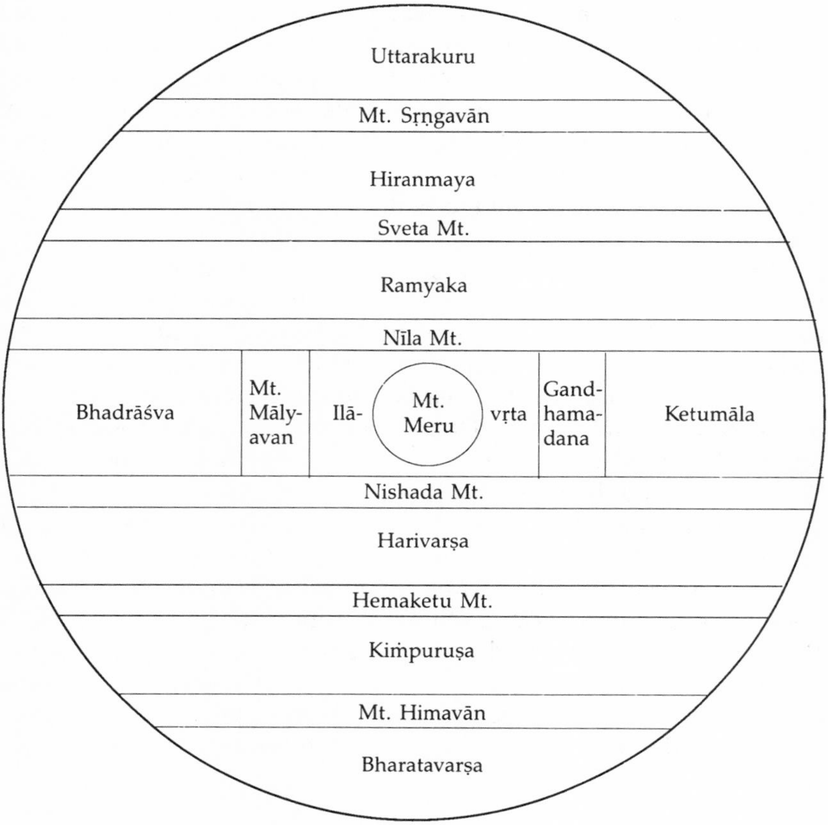

Figure 4 The Territories (Varṣas) of Jambudvīpa

sand; and the Kali age one thousand: so those acquainted with antiquity have declared. The period that precedes a Yuga is called a Saṅdhyā, and it is of as many hundred years as there are thousands in the Yuga; and the period that follows a Yuga, termed the Saṅdhyāṁśa, is of similar duration. The interval between the Saṅdhyā and the Sandhyāṁśa is the Yuga, denominated Krita, Treta, &c. The Krita, Treta, Dwapara, and Kali constitute a great age, or aggregate of four ages; a thousand such aggregates are a day of Brahmā, and fourteen Manus reign within that term . . . Of such days and nights is a year of Brahmā composed; and a hundred such years constitute his whole life. (*Vi.P.* I.3, pp. 20–23)

Basically, for our understanding of the cosmology, there are four important divisions:

1. *A lifetime of Brahmā,* which appears to encompass the totality of time, beginning with the *prākṛtasarga* and ending with the *prākṛta* or elemental *pralaya.* Although the Hindu notion of time is generally regarded as cyclic and never-ending, the texts do not indicate or allude to the existence of more than one lifetime of Brahmā, that is, to a transmigrating Brahmā or to many Brahmās. However, there are expressions of time that exist outside or independent of the measurement of Brahmā's life from the bhaktic viewpoint; for example, Viṣṇu is said to be time [kāla] itself, and in several Purāṇas the entire concept of the measurement of time is exploded when it is said that the lifetime of Brahmā really corresponds to a nimeṣa, or blink of the eye of the supreme Puruṣa, who is Viṣṇu, Śiva, or Kṛṣṇa.[16] This image becomes even more intriguing when one recalls the frequent descriptions of the characteristics of a god, such as in the Nala episode of the *Mahābhārata* (Mbh. III.50–78), which states that a telltale characteristic of a god is that he does not blink. However, in terms of the traditional cosmological framework, the boundaries are formed by the beginning and end of Brahmā's life.

2. A *kalpa,* or one day of Brahmā's life, is the division by which destruction and recreation are regulated. The etymology of the *kalpa* comes from the root √*klṛp,* which means "to become, to happen, to set in order, to frame or form," and so on. So tied up with the activity of creating or structuring is the term *kalpa* that the night of Brahmā, which is of equal duration as a kalpa, is never so called because it is a period of inactivity.

3. *Yuga* refers to two time spans, one encompassing the other; the four yugas—Kṛta, Treta, Dvāpara, and Kali—each of different length, and the mahāyuga or caturyuga, which constitutes one set of the smaller four. The real cyclicity of Hindu time is most pronounced within the concept of yugas.

Whereas the other divisions of time (e.g., day and life of Brahmā) seem to have had a fairly constant measure from their appearance in the Purāṇas, the notion of the yuga and its exact duration remained in flux for some time. Coming from the root *yuj,* lit. "to yoke or join or fasten," Monier-Williams defines yuga as "a yoke, team; a pair, couple, brace; a race of men, generation; a period or astronomical cycle of five (rarely six) years, a lustrum; an age of the world, long mundane period of years."[17] It seems that, coming from both a model of human generation and a period of revolution of heavenly bodies, yuga came to signify a *period of time* of varied length. In both cases, too, it is clear that "a yuga is only one in a chain of evolutions or revolutions that continue successively and endlessly on."[18]

The length of each yuga seems to have undergone several

changes; at first, each yuga was said to be 1,000 years long; then each yuga was expanded to 1,200 years long, and finally, the idea of declining yugas was adopted, showing in all likelihood the influence of the dice game on yuga computation; that is, the names of the yugas, Kṛta, Treta, Dvāpara, and Kali refer to the throws of the dice in an ancient dice game in which they signified the numerical series 4, 3, 2, 1.[19]

By the time of compilation of the Purāṇas, there seems to have been general agreement on the duration and appellation of the yugas; each is preceded by a "dawn" [*saṅdhyā*] and followed by a dusk or twilight [*saṅdhyāṁśa*], so they are computed in the following manner:

NAME	DAWN	YUGA	DUSK	TOTAL
Kṛta	400	4,000	400	4,800 divine years
Treta	300	3,000	300	3,600 divine years
Dvāpara	200	2,000	200	2,400 divine years
Kali	100	1,000	100	1,200 divine years
Total				12,000 divine years

The significance of the dawn and twilight framing each yuga is unclear; most obviously it seems to be an attempt to "microcosmize" each yuga to a greater time period (e.g., the kalpa), which was preceded by the "dawn" of a new creation and the "twilight" harkening a destruction. Further, possibly the entire time system *was* on a much smaller scale, and the dawn and dusk separating each yuga from the next are vestiges of this:

> At the end of the last Kali Yuga of a kalpa, the heat of the sun dries up the whole earth; and by it the three worlds are set on fire and consumed. At last enormous clouds appear and rain for hundreds of years, and deluge the whole world till the waters inundate heaven. As the latter signs are frequently alluded to, in the form of similes in the Epics, etc., as occurring at the end of a yuga (instead of at the end of a kalpa), it is most probably that originally the yuga ended with the destruction and consequently began with the creation of the world.[20]

There is both imagery evocative of the end of a kalpa at the end of the yuga (Kṛta, Treta, etc.) and at the end of the Mahāyuga: "the dusk could be a less complete resorption than the "night" of Brahmā which separates two kalpas. In all cases, the passage of a mahāyuga (or group of four yugas) to another should imply a certain form of resorption, a regression to a state of chaos which will permit a recreation of the golden age."[21] And further, "the fact all the more remarkable that, in the enumeration of units of time, each yuga is given as if preceded and followed by a dusk, the term *saṅdhyā* evoking that of the *pratisandhi* which also designates the cosmic resorption between two kalpas."[22] This becomes especially important with respect to the role of the avatāras in the cosmology, as will be seen.

4. *Manvantara,* or ages of Manu, is another fashion in which the same period of time encompassed by a kalpa is also computed. The intent of this measurement is more quasihistorical or genealogical than cosmological; and this is reflected in the inclusion of the computation of kalpas and yugas in the two topics or *lakṣanas* of the Purāṇas concerned with creation [*sarga* and *pratisarga*], although manvantara is a separate topic unto itself and also concerns itself with the development of long genealogical lists, tracing the descendants of each of the seven *Manus* or primal ancestors who have thus far appeared on earth. Further, the idea of manvantara seems artificially superimposed on the kalpa-yuga system, as there are said to be fourteen manvantaras, each consisting of seventy-one caturyugas, in a kalpa, but the multiplication leaves a remainder of six caturyugas.

Thus, there seem to be three broad conceptions of time:

1. *Cosmic time* is measured by days of Brahmā or kalpas, in other words by a pendulum swing between the two points of creation and dissolution, the interim between each being of equal time.
2. *Sociocosmic time* is measured by yugas, which pertain to human existence but, as we shall see, are tied to the cosmic processes. This is a cyclical conception of time marked by four divisions or interruptions of uncertain significance.
3. *Historical time* is expressed by the manvantara system, which, although grafted onto the cosmic scale, has no integral place in the strictly cosmological speculations themselves.[23]

Pralaya

As there is a primary creation at the beginning of Brahmā's life and a secondary creation at the beginning of each kalpa, so are there complementary dissolutions [*pralaya*] of the world at the close of each kalpa and a final destruction at the end of Brahmā's life.[24]

We will see that, in a sense, the pralaya has more import in terms of what it means for the human individual than does the creation. This is simply because, in the framework of the cosmological soteriology, only during the pralaya can the human ātman achieve freedom from rebirth and absorption into the absolute.[25] As Biardeau says, "In other words, the final perspective and the ultimate reason for the resorption of worlds seems to be the deliverance of beings."[26] The accounts of the pralaya concern themselves as much with the journey of the liberated through the higher spheres as they do with the depiction of the physical cataclysm in the triple world; in fact, the naimittika pralaya seems to consist of two parts, the explanation of the destruction of the triple world and the description of the activities of the saved in the higher realms.

The pralaya that occurs at the close of each kalpa is termed *naimittika,* meaning occasional or incidental. At the close of the one-hundredth Kali yuga, a dearth ensues, killing off all beings on earth. Then Viṣṇu in the form of Rudra, or Rudra himself, descends and enters the seven rays of the sun and burns so as to dry up the entire earth. Then he sets fire to the triple world and the nether worlds, reducing them to ashes, and subsequently breathes forth heavy clouds of diverse colors, which in turn send down torrents of rain. Having inundated the triple world with water, a wind blows to disperse the clouds. This accomplished, the destroyer reclines on Śeṣa, the serpent couch and sleeps on the waters as Nārāyaṇa for a night of Brahmā.

During the pralaya, there is a great deal of movement among the survivors of this cataclysm. Those living on earth, of course, perish. The inhabitants of the two upper spheres of the trailokya, Bhuvar and Svar, flee their abodes for the Maharloka when the flames begin to devour the trailokya. As the heat gets more intense they, along with the inhabitants of the Maharloka, ascend to the Janaloka. The night is spent by these personages chanting hymns of praise to the sleeping Nārāyaṇa. When the new kalpa dawns, they will be reembodied in a subtle form, *mahāsiṣṭha,* in one of the three or four upper lokas,[27] but it is clear they have escaped the transmigratory cycle; they will not be born in a corporeal form on earth. It is unclear exactly how these liberated souls reach the Brahmaloka. All that is said is that they must oscillate between the Maharloka or Svarloka and the Tapaloka or Janaloka for the duration of ten kalpas before they can reach the Brahmaloka: "But then, the inhabitants of the two worlds, whose authority was established, surrounded by the flames, they go to the Maharloka, O Great Sage. Then, afflicted by the great heat, from that world, they go further to the Janaloka, revolving ten times, desiring the highest [realm]."[28]

Thus it appears that, having gone no further than the Jana- or Tapaloka for ten naimittika pralayas, on the eleventh occasion they would ascend finally to the Brahmaloka to join its holy inhabitants in the contemplation of the sleeping Nārāyaṇa.

The dissolution that occurs at the end of Brahmā's life is termed *prākṛta* or elemental *pralaya*. It is simply the reverse process of the *prākṛtasarga*, modeled along the lines of the yogic resorption into the absolute. It is a swallowing up of each cosmogonic principle in backward succession so all that remains is undifferentiated chaos [*pradhāna*] and the supreme Puruṣa, Brahmā, the *kṣetrajña*. In terms of soteriology, *ultimate* and total liberation comes only at this point, the end of Brahmā's life, when all those who have reached the Brahmaloka during the past 36,000 kalpas are completely resorbed into and united with Brahmā, never to become part of Pradhāna again: "Those who are emancipated, they are considered as not returning back; because they are devoid of any quality, because of their departure at the end of the universe, they are soul-less."[29] Those inhabitants of the Brahmaloka absorbed into Brahmā at the end of his life are called *kṣetrajña*, bringing us back full circle to that epithet which describes Brahmā at the beginning of the *prākṛtasarga;* that is, *kṣetrajña*.

Thus, the meaning of the life of Brahmā, the numerous creations and destructions, becomes clearly and ultimately a soteriological one and a statement of the most serious nature with regard to the supreme deity of the bhaktas; that he, Viṣṇu, in his various forms as Brahmā, the boar, Rudra, Nārāyaṇa, creates, preserves, and destroys the universe, that he lives out his nearly incalculable life, only to provide his devotees with the chance to gain liberation.

A Twofold Interpretation of the Cosmology

Viewing the cosmology (i.e., creation, divisions of time and space, destruction) as an integral system that unfolds a soteriology as well as a theory of the nature of the universe, it can be seen as dividing itself into two distinct modes or categories that were referred to earlier with regard to the cosmogonies; that is, sociocosmic and cosmic. To render the most meaningful interpretation of the cosmology and its soteriological intent as a context for the appearance of the avatāras, it must be understood thoroughly within these two structures, the sociocosmic and cosmic.

Sociocosmic

The notion of the smaller or sociocosmic universe is integrally tied to the Purāṇic notion of dharma. Dharma, in its cosmological sense, appears to be an intangible that pertains to sociocosmic time and space. That is, the quality and "quantity" of dharma is governed by the progressive decline of the four yugas, from Kṛta to Kali and, conversely, what distinguishes each yuga from the next, besides its duration, is the status of the dharma in that yuga.

Complimentarily, the sociocosmic realm can be seen spatially as including those spheres in which dharma is of consequence; that is, the triple world.[30] The inhabitants of the earth are ruled by dharma; and the inhabitants of heaven, the gods, are the regulators of the dharma. In this way, the Purāṇic conception of dharma seems to be a reformulation, in a limited sense, of the Vedic concept of *ṛta:*

> The cosmic order or law prevailing in nature is recognized under the name of ṛta (properly the "course" of things), which is considered to be under the guardianship of the highest gods. The same word also designates "order" in the moral world as truth and "right," and in the religious sense as sacrifice or "rite."[31]

In fact, the sociocosmic realm is a very Vedic universe, as it encompasses the old triple world of the Vedas as well as keeping the old Vedic gods who did not later rise to supremacy (e.g., Indra, who is the king of heaven and sovereign of the trailokya, the Aśvins, Maruts, Bṛhaspati, etc.) as the inhabitants of svarga, the guardians of the dharma, and the recipients of the sacrifice. This Vedic and hence sacrificial imagery is brought to the fore in the re-creation of the triple world, that is, the first half of the *pratisarga,* in which Brahmā, in the form of a boar, rescues the earth and refashions the triple world: the boar is called the sacrificial boar; *yajñavarāha* or *vedayajñavarāha,* the symbol of the sacrifice par excellence, the parts of whose body are analogized to the different parts of the sacrifice: "for thy feet are the Vedas; thy tusks are the stake to which the victim is bound; in thy teeth are the offerings; thy mouth is the altar; thy tongue is the fire; and the hairs of thy body are the sacrificial grass" (*Vi.P.* I.4, p. 28).

Although the *naimittikapralaya,* the destructive counterpart to the *pratisarga,* is spaced by kalpas, which are "cosmic" measurements of time, it still maintains a sociocosmic sense in that it *is* the counterpart of the *pratisarga,* by being the destruction of the triple world that is created at the beginning of each kalpa; that is, it is "sociocosmic" because the destruction pertains only to the triple world.

Cosmic

The "cosmic" universe represents a move beyond the Vedic-sacrificial universe to the Upaniṣadic-Saṁnyāsic, and finally bhaktic ideals. Cosmic time is recorded by the lifetime of Brahmā and his days or kalpas. Its spatial realm is the four higher lokas, the worlds that remain untouched by the *naimittikapralaya*. Its inhabitants are those who seek and gain freedom from the cyclicity of the sociocosmic realm and union with the absolute. The cosmic creation, *prākṛtasarga*, unfolds completely in yogic imagery; and its creator, the supreme Puruṣa, Brahmā, emits the cosmos at the beginning of his life and resorbs it at the end, in the same rhythm as the yogin performs his prāṇayāma, and with the same purpose in mind, on a cosmic scale; that is, extinction of material reality and absorption into the absolute.[32]

Qualifications

Before this twofold classification is schematized, attention should be given to the role of the deities involved in the cosmology. Ideally, this will begin to give us a sense of the nature of Viṣṇu's role and action in the cosmology.

Through his persona of Nārāyaṇa, Viṣṇu remains a constant and eternal fixture in the cosmos, despite its flux. Yet in a characteristically Hindu paradox, Nārāyaṇa, through his ability to generate or become other deities involved in the cosmic processes, himself effects the various transitions that keep the cosmos in flux.

The cosmic processes are executed mainly by Brahmā; he instigates and oversees the emanation of creative principles from Pradhāna, his meditation completes the primary creation, and he alone resorbs the world at the end of his life. Several metaphors, however, hint at a kinship or possible identity of Nārāyaṇa and Brahmā, and at a role for Nārāyaṇa in the cosmic processes as well; their common epithet of Puruṣa; the role of the waters (Nārāyaṇa's domain) with respect to the nurturing of the Brahmāṇḍa.

Clearly Viṣṇu-Nārāyaṇa is in control of the sociocosmic processes, but in a once- or more-removed fashion; Viṣṇu-Nārāyaṇa recreates the triple world through the form of a boar or, significantly, through the form of Brahmā, born from Viṣṇu's lotus-navel, who becomes a boar. Analogously, at the end of a kalpa, Viṣṇu becomes Rudra to actually destroy the triple world, and remains asleep in *yoganidrā* during the ensuant night of Brahmā and journey of the

	COSMIC	TRANSITIONAL/ ETERNAL	SOCIOCOSMIC
Creation	Prakṛtasarga ⟵ yogic emission BRAHMĀ	⟶ NĀRĀYAṆA→(Brahmā)→ awakens	SACRIFICIAL BOAR Pratisarga
Time ↓	Kalpa or day of Brahmā (Brahmā's life)	Blink of an unblinking eye	Yugas and units of yugas
Its Determinant	Creation and destruction (Natural processes)		Dharma and its decline
Space	Four higher lokas	Paramaṁ padam	Triple world a) earth, atmosphere,

			heaven or b) heaven, earth, nether worlds
Destruc-tion	Prakṛtapralaya yogic resorption BRAHMĀ	NĀRĀYAṆA ⟶	Naimittikapralaya a) RUDRA: destruction of trailokya b) ascension of souls,
		NĀRĀYAṆA asleep ⟶	contemplation of

The position of the columns is not conceptually accurate; if it were possible, they would be drawn as follows:
1. sociocosmic world as egg or double pyramid
2. cosmic world as overarching umbrella
3. transitional-eternal as umbrella over 1 and 2 but also as an essence in flux pervading 2.

Figure 5 Schematization of Purāṇic Cosmology

souls. It is as the recumbent Nārāyaṇa that Viṣṇu preserves the worlds, holding them within himself. Throughout this night of sleep, Nārāyaṇa alone remains watchful, meditating on those who will make their journey toward liberation during this night. Thus, Viṣṇu maintains the cosmos through the creator, Brahmā, and the destroyer, Rudra, and through his role as Nārāyaṇa during the cosmic night, and as Viṣṇu, the preserver, during the kalpa. Thus, between the two parts of the classification, cosmic and sociocosmic, rests another structure which is both transitional and eternal; epitomized by Nārāyaṇa, who pervades the cosmos by his presence in every transition in its cycle, and who remains eternal, transcendent, epitomized in space by his *paramaṁ padaṁ,* in time by the blink of an eye that never blinks. Now we can schematize the entire cosmology in a meaningful fashion with regard to structures of time, space, creation, and deity (see Fig. 5).

What then of the expanding Purāṇic universe and the changing role of its deities? A tension is generated by a cosmology that places god at the vast boundaries of the spatiotemporal universe and a theology that beckons the follower to draw intimately near to that god; a cosmology that expands, ultimately transcending the territories of dharma and karma, and an ethic that attempts to uphold those principles. Without a mediating solution, the idea of bhakti, which blossoms in the Purāṇic myths in view of the total cosmology, would be completely untenable. For bhakti, there is a need to both integrate the three levels of the cosmos meaningfully and to reduce the problems created by the bhakti ideals. How is this to be done? Enter the avatāras.

Notes

1. In fact, this subject matter is believed to constitute only approximately one-fortieth of the Purāṇa texts. For complete discussion of the five topics, see W. Kirfel, *Das Purāṇapañcalakṣana* (Bonn: Kurt Schroeder, 1927).

2. Biardeau, "Études de mythologie hindoue I," *BEFEO* 54, no. 20; hereafter *EMH.*

3. Cornelia Dimmitt, in *Classical Hindu Mythology,* C. Dimmitt and J. A. B. van Buitenen, (Philadelphia: Temple University Press, 1978), p. 16.

4. See W. Kirfel, *Das Purāṇa Pañcalakṣana,* (Bonn: Kurt Schroeder, 1927), pp. 1–136.

5. Although technically there are fourteen vertical divisions, seven upper lokas and seven nether worlds, in most cosmological speculations the nether worlds are included in the triple world, usually as part of the earth, and are never referred to as *lokas,* but rather as *pātālas* or *atalas.*

6. Cf. also *Mark.P.* 47.65–67.

7. Jan Gonda, *Loka: World and Heaven in the Veda* (Amsterdam: N.V. Noord-Hollandische Uitgevers Maatschappij, 1966), p. 35.

8. Macdonnell, *Vedic Mythology,* (Delhi: Motilal Barnasidass, 1974 [1898]), pp. 8–9.

9. Ibid., p. 168.

10. The *Vāyu Purāṇa* peoples the Tapaloka with the sons of Brahmā who, after many rebirths, become Vairājas in the Brahmaloka.

11. Cf. *K.P.* 1.38.1–44; 1.43.1–48.24; *A.P.* 107.1–108.66; 118.1–120.42; *G.P.* 1.54.1–57.6; *N.P.* 1.3.37–46; *P.P.* 3.3.1–6.42; *Br.P.* 18.1–24.26; *Brmd.P.* 1.14.1–20.58; *Bhv.P.* 2(1).3.1–4.23; *Bhg.P.* 5.16.1–26.40; *M.P.* 112.1–122.64; *Mark.P.* 50.15–52.23; *L.P.* 1.45.1–53.62; *Var.P.* 74.1–89.7; *Vām.P.* 11.31–13.58; *V.P.* 1.33.1–49.186; *Vi.P.* 2.2.1–6.51; *Vidh.P.* 1.4.1–13.13; *S.P.* 5.15.1–18.77; *Sk.P.* 1(2)37.1–87; 3(3)29.37–44; 6.261.36–53; 7(1)11.6–44; *Mbh.* 6.5–12.52.

12. In fact, the Buddhist cosmology, especially as presented in the *Abhidharmakośa,* also appears to be contending with the two alternatives, *caturdvīpa* and *saptadvīpa,* however the schematization of the two into one cosmology is different in the Buddhist than the Purāṇic. (I am indebted to my colleague Randy Kloetzli for pointing this out.) Thus, Jambudvīpa, as India, and the three other islands are located outside the seven-ringed continents and are much further away from Mt. Meru, the *axis mundi.* The Purāṇic and Buddhist cakravala cosmologies bear other interesting similarities, such as the length of life in different lands and karma as the length determinant in Jambudvīpa (cf. W. Kirfel, *Die Kosmographie der Inder* [Hildeshelm: George Olms Verlagsbuchandlung, 1967], p. 58), the declining length of life according to the passage of time, etc. In fact, a comparative study of the whole problem of the relation of the appearances of Buddhas to the cosmology and the relation of the appearances of avatāras to the Purāṇic cosmology would probably yield significant fruit.

13. Rai Krishnadasa, "Purāṇic Geography: Chatur-dvīpa and Saptadvīpa," *Purāṇa* 1, no. 2 (1960):203.

14. H. H. Wilson, *The Vishnu Purāṇa* (Calcutta: Punthi Pustak, 1961 [originally published 1840]).

15. Cf. *A.P* 122.1–24; *N.P.* 1.5.21–31; *P.P.* 1.3.2–23; *Brmd.P.* a.5.4–16; 2.7.70–73; *Brmd.P.* 1.7.95–116; 1.29.1–43; 3.2.91–110; *Bhg.P.* 3.11.6–38; *Mark.P.* 43.23–44; *L.P.* 1.4.1–43; *V.P.* 1.57.1–38; 2.38.211–227; *Vi.P.* 2.8.60–83;

6.3.6–12; 1.3.5–28; *Vidh.P.* 1.72.1–73.19; *Ś.P.* 2(1)10.16–25; 7(1)8.1–31; *Sk.P.* 1(2)39.47.66; 2(1)36.30–34; 2(1)6.194.11–31; 7(1)105.33–39; 7(1)7.18.1–17; *Mbh.* 12.231.1–32; 3.188.17–29; 12.311.1–7.

16. Biardeau, *EMH* 1:44.

17. Monier Monier-Williams, *A Sanskrit-English Dictionary* (Oxford: Oxford University Press, 1970), p. 854.

18. Cornelia Dimmitt Church, "The Yuga Story: A Myth of the Four Ages of the World as Found in the Purāṇas" (dissertation, Syracuse University, 1970), p. 72.

19. For more complete discussion of the development of the yuga concept, see D. R. Mankad, *Purāṇic Chronology* (Anand: Gangajala Press, 1951); "Manvantara Caturyuga Method," *ABORI* 23 (1942):271–290; "The Yugas," *Poona Orientalist* 6 (1941):206–216; A. B. Keith, "The Game of Dice," *JRAS* London (1908):823–828; *Purāṇa* II (1969); and for a more complete discussion of the yuga story and its interpreters, see Church, ibid.

20. Hermann Jacobi, "Ages of the World (India)," *ERE* 1:207.

21. Biardeau, *EMH* 1:22, n. 2.

22. Ibid.

23. For the useful terms *cosmic* and *sociocosmic*, we are indebted to Biardeau, *EMH* 1:22f.

24. Cf. *K.P.* 2.43.1–44.30; *A.P.* 368.1–27; *G.P.* 1.216.1–12; *P.P.* 1.41.48–73; *Br.P.* 231.1–233.75; *Brmd.P.* 1.6.43–77; 3.1.119–3.113; *Bhg.P.* 12.4.1–43; *M.P.* 165.1–24; *Mark.P.* 43.1–24; *V.P.* 2.38.132–40.135; *Vi.P.* 6.3.1–7.106; *Vdh.P.* 1.74.1–79.30; *Mbh.* 3.188.66–88; 12.233.1–19; 12.331.1–312.17.

25. Significantly, the Purāṇas refer to mokṣa, or individual liberation as *Ātyantika pralaya* (*Vi.P.* VI.3, p. 493), and to physical death as *nitya pralaya* (*Bhg.P.* I.3). The three or four pralayas are usually described one after the other, i.e., Naimittika, Prākṛta, Ātyantika, and Nitya, indicating that they are regarded as different types of the same phenomenon, dissolution, pralaya.

26. Biardeau, *EMH* 3, *BEFEO* 55 (1969):33.

27. Biardeau, *EMH* 3:38.

28. *tatas tāpaparītās tu lokadvayanivāsinaḥ*
kṛtādhikārā gacchanti maharlokam mahāmune
tasmād api mahātāpataptā lokāt tataḥ paraṁ
gacchanti janaloka daśavṛttyā paraiṣinaḥ

(*Vi.P.* VI.3.28–29)

29. *tatraiva parinirvāṇāḥ smṛtā nāgāminas tu te*
nirguṇatvānirātmanaḥ prakṛtyante vyatikramāt

(*V.P.* II 40.45)

30. The nether worlds seem to be in some sense included in the triple world, as they are burned in the pralaya and are the abode of the demons, whose goal it is to usurp heaven and thereby gain control of the dharma.

31. Macdonell, *Vedic Mythology.*

32. The yogic and Upaniṣadic imagery of creation is far too complex to enter further into here; see Biardeau, *EMH,* vols. 1–3.

5

Myths of the Narasiṁhāvatāra: Motif Analysis and Discussion

In turning to the analysis of the myths themselves, we are faced with the enigma of Narasiṁhāvatāra, whose ferocious and sanguinary appearance surprises not only the unsuspecting characters within the myth, but ourselves as well. As was obvious from the meagre evidence for the development of such a form in the Vedic and Brāhmaṇic literature, we are not confronted here with the scholar's fantasy of smooth and clear development such as is found in Vāmana; to the contrary. The earliest evidences of the myth (which include the man-lion figure) appear within the textual boundaries of this study, in the *Mahābhārata,* which, although brief in its telling of the myth, obviously knows the basic structure well. In other words, we begin with a functioning myth and watch its permutations; how the myth arrived at its rudimentary form, and where the figure of the man-lion came from remain unsolved mysteries.[1]

Our "text," then, is composed of eighteen versions of the Narasiṁhāvatāra myth, and our purpose is to analyze each version to expose its unique treatment of the myth, its particular permutations of structure and language, and to bring to attention the meaning inherent in the mythical structure and the subtleties of its language.

To make a discussion of eighteen myth versions less cumbersome, some organizational principles have to be imposed; we have tried to adopt principles here that seem to develop from the texts themselves. Basically, there are two.

First, through careful reading of the myths, it became clear that many of them were similar or identical to one or two others in either structure or in both language and structure. That is, although we might find three myths in *Harivaṁśa, Padma Purāṇa,* and *Matsya Purāṇa,* when subjected to parallel text construction, a method adopted from Willibald Kirfel,[2] they proved to be one myth known to three separate poets, either through a common text kernel or borrowings from one of the texts themselves. This occurs in three cases, reducing what at first appeared to be eight versions to three, allowing for minor variation in word choice or order.

There were also cases where it was evident that, although the poets of different versions were not working with a common text, the version of the myth each knew was structurally the same; all the basic elements that moved the tale were identical, but each myth was obviously an individual's work, not a wholesale borrowing of another text. Texts that fell into this category were grouped together for the sake of a more coherent discussion of the myths; they were never understood as being *one text.*

Thus, given these two factors, the eighteen versions can be arranged more manageably into seven groups. Where several versions are basically one text, they are grouped together and indicated as such. Where structural similarity exists, allowing for minor differences, those texts are grouped together, their differences exposed.

The second principle of organization is one of ordering the presentation of the texts or text groups in a meaningful way. Our method is one not governed by "historical" or chronological relationships between the contexts of each text (i.e., between epics and Purāṇas) and between the texts themselves, but rather by that sequence of texts which allows us to expose the full range of the myth itself. Through examination of the myths it became clear that central structural changes pivoted around one character in the myth, the Asura Prahlāda. As he assumes a greater role in the myth, the structure and tone shift, until the entire motivational machinery is changed to center on him. This movement significantly altered the characterization and role of the avatāra in the myth as well, as will be shown. Prahlāda's role showed diversity enough to gauge the changes in several stages, and the sequence of texts emerged in distinct relationship to the way in which Prahlāda was characterized.

The advantages of such a method of organization seem several;

although some myths found in texts thought to be "later" historically than others are presented as preceding them in our discussion,[3] they are arranged to show a progression that has relevance not only to the myth itself, but to an overall historical change in religiosity as well; that is, the development of bhakti, which is expressed predominantly in the myth through the vehicle of Prahlāda. That *this* development has particular meaning for our study of the avatāra hardly needs mention.

Thus we will be examining seven text groups in such a way as to highlight the overall development of the myth with regard to its religious rather than historical context and to bring to light the character and nature of the Narasiṁhāvatāra and the meaning of his myth, using the set of five motifs (see Chapter 1) as signposts toward our goal.

Myth Analyses

Mahābhārata 3.272.56–60 (CE 3.100.21a); Bhāgavata Purāṇa II.7.14; Agni Purāṇa 4.2–3

These first three versions are what we call *compressed myths.* Rather than represent a full myth, in which mythological language is employed and one is meant to be drawn into the tale, the *Mbh., Bhāg. II,* and *Agni P.* variants each give us a summary of the myth in restrained and streamlined language; they are *references to* the myth, quickly recapitulating the essentials of the story line. For this latter reason they are included among the texts; they give a clear picture of what the poets of these three texts saw as the pertinent details, characters, and actions that structure the myth. They represent the myth stripped of its language and pared down to bare bones; and for this reason, they hold our interest.

Mbh. 3.272.56–60. This is the chronologically earliest evidence of knowledge of the Narasiṁhāvatāra myth within epico-Purāṇic literature. A curt four *ślokas* long, and reduced to a half *śloka* in the Critical Edition, the myth occurs in a brief recounting of several of the descents of Viṣṇu. The myth supplies no explanation of motivation; just that Viṣṇu, having made half his form man and half lion, went to Hiraṇyakaśipu's hall and "sounding like a cloud, resembling a multitude of dark clouds" (images found frequently in subsequent myths), he tore the Asura apart with his nails.

It is interesting to note that in this myth, after becoming Narasiṁha, the god touches one hand with the other [*pāṇiṁ saṁspṛśya pāṇinā*], an act that seems to have no particular meaning in this version (and many others) but may reflect the link between the boon in the Indra-Namuci pact of the Brāhmaṇa myth (see Chapter 3, p. 39) and the Narasiṁha myth; in *ŚB* XII.7.3.1–4, Indra promises not to slay Namuci with the palm of the hand or the fist.

In all, this short version of the myth seems to be a summation, drawing on a wider knowledge of the tale that is kept in reserve, rather than presenting us with the myth in what might be its most rudimentary form.

Bhāg.P. II.7.14. The Narasiṁha myth is recapitulated during a brief description of all of Viṣṇu's avatāras, which at this place in the *Bhāgavata* number twenty-two. Narasiṁha appears as the twelfth manifestation, preceded by that of the tortoise and followed by Viṣṇu on Garuḍa who saves an elephant from a crocodile.

The myth is sufficiently short to present here in its entirety:

> The Lord then assumed the form of Nṛsiṁgha and tore into pieces with His nails the Lord of the Daityas, Hiraṇyakaśipu by name, who was approaching the celestials with a dreadful club in his hand. Hari thus removed a great fear from the minds of the gods. In this form His face worn [sic] a very dreadful sight by reason of the rolling eye-brows and grinding teeth.

It is a condensation lacking in elements one would have expected to find in the *Bhāg.P.*, given the elaborate amplification the myth receives later, in *Bhāg.P.* VII.2–10.47. The boon is lacking, and although we find it often assumes lesser importance in myths that center around the figure of Prahlāda as bhakta, any mention of him is curiously lacking here, in what is probably the most Vaiṣṇava-bhaktic of all Purāṇas. The instrument of death is traditional, being the nails or claws usually used to circumvent the conditions of the boon, but the reason for Hiraṇyakaśipu's murder is pitifully dull; he was bullying the gods with a club. Perhaps, this description is based on a piece of iconography, which emphasizes the terrifying countenance of Narasiṁha as he tears the Asura apart.[4]

Agni P.4.2–3. The *Agni Purāṇa* retelling occurs as well in a description of Viṣṇu's avatāras, which begins classically with the fish manifestation and places Narasiṁha, as tradition does, after the tortoise and boar.

Again, our compressed myth is short enough (two *ślokas*) for easy recital:

> Hiraṇyākṣa had a brother by name Hiraṇyakaśipu. Having vanquished the celestials he occupied all their possessions and monopolized their share in the sacrificial offerings. Having assumed the form of a man-lion he killed them together with all the Asuras and reestablished the Suras in their own stations. Narasiṁha was then worshiped by the celestials.

Here again, the boon is completely omitted. What is emphasized, more explicitly here than in the *Bhāg.P.* version (although there the central concern is the same) is the welfare of the gods as guardians of the trailokya, inhabitants of heaven, and proper recipients of the sacrifice—all very orthodox, brahminic concerns, free at this point from the superseding universe of bhakti. The rhythm stressed here is not that of the yugas or pralaya (kalpa), but of the upside-down–rightside-up oscillation that characterizes the relationship between the Devas and Asuras.

Brahmāṇḍa Purāṇa 2.5.3–29; Vāyu Purāṇa 67.61–66

The two variants that appear in the *Brahmāṇḍa* and *Vāyu Purāṇas* are markedly similar; that the two texts themselves are rooted in a common text kernel has been noted by Pargiter[5] and Kirfel,[6] the latter of whom reconstructed the Narasiṁha myths in both texts in parallel fashion for easy comparison.[7] Swain contends that the Narasiṁha myth found in the *Vāyu* is closer to the original kernel, the *Brahmāṇḍa* redactor having "improved" upon the story with a few embellishments.[8] Our concern is not with primal proximity but with the two texts as we have them now (see Appendix I for *Brahmāṇḍa* translation).

Both myths begin abruptly with the austerities of Hiraṇyakaśipu, which are seemingly without motivation, lasting for 100,000 years, and culminating in the granting of a boon by Brahmā. Here the texts differ on the actual words and terms of the boon. The *Vāyu* is more terse and does not emphasize the neither-nor fabric of which the boon is often made: "Immortality and inviolability from all beings. Having conquered the gods with yoga, to become the god of all. Dānavas, Asuras, and gods must be equal, and I must possess the great sovereignty of Maruti. Give me this wish" (*Vāyu P.* 67.62). The conditions here, although beginning like the *Brahmāṇḍa* with invincibility and immortality, become curiously modest and humorously democratic. In no other variant does the demon suppress the desire to literally put down the Devas. The wish for sovereignty of Maruti is strange and unique, its exact meaning unclear. Maruti, according to M. Monier-Williams[9] is only a patronymic of Dyutana, Bhīma, and Hanumat. Marutī (long *ī*) refers to the northwest quarter and the constellation Svāti; but that is not the form we have here. Maruti can also refer to Vāyu and may have specific meaning in this text because it comes from the *Vāyu Purāṇa*.

The *Brahmāṇḍa* boon begins with the same words about invincibility, immortality, and conquering the gods through yoga. Here it diverges, supplying a more elaborate, more typical set of conditions: "I will make the sovereignty endowed with strength and vigor. Dānavas and demons, gods together with celestial singers, all these must be my subjects, close at hand, and serving me. Inviolable by wet or dry, by night or day" (*Brahmāṇḍa P.* 2.5.16–17). The narrator's comment immediately following is instrumental in exposing the fabric of such a boon: "Then, having been spoken to, Brahmā gave the boon possessing interstices [*saṇtaraṁ varaṁ*]" (2.5.18). The boon, which seemed to blanket all threat to power in the *Vāyu*, is so constructed here as to intimate those loopholes through which the man-lion leaps. This particular myth (the *Brahmāṇḍa*) does not allow the subtlety of the neither-nor language to suffice and exposes the obvious for the reader, forecasting the future. Although gods and demons seem to be set on equal footing here as well, the malice is revealed—all shall be as slaves to Hiraṇyakaśipu's throne.

The *Brahmāṇḍa*, developing the Asura's feeling of power, continues in phrases that are commonplace in subsequent myths. Hiraṇyakaśipu, not content to leave well enough alone, exercises his power by becoming significant elements in the cosmos: "In heaven, he became the sun, moon, and wind" (2.5.20b–21a) and on earth, took on functions of all three castes: "He became the herdsman, the shepherd, and the cultivator, he became the knower of all the worlds, giving interpretations of the mantras; Leader, protector, preserver, giver of the sacrifice and sacrificer" (2.5.21b–22). Moreover, his quest for power hints at going beyond the trailokya to a more daring attempt at supremacy; the vehicle through which Hiraṇyakaśipu wins his power, yoga (*Brahmāṇḍa P.* 2.5.15), is already a more threatening force than the conventional "trailokic" means, battle and physical prowess.[10] And as a further affront to Viṣṇu's specific powers, the myth relates that Hiraṇyakaśipu, "having *pervaded* [*vyāpya*] the world, everything standing and moving, he lived in many forms" (2.5.19b–20a).

Thus, although in the *Vāyu* and *Brahmāṇḍa* texts Hiraṇyakaśipu achieves a sovereignty over the trailokya that is cosmologically improper, there is little of the unabashed malevolence in his actions that we find in subsequent myths. Moreover, this affront, explicit in the *Brahmāṇḍa*, implicit in the *Vāyu*, goes beyond the trailokya to Viṣṇu and *his* sphere of power, to the universe of bhakti and its master. Biardeau notes this with a keen eye: "It is therefore not simply the dharma which is in question, but the dharma integrated into the hierarchical structure of bhakti, where Viṣṇu is the only sovereign lord."[11]

The jump from Hiraṇyakaśipu's full-blown power to his abrupt demise at the hands of Narasiṁha, from this point of view, is more understandable. The cosmological inversion of Devas and Asuras is there, but understated. However, the combined force of Hiraṇyakaśipu's threat to the trailokya, the sacrificial, orthodox world and to Viṣṇu's power, encompassing the universe of bhakti, warrants the swift and violent murder by Narasiṁha. In this simple form of the myth, from which Prahlāda is totally absent, we have a hint of the concerns on which the myth will eventually focus.

The murder "weapon" in both texts, is the traditional one: Hiraṇyakaśipu is torn apart by the nails of the man-lion. That this method is one that circumvents the conditions of the boon is made known by both the *Brahmāṇḍa* and the *Vāyu* ("Then he who was very strong, battling him with his arms, tore apart the demon with his nails, because they are neither wet nor dry" [*Brahmāṇḍa* 2.5.29; *Vāyu* 67.67]). Even though the latter does not specify those conditions in its account of the boon, it is either obviously aware of them or is drawing from the "text kernel" or common knowledge.

Harivaṁśa 41; Brahmā Purāṇa 213.44–79; Viṣṇudharmottara Purāṇa I.54

These three versions are structurally and semantically as close to one another as the *Vāyu* and *Brahmāṇḍa*, as parallel text reconstruction has shown. This procedure revealed that the *Brahmā P.* and *Harivaṁśa* versions are more similar to each other than to the *Viṣṇudharmottara*, which supplements the end of the myth with a great deal more description of the terrifying appearance of Narasiṁha and his battle with the Daityas, and differs in several details as well. Barring this major exception, however, one can see from studying the parallel presentation of the texts that there are only minor differences—a different word choice for the same meaning, the order of *ślokas* reversed; in the end, these are three remarkably congruent texts, given the many hands through which they may have passed.

The *Harivaṁśa* and *Brahmā P.* texts begin by setting the action in the classical temporal frame, that is, in the Kṛta Yuga [*purā kṛtayuge*]. Although that time frame is taken for granted in scholars' lists of the appearances of the avatāras, surprisingly this is one of only a few places in the myth itself that it is actually stated. The *Vdh.* text omits this and instead sets the action by referring to the murder of Hiraṇyakaśipu's brother, Hiraṇyākṣa, as the impetus for the former's austerities to gain power for revenge.

In all three texts, the action begins with Hiraṇyakaśipu's severe austerities which last, in the *Br.* and *HV,* 11,500 years, and in the *Vdh.*, 11,000. The significance of these numbers is unclear, except that both are close to the length of a Mahāyuga, 12,000 years; this may be an additional device to create the aura of preeminent pralaya, an aura that surrounds the appearance of each avatāra and is inherent in the dawn-dusk interval between each yuga (the Narasiṁhāvatāra is said to appear at the *end* of the Kṛta Yuga).

Impressed with Hiraṇyakaśipu's tapas, Brahmā arrives with entourage and grants the boon. The basic conditions are the same in all three myths and show a marked expansion from the *Vāyu-Brahmāṇḍa* myths. The Asura seeks to assure his invincibility by saying he may not be killed by gods, demons, Gandharvas, Yakṣas, snakes, Rakṣases, men, or Piśācas, nor cursed by ṛṣis; to be killed neither by weapons, swords, rocks, or tree, by neither wet nor dry (high nor low in the *Br.P.*). The *Br.P.* and *HV* add a loophole, a variation on the Brāhmaṇic prototype; that he who is able to kill the demon with one stroke of the hand will be his death. It is interesting to note that the ideal method of slaughtering the sacrificial animal is by one clean stroke.

In the second half of the boon Hiraṇyakaśipu expresses his desire to encompass the universe, taking the form of its various elements. This wish, compact in the *Vāyu-Brahmāṇḍa* versions, is elaborated on in all three texts: to be the sun, moon, wind, and fire, water, air, ether, and the universe itself (or ten regions); to be anger and lust, and, significantly, to be Varuṇa, Indra, Yama, and Kubera, the four *lokapālas* or guardians of the West, East, South, and North, respectively; also, to be a Yakṣa and leader of the Kiṁpuruṣas (both attendants of Kubera). In other words, Hiraṇyakaśipu's desire is to both surround and penetrate the universe, to take on all its various forms, recalling the sacrificial victim par excellence, Puruṣa.

Understandably enough, the gods are upset by Brahmā's gift of the boon, and question him. But as Biardeau points out, Brahmā,

> as a personification of brahman-Brahman, is linked to the Vedic Revelation, to the world of sacrifice and, more generally, of karman to a world where each act is done for a precise result and should produce this result. . . . Brahmā, the science of action in person, finds himself constrained to "give" that which the act must produce. That is why he cannot oppose even the most unreasonable requests.[12]

As a personification of the orthodox universe, he must play according to its rules. But Brahmā promises eventual victory for the gods: "By all means is the fruit of his tapas to be attained by him; but, at the end of his tapas, Viṣṇu, the Blessed One, will become his conqueror" (*Br.P.* 2.3.64; *Vdh.P.* I.54.21; *HV* 41.63).

The oppression perpetrated by the Asura, "made arrogant by the granting of the boon," is described in these myths. No sooner is the boon received than does Hiraṇyakaśipu begin his reign of terror, harassing people, overpowering the tapasic munis in their hermitages, and conquering the gods, ousting them from heaven, and usurping their sovereignty over the trailokya. The inversion of dharma in the trailokya is complete; Hiraṇyakaśipu made the Daityas deserving of the sacrifice and the gods undeserving.

With this last straw, the gods prevail upon Viṣṇu as the solution to the problem, notably praising him first as the sacrifice or master of the sacrifice. Viṣṇu responds by taking the man-lion form and confronting the evil demon. In the *Br.P.* and *HV* versions, the description of this form is brief and reminiscent of the *Mbh.* texts. "Looking like a dark cloud, sounding like a dark cloud, glowing with the energy of a dark cloud, and swift as a dark cloud" (*Br.P.* 213.78; *HV* 41.78). The imagery recalls both the monsoon and the pralaya, a common yoking of metaphors. Fulfilling the conditions of the boon and its loophole, in the *Br.P.* and *HV* Narasiṁha kills the Daitya with one hand, an alternative to the usual clawing sequence.

The *Vdh.* myth deviates after the Narasiṁha form is fashioned, and begins to supply us with some of the full-blown pralayic imagery we find in many of the subsequent versions; the description of Narasiṁha goes beyond the dark cloud and is full of light and fire, recalling again both the storm and the destruction. In several phrases, the likeness of this terrifying theophany to the pralaya itself (or to the traditional lord of the pralaya, Śiva) is explicit: "His tongue was moving up and down, to and fro, appearing and disappearing, and it quivered like the lightning of the cloud at the end of the pralaya [*pralayānta*]" (*Vdh.P.* I.54.40); "having flaming breath which, going in and out, sounded like the cloud at the end of a kalpa [*kalpānta*]"

(*Vdh.P.* I.54.42a). Another provocative metaphor recalls the pralaya and Śiva's association with it as well: "having the lustre of the submarine fire [*vaḍavānala varcasaṁ*] to consume the great ocean of Daitya troops" (*Vdh.P.* I.54.35b). As O'Flaherty has noted, "The fire of doomsday is said to have the form of a mare (*vaḍava*) at the bottom of the ocean; inextinguishable flames issue from her mouth. . . . Eventually, this fire of the underworld will destroy the universe, at the end of an aeon."[13] She further notes that often Śiva engenders the mare-fire with a blast of his third eye; other times there are references to Śiva as the mare-fire itself.

This fierce apparition of Viṣṇu shatters the *sabhā* of the demon (as it often does in other versions) and after a swift victory over the Daitya troops, he takes Hiraṇyakaśipu on his lap and tears open his chest, a scene portrayed in many iconographic images. The myth is subtle and leaves it to the reader to connect the man-lion form and his mode of murder with the conditions of the boon, unlike the *Br.P.* and *HV* versions.

In these three versions, the emphasis is on the order and safety of the trailokya and has less to do with the bhakti universe than the *Vāyu* and *Brahmāṇḍa* discussed previously. The malice of Hiraṇyakaśipu is inflicted on the inhabitants of earth and heaven and on that sacred act which binds them together, the sacrifice. Viṣṇu is appealed to as, among other things, the sacrifice or its master, and acts primarily to restore order to the triple world. Even in Hiraṇyakaśipu's wish to be different gods and elements, those he chooses pertain to and even border the trailokya. The *words* about pervading the world and living "in many forms" do not appear in these versions. Although Hiraṇyakaśipu wins his boon through tapas, it is tapas seen by Brahmā as karman, an act that, like any other, yields fruit.[14]

This side of the Narasiṁha myth, which speaks to the dharmic concerns of the trailokya and the alternating rhythm of daivāsura relations, is well developed in all three myths. The aspect of the myth that highlights the destructive, pralayic nature of the Narasiṁhāvatāra and addresses itself to a grander, cosmic rhythm begins its development in the *Br.P.*, *HV*, and especially in the *Vdh.P.*, and comes into its own in subsequent myths.

Śiva Purāṇa II.5.43; Kūrma Purāṇa I.15.18–72.

In these two versions, we are introduced to the figure of Prahlāda for the first time in the context of the myth, and the element of *darśana* begins to figure into the structure of the myth. The versions are similar basically in their treatment of this aspect, but show no other structural or semantic similarities to suggest they draw from a common kernel; it is for our own analysis that we group them together.

The *Śiva P.* version makes clear the malicious and power-hungry nature of Hiraṇyakaśipu from the start. After the death of his brother at the hands of the boar avatāra, the Asura, "always fond of enmity with Viṣṇu that he was" (*Ś.P.* II.5.43.5a) wreaked such havoc on the trailokya that the gods were forced to abandon heaven and roam the earth incognito (recalling the fate of the Pāṇḍavas in the *Mbh.*). After this incident, the myth continues in its usual way with the tapas of Hiraṇyakaśipu. The cosmological significance of this act is made explicit here for the first time. The fiery power of the Asura's tapas is clearly pralayic in its threat of destruction: "The smoking fire of penance springing from his head, spreading all around scorched the worlds all round above and below. The gods [who had returned to heaven], scorched by that, abandoned heaven and went to Brahmā's region" (*Ś.P.* II.5.43.12–13a). Likewise, the fire that inaugurates the pralaya sends the gods to higher regions for safety.

Brahmā arrives at Hiraṇyakaśipu's dwelling and grants the boon according to the Asura's terms:

> O creator, O lord of subjects, never may I have the fear of death from weapons, missiles, thunderbolts, dry trees, mountains, water, fire, or onslaught of enemies—gods, Daityas, sages, Siddhas, or in fact from any living being created by you. Why should I expatiate on it? Let there be no death for me in heaven, on earth, in the daytime, at night, from above or below, O lord of subjects. (*Ś.P.* II.5.43.16–17)

The boon granted, Hiraṇyakaśipu sets about his usual work; he "disturbed all righteous activities and defeated all the gods in battle" (*Ś.P.* II.5.43.20b). The gods go directly to Viṣṇu, reclining on the Milk Ocean, who promises to kill the demon.

Viṣṇu assumes the man-lion form, described in majestic and terrifying imagery: "powerful like the fire at the time of dissolution. He was identical with the universe" (*Ś.P.* II.5.43.27a). Notably, he leaves on his mission "when the sun was about to set." Seeing him arrive at the city of the Daityas and make a powerful entrance by "smashing and crushing" many of the inhabitants, Prahlāda, heretofore unmentioned, remarks to his father Hiraṇyakaśipu that the "universe-formed lord," Viṣṇu, has come as Narasiṁha, and submission is the best tact to take. Prahlāda's concept of the universe-formed lord, in subsequent versions, is developed into a *Gītā*-esque vision of the universal theophany. Here we are at the inception of Prahlāda's role as the seer of the avatāra's true nature, which he plays not only in this myth but also in that of the Vāmanāvatāra (see Chapter 6).

As might be expected, Hiraṇyakaśipu pays no heed to his son's advice and orders his troops to a full attack. The fate of those soldiers is described in a metaphor that is used constantly as well in Vāmana's destruction of the Asura troops and in the *Gītā*'s theophany of Viṣṇu swallowing up the Kauravas and their allies: "At his behest the leading Daityas who desired to catch the lion approached him but they were burnt in a trice like the moths in the blazing fire attracted by its colour" (*Ś.P.* II.5.43.33). It is an image of the fire that attracts and consumes, that swallows up the world and its inhabitants at the pralaya. This doomsday quality is expressed temporally as well by the poets' phrase that the fight lasted "a day according to the calculation of Brahmā" (*Ś.P.* II.5.43.35a), that is, a kalpa, after which the pralaya ensues according to cosmological theory (see Chapter 4). At the end of this period of time, the battle ends suddenly as Hiraṇyakaśipu is seized and clawed apart on the knee of Narasiṁha.

Before parting, Narasiṁha rewards the wise Prahlāda by crowning him king, inaugurating a relationship that eventually will become the very raison d'être of the myth.

The *Kūrma Purāṇa* myth begins in the traditional manner but offers some unique additions that brilliantly help to elucidate the basic conflicts of the myth, the meaning of Prahlāda's budding role and, in a kind of epilogue, an insight into the nature of Narasiṁha. In the context of a telling of the Daitya genealogy, we are introduced to Hiraṇyakaśipu who, "by propitiating the lord Brahmā Parameṣṭhin, and eulogizing him with various prayers, the demon Hiraṇyakaśipu, possessed of great strength and prowess, saw the Lord and received divine boons [*varān divyān*] (*K.P.* I.15.19). No mention is made of the terms of these boons. In a blink of the eye, the gods, oppressed by the demon's army, go first to Brahmā and then to Viṣṇu in his dwelling on the northern bank of the Milk Ocean.[15] The gods, recounting their plight to Hari, allude to the nature of the boon: "He [Hiraṇyakaśipu] is [by the boon of Brahmā] unslayable by all the beings except by thee" (*K.P.* I.15.31a). To solve the problem, Viṣṇu acts in a way unique to this version of the myth; he creates a Puruṣa to kill the demon. As the Puruṣa approaches the enemy camp, he is attacked by the Asura army, which includes Prahlāda. These soldiers, sons of Hiraṇyakaśipu, recognize the Puruṣa to be "indeed that god Nārāyaṇa" (*K.P.* I.15.41) but are nonetheless undeterred from battle. Vanquishing the sons easily, the Puruṣa, however, is badly wounded by the father and repairs to Viṣṇu. In his stead, Hari now assumes the

Narasiṁha form through yogic meditation. Arriving at the demon city, the man-lion dramatically eclipses his predecessor: "He seemed like the fire at the time of pralaya [*yugānta*]" (*K.P.* I.15.51b). Prahlāda, the eldest son, is dispatched to do battle with the enemy, but is again quickly defeated. Watching the battle progress from the sidelines, Prahlāda sees the man-lion escape the Pāśupata weapon (which is, notably, Śiva's weapon) unharmed and, in a flash of insight, he "knew the lord to be the all-souled eternal Nārāyaṇa" (*K.P.* I.15.57b). Unlike his earlier recognition of Puruṣa, this brings knowledge, an instantaneous conversion, and an outpouring of bhakti. Futilely trying to sway his father from further battle, Prahlāda watches as the man-lion tears Hiraṇyakaśipu to pieces with his claws. Prahlāda's brothers suffer a puzzling fate: "The other sons headed by Anuhrāda and thousands of demons were led to the valley of death [*yamālayaṁ*] by the lion produced from the body of the man-lion" (*K.P.* I.15.70). The full meaning of this act is difficult to discern, but we are helped by another glimpse of this aspect of the man-lion, in a kind of epilogue to the myth, which does not follow immediately but occurs late in Chapter 15, in the myth of the Asura Andhaka. The same episode occurs in *Matsya Purāṇa* 179, several chapters after its version of the Narasiṁha myth, and in *Garuḍa Purāṇa* 241, although no Narasiṁha myth proper appears in that text.

Andhaka, son of Hiraṇyākṣa, develops an ardent fancy for Umā, Śiva's wife. Struck in battle over her with Śiva, Andhaka creates thousands of other Andhakas capable of vanquishing Śiva.[16] With Śiva seeking shelter at his side, Viṣṇu aids the god, creating "a hundred of excellent goddesses for the destruction of the demons" (*K.P.* I.15.135). They easily kill the little Andhakas and send their creator running. Finally, after yet another battle, Andhaka repents and pays homage to the gods and Umā.[17]

Yet Viṣṇu's creation, the goddesses or Matṛkās (mothers), as they are called, needs to be dealt with. Having gone with the Bhairava form of Rudra to the nether region (here *pātālaṁ*), "where that destroying form of Viṣṇu, invested with darkness, Hari in the shape of a man-lion, the unmanifest lord abides" (*K.P.* I.15.220), the Matṛkās are afflicted with hunger and begin to eat up the entire trailokya. Śiva is powerless in coping with them but, beckoned back by Viṣṇu-Narasiṁha, in the latter's presence "all the matriarchs bent on destruction bestowed their power upon Bhairava, Śambhu of excessive strength" (*K.P.* I.15.228).[18] Viṣṇu, linking himself to Śiva in a rare alliance, instructs them that only Kāla, a form of himself and a former one of Rudra, is the proper destructive agent: "It is that unassailable lord Kāla, destroyer of the world, who in the form of Rudra would devour the entire world at the end of the age [*kalpānte*]" (*K.P.* I.15.233).[19] Through these episodes we can begin to see a distinct interconnection between the man-lion and Śiva, destruction, and death—all linked here uniquely by the vivid image of the bloodthirsty goddesses. Here, Narasiṁha emerges as the master of controlled destruction, destruction in its proper time and place; such will not always be the case.

Matsya Purāṇa 161–163; Padma Purāṇa (Uttara) V.42; Harivaṁśa 226–233 [III.41–47]

As M. V. Vaidya notes,[20] these three versions appear to be elaborations on the *Harivaṁśa* 41 and *Brahmā Purāṇa* 213 texts. The inflated length of the texts is due primarily to the insertion of an ornate and long-winded description of Hiraṇyakaśipu's *sabhā*[21] and another listing the names of countries and rivers shaken by Hiraṇyakaśipu's wrath. Other elements have been added as well that are more pertinent to our discussion.

The three versions are in substantial verbal agreement and structurally the same, as our parallel-text reconstruction has shown. Most differences appear to be minor, alternate word choice, inverted phrase order; small but significant changes made from one version to the next shall be pointed out in discussion. As in the case of the *HV* 41–*Br.P* 213–*Vdh.P.* I.54 text, we are able to discuss the three cotemporaneously.

As in their shorter predecessors (just listed), all three versions set the myth in the Kṛta Yuga and begin with the tapas of Hiraṇyakaśipu, which lasts 11,000 years in the Purāṇa versions and, as before, 11,500 in the *Harivaṁśa*. Brahmā arrives as usual, with his entourage and grants the boon, the conditions of which remain the same as those in the short versions, with the exception of the *Harivaṁśa*, which adds two *ślokas:*

> That I shall not die in heaven nor in the nether regions, not in the air nor on earth, neither during the day nor at night. I may only succumb under the force of one who, in the middle of my officers, soldiers, and animals which serve for vehicles, triumphs over me by the power of his arms. (*HV* 226.15–16)[22]

The myth proceeds as it does in the short forms, with Brahmā's explanation of the inevitability of Hiraṇyakaśipu's harvest of the fruit of his tapas, and the promise of Viṣṇu's intercession. The reign of terror begins: the triple world comes under the demon's sway, heaven becomes his dwelling, and the gods are ousted from the sacrifice in favor of the Dānavas. The myth makes an important point concerning Hiraṇyakaśipu's motivation: he acts through the intoxication of the boon and is "impelled by time [*kāladharmiṇā; kāladharmataḥ* (*M.P.*)]." The gods repair to Viṣṇu, the "sacrifice itself," who creates his man-lion form and leaves for the demon's dwelling. It is interesting to note that, although no "loophole" in the boon exists in these versions concerning death by the blow of one hand, the man-lion nevertheless grasps one hand with the other at this point in all three versions.

At this place in the myth the long description of Hiraṇyakaśipu's dwelling is inserted. At its conclusion, Hiraṇyakaśipu sees Narasiṁha, "having arrived like the wheel of time, having the form of a man-lion, covered with ashes like the god of fire" (*M.P.* 162.1; *HV* 228.1; *P.P.* V.42.84).[23] Now the three texts make a significant addition; Prahlāda, the "mighty son of Hiraṇyakaśipu," sees the man-lion as no other Asura does. The *Padma* version relates that "Prahlāda saw the lion-god who had arrived with the divine form" (*P.P.* V.42.85b).[24] However, the *Harivaṁśa* and *Matsya* reading is significant: "With a divine eye [*divyena cakṣuṣā*] Prahlāda saw the lion-god who had arrived" (*M.P.* 162.2b; *HV* 228.5b). Implied in this verse is proof of some already existent relationship between Prahlāda and Viṣṇu that, given Prahlāda's subsequent vision of the man-lion's theophany, draws strong associations with Arjuna's role and experience in the climactic eleventh chapter of the *Bhagavad Gītā*.

In essence, Prahlāda sees the entire universe contained in the body of the man-lion. Sensing the horror and inevitable destruction this figure will bring ("My mind predicts that this is horrible and will cause the end of the Daityas" (*P.P.* V.42.88; *M.P.* 162.5; *HV* 228.8]), Prahlāda's account of his vision subtlely supersedes the claims of his father's boon; as Hiraṇyakaśipu aspired to become the moon, sun, stars, and even the Lokapālas, here Prahlāda sees all these and more within Narasiṁha's form. Not only the guardians of the trailokya reside there, but their cosmological superiors as well, Brahmā and Śiva. Hiraṇyakaśipu is reduced to insignificance as all those he claimed inviolability from, all those he deigned become, are revealed as but parts of this man-lion's universal form.

> The moon with the stars, the Ādityas together with the rays of light, Kubera and Varuṇa, Yama and Śakra, lord of Śacī, Maruts, gods and Gandharvas, ṛṣis and ascetics, Nāgas, Yakṣas and Piśācas, Rakṣases of terrific prowess, Brahmā, the gods, and Paśupati, all those standing and moving wander about on his brow. (*P.P.* V.42.90–92; *M.P.* 162.7–9; *HV* 228.10–12)

And, as Arjuna saw the Kauravas swallowed up by Kṛṣṇa's terrible form, Prahlāda sees the Daitya hosts contained as well in this all-form. What Prahlāda sees, however, in his private vision, is not dominated by destruction. The eternal dharma, intellect, enjoyment, truth, tapas, and self-restraint add balance to the horrifying visage of the man-lion.

The *Harivaṁśa* records the effect this *darśana* has on Prahlāda: "he lowered his head and plunged into virtuous meditation" (*HV* 228.17). And now Prahlāda, previously called mighty [*viryavān*] is now described as very wise [*mahāmatiḥ*].[25]

Prahlāda's recital of his vision has no effect on his father but to spur him on to battle with even greater appetite, and the poets give full reign to martial vocabulary in the ensuing description of the fight. During this episode, pralayic imagery is at its best. Narasiṁha roars "openmouthed, like time itself" (*M.P.* 162.17) or "like Yama, king of Death" (*P.P.* V.42.100; *HV* 229.4), and is likened to the sacrificial fire: "Hiraṇyakaśipu hurled these weapons at Narasiṁha like an oblation into the blazing fire" (*M.P.* 162.28; *P.P.* V.42.111; *HV* 229.17). And then "the ocean of Daitya troops, stirred up by the gale of anger, washed over everything like the ocean washed over Mt. Mainaka" (*M.P.* 162.30; *P.P.* V.42.113; *HV* 229.19), precisely the same sequence of events, fire followed by flood, that characterizes the pralaya.

The poets continue. The world is covered with darkness, and the seven winds blow, "all announcing a catastrophe" (*M.P.* 163.3; *P.P.* V.42.124; *HV* 230.5). "All the planets which become visible in the destruction of all the world, all these were seen in the sky roaming as they pleased" (*M.P.* 163.34; *P.P.* V.42.125b–126a; *HV* 230.6b–7a). Then the sun becomes pale, a dark twilight cloud appears, and "seven horrible dim suns appear in the sky"[26] (*M.P.* 163.37; *P.P.* V.42.129; *HV* 230.10) and "All the planets rose up together by degrees, horrible planets which come at the end of a yuga" (*M.P.* 163.39b–40a; *P.P.* V.42.131b–132a; *HV* 230.12b–13a). Everything points to impending disaster: "The images of all the gods open and close their eyes, laugh and cry and moan profoundly, throwing smoke or flames as if they announce the end of the world" (*M.P.* 163.44–45; *P.P.* V.42.137–138; *HV* 230.17–18). Nature goes awry, fruits bear fruit, flowers bear flowers, rivers run backward.

At this point the *Harivaṁśa* interpolates, introducing the figure of Śukra, preceptor of the Asuras, to whom Hiraṇyakaśipu turns to interpret the omens (as if any interpretation is needed). Predictably, Śukra warns that he will lose his throne and his life; indeed, the danger is great.

Hiraṇyakaśipu fights on, unabashed. The poets expound, in a

long and tedious geographical description, on what is shaken by this battle and the fury of the demon.

Quickly, now, the battle draws to a close as Narasiṁha, armed with club and trident (respectively, Viṣṇu's and Śiva's weapons)—or, in the *Harivaṁśa,* significantly, with the vajra, Indra's weapon, and trident—attacks Hiraṇyakaśipu and gores him to death with his nails. This most destructive act initiates a renewed peace in the universe: "And the earth and time, the moon and ether, the planets and the sun, all the regions, the rivers and mountains and the great oceans became clear at the destruction of the son of Diti" (*M.P.* 163.95; *P.P.* V.42.187; *HV* 232.14). And Viṣṇu, well praised by the gods and other celestials, puts aside his man-lion form and returns to his abode on the Milk Ocean.

Śiva Purāṇa III.10–12; Liṅga Purāṇa I.95–96.

These versions hold two things in common: first and most important for our discussion, they represent a change in the motivational structure of the myth, which now comes to pivot around the figure of Prahlāda; and second, they present us with a decidedly Śaivite twist to the ending of the myth that, like the Matṛkā episode of the *Kūrma, Matsya,* and *Garuḍa Purāṇas,* affords us insight into the relationship between Śiva and Narasiṁha. The two versions are not identical semantically; indeed they offer quite a bit of variety although the structuring principles are the same. The endings, unique to these two versions, are in near semantic agreement.

The *Ś.P.* tells the myth in the context of Śiva's incarnations. It begins traditionally with Hiraṇyakaśipu's tapas (10,000 years) and his boon, declared simply to Brahmā: "None of your creation shall kill me" (*Ś.P.* III.10.13). The demon conquers the trailokya, harasses the gods, violates all virtuous rites, and oppresses brahmins. Yet it is now another act of malice which spurs Viṣṇu to action: "When the king of the Daityas hated his own son, Prahlāda, Viṣṇu became his particular enemy" (*Ś.P.* III.10.16). Taking a form and paying heed to specifications of time and space that no longer exist in this myth's version of the boon, "Viṣṇu came out from a pillar in the hall at dusk, in the body of a man-lion, with great fury" (*Ś.P.* II.10.17). With haste he takes the demon king to the threshold and tears open his stomach with his claws.

Dispensing with the formerly essential structure of the boon altogether, the *Liṅga Purāṇa* myth begins with a description of Prahlāda as a Viṣṇubhakta. After repeated efforts on Hiraṇyakaśipu's part to sway his son from Viṣṇu's to his own worship, the Asura king vows to have Prahlāda put to death. We have here, in unadorned form, the final phase through which the myth passes.

As in the *Śiva Purāṇa* version, this affront to his own bhakta causes Viṣṇu to become the man-lion and kill Hiraṇyakaśipu. Arriving at his palace "like the fire of annihilation at the close of the yugas, he harassed the leading Daitya" (*L.P.* 95.17b) splitting him open with his claws.

At this point, in both the *Śiva Purāṇa* and *Liṅga Purāṇa* myths, a subtle shift of events begins. In other versions, the tapas of Hiraṇyakaśipu took on a threateningly destructive tone, and Narasiṁha, in a properly pralayic role, wiped him out, inaugurating a new sense of order. But in this Śaivite context, roles begin to change; after he slays Hiraṇyakaśipu, Narasiṁha himself becomes a threat of pralayic proportions:

> On seeing Narasiṁha, Devas, Asuras, Nagas, Siddhas, Sadhyas, Viṣṇu [?], Brahmā, and others left off their courage and strength and went off in different directions in order to protect their lives. When they had gone, the lord Narasiṁha who had a thousand shapes, who had all feet and all arms, who had a thousand eyes, whose three eyes were the moon, sun, and fire, who was the wielder of Māyā, remained there enveloping everything. (*L.P.* I.95.19–20)

> Though the Lord of Daityas was killed, yet the gods did not derive any pleasure. The fiery fury of the man-lion did not subside. The entire universe was again excited by that fiery splendour. The gods were miserable. Saying "What will happen now?" they kept themselves at a safe distance from fear. (*Ś.P.* III.10.25–27a)

In the *Śiva Purāṇa* myth, Prahlāda is sent in to cool Narasiṁha down. He cools his heart, but the "flame of fury" does not subside. Now the gods go to Śiva for refuge, praising him with epithets, among which is *Vāmana* (*L.P.* I.95.46), completing the inversion begun when they praised Narasiṁha as *Paśupati* (*L.P.* I.95.30). Śiva calls forth one of his own terrifying forms, Vīrabhadra, "the cause of the Great Dissolution" (*L.P.* I.96.4). Śiva-Vīrabhadra attempts to calm Narasiṁha, who rages more furiously: "I am now going to annihilate the universe of mobile and immobile things. . . . I am Kāla, the cause of destroying the worlds" (*Ś.P.* III.11.27; *L.P.* I.96.27; *Ś.P.* III.11.35; *L.P.* I.96.34). As they banter back and forth about the superiority of each one's destructive power, Śiva takes on a new form, the awful Śarabha, a horrifying winged beast that binds Narasiṁha and flies off with him clutched in its talons. Narasiṁha concedes the fight, acknowledging his own arrogance and praising Śiva's power. Śiva-Śarabha destroys the man-lion and, in the *Liṅga* version: "Just as water mixed with water, milk with milk, and ghee with ghee, all merge into one, in the same manner Viṣṇu has merged into Śiva" (*L.P.* I.96.12).

Thus these two versions, which, in haste, might be dismissed as Śaivite revision of a powerful avatāra myth, have important elements for our understanding of both the development of the myth and the character of Narasiṁha. In these versions we see, for the first time, how the theme of Viṣṇubhakti will come to radically alter the mythological structural elements and move the focus of the myth from trailokic, dharmic concerns to those of the larger universe of bhakti. These changes have as their focus the budding character of Prahlāda, who provides us with an even more radical example of the all-encompassing circle of bhakti than does Rādhā, as Biardeau remarks: "At the same time, one shouldn't forget that the devotee is an *Asura,* and thus the salvation brought by devotion to Viṣṇu has a universality which the narrow brahmanic conception of deliverance didn't have."[27] The relationship between Prahlāda and Viṣṇu as bhakta and saviour, which was developing but still marginal in previous myths, now moves center stage to alter the motivational structure. As Paul Hacker remarks, "Yet Prahlāda continues to still be the center of the story."[28] Viṣṇu's concern for the gods, the trailokya, its dharma, and sacrifice is now superseded by the larger universe of concerns of Viṣṇu and his bhaktas. This move in cosmological and theological levels remains in place for the rest of the myths we shall discuss.

If the *Śiva* and *Liṅga Purāṇa* myths mark the turning point in structure, they are equally important in what they reveal about the nature of this man-lion and his relations with Śiva. We noted earlier that the Śaivite ending common to the *Liṅga* and *Śiva* versions displayed a subtle shift in Narasiṁha's role. In other versions, Narasiṁha plays a correct and timely destroyer to Hiraṇyakaśipu's improper attempts at inversion and destruction. He also punishes the demon for overstepping his boundaries, for threatening to become what only Viṣṇu is. Here in a curious epilogue the poets have put the man-lion in Hiraṇyakaśipu's place as untimely destroyer and arrogant pretender to divinity, and Śiva in Narasiṁha's place as proper and true destroyer; a switch that can be represented formulaically:

Hiraṇyakaśipu : Narasiṁha = Narasiṁha : Śiva

The resonance between these two sets of relationships is made even clearer when Śiva binds Narasiṁha, who then becomes a Śiva-bhakta, just as Narasiṁha threatens but then converts Hiraṇyakaśipu in the *Viṣṇu Purāṇa* version.[29]

The competitive closeness of nature between Śiva and Narasiṁha is displayed many times in this epilogue: the exchange of epithets (*Paśupati* for Viṣṇu, *Vāmana* for Śiva), the supercilious argument over who is the true destroyer, as well as an image issuing from the *Ś.P.* myth that is also recorded in the *Bhāgavata Purāṇa* and *Skanda Purāṇa* myths, in folk versions, and in countless iconographical images—that of Narasiṁha appearing instantly from a pillar. The pillar, whose numerous sacrificial associations shall be discussed later, has a close counterpart in Śiva's liṅga: "The iconography shows him bursting from the pillar like Śiva whose human form appears on opening the liṅga [*liṅgodbhavamūrti*]."[30] This calls to mind as well the description of Narasiṁha in *L.P.* I.95.20, cited earlier, in which he is said to have three eyes, a traditional characteristic of Śiva.

Through these "aberrations" that the texts sometimes afford us, we are given a glimpse into the nature of Narasiṁha: from the Śaivite point of view, he is too Rudraic for comfort; from others, such as the Andhaka episodes of the *Kūrma* and *Matsya*, this man-lion out-Śivas Śiva. In either case, the point is clear; through the vehicle of Narasiṁhāvatāra in these particular myths we are at one of the closest junctures of the paths of the two great Hindu gods, Viṣṇu and Śiva.

Skanda Purāṇa VII.2.18.60–130; Bhāgavata Purāṇa VII.2–10.47; Viṣṇu Purāṇa I.16–20

These last three versions represent the culmination of that slow transformation from a mythological mode of expression of the Narasiṁhāvatāra to a mythologically framed vehicle for the outpourings of bhakti teachings, coming from the mouth of its most popular Purāṇic advocate, Prahlāda. We have moved from the Narasiṁhāvatāra myth to, as the *Viṣṇu Purāṇa* aptly titles it, *Prahlādacarita*, "The Tale of Prahlāda." This new centrality is reinforced, in the *Bhāgavata* and *Viṣṇu Purāṇa* versions, by the fact that the myth does not appear in a sequence of avatāra myths but, in the former, as a pick-me-up told by Sukadeva to King Parikṣit, whose faith in Hari is plagued by doubts and, in the latter, in the context of a Daitya genealogical section.

We turn first to the *Skanda* version, perhaps the most problematic in its poor construction. The *Viṣṇu Purāṇa* and *Bhāgavata Pur-*

āṇa versions shall be discussed together, as their communality and complementarity are more easily shown, especially with the help of previous, able scholarship.

That the *Skanda Purāṇa* version is not well known is clear from Paul Hacker's silence on it in his otherwise extensive study of Prahlāda in the man-lion and other myths.[31] The myth itself, situated in a Purāṇa too cumbersome for adept handling and too corrupt for fluid translation, at least at our hands,[32] is nestled in an incredibly long and even more problematic version of the Vāmana myth (see Chapter 6), which digresses for 150 *ślokas* to recount the *daśavatāra* myths.

The Narasiṁha myth begins here by establishing the malicious actions of Hiraṇyakaśipu who, "having violated the law, established the sovereignty on earth, having vanquished the chief of gods" (*Sk.P.* VII.2.18.64). His greed not yet sated, he begins to covet heaven and torment his son Prahlāda. As the poet unfolds the virtuous character of Prahlāda and his disrespect for his father's rule, the boon is abruptly introduced; to wit:

> While he [Prahlāda] was being taught, he was angry [thinking], "The Daitya does not honor the gods because of the sovereignty of the two worlds." Pleased with his [Hiraṇyakaśipu's] austerities, Lord Brahmā granted him a wish. "Immortality from the gods and men, O Best of Gods. May my death be from no one. If it may be, may it be from Viṣṇu, who may be somewhat lion, somewhat man." (*Sk.P.* VII.2.18.67–69)

The superfluous nature of the boon is made clear by Hiraṇyakaśipu's foretelling of his own death by the avatāra. The myth, once made ingenious by deft circumvention of the pact, is now, at least in its craft and subtlety, dull. Its concerns have definitely shifted.

The focus is clearly on Prahlāda, whose character as a Viṣṇu-bhakta now unfolds. Probably drawing on the *Viṣṇu Purāṇa* and *Bhāgavata Purāṇa* versions, the *Skanda* hastily relates Hiraṇyakaśipu's futile attempts to have his son put to death by sword, elephants, snakes, water, and fire, for the crime of devotion to Hari. Unmoved by his father's own threat to decapitate him, Prahlāda delivers a caustic speech (unlike those in the *Bhāgavata* and *Viṣṇu*) on the vileness of biological family in contrast to the true family of Hari; a description of which is full of Sāṁkhyan imagery.[33]

Hiraṇyakaśipu, having heard enough about Viṣṇu's omnipresence, delivers the final ultimatum; make Hari appear from a palace pillar or die by the sword. Fixed in final meditation on Hari, a garland comes from the sky and alights on Prahlāda's neck, and with that, an awful sound issues from the pillar, and Narasiṁha appears from within it, swiftly seizing the demon and tearing him to shreds with his nails, as the demon himself had predicted.

The *Skanda* myth is moved essentially by the same elements as the *Bhāgavata* and *Viṣṇu* versions, but lacks their richness. It seems caught between the original concerns of the myth and the now overriding ones of bhakti and fails to achieve a meaningful integration. The *Bhāgavata* and *Viṣṇu* versions are more successful.

As mentioned earlier, both versions make no bones about their central concern: this is a story about Prahlāda, the exemplary Viṣṇu-bhakta. To intensify the struggle of the devotee against the violent ignorance of Hiraṇyakaśipu and to bring to the fore the gentleness of Viṣṇu, which is personified in his soulmate, the devotee Prahlāda is no longer of soldiering age, but a young lad of approximately five years.

> The basis for the harsh effects is the almost ingenious idea of letting Prahlāda appear as a child. Already present in the previous development of the figure of Prahlāda were his titanic origin and the extraordinarily effective framework that emphasized, by sharp contrast, his virtuousness and wisdom in their uniqueness.[34]

It is the kind of twist that bhakti mythology delights in taking throughout the Purāṇas: the gopis—low-born, ignorant infidels (women!), are model devotees; a little demon boy is wise, selfless, and, as we shall see, identical with Hari himself. Each example goes to stress the universality of the god and his circle.

Both myths begin with Hiraṇyakaśipu's reign of terror, though each is motivated differently: in the *Bhāgavata,* the demon is seeking revenge for his brother's death, which he felt was met with unjustly: "My best friend and beloved brother has been slaughtered by my puny adversaries, with whom Hari, though professing impartiality, has sided attributing his action to their devout worship unto him" (*Bhg.P.* VII.2.6).[35] In the *Viṣṇu Purāṇa* Brahmā's boon (the conditions of which are not elaborated) gives Hiraṇyakaśipu free rein to wreak havoc. In both cases damage is done: he ordered the demons "to fall to slaughtering those who are engaged in sacrifices, religious penances, vows, Vedic recitations and acts of charity because Vishnu himself is identified with the religious observances of the twice-born ones" (*Bhg.P.* VII.2.10) or, as in many versions, "He had usurped the sovereignty of Indra and exercised of himself the functions of the sun, of air, of the lord of waters, of fire, and of the moon. He himself was the god of riches, the judge of the dead; and he appropriated to himself, without reserve, all that was offered in sacrifice to the gods" (*V.P.* I.17.2–3).

In each case the gods are chased from heaven and forced to wander the earth incognito. Here the *Bhāgavata* inserts Hiraṇyakaśipu's tapas and boon in full cosmological context. The gods had returned to heaven, and Hiraṇyakaśipu was absorbed in his austerities. But, "Only a short time thereafter, a smoky fire emitted out of the Daitya's head as a result of his severe religious austerities, and that fire spreading in all directions began to scorch the higher, middle, and lower regions" (*Bhg.P.* VII.3.4), causing the gods to retreat to the Brahmaloka.

But the demon threatens not only the trailokya and the orthodox laws of time and space, which it conjures with such imagery, but demands to supersede it:

> As the great Parameṣṭhin [the Creator of the Universe] [Brahmā], having created the mobile and immobile Universe by virtue of his rigid penances and yoga, now sits supreme on his own throne, so will I ensure a similar high position for me by strictly observing the ever-growing asceticism and yoga: Otherwise, I will with my prowess upset the laws of this Universe because Time and Soul are eternal. What is the good of attaining to the state of Vishnu and others which disappears with the lapses of time at the end of a kalpa. (*Bhg.P.* VII.3.9–11)

It is now not enough for the demon to become Indra, he must be Brahmā.

Biardeau clarifies the meaning of these demands in her masterful analysis of these two versions of the myth.[36] Hiraṇyakaśipu asks for two things, which are basically incompatible. He asks to become Brahmā, personification of the orthodox, upaniṣadic ideal of deliverance that presupposes a monistic goal, realization of the unity of ātman and Brahman; yet he also wants that transcendence in a definitively personal and individual way, he wants equality with Brahmā to yield for him an absolute and eternal power over the universe. "It is Hiraṇyakaśipu, king of *Asuras,* he and he alone, who wants to be equal to Brahmā and assured of perpetual power. It is therefore a question of the appropriation of the idea of deliverance for personal and worldly ends, of equality with Brahmā which will make him absolute monarch of the three worlds."[37] Brahmā, slave to the laws of karma, grants the aggressor a boon, that his death not come "from any being of thy [Brahmā's] creation" (*Bhg.P.* VII.3.33), and the conditions are further classically delineated.

With Hiraṇyakaśipu oppressing the worlds as in the *Viṣṇu Purāṇa*, the *Bhāgavata* poets give us a clue to the action to come, whereas the Viṣṇu is silent, concentrating its attention on the boy Prahlāda. In the *Bhg.P.*, the gods hear this pledge from Viṣṇu, to whom they have gone for help:

> He meets a hasty destruction who reviles the gods, scriptures, kine, Brahmanas, pious persons, religious rites, and myself. Though the Daitya king Hiraṇyakaśipu has been made powerful by boons, yet I will slay him when he will persecute his own son, the high-souled peace-loving, and foe-less Prahlāda. (*Bhg.P.* VII.4.26–28)

At this point both texts turn to Prahlāda, who is portrayed as the perfect Viṣṇu-bhakta, and serves as the mouthpiece for long discourses on devotion to Viṣṇu. Both myths include episodes of Prahlāda's "scandalous" declarations of Hari's supremacy in front of his father followed by the unsuccessful attempts by the gurus (Saṇḍāmarkau, the quizzical sons of the preceptor Śukra) to brainwash the boy with knowledge proper to a Daitya prince; when these lessons fail, Hiraṇyakaśipu tries to have the boy put to death by the same methods enumerated in the *Skanda Purāṇa* myth, all to no avail. Prahlāda, shuffled back to the gurus for lessons in dharma, artha, and kāma, reverses the roles and instead instructs his young classmates in Viṣṇu-bhakti, quickly converting them.

Fearing the undermining of his power by his own son, Hiraṇyakaśipu takes more drastic measures to stop Prahlāda. Here the versions differ, but appear complementary. In the *Vi.P.*, Hiraṇyakaśipu has Prahlāda bound and thrown into the sea, piling boulders on top of him. But it is precisely in this state of bondage that liberation comes to Prahlāda:

> Prahlāda is thrown into the sea, tied by serpents: the image is transparent, because the "ocean of saṁsāra" is so familiar to us. Prahlāda finds himself in a state of bondage, another expression of the bonds of transmigration, and his father adds masses of rocks to hold him more securely as a prisoner at the bottom of the sea. But he doesn't know that the bhakta can, in all situations, praise Viṣṇu, even in the most complete state of bondage, and that his devotion is liberating.[38]

The irony of the inversion is total; that situation which Hiraṇyakaśipu intended to be most oppressive became instead one of mokṣa, liberation: "Thus meditating upon Viṣṇu, as identical with his own spirit, Prahlāda became as one with him, and finally regarded himself as the divinity. . . . As soon as, through the force of his contemplation [*yogaprabhavāt*] Prahlāda had become one with Viṣṇu, the bonds with which he was bound burst instantly asunder" (*Vi.P.* I.20.1,3). And Viṣṇu appears to him, not as Narasiṁha, but "clad in yellow robes," the traditional garb of Kṛṣṇa, god of bhakti par excellence, and the yogin, "recalling that the god of bhakti is also the supreme yogin."[39]

The *Bhāgavata* presents us with a more traditional climax. At his wits' end, Hiraṇyakaśipu is ready to decapitate his virtuous son, conjuring up a sacrificial scene.[40] Striking a nearby pillar with his fist in rage, the demon king is shocked to hear an awesome sound issue forth from the column, and then the terrible Narasiṁha form. Again, a sacrificial image is flashed, this time inverting master and victim. The word used for pillar, *skambha,* means "stake" as well, and Viṣṇu's association with that sacrificial stake has been well documented.[41] Blood thirsty as the avatāra seems, in his subsequent disemboweling of Hiraṇyakaśipu and wearing his entrails as a garland, the murder assumes a religious and redemptive value, performed as a sacrifice:

> Thus, the appearance of Viṣṇu in the pillar signifies—even in remote fashion—a sacrifice where Prahlāda was almost the victim; the avatāra therefore finds that he commits a murder as one kills a sacrificial victim. It is the very model of the violent act which Narasiṁha thus gives us, conforming to the doctrine of the *Bhagavad Gītā.*[42]

After Prahlāda's liberation in the *Vi.P.,* he is granted a boon by Hari and asks for a pardon for his father, that he might attain "liberation from existence" after his immanent but inconsequential death at the hands of Narasiṁha ("After his father had been put to death by Vishnu in the form of a man-lion, Prahlāda became the sovereign of the Daityas" [*Vi.P.* I.20] is the only mention of the murder). As Biardeau points out, this episode completes the complementarity between the variant sections. As the sacrificial victim in the *Bhg.P.* myth, Hiraṇyakaśipu is assured liberation: "It is, besides, the sacrificial nature of this violent act accomplished for the good of the worlds which gives the victim a chance of salvation."[43] Without such a scene, the *Vi.P.* needs to supply something extra to make the same point; that in bhakti even the criminal can be saved. As Biardeau sums it up: "The pillar and the conversion of the wicked one obtained by the bhakta seem to play equal roles, to the point that the presence of one of the themes excludes the other."[44]

In the end, these two versions, though similar in the structural centrality they give to Prahlāda and in the sameness of doctrine preached by the demon bhakta, give us two different understandings of bhakti through their treatment of Narasiṁha. With respect to this, the *Vi.P.* is most extreme; in Hacker's succinct words, "But the avatāra has really become superfluous here!"[45] One must disagree with Hacker's belief that this is due to the poet's lack of knowledge about Narasiṁha; the myth is simply structured around new issues, and those events that heralded the descent are now negligible in *this* poet's understanding of bhakti. The boon is referred to only in briefest terms, and the oppression of the trailokya by the Asura brings *no* response from its classical preserver, Viṣṇu. The poet is concerned only with the propagation of bhakti and its significantly typical advocate, Prahlāda. That the boy, appearing helpless and demuring, but in fact invincible and uncannily wise, recalls the image of the young boy Kṛṣṇa is hardly accidental. The long discourses by Prahlāda on the identity of all things, especially the presence of Viṣṇu in all things, which finally culminate in his own identity with Hari, lifting him out of the ocean of saṁsāra to liberation, questions the necessity of the avatāra at all. When Viṣṇu finally does appear, it is in a universal, not particularized, form. When bhakti reaches its most transcendent level of meaning, and concerns itself only with liberation, as it does here, the role of the avatāra becomes, as Hacker says, superfluous.

The *Bhāgavata* myth is, in this frame, richer, multivalent, and portrays bhakti at perhaps its fullest expression. Although Prahlāda's peril structures the myth, the Asura's tapas and boon (and hence the man-lion form) still have meaning. Viṣṇu expresses his concern for all of the universe in his promise of redress; for the trailokya and its inhabitants, and also for those liberated ones like Prahlāda who dwell in the sphere of bhakti. He acts on *both* their accounts. In the *Vi.P.* we encountered a bhakti that transcends and perhaps transgresses or ignores dharma; the *Bhāgavata,* however, presents a bhakti that integrates dharma. Therefore the avatāra, which the *Bhagavad Gītā* inextricably binds to dharma, is still an integral part of the *Bhg.P.* myth, but not that of the *Vi.P.*: "It is evidently this renewal and this return of dharma within bhakti which permits Viṣṇu to be the supreme god and the avatāra, he who delivers individuals from the world of rebirth and assures the perpetuity of that same world in coming to restore its troubled order."[46] More meaningful now is the liberation of Hiraṇyakaśipu through sacrifice is the *Bhg.P.*, through grace in the

Vi.P. In the *Bhg.P.*, Narasiṁha's meaningfulness to every level of being in the universe is underscored as various groups or persons thank him for the particular effect his action had on their lives: Indra, predictably, appreciates getting back the sacrificial portions; the sages, their austerities; the Pitṛs, their oblations; the Nāgas, their gem crowns; and so on. But now, in a concluding incident on which the *Ś.P.* II.10–12 and *L.P.* I.95–96 myths seem to draw, Prahlāda is called forth as the only one capable of nearing the raging Narasiṁha and quelling his fury, with a simple gesture of devotion. Bhakti triumphs here and takes its place at the top of a universe that it transcends yet still pervades. In such a universe, the avatāra lives.

Understanding Narasiṁha

"Narasiṁha is one of the avatāras who lends himself the least to analysis of his being."[47]

The Motifs

Examination of the motif table (Fig. 6) will give the reader a quick and basic idea of how often the five motifs actually occurred in each version of the myth. From this preliminary checking we move on to interpret these occurrences.

Special Relationship with Indra. As can easily be seen, the eighteen versions supply us with no outright statement that exhibits evidence of a special relationship between Indra and the avatāra. Even references to Indra as the king whose kingdom is overthrown by the Asura, or of Narasiṁha restoring the kingdom to Indra after slaying Hiraṇyakaśipu, are conspicuously absent.

This occurrence (or nonoccurrence) speaks, however, through its silence. One is reminded again of the structural prototype of the myth, the Indra-Namuci myth of the Brāhmaṇas, in which, curiously, Indra, in a type of predicament in which he so often relies on his faithful ally Viṣṇu, seeks help from the Aśvins and Sarasvatī. It is a myth that, at least for its Brāhmaṇic redactors, finds room for only half of an established duo. It is interesting to note that those gods to whom Indra goes for aid are decidedly "third function" in Dumézil's terminology, or evocative of the vaiśya aspect of society; the brahmin element, epitomized by Viṣṇu as the sacrifice (in the Brāhmaṇas), has no place here.

TEXT	R.I.	C.S.	M	A.T.	L.L.
MBH. 3.272.56–60 [CE 3.100.21A]					
HARIVAṀŚA Ch. 41					x
Ch. 226–233		x			
AGNI PURĀṆA Ch. 4.2–3					
BRAHMĀ PURĀṆA 213.44–79					x
BRAHMĀṆḌA PURĀṆA II.5.3–29					x
BHĀGAVATA PURĀṆA II.7.14					
VII.2–10.47		x	x	x	x
KŪRMA PURĀṆA I.15.18–72		x		x	
LIṄGA PURĀṆA I.95		x			
MATSYA PURĀṆA Ch. 161–163		x			x
PADMA PURĀṆA V.42		x			x
ŚIVA PURĀṆA II.5.43		x			x
III.10–12		x			x
SKANDA PURĀṆA VII.2.18.60–130					x
VIṢṆU PURĀṆA I.16–20					
VIṢṆUDHARMOTTARA PURĀṆA I.54		x			x
VĀYU PURĀṆA 67.61–66					x

R.I. = special relationship with Indra
C.S. = cosmogonic scenario
M. = mediating power and activity
A.T. = action through trickery
L.L. = loophole in the law

Figure 6 Motif Index for Narasiṁhāvatāra Myths

Thus, if we understand that Indra's absence in our epic and Purāṇic myths may indicate that Viṣṇu, as Narasiṁha, wholly takes over Indra's role, we begin to see an image of the character of this avatāra: Indraic—martial, royal, kṣatric—a powerful warrior. In connection with this, an examination of the avatāra's epithet, Narasiṁha, is appropriate. Biardeau supplies an insight:

> Let us already note that the name of *Nara-siṁha,* if one goes back to the myth, must be translated as 'man-lion,' since Viṣṇu appears in a half-human, half-leonine form; but the epithet *narasiṁha,* historically very frequent, is a royal epithet, which signifies "lion among men," the lion being the king of animals (one has the symmetrical epithet of *narendra:* "Indra among men," Indra being the king of the gods).[48]

Thus faced with such a characterization, the presence of Indra in the avatāra myth might result in a superfluous doublet, detracting as well from the surprise of such a figure in a line of avatāras that, until this point, have presented us with cosmogonic, sacrificial, brahminic figures (i.e., the fish, tortoise, and boar).

Hence, although Indra is totally absent from the myth, such an absence in actuality highlights the intimate bond between the two gods; Indra is much alive in the figure of this man-lion, or lion among men.

Cosmogonic Scenario. There can be no question, after the analyses of the different versions of the myth, that we are faced with a scene that is blatantly evocative of the destruction, the pralaya. This destructive scenario is produced by two acts.

First, occurring less frequently, is the impending destruction threatened by the tapas of Hiraṇyakaśipu. This is pronounced in the *Bhg.P.* VII.2–10 version (cf. *Bhg.P.* VII.3.4ff.; see pp. 92ff for discussion), and the *Ś.P.* II.5.43 version (cf. *Ś.P.* II.5.12–13, see pp. 82–86 for discussion), when a pralaya-like fire is emitted from the demon's head, causing the gods to flee upwards. Brahmā's granting of the boon can also be interpreted in light of this: "Brahmā must give all of that to put an end to the danger of the conflagration of the worlds, but the asura will immediately turn his power against Viṣṇu and the cosmic order he protects."[49] Hiraṇyakaśipu's impending pralaya is dangerous, as it is improper; it issues from tapas done for selfish purposes, and it threatens the very cosmic order of which pralaya *should* be the regulator. Cosmologically, it is a destruction out of place and must be averted.

The second destructive scenario is the dominant one, that initiated by the coming of the avatāra, Narasiṁha. That this is a cosmologically proper time, place, and agent of destruction is made known by the poets.

Temporally, the descent of the man-lion is placed at the end of the Kṛta Yuga (cf. *M.P.* 161.2; *P.P.*V. 42.2; *HV* 226.2; *Br.P.* 213.44; *HV* 41). The affinity of the end of the yuga with the end of the kalpa as evocative of the pralaya and intensified by the twilight-dawn frame between each yuga and the next has been previously documented and discussed (see Chapter 4). Biardeau calls this interyuga period "the profound structure which is the echo of the pralaya,"[50] and ties a tight knot between this period and the avatāra:

> It is evidently the whole interest of the structure in yugas which punctuates the appearance of the avatāra: it permits the inser-

tion of this work of death and recreation into the framework of cyclical time which assures the perpetuity of the world of transmigration, and the action of the avatāra must, therefore, symbolically represent the analog of the pralaya and recreation.[51]

Set in a proper temporal frame for a destruction, the end of the yuga, in its twilight, the appearance of Narasiṁha is invariably described in terms that openly liken him to the pralaya itself and to its agents. These have been given in the analyses of the versions, and we need not do more than recapitulate. Narasiṁha is explicitly likened to the pralaya or yugānta itself in the *Bhg.P.* VII.2–10, *L.P.*, and *K.P.* versions; he is said to appear like kāla or the fire of destruction, both agents of the pralaya, in the *M.P.*, *PP.*, *HV* 226ff., *Ś.P.* II.5.43, and *K.P.* versions; and we find extensive pralayic sequences and imagery in the *M.P.*, *P.P.*, *HV* 226ff., and *Vdh.P.*, versions. In all, an image of the pralaya being at hand, or the arrival of Narasiṁha inaugurating an event of meaning equal to the pralaya, and an unquestionable image of Narasiṁha as the master of such a destruction, are not only present in the versions, but also climactically central to many of them. Again, the point is made in sharp contrast to the preceding avatāras, all with creative, life-supporting intent.[52] That this terrifyingly destructive form commonly recalls not Viṣṇu, but his complementary opposite, Śiva, is a phenomenon on which the poets play at times with brilliant subtlety. What we are faced with is a very un-Viṣṇu-like Viṣṇu—destructive as opposed to a normally creative god, kṣatric to a traditionally brahminic god, and Rudraic: all of these potentially antagonistic sets could coexist only under the encompassing view of Viṣṇu-bhakti, which ultimately sees all things as proliferations of the Supreme nature of Viṣṇu.[53]

There is little doubt, then, that this motif of a (in this case) destructive cosmological scenario has considerable, if not central importance for understanding the nature of Narasiṁha. This may be further brought to light in a discussion of the destructive image particularized in the Śiva-esque character of the avatāra, a subject that has obvious ramifications beyond the literary confines of myth into its cultic counterpart. Such a discussion will close the chapter.

The Triad of Liminal Motifs. The myths show Narasiṁha as having no special function or position of mediation. This, of course, does not take into consideration that his role is one of intervention in a conflict between the gods and demons and, as such, perhaps, is one of "mediation" between them; but it is always clear that Viṣṇu is on the side of the gods, being one of them, although their superior as well.

This professed partiality brings us to the next motif in this triad, action through trickery. Viṣṇu's role in the drama of the myth is viewed as one of deception or trickery in *Bhg.P.* VII.2.6, but it is seen in such a light expectedly by Hiraṇyakaśipu, who feels that Viṣṇu had some commitment to impartiality that he violated, duping the demons. This seems to be nothing more than a doublet to King Parikṣit, whose own doubts about Viṣṇu's impartiality spurred the bard to tell the tale of Narasiṁha.

Of the "liminal" motifs, clearly the "loophole in the law" occurs with significant frequency. The motivation for finding such a "loophole" or interstice in a seemingly watertight dilemma comes in all cases from the conditions of the boon granted by Brahmā to Hiraṇyakaśipu. In eleven of the eighteen versions the Asura's proclamation renders him invulnerable to what appear to be all categories of beings under all temporal and spatial conditions. It is often couched in very "liminal" language of neither-nor terms. For example: "Not devas, asuras, nor gandharvas; neither yakṣas, snakes, nor rakṣases, neither men nor piśācas may kill me, O Best of Gods, nor ṛṣis by cursing me. Neither by arrow nor by sword, mountain, nor tree, neither by dry nor by wet, neither by day nor by night" (*M.P.* 161.11–13). The Narasiṁhāvatāra circumvents the boon, finds the loophole in the law, in various ways, according to the different versions. Most basic is the man-lion form itself, which is obviously neither man nor beast, but some of both. And in all but two versions (*Br.P.*, *HV* 41) where the "murder weapon" is identified, Narasiṁha's claws or nails are used; only the *Brahmāṇḍa Purāṇa* explains why; "because they are neither wet nor dry."

Other versions are more deliberate in pointing out Viṣṇu's cunning in circumventing the boon; *Bhg.P.* VII.2–10 mentions that Hiraṇyakaśipu is killed on the threshold of the palace because that version of the boon included neither indoors nor out of doors. Both *Ś.P.* versions mention that Narasiṁha came at dusk, but only *Ś.P.* II.5.43 supplies the motivation; Hiraṇyakaśipu had stipulated that he could be killed neither by day nor by night.

Several versions remove any element of suspense and cunning by making the Asura include his own loophole; the *Skanda P.* myth shows the demon prophesying that he will be killed by Viṣṇu, who will be "somewhat lion, somewhat man." In the *Brahmā P.* and *HV* 41 versions Hiraṇyakaśipu announces that he will be slain by one stroke of the hand. The *Brahmāṇḍa P.* is more subtle, just saying that the boon "possessed interstices."

All in all, the myth fails to highlight the cunning and tricksterlike character one expects to find once the boon is made. The cunning of the man-lion as the loophole is never dwelt on; the connection between his form and the conditions of the boon are rarely stated outright. Perhaps the poets possessed more subtlety than we do. In any case, what becomes clear is that the emphasis of the myth has shifted from that of its precursor, the Namuci myth, with the replacement of Indra by Narasiṁha. The cunning and liminality of the avatāra as it is derived from this triad of motifs clearly is not central to the myth, although it may have produced some of the most memorable elements. It is true that the boon, in the early and middle versions of the myth (in terms of our own developmental organization), provides the structuring motivation for the action of the myth. But as bhakti comes to dominate the story the boon loses its function and, in some versions, its meaning. In the *Liṅga P.* version, it is totally absent. With the boon going or gone, the raison d'être of the avatāra itself must change. Thus to understand the function and nature of Narasiṁha not as static but as changing as the myth shifts its focus, we must turn now to analyze how the avatāra functions: what are his concerns throughout the course of the myth?

The Function of Narasiṁha

As was briefly mentioned in the opening of this chapter, the changes in the myth's structure basically are initiated by the development of the figure of Prahlāda. As the budding bhakta gains in importance, the motivation that brings the avatāra down shifts from Hiraṇyakaśipu's reign of terror caused by the boon to the particularized threat on Prahlāda's life by the same demon. The basic elements of activity remain the same: Hiraṇyakaśipu is evil, Viṣṇu appears as the man-lion to kill him and restore peace. Yet those elements that trigger Viṣṇu's descent, by which he is motivated to act, reveal a world of meaning about Narasiṁha in particular and the avatāra form more generally.

In the "early" and "middle" versions, those in which the boon plays a significant role and Viṣṇu is heralded by the gods to help, the concern that motivates Viṣṇu to *avatārati*, to descend, are specifically *trailokic.*[54] Viṣṇu acts on behalf of the triple world, which has been turned topsy-turvy by the malevolent demon. The gods have been chased from heaven, the Asuras have claimed it as their own, Hiraṇyakaśipu has become king of the trailokya and has usurped the gods' shares of the sacrifice. In short, he has replaced dharma with adharma. Thus Viṣṇu acts in classic avatāra form, to protect the dharma, to right wrongs, to put everything back in proper cosmological balance. In these situations, the avatāra is a vivid character, playing clearly the integral role in the myth.

When Prahlāda's peril comes to substitute for Hiraṇyakaśipu's general adharmic activity as that which motivates the god to act, Viṣṇu's concerns shift accordingly, expanding to a higher plane. Although he is concerned with the Asura's travesty on the trailokya, he is moved to act by Prahlāda's crisis. The *Bhg.P.* expresses the god's sentiments perfectly:

> He meets a hasty destruction who reviles the gods, scriptures, kine, Brahmanas, pious persons, religious rites, and myself. Though the Daitya king Hiraṇyakaśipu has been made powerful by boons, yet I will slay him when he will persecute his own son, the high-souled, peace-loving and foeless Prahlāda. (*Bhg.P.* VII.4.26–27)

The *Vi.P.* and *Sk.P.* are less poetic—Viṣṇu simply appears when Prahlāda is in danger. Viṣṇu's concerns have moved to a higher sphere, to his bhaktas, whose ultimate allegiance goes beyond the sacrifice, beyond Indra and the gods, to devotion to Viṣṇu. The bhakta's concerns transcend dharma and karma, as Prahlāda eloquently explains to us. Cosmologically and theologically, we are on a higher plane.

What is significant is the change in the avatāra's role as bhakti predominates the myth. Note that Viṣṇu appears to Prahlāda in the *Vi.P.* clad in yellow robes, and that the appearance of the man-lion has been reduced to one sentence. In the *Sk.P.* and *Bhg.P.* VII versions the man-lion appears to kill Hiraṇyakaśipu, but Prahlāda's long monologues on Viṣṇu-bhakti predominate the text now. Although Narasiṁha murders in the same gory fashion in these two myths, the emphasis is clearly on the rewards of Viṣṇu-bhakti, that is, Viṣṇu's grace and devotion to his devotees, not on the destructive nature of the avatāra. The evil Asura is even absolved of his sins and granted emancipation after death in the *Vi.P.* and *Bhg.P.* VII episodes. We are far from the relentless, Rudraic destroyer.

This shifting in the concerns and role of Narasiṁha seems to speak to the issue of the function of the avatāra itself. Biardeau has noted that the cults which worship Narasiṁha know him chiefly through the *Vi.P.* and *Bhg.P.* VII versions and local variants based on those, and that although Narasiṁha is a startlingly sanguinary form of Viṣṇu, his cult, in sharp contrast, is devoid of these bloody aspects. "Furthermore, the violence is in the [classical] myth, but it is totally absent from the cults."[55] We surmise from this fact that as bhakti predominates, the Narasiṁha we knew in the height of the myth's development recedes. What this suggests about the avatāra is that it is liminal in a way that was not suspected. The avatāra form seems to bridge the transition made from an emphasis on orthodox, Vedic and Upaniṣadic religion to bhakti; from strictly trailokic concerns to those of a larger universe that encompasses and transcends the former. The avatāra represents the new god of bhakti still primarily concerned with the orthodox world: dharma, svarga, and sacrifice. He is the Supreme god but sufficiently diversified into as many roles as there are needs. Through the vehicle of the avatāra, Vaiṣṇava bhakti is able to assert the identity of Viṣṇu with all aspects of life: creation, destruction, Brahmā, Śiva, brahmin, kṣatriya, trailokya, Viṣṇuloka. In the late Narasiṁha myths, Prahlāda convinces us of this fundamental identity through his discourses; the avatāra, as Hacker remarked, is "superfluous."[56] Viṣṇu's appearance out of avatāra garb in the *Viṣṇu Purāṇa* is natural in this context. The transition to bhakti is complete, the work of the avatāra done. The *Bhg.P.* VII version, as mentioned before, has not gone this far, but brilliantly shows the avatāra in transition between the two worlds and the direction in which he points.

The Nature of Narasiṁha

Given the changes through which the advent of bhakti puts Narasiṁha, we must in the end come back to view him at the height of his splendour and speak about his nature as a constant, as well as in flux. Through the examination of the motifs, we were exposed to what seem to be basic elements of his character. The trickster was absent; in his stead was a vision of the master of destruction. The Rudraic element in this avatāra appears almost central through the imagery. The *Kūrma Purāṇa*'s description of the "lion" half of Narasiṁha leading the Asuras to the valley of death (pp. 82ff.) makes a clear connection and recalls Śiva's association with the land of death, the cremation grounds. The Matṛkā episodes situate Narasiṁha in the regions below. Together, these associations link him as well to the goddess; the Saptamatṛkās are widely worshipped in connection with the goddess (as well as with scenes of blood sacrifice), and we find that the goddess herself is associated with the south, the realm of death, and often is portrayed with the lion as her *vāhana* or vehicle.[57] Through this network of multidirectional connections, Narasiṁha emerges not only as a Śivaesque Viṣṇu, but as a powerful representation of the *totality* of godhead, goddess included.

Those Śaivite adaptations of the myth discussed earlier[58] intensify this element by creating a confrontation between Narasiṁha and Śiva; as there cannot be two Indras in the myth, there can be only one Śiva, one destroyer. In the Śaivite fantasy, Śiva is the victor, the true destroyer, and Narasiṁha is the "improper" bringer of pralaya; in the Vaiṣṇava-oriented Matṛkā episodes of the *Kūrma, Garuḍa,* and *Matsya Purāṇas,* Narasiṁha is more fit for the role of destroyer, and Śiva's destruction of the Andhakas through the Matṛkās has backfired on him; through his creation (the Matṛkās), he has become an improper agent of destruction, threatening to devour the triple world.

But within the confines of the traditional myth, Narasiṁha is an eminently successful figure; arriving on the scene to bring about a properly timed pralayic interlude, shedding light on one face of Viṣṇu as yet unseen but that had to be revealed.

As each avatāra reaches out to join Viṣṇu to another plane of divinity or humanity, "Narasiṁha" is perhaps the most difficult and precious of unions to achieve. "But one can also see in the two parts of the name, *nara* and *siṁha,* the mark of his dual nature: as nara he is therefore the Puruṣa Viṣṇu while siṁha is consequently the name of his terrible, rudraic aspect [and we would add, 'goddessesque']."[59] The poets, through their craft, have revealed yet another meaning to Viṣṇu, the Supreme Yogin, through that awesome yoking perfected in Narasiṁha.

Notes

1. The late A. Eschmann pointed to a leonine deity of "tribal" origins associated with a tribal Narasiṁha in his "girija" or mountain-born aspect as the origin of the Jagannatha-related Narasiṁha in her "The Vaiṣṇava Typology of Hinduization and the Origin of Jagannatha," in *The Cult of Jagannatha and the Regional Tradition of Orissa,* ed. A. Eschmann, H. Kulke, and G. C. Tripathi (New Delhi: Manoher Publications, 1986).

2. Kirfel, *Das Purāṇa Pañcalakṣana* (Bonn: Kurt Schroeder, 1927). Parallel text reconstructions of the Narasiṁha myth found in *Brahmā Purāṇa* 213.44–80, *HV* 41.44–80, and *Vdh. P.* I.54 can be found in Deborah Soifer, "Beast and Priest: A Motific Study of the Narasiṁha and Vāmana Avatāras in Cosmological Perspective" (Ph.D. dissertation, University of Chicago, 1978).

3. Such is the case, for instance, for the *Ś.P.* III.10–12 myth, which is later and even seems to draw on the *Bhāgavata Purāṇa,* which is the final text to be examined.

4. In fact, two of the most common iconographic images of Narasiṁha are the combat of Hiraṇyakaśipu and Narasiṁha and Narasiṁha disemboweling Hiraṇyakaśipu with his claws; cf. Biardeau, "Narasiṁha, mythe et culte," in *Puruṣārtha: Récherches de Sciences sociales sur d'Asie du Sud* (Paris: Centre d'Etudes de l'inde et de l'Asie du Sud, 1975), p. 50.

5. F. E. Pargiter, *Ancient Indian Historical Tradition* (Delhi: Motilal Banarsidass, 1962), p. 23.

6. Kirfel, *Das Purāṇa Pañcalakṣana*, pp. x–xiii.

7. Ibid., p. 193.

8. A. C. Swain, *A Study of the Man-Lion Myth in the Epics and Purāṇa Text* (Poona: University of Poona, 1970), p. 39.

9. Monier Monier-Williams, *A Sanskrit-English Dictionary* (Oxford: Oxford University Press, 1970), p. 812.

10. On the role of Viṣṇu as Supreme Yogin who absorbs the trailokya in the pralaya, see Biardeau *EMH* I–III.

11. Biardeau, *EMH* 4:180.

12. Biardeau, "Narasiṁha: mythe et culte," p. 39.

13. Wendy D. O'Flaherty, "The Submarine Mare in the Mythology of Śiva," *JRAS* no. 1 (1971):13.

14. Biardeau, "Narasiṁha: mythe et culte," p. 39.

15. This is a very standard procedure and a puzzling one, spatially; the gods go vertically to the top of the universe, the Brahmaloka, and then horizontally to the sixth of seven circular oceans, Kṣiroda or Milk Ocean. Viṣṇu seems to be the only supreme god who has horizontal as well as vertical cosmological relevance (the dwelling of the varāhāvatāra is said to be the Lokāloka Mt., the border of the horizontal universe).

16. So reminiscent of Walt Disney's animated rendering of "The Sorcerer's Apprentice."

17. In the *Matsya* version, Śiva creates the Matṛkās expressly to drink the blood of the Andhaka demons. When they can drink no more and the demons again begin to multiply, Śiva seeks Viṣṇu's help, and he creates Suṣka-Revantī, who "in a moment drank the blood of all the Andhaka demons" (*M.P.* 179.36). In the *Garuḍa* version, Śiva creates the goddesses.

18. In the *Matsya* text, beckoned by Śiva to restrain the hungry Matṛkās, Viṣṇu, appearing as Narasiṁha, creates his own band of blood-thirsty mothers, who subdue those created by Śiva. The latter take refuge in Viṣṇu, who explains that their place is with Śiva and their function to protect "His Raudra Devī."

On the relationship between Narasiṁha and the Śaiva deity Bhairava-Ekapāda in the formation of the Jagannatha-related figures in Orissa, see A. Eschmann, H. Kulke, and G. C. Tripathi, "The Formation of the Jagannatha Triad," in *The Cult of Jagannath and the Regional Tradition of Orissa.*

19. In the *Garuḍa Purāṇa* version, while the Matṛkās go berserk, Śiva, their maker, meditates on Narasiṁha, who comes and "caused the Matṛkās to be merged in his person." Here the transfer is in the opposite direction.

20. M. V. Vaidya, "The Palace of Hiraṇyakaśipu," *ABORI* 23 (1942):610.

21. Cf. ibid., in which he concludes that much of this description is borrowed from the *Mbh.*'s account of the divine sabhās of Indra, Yama, Varuṇa, Kubera, and Brahmā (*Mbh.* II.7.ff).

22. This same verse is extra to the *HV* 41 version as well; however, it speaks of one who will triumph with the "blow of one hand" instead.

23. This also calls to mind the Śaiva sectarians who smear themselves with ashes.

24. Swain's understanding is "Prahlāda with his divine form had the vision of the Man-lion," *A Study of the Man-Lion Myth in the Epics and Purāṇa Text,* p. 43.

25. Ibid., p. 43.

26. Compare with *Viṣṇu P.* VII.III's description of the pralaya: "The seven solar rays dilute to seven suns."

27. Biardeau, "Narasiṁha, mythe et culte," p. 41.

28. Paul Hacker, *Prahlāda: Werden und Wandlungen einer Idealgestalt* (Weisbaden: Akademie der Wissenschaft und der Literatur No. 9, 1959), p. 22.

29. Hacker remarks that the Śarabha configuration is brought in as a contender against Prahlāda (p. 22), in terms of the character able to calm Narasimha. Structurally, he is correct: Śarabha replaces Prahlāda, but the meaning of the episode seems wider than that.

30. Biardeau, *EMH* 4:197. Biardeau notes further a myth in which Viṣvaksena, a Viṣṇubhakta, is made to worship the Śivaliṅga: "The lord then wants to kill him [*Viṣvaksena*] and Narasiṁha comes out of the liṅga, breaking it, and burns the evil lord with the fire of his eye" (*EMH* 4:197).

31. Cf. Hacker, *Prahlāda: Werden und Wandlungen einer Idealgestalt.*

32. Perhaps I am not alone: the Gurumandel Series translation begun in 1960 is incomplete and seems not to have published further volumes after approximately 1970.

33. "Prakṛti is our mother, buddhi is our sister, then Ahaṁkāra is born, who is known as 'I.' The tanmātras, my own five brothers who go together with me. This is my nature, the Vikāra is my kinfolk. He who is the twenty-fifth puruṣa is the bearer of these. He is my father, in my body does Hari reside as supreme Soul" (VII.2.18.100–102).

34. Hacker, *Prahlada: Werden und Wandlungen einer Idealgestalt.*

35. This same "partiality" sparked Parikṣit's doubts about Viṣṇu, leading Sukadeva to recite this myth about Prahlāda to him.

36. Biardeau, "Narasiṁha, mythe et culte," pp. 35–48.

37. Ibid., p. 36.

38. Ibid., p. 44.

39. Ibid.

40. "It is a frequent form of execution in the myths and it evokes the execution of victims in bloody sacrifices which the cult of certain divinities includes," ibid., p. 43.

41. Jan Gonda, *Aspects of Early Viṣṇuism,* (Delhi: Motilal Banarsidass, 1969), pp. 81–84.

42. Biardeau, "Narasiṁha, mythe et culte," p. 43. Although she acknowledges an association between Narasiṁha and the sacrifice through his disemboweling of Hiraṇyakaśipu, Anncharlott Eschmann sees the significance of the pillar in the myth as being related, at least in Orissa, to wooden posts in Orissi folk religion, some of which represent the tribal goddess Khambheśvari and are also marked with images of Narasiṁha. See A. Eschmann, "The Vaiṣṇava Typology of Hinduization and the Origin of Jagannatha," pp. 109–112.

43. Ibid.

44. Ibid., p. 45.

45. Hacker, *Prahlāda: Werden und Wandlungen einer Idealgestalt,* p. 594.

46. Biardeau, "Narasiṁha, mythe et culte," p. 42.

47. Biardeau, *EMH* 4:177.

48. Biardeau, "Narasiṁha, mythe et culte," p. 32.

49. Biardeau, *EMH* 4:177.

50. Ibid., p. 182, n. 4.

51. Ibid., p. 182.

52. Cf. Biardeau, "We have already made it clear that the cosmogonic themes transposed onto avatāra myths could effectively put more of the accent on the creator, or Viṣṇuic aspect" (*EMH* 4:183).

53. "It is Viṣṇu alone who must accomplish the functions which were divided between Rudra-Śiva or *Kālāgni* on one hand, and Nārāyaṇa-Viṣṇu sleeping, then taking the form of Brahmā in order to create, on the other hand. The avatāra thus reunites in himself two aspects of divinity which until now had remained opposed and complementary. It is Viṣṇu, undoubtedly, but endowed with a 'terrible' component, which we will call 'Rudraic,' without having to justify it from now on" (*EMH* 4:183). (We are indebted to Biardeau for bringing these sets of opposing characteristics into sharper focus.)

54. For a full discussion on what this term encompasses, see Chapter 4.

55. Biardeau, "Narasiṁha, mythe et culte," p. 32.

56. See p. 103.

57. Alf Hiltebeitel, "The Indus-Valley 'Proto-Śiva,' Reexamined through Reflections on the Goddess, the Buffalo, and the Symbolism of Vāhanas," *Anthropos* 73 (1979):767–797.

59. *L.P.* I.95–96; *Ś.P.* III.10–12; see pp. 89ff.

59. Biardeau, *EMH* 4:197.

6

Myths of the Vāmanāvatāra:
Motif Analysis and Discussion

Encountering the Text

The corpus of Vāmanāvatāra myths presents itself as a strikingly different text from its predecessor, both in form and content. We can surmise with relative certainty that the Vāmana myth was known more widely and well than the Narasiṁha tale; several factors point to this conclusion. We have found thirty versions of the myth, nearly double the number of man-lion myths. Further, among these thirty only two proved to be identical to two other texts from different Purāṇas; that is, the *Vāyu Purāṇa* 98.59.88 and *Brahmāṇḍa Purāṇa* II.73.75–87 versions were identical, and the *Harivaṁśa* 41 and *Brahmā Purāṇa* 213.80–115 texts were doublets.[1] This reduces the number of actual texts to twenty-eight; the same phenomena was more common to the Narasiṁha text, reducing the number of those versions from eighteen to twelve. Rather than rely on an already existent written text or reduplicate the exact words of another poet, the authors of the Vāmana myth seem to have been familiar enough with their tale to feel secure in independent invention, if we may conjecture about such a shadowy process.

There are other reasons to suppose a widespread familiarity with the myth. Vāmana, unlike Narasiṁha, was not a new figure in epico-Purāṇic literature, as we have shown. The dwarf was known as a form of Viṣṇu since the Brāhmaṇas, likewise, the Trivikrama or thrice-stepping form of the god was present since the *Ṛg Veda.* In short, nearly all the elements basic to the myth were common knowledge at the beginning of the period with which we are concerned; the myth, therefore, was in a much less fluid state than that of Narasiṁha.

For these reasons, and others that will become apparent as we progress, the myth shows far less development within the versions under study than did its predecessor; in fact, the Vāmana myth is lacking a clear line of successive stages. This is not to say that all the versions are identical (a fool's gold in the Purāṇas), but that, for the most part, they appear to be "minor" variations on the same basic theme. The myth is never radically altered, and it would be safe to suggest that nearly any version could be picked and exhibited as "typical."

Such being the case, the presentational scheme developed for the Narasiṁha myth would not fit this material. The motivational structure never shifts here, and although many elements change from version to version, those changes do not alter the structure of the myth. Rather than a changing central figure around whom the myth pivots (such as the gradual replacement of Hiraṇyakaśipu's tyranny by Prahlāda's devotion in the Narasiṁha myth), the myth seems to break down into a handful of basic elements, not unlike Lévi-Strauss's concept of mythemes. The difference here is that, whereas Lévi-Strauss uses mythemes to refer to action (although he refers to them as *relations*), the variables in our myth seem to exist in terms of roles and characterizations as well (e.g., the nature of Bali's reign, Śukra's role, Bali's fate, etc.). It is in this context that we refer to the basic elements of the myth as mythemes.

Given a basic set of mythemes, the versions appear to us as if constructed via a mix-and-match process that allowed the poets a little variety and room for individualism (although we doubt this was the actual "method" employed). What prompts us to believe, however, that there is not a great deal of method in the madness is that, although one poet changes two elements in a myth, another may change the first and not the second; to clarify through example, the *Vāmana Purāṇa* 49–65 and the *Padma Purāṇa* Uttara 266–267 versions both describe Bali's reign as dharmic, characterizing it as a Satya Age, but the *P.P.* omits Prahlāda altogether, yet the *Vām.P.* version gives him a decisive role. In other words, each mytheme or element seems to be independent of the others, usually (but not always) within the boundaries that logic dictates.

This is not to say that there are no meaningful patterns within this endless amount of variation. We can discern several basic patterns that arise out of the multitudes. Again, these do not change the action and structure of the myth, but they are no less important in pointing out the poet's vision of the concerns that beckon the avatāra.

There are three patterns, and with Wendy O'Flaherty's help[2] we can clarify them and see their context within basic structures in Hindu thought. The first situation that prompts the avatāra takes as its context the classic daivāsura struggle: Bali is a typical demon, true to his svadharma; he wants to cause trouble, to usurp the sovereignty of the trailokya, to steal the sacrifice. Likewise he is ignorant of Viṣṇu's supremacy and strength. This, as O'Flaherty notes, is typical of the concerns of the Vedic period and recall as well the earliest "germ" of the Vāmana myth, *ŚB* I.2.5.1.ff. These concerns are still voiced in such versions as *Rām.* I.29; *A.P.* 4.4–11; *Sk.P.* VII.4.19.10–14.

The second situation presents us with a skewed version of the daivāsura conflict: Bali is now characterized as a virtuous Asura; that is, one who violates his svadharma (to be evil) to honor sanātana or eternal dharma (to be evil is Evil; one must be good). This still poses a threat to the gods; perhaps a more serious one, for "a demon who tries to 'be good' is violating his svadharma, paving the road for his own ruin as well as for the obstruction of cosmic order."[3] In myths such as these, Bali is shown as a dharmic king, outdoing even Indra. Sometimes Bali is said to have been able to win heaven through a boon given by Brahmā in reward for his austerities. Such is the case in *HV* 248–256, and *Vām.P.* Saro.2–10. This type of situation echoes the concerns of the post-Vedic period, when power was won through asceticism and virtue.[4]

The final characterization finds Bali as a Viṣṇu-bhakta who willingly gives up his kingdom to Viṣṇu in an act of renunciation motivated by bhakti. We find this in such versions as *P.P.* Sṛṣti 25, *Bhg.P.* VIII.15–23, *Bhg.P.* IV.76.1–27, and it is obviously characteristic of the period of bhakti that, as O'Flaherty notes, "resolves the conflict between gods and good men or demons by reintroducing the Vedic concept of dependence on the gods."[5] Although O'Flaherty is correct in linking this concept of dependence on gods with bhakti, as characteristic of what is new (or renewed) in bhakti, she neglects that in its fullest meaning bhakti comprehends the other levels as well; herein lies the reason for finding all three levels present in the Purāṇas, themselves "bhakti" texts.

These characterizations are helpful in setting some of the mytheme variations in a meaningful context. It must be stressed, however, that they do not structure all the mythemes in any one version, necessarily. The poets are full of surprises. For instance, in *P.P.* Sṛṣṭi 25, Bali conquers the world honorably through Brahmā's boon (second level: sanātana dharma, tapas, etc.). Yet once king, his reign is characterized as adharmic (first level: svadharma); still at the end of the myth Viṣṇu grants Bali a boon for his truthfulness, and he chooses death at Viṣṇu's hands (i.e., mokṣa: liberation achieved through Viṣṇu's personal intervention), a purely bhaktic goal.

Thus, given the unique nature of the Vāmana versions, we obviously cannot apply the same principles of organization used for the Narasiṁha presentation. We could maintain no logical system of meaning (nor stamina) through individual presentation of the twenty-eight versions. Instead we will discuss the variations on six mythemes which raise issues and concerns basic to the meaning of the myth:[6]

1. How Bali attains the sovereignty
2. The nature of Bali's reign
3. How Vāmana is described
4. Prahlāda's role, Śukra's role
5. Completion of the three steps
6. Bali's fate

As stated, the three situational levels cannot structure our analysis, but provide one larger reference of meaning in which the myths may be set.

The Analysis

How Bali Attains the Sovereignty

The myth presents us with three different views of how Bali attains sovereignty over the trailokya. The first is typical of O'Flaherty's first stage. The Asura, true to his own svadharma, causes trouble by defeating the gods by force and ousting them, with Indra at their head, from heaven. The Asuras' victory comes as no surprise, for, as elder brothers to the gods, they have been classically depicted as their superiors in physical strength, such as was the case in the Brāhmaṇas. This explanation is offered in thirteen of the versions.[7] In most of these, there is little elaboration given to this victory; for example:

> At that time, Bali, the son of King Virocana, conquered Indra and other devas, together with the deities of the wind and he ruled over the three worlds. (*Rām.* I.29.3)

> The mighty Daitya named Bali, who was strong and invincible, by him were all the godly troops made to abandon the palace of the gods. (*Bhg.P.* IV.76.3)

The *Skanda Purāṇa* (VII.4.19.10–14) is unique in giving us a date for this victory, "at the end of the Kṛta Yuga" (*Sk.P.* VII.4.19.11). In all, the poets do not dwell on the details of the conquest; it is not important how it happened, but that it happened.

As a consequence of their defeat, the gods usually go directly to either their parents, Aditi and Kaśyapa, or to the grandfather Brahmā for refuge. However, in two versions, *N.P.* I.10–11 and *Sk.P.* V.1.74, they wander on the earth disguised as mortals, as was also sometimes the case in the Narasiṁha myth (and that of the *Mahābhārata* as well).

The second group of texts explains that Bali won his crown following in the footsteps of his great-grandfather Hiraṇyakaśipu; by obtaining a boon of invincibility from Brahmā in reward for his tapas.[8] This method of attaining the sovereignty corresponds to O'Flaherty's second stage, where ascetic practice and virtue become the primary means of gaining power; Bali is virtuous in his austerities, but employs the power yielded by the fruit of such action toward typically Asuric ends. Perhaps this alteration in the myth was coterminous with the creation of Hiraṇyakaśipu's parallel role in the Narasiṁha myth.[9]

The conditions of Brahmā's boon are spelled out in *Vdh.P.* I.55, *P.P.* Sṛṣṭi 25; and *Vām.P.* 52; Bali[10] is given "invincibility, unconquerability in battles between the gods and demons" (*Vdh.P.* I.55.3). *HV* 248–257, in its characteristically poetic elaboration, reminds Bali of his privileged position through the mouthpiece of Prahlāda, the Asura's grandfather:

> O Prince of Asuras, are you not the fire, wind, sun, water, the moon, constellations, celestial regions, atmosphere, and earth, past, present, and future? That is a privilege you have received from divine Svayambhū [Brahmā]. Hasn't this god accorded you the title of Indra, the right to wear the camara, triumph of battle, the kingdom, power, the force of an innumerable army, domination of all beings, preeminence, the sovereign virtue of yoga, heroism in combat, immensity, agility, all precious qualities? In

> fact, O King of the Daityas, your destiny is to vanquish the gods and their followers. (*HV* 248.3ff.)[11]

When the battle follows, Indra hears a mysterious voice that tells him of Bali's boon, but goes on to say that one day Bali will meet his vanquisher in one whose description fits only Viṣṇu. Indra and the gods withdraw from battle.

The *Vām.P.* Saro.2–10 and *Mbh.* 12.326.72–76 versions express knowledge of some kind of invincibility Bali possesses; in the *Vām.P.* version Aditi tells Indra that "He [Bali] can be killed in the battle field only by Viṣṇu—by him alone" (*Vām.P.* Saro.3.5), and the *Mbh.* says that Bali is unslayable by all the gods.

The third agent of Bali's victory is unique in coming from a source of power not directly his own. The *Bhg.P.* VIII.15–23 version relates that Bali became extremely powerful through the Viśvajīt sacrifice performed for him by his preceptor, Śukra. In fact, through this sacrifice Bali, essentially, is "Indracized": "When the proper oblation of havi was offered into the sacrificial fire, there arose immediately from the fire a golden chariot like those of Indra, and one pennon having the emblem of a lion—as well as a celestial bow having a golden frame, two quivers filled with unending arrows and celestial armour" (*Bhg.P.* VIII.15.3–6). Bṛhaspati, the Devas' guru, aware of what has occurred, tells Indra

> I know the cause of the increase of power of your enemy. He is the disciple of the race of Bhṛgu; and he has been embued with energy by the descendant of Bhṛgu [Śukra], conversant with the knowledge of Brahman. Save the Lord Shree Hari, neither thyself nor anyone equal to thee shall be able to vanquish the powerful Bali. . . . He has gradually acquired power through the energy of the Brahmanas. By insulting them, however, he shall be consumed along with his kinsmen. (*Bhg.P.* VIII. 15.28,29,31)

This is a twist to the story with which the *Bhāgavata* poets evidently are familiar from the *Mahābhārata,* which knows of Bali outside the Vāmana myth.[12] Tripathi takes note of this: "From scattered passages in the *Mbh* we can gather the following about him: namely, he had received his kingdom by the grace of the brahmans. Later on he became arrogant, offended the brahmans, and ordered his subjects to venerate him instead of the gods."[13]

One myth is ambiguous about how Bali attains the sovereignty in heaven, or even if he does. *Sk.P.* VII.2.14–19 relates that Bali became the sovereign of the earth. But because Bali's reign is so dharmic, Indra (egged on by that celestial troublemaker, Narada) seeks out Viṣṇu for help, saying "All the world has gone to the Devaloka, O Keśava" (*Sk.P.* VII.2.14.73a). We can interpret such a difficult statement to mean that due to Bali's virtuousness as king, the earth has become like heaven, and Bali, Indra's double. The problems that arise from Bali's sovereignty, once established, bring us to our next discussion.[14]

The Nature of Bali's Reign

With Bali's conquest of heaven, either by physical force or ascetic virtue, Indra is out of a job and the gods are bounced from their own home. This in itself creates an emergency, warranting Viṣṇu's descent without much further elaboration on the crisis. But many of the versions pause to describe Bali's reign and how the trailokya fares under his rule. Again we find a Bali devoted to his asuric svadharma (which is adharma) or another, more frequently devoted to sanātana dharma. From the gods' point of view, neither makes a suitable king.

P.P. Sṛṣṭi 25 is the only version to be explicit about the Asura king's (Bāṣkali in this case) ways. The myth relates that the Dānava, having conquered heaven, immediately made the Asuras the enjoyers of the sacrificial shares. Indra, lamenting the situation to Brahmā, explains further,

> With those who do not observe anything connected with Veda and Śruti, the rituals do not go on. . . . rescue us who are drowning in misery, by mentioning a way by which our might may increase, having seen the bad condition of this world, as mentioned to you by me, where neither studying the Vedas nor calling for sacrifices [exists], desisting from auspicious celebration, where the chain of study is abandoned, where livelihood and family life have been given up, deprived of justice, nothing but breath remaining, the world has attained suffering and even worse conditions. (*P.P.* Sṛṣṭi 25.28b,34b–37a)

Here Bāṣkali succeeds in inverting the trailokya and its order. He has made heaven the nether world and has made dharma adharma. The world has been turned on its proverbial ear, and through Indra's apparently conflicting statements about the fate of the sacrifice (the Asuras have taken over; the Asuras have abandoned it), we view two images of the danger at hand, inversion and destruction: dharma, inverted in the Asuras' usurpation of the sacrifice, has been molested; but with the Asuras' abandonment of dharma (and especially its instrument, the sacrifice), the threat seems worse, for in cosmological terms dharma is the glue that holds the universe together, and now it threatens to become unstuck. The language of the myth is reminiscent of many versions of the Narasiṁha myth, where Hiraṇyakaśipu uses ascetic virtue to gain a boon that he uses toward traditionally asuric, adharmic ends.

Many texts[15] are silent on this issue, as a good number of these did not describe how Bali attained his sovereignty. It does not seem unlikely that these versions implied, with Bali's reign, all those antiqualities an Asura would usually possess; many of these texts are chronologically "early"[16] and well may reflect the first stage (according to O'Flaherty), where demons act like demons.

Many texts, however, delight in complicating the story with a typical Purāṇic twist, making Bali a dharmic king. Several content themselves with a description of Bali himself, such as *Vdh.P.* I.55, which praises Bali as "the soul of dharma" (I.55.2) and "most excellent of supporters of dharma" (I.55.16), or as "prudent and pious, versed in the knowledge of Brahmā," in *K.P.* I.16.12. *Sk.P.* V.1.74 recalls the illustrious grandson Bali, describing his reign:

> While he was protecting his subjects properly, while he was nourishing them properly, there was not one who was short-lived, nor stupid, nor foolish, nor ill, nor wicked, nor sonless, nor devoid of wealth. A great king, world guardian, sacrificer and giver of great gifts, the earth, consisting of seven islands, was always protected by him. (*Sk.P.* V.1.74.18–20)

Two texts lend an air of validity to Bali's reign with the appearance of Śrī-Lakṣmī, sovereignty incarnate, before Bali's throne. In *Vām.P.* Saro.2.14b fickle Lakṣmī praises Bali, admitting "I am pleased with you on the defeat of Indra. May you prosper!" In *HV* 250 the goddess expresses the same sentiments, and in *Vām.P.* 49 Lakṣmī discourses to Bali enigmatically on the fourfold classification of men, colors, gods, qualities, treasure, and so on, calling attention to the fact that she, incorporating within herself all the royal and kṣatric virtues as Jayaśrī, has come to "enter the place of Bali." In all three places, Lakṣmī brings with her an entourage of goddesses personifying royal attributes, who come as she does, to reside at the court of the new king.

Sk.P. VII.2.14–19, in which Bali's sovereignty is established on earth, recreates a Hindu paradise in describing life under Bali's rule:

> The earth was producing crops without cultivation and was possessed of good water and endowed with corn. The flowers smelled and the fruits were juicy, trees bore fruit at the top and there was honey in each lotus. All the brahmins knew the four Vedas, the kṣatriyas were skilled in battle, the vaiśyas were intent upon tending cattle, and the śūdras intent on serving. The people were good mannered, free from plague and disease, all were well-fed, always happy, and always active. (*Sk.P.* VII.2.14.8b–11)[17]

Without calling it so outright, what we have here is a description of the Satya (Kṛta) Age, the Golden Age. *HV* 248–257 alludes to this same phenomenon with a standard metaphor: when Bali was king, "Dharma was supported by four feet, and adharma had none" (*HV 250.4*). *Vām.P.* 49–65 imaginatively notes Bali's dharmic reign, while at the same time masterfully calling attention to the danger of such a state. Having set the myth at the beginning of the Kali Age, the poets focus on the plight of time itself: "Finding the world following the path of virtue as in the Satya Age, Kali looked up to Brahmā, following his nature. . . . 'O Chief of Gods, my nature has been destroyed by Bali.' To him the venerable Yogin said, 'It is not your nature only, but that of the entire world that has been destroyed by that mighty one' " (*Vām.P.* 49.2,4–5). Thus Bali, by dedicating himself to absolute, sanātana dharma, has transgressed an even higher cosmic law, time itself. This adds a new dimension to the havoc the "well-meaning" demon wreaks on the world; making things static in an unceasingly dynamic world. Sanātana dharma, Good with a capital G, may be absolute, but time makes increasingly less space for it. This daring act of Bali's, to alter the very nature and order of time, seems even a more serious threat than usurping heaven. Indeed, it addresses itself not only to the sociocosmic (trailokic) but to the cosmic as well.[18]

Several other myths raise Bali's virtuosity to an even higher step and add to it a new dimension of meaning through the introduction of (O'Flaherty's third stage) bhakti. *P.P.* Uttara 266–267 attributes Bali's dharmic nature to the fact that he was "the beloved bhakta of Hari" (*P.P.* Uttara 266.2). In *Br.P.* 73 and *HV* 41.79–103, identical texts, Viṣṇu reveals to the distressed gods that "the Daitya Bali is my devotee" (*Br.P.* 73.19) and that he [Viṣṇu] will remedy the situation without bloodshed. *N.P.* I.10.30 states that "Bali, wholly devoted to Nārāyaṇa" led a virtuous reign, complete with sacrifices to the gods. This twist, although making little sense within the context of the myth so far, sets us up for a dénouement that allows Bali to prove his devotion to Viṣṇu by grateful submission. It also eliminates the need for a frequent mytheme that occurs later in the sequence of the story, Prahlāda's intervention.

One version, *Bhg.P.* IV.76.1–27, escapes our categorization, and seems to combine use of the second and third levels of power, tapas and bhakti. In a statement that in part recalls Brahmā's words about Hiraṇyakaśipu, Viṣṇu tells the gods "I know the Daitya Bali, son of Virocana, thorn of the tripleworld. Through tapas, his soul was transformed; he is peaceful, restrained, and lord of his senses; he is devoted to me, his life is mine, his promise is true, and he is mighty. After a long time, there will be an end to his tapas." (*Bhg.P.* IV.76.4b–5). Though Bali is devoted to Viṣṇu, his bhakti is not the transcendent kind. His tapas is still subject to the laws of karma, and thus his fall from grace just a matter of time. It is a passage indicative of the myth in general, which strives for but never really succeeds in becoming a proper vehicle for bhakti's most transcendent teachings, as does the Narasiṁha tale. Its roots are too deeply entrenched in a tradition of brahmins and sacrifice. To wit, the dwarf himself.

The Description of Vāmana

With Bali reigning undaunted in heaven, the gods set out in search of help, joined by their mother Aditi and sometimes their father, Kaśyapa. Seeking advice first from Brahmā, they either go together or Aditi goes alone to practice tapas to incur the presence and favor of Viṣṇu. It is of note that in *HV* 252 Brahmā directs them to Viṣṇu's dwelling, "Amṛta" on the bank of the Milk Ocean. Recording their speedy voyage, the poet says this: "In an instant they had crossed all the oceans, mountains, and rivers of the earth. They saw a horrible region, deserted, deprived of sunlight, and plunged in a profound darkness." This region marks the edge of the horizontal universe, the Lokāloka Mountain, and again, as we saw in the Narasiṁha myth, Viṣṇu's dwelling is at the most transcendent point of the universe, be it vertical or horizontal.

Through penance, Aditi (sometimes joined by the gods) wins a boon from Viṣṇu; that he will be born as her son, the younger brother of Indra, to win back the sovereignty for Śakra and reinstate the gods in their proper dwelling.[19] Sometimes she specifies that he be born as a dwarf. Often Aditi must carry the fetus for a thousand years or, alternately, her tapas has lasted a thousand years; but after a long period of one kind of discomfort or another, Viṣṇu is born from Aditi.

Besides those myths mentioned later (note 19) in which Viṣṇu is not born from Aditi at all, two myths tell of Viṣṇu's birth from Aditi, but not as a dwarf. *K.P.* I.16 states that Viṣṇu was born *as Upendra,* and subsequently goes to Bali's sacrifice, "assuming the form of a dwarf" (I.16.48). In *Mbh.* III.13.23–25, Viṣṇu is born and remains a child, a younger brother of Indra, and in *Mbh.* 12.340 he is said to be born as the twelfth Āditya.

With these exceptions, then, Aditi gives birth to a dwarf. Given that this is a miraculous birth—the first time that Viṣṇu as avatāra is born, and the superstitious wonder of the birth of a dwarf—the descriptions given by the poets are curious in their lack of to-do about the dwarfishness of this dwarf. In fact, only two versions bother to give any real details of his appearance as a dwarf; and one is *Sk.P.* VII.2.14–19 in which, as mentioned previously, Viṣṇu is not born from Aditi but cursed to become a dwarf for having laughed at the Vālakhīlyas, dwarfs themselves. The description is nonetheless noteworthy: "A brahmin knowing the four Vedas, a pilgrim to tīrthas, he had a big belly, dwarfish limbs, crippled feet, and a great head, a big jaw, fat calves, thick neck and was very lustful. He was wearing white clothes, a single lock of hair, carrying a parasol and a water jar" (*Sk.P.* VII.2.14.81–82). *Vdh.P.* I.55 gives an abbreviated description: "the illustrious and charming dwarf who was endowed with short and corpulent limbs, and was splendid with the black antelope skin, twisted locks of hair, staff, and water jar" (*Vdh.P.* I.55.16b–17). Even in these passages, which give us some idea of his dwarfish nature, another characteristic is stressed equally or more and is always described in all those versions that afford us any detail: the dwarf's decidedly *brahmin* nature. In five versions, he is described as bearing the signs or carrying the implements which mark him as a brahmin. In *P.P.* Uttara 266, "the god, knowing all the Vedāṅgas, the lord was marked by [the marks of] the belt, staff, and dress." *HV* 256 outfits him with the mauñja belt, sacred thread, parasol, staff, black antelope skin, and tonsured hair, as does *Bhg.P.* VIII.18, minus the tonsure. The *Kūrma Purāṇa* states: "Wearing a black-coloured deerskin and sacred thread, and holding a Palāśa rod, the brahmin with matted hair and besmeared with ashes came thither reciting the Vedas" (*K.P.* I.16.49). *Sk.P.* V.1.74 mentions that he approached Bali's sacrifice reciting mantras from the four Vedas, and even *Mbh.* III.271, as early and abbreviated a version as it is, takes care to note that Vāmana held the staff and water pot, wore matted locks and the sacred thread.

In six other versions, Viṣṇu receives his brahmin accoutrements in postpartum jātakarma and upanayana ceremonies, as mentioned in *Bhg.P.* IV.76.16–18: "Kaśyapa, the wise Prajāpati, performed his

[Vāmana's] saṁskāras, including the jātakarma and other ceremonies." The *Matsya Purāṇa* provides a full account of the ceremony:

> Then Brahmā giving the black antelope skin to Hṛṣikeśa, Bṛhaspati gave the Blessed One the sacred thread, Marici, son of Brahmā, gave the Aṣaṭha staff, and Vasiṣṭha the water jar, Angiras a broom of kuśa grass, Pulaha a rosary string, Pulastya two pure garments and the Vedas, adorned with "oṁ" and accents, all the śāstras and the utterances of Saṁkhyā yoga. Having matted hair, holding a stick, parasol, and water jar, Vāmana, comprehending in him all gods, reached Bali's sacrifice.

Vām.P. 62 states that Bharadvaja, a descendant of Bṛhaspati, performed the jātakarma and upanayana ceremonies, in which many of the same brahmin accoutrements as mentioned in the *M.P.* are given, but some by different persons (e.g., King Raghu gave the parasol, Nṛga gave a pair of sandals). *Rām.* I.29, *Br.P.* 73, *Brmda.P.* II.73.75–87, and *Sk.P.* VII.2.14–19, although lacking in description, still call Vāmana a brahmin. All of this makes it undeniably clear that Viṣṇu, as Vāmana, is a brahmin; a fact that merits more emphasis from the poets than does his dwarfish nature. The reasons for this may be several: to maintain the logic of the story line, Viṣṇu must appear at Bali's sacrifice as a brahmin if he is to be entitled to a gift from the sacrificer. Other motives, to which we will return in depth later, have their roots deep in the history of the myth; this is the epico-Purāṇic development of that Brāhmaṇic myth in which Viṣṇu *was* the sacrifice itself and won the world from the Asuras through the power of the sacrifice. It is also a myth that was fashioned by the hands of the orthodoxy since Vedic times and remains a myth basically devoted to their concerns.[20]

Thus, as Biardeau comments, "Vāmana . . . appears as a pure brahmin"[21] with one important exception which she, too, notes. Among all that brahmin paraphernalia accorded Vāmana, several versions[22] include a parasol. Surely not a brahminic symbol, "We know certainly that the parasol is a royal attribute par excellence."[23] This regal quality is enhanced even more in *Vām.P.* 62, when it is given to Vāmana by King Raghu, an ancestor of Rāma Dāśarathi and the only nonbrahmin to participate in the initiation ceremony. Furthermore, Biardeau deftly points out, the iconographic image of the parasol is evocative of both the lotus and discus; again, both royal symbols: "Therefore, the parasol becomes, at the same time, a kṣatriya component."[24] And, for Biardeau, this signifies that Vāmana is the rightful sovereign of all the earth. We see perhaps another meaning. If we recall the Vedic antecedents to the myth discussed previously (Chapter 2), the firm alliance of Indra and Viṣṇu in demon-slaying comes to mind, as well as the connection of Viṣṇu's three steps with this. Now Viṣṇu, as Vāmana, having eclipsed Indra in importance, conquers the demons alone, but, as the myth makes clear (see later, section on motifs), *for Indra.* It is worth noting, in this context, that in the two versions (*Vdh.P.* I.21; *P.P.* Sṛṣṭi 25) in which Indra accompanies Vāmana to Bali's sacrifice, the parasol is absent. Thus it seems, given the background of the myth, that Vāmana acts not as rightful sovereign of the earth, but in his stead; the parasol evokes Indra's rightful kingship, which his faithful ally has come to defend.

One other characteristic stands out in the poets' depiction of this avatāra: Vāmana is quite often called a *boy* [*baṭu*]. This occurs in eight versions,[25] and in the *Mbh.* III text it is used to the exclusion of Vāmana; thus in these eight texts, Viṣṇu is born as a brahmin-boy-dwarf. The reasons for this additional diminutive might be several: for the sake of logic, as he is just born; to reinforce the structural element of smallness on which Vāmana's "trick" depends; to emphasize that quality of Vāmana's which proclaims "don't judge a book by its cover"—the small, innocent, unlearned character of a boy-dwarf in contrast with his knowledge of the sacrifice and his theophany. The boyishness also evokes Viṣṇu as Balakṛṣṇa.

This near interchangeability in function of boy and dwarf highlights once again that the dwarfness (rather than smallness) of Viṣṇu does not seem to play as significant a role in the myth as one might have suspected. In only two versions does that particular aspect of his nature come into play; in *Sk.P.* VII.2.14–19 Śukra warns Bali about the laws that forbid him to let Vāmana enter the sacrificial arena: "All brahmins who are miserable, blind, wretched, and so on are to be honored *at the entrance,* as well as those who are deaf, dwarfed, humpbacked, diseased, and cruel" (*Sk.P.* VII.2.18.223). And in the *Vām.P.* 52 myth, the dwarf plies his case to the demons, saying he is poverty stricken because his brother tricked him out of his share of their father's estate with these words: "A hump-backed, a dwarf, a lame person, a eunuch, a leper, a madman, a blindman; these people have no share in property" (*Vām.P.* 52.64). With these exceptions, then, Viṣṇu's dwarfishness, that is, as a freak of nature, has little meaning in the myth; it almost seems that his petite size as dwarf or boy is structurally relevant only to the myth. Yet we must also keep in mind, once again, our Brāhmaṇic roots in which Viṣṇu was both dwarf and sacrifice, and return to this problem at a later point.

As the myth shifts its attention back to the Asura camp once again, we learn, in all versions,[26] that Bali is about to or has just commenced a sacrifice. In many myths[27] it is specified to be an Aśvamedha ceremony; others mention a twelve-year sacrifice or, significantly, that Bali is beginning the last of one hundred sacrifices. The meaning seems to be clear: not only is Bali unfit as the sacrificer, but especially he is not the proper person to receive the gift that the sacrifice will bestow, universal sovereignty. To perform 100 horse sacrifices[28] is to become Indra, "Śatakratu":

> But Indra prides himself on being the god of a hundred horse sacrifices [*śatakratu*]; originally this must have indicated a god to whom a hundred sacrifices were to be performed, but when the gods were recast as sacrificers as well as recipients of the sacrifice, the name was reinterpreted to mean "one who has performed a hundred sacrifices."[29]

Thus it seems that, until Bali performs the sacrifice, his sovereignty is not fixed; with the completion of the sacrifice, however, all will be lost: Bali will become Indra.

The Roles of Prahlāda and Śukra

In many versions of the myth we find Prahlāda, now the aged and, usually, wise grandfather of Bali. With the exception of *HV* 41.79–103/*Br.P.* 213.80–105 and *Brmda.P.* II.73.75–87/*V.P.* 98.59–88, in which Prahlāda is named as one of the demons battling Viṣṇu's theophany, and *HV* 248–257, in which Prahlāda tries to prevent Bali from giving land to Viṣṇu because he is not a brahmin boy but the man-lion returned,[30] Prahlāda's nature and role remain constant: he is an Asura with a bhakta's knowledge of the all-encompassing power of Viṣṇu and a properly devotional attitude.[31]

When Bali notices that the Asuras have become lacklustre, devoid of tejas, he consults his grandfather to find the cause. Through meditation, Prahlāda sees Viṣṇu residing in Aditi's womb, about to be born. His vision of Viṣṇu is properly theophanic, all the universe is contained within his body.[32] After Prahlāda has impressed upon the young king the absolute power of Viṣṇu, Bali foolishly denies that any of his demon warriors are not as strong as Viṣṇu and could not vanquish him in battle. Enraged by his own grandson's blasphemous ignorance, Prahlāda rails against him, and finally curses him to fall from power, losing his kingdom: "As the words you have said, O Reviler of Viṣṇu, are more serious than the cutting off of my own head, you should lose your kingdom and fall" (*Vām.P.* Saro.8.48).[33] Thus Prahlāda, as in the most "bhakticized" versions of the Narasiṁha myth, acts as Viṣṇu's agent. Even though Bali, realizing his wrongdoing, apologizes and Prahlāda forgives, the power of the curse supersedes its transmitter and Prahlāda's angry words must stick. The deed done, the coming of the avatāra is nearly superfluous.

Śukra, as spiritual preceptor of the Asuras, plays an integral role at Bali's sacrifice. The counterpart of Bṛhaspati, the Asura brahmin Śukra has a svadharma-sanātana dharma conflict all his own.[34] As a brahmin sage, Śukra has a privileged vision of the sacred, but he uses that vision toward demonic ends: "Śukra recognizes Viṣṇu in his dwarf disguise because Śukra alone among the demons has true spiritual insight [Prahlāda?], but he uses this insight to warn Bali and the demons not to promise Viṣṇu anything lest Viṣṇu take away his entire kingdom."[35] In fourteen versions of the myth, Śukra's warning is either referred to[36] or incorporated into the narrative.[37] The warning itself takes on various forms; as mentioned earlier (see the preceding subsection, description of Vāmana), in *Sk.P.* VII.2.14–19 Śukra tells Bali not to allow Vāmana to enter the sacrificial enclosure because he is a dwarf; *Br.P.* 73 is less forthright, with Śukra just advising Bali to consult with him before giving anything to the dwarf. In the remainder of the versions, however, Śukra makes his feelings known in no uncertain terms; he views Viṣṇu's coming as full of malintent.

> "This is Viṣṇu, the highest lord Hari, who has come as requested by the gods to acquire the entire earth from you through deception" (*P.P.* Uttara 267.176).

> "He [Viṣṇu] knows what is suitable for the good of the gods and not the law" (*P.P.* Sṛṣṭi.25.161).

> "In the form of a dwarf and the appearance of a young brahmin, he tries to trick you to serve Indra, his friend" (*HV* 256.168).[38]

Śukra is so adamant in preventing Vāmana from receiving the gift, that in *N.P.* I.10–11, a version often duplicated in folk traditions, Śukra tries to prevent Bali from pouring the water that ceremonially seals the offer he had made to Vāmana and is blinded by Viṣṇu with a blade of grass turned into a deadly weapon. In several cases, when Bali characteristically rejects Śukra's advice, either because it is simply improper to refuse any guest at a sacrifice or because he now recognizes Viṣṇu's superiority and welcomes him (in many cases thanks to

Prahlāda), Śukra is so enraged at his pupil's disobedience that he curses him to lose his kingdom, as in *Sk.P.* I.1.19.108–109a: "'Having overstepped my words, O Victorious One, you wish to give. You are wicked, fool! Because of that, you shall be destitute of wealth.' And then he cursed his pupil."[39]

In this respect, we can see the roles of Prahlāda and Śukra as complementary opposites: Prahlāda transmits knowledge of Viṣṇu's benevolence to Bali (bhakti), who rejects it (svadharma) and is then cursed by Prahlāda. Śukra transmits knowledge of Viṣṇu's malevolence (svadharma) to Bali, who rejects it (sanātana dharma-bhakti) and is then cursed by Śukra. In this they personify the concerns of the avatāra himself, who arrives not only for the gods' welfare, but also to censure Bali, who has committed an offense against one of these three truths, according to which version is read.

Viṣṇu's Steps

After Vāmana's request for just three steps of land (usually for a fire hut, so he can sacrifice) has been granted, the water poured into his palm, he miraculously abandons his diminutive stature to become giantesque (see later discussion of motifs: Cosmogonic Scenario). In approximately half the versions,[40] he re-creates an act with which, by now, we are quite familiar; he takes three steps, encompassing the universe, winning it back for Indra and the gods. But unexpectedly, in ten versions the steps are not the dénouement, but precipitate yet another conflict. In these, there is not room enough in the universe for Viṣṇu to take all three steps; the second brings him to (or through) the shell of the Brahmāṇḍa at the Brahmaloka, in many cases even piercing it with his toe. This presents a new problem for Bali, whose responses are several.[41]

When Viṣṇu comments to Bali that, in fact, the latter has not delivered what he had promised (thus violating the sanātana dharma of the power of one's word), Bali rather cunningly (although in the spirit of a bhakta, too) replies that he cannot give what Viṣṇu, creator of the universe, has not made.[42] In *Vām.P.* 62 Bāṇa, Bali's son, answers likewise in his father's stead, adding brashly that Viṣṇu was not giantesque when he asked for the steps. In *Sk.P.* I.19.9 he goes even further, saying "Those who are wise do not win through deceit!" In many of these versions, Bali's binding is explained as punishment for his failure to keep his word. In three other versions[43] Bali proposes a solution that shows him in the undeniably submissive posture of a bhakta. To keep his word and show his devotion to Viṣṇu, he proposes that the third step be taken on his head or his back. Viṣṇu does so, and in two cases rewards Bali for his selfless devotion. *Sk.P.* I.1.18–19 combines both traditions, with Garuḍa threatening Bali with fetters for violating his promise, at which point Vindhyāvali, Bali's wife, intervenes, saying he should take the three steps on her own, her son's, and her husband's head. This solution of striding on the new devotee's head, especially for the third step, is significant, for it subtly identifies the *paramaṁ padaṁ,* the Vedic place of Viṣṇu's highest step, the Purāṇic Viṣṇuloka, with the devotee himself, uniting the transcendent and immanent.

Bali's Fate

The steps taken and the worlds regained for the gods, only Bali remains to be dealt with. Again, his misdeeds and the punishments they bring can be related to the three "dharmas." First, Bali must be punished because he carried out his svardharma, which necessitated adharma; that is, he transgressed his territorial and occupational bounds as an Asura by leaving the nether worlds, his proper home, usurping heaven and the sovereignty over the trailokya and, in some cases, stealing the gods' shares of the sacrifice. This is an issue at stake in nearly all the versions, regardless of what is additional. In retribution for this violation of dharma, Bali is sent back to from where he came, specifically Pātāla or Sutala, two of the nether worlds. In several myths, he also is bound there, recalling another myth from the *Mbh.* in which he was bound and thrown in a cave for offending brahmins (*Mbh.* XII.220.18). Thus we see that although it is the Asura's svadharma to be adharmic, from the point of view of dharma, this activity is *properly* carried out within the Asuras' *own* space, the nether worlds.

In several cases,[44] where Bali has been a threat due to the dharmic nature of his reign, the description of his punishment of a forced return to asuric (i.e., adharmic) life-style includes an ingenious elaboration on what Bali's pleasures will be in the nether worlds:

> Gifts not conformable to law, śraddhās not sanctioned by the Vedas, and sacrifices performed without faith will bestow merit on you. And sacrifices without the payment of the Dakṣina, ceremonies performed without the sanction of religious law, and study without the necessary vow of brahmacarya, worship

> without water, religious rites without Darbha grass, and sacrifice without ghee will produce the desired results for you, O Bali. (*Vām.P.* Saro.10.78–80)

Thus, to a proper Asura (loyal to svadharma), all that is normal or dharmic seems inverted, and likewise are their practices exactly the opposite of what is correct. Given their subterranean residence, one is reminded of the naiveté of childhood that pictures the inhabitants of Antarctica standing miraculously upside down and doing everything backwards.

Although Viṣṇu effectively puts Bali back in his proper place, he nevertheless often promises him another chance to become Indra, to be sovereign of the triple world. In seven versions[45] Viṣṇu promises that when the next Manvantara arrives, Bali will become Indra. In so doing, he reveals to us an important point: although an Asura's attempt to usurp heaven, become Indra, steal the sacrifice—in short to become daivic—is an inversion of the normal order and must be stopped, it nevertheless is a constant occurrence, indeed an oscillating rhythm that seems to be basic to the cosmos.[46]

Bali's banishment to Pātāla, and especially his binding, additionally can be seen as retribution for his violation of sanātana dharma, for not keeping his vow of a gift of three steps to Viṣṇu, as previously mentioned.

Finally, in remembering the instances of Prahlāda's curse, Bali's punishment, specifically his loss of the sovereignty, can be seen as just desserts for his transgression against Viṣṇubhakti. Yet in a typically bhaktic inversion, Viṣṇu also rewards Bali, placing the value of his newly found devotion far above his misdemeanors. For instance, in *K.P.* I.16.1–69, the version in which Bali accepted Viṣṇubhakti when Prahlāda preached it, Bali attains mokṣa in the end. Likewise in *P.P.* Sṛṣṭi.25, when Viṣṇu's steps are unfulfilled and the Asura responds about Viṣṇu as creator, he is rewarded with a boon and chooses death at Viṣṇu's hand (i.e., bhakti mokṣa).

The treatment of Bali's fate concludes the myth meaningfully by highlighting the concerns of each version through its individual handling of the same problem. Through the examination of these, it is beginning to be evident that the central thrust of the myth is at the necessity for maintaining the cosmological status quo, whether it is expressed through Bali's bringing of adharma into the realm of dharma through a typically asuric conquest and reign in heaven or through his violation of asurasvadharma or "cosmic" laws regulating time and dharma, expressed in his "daivic," dharmic conquest and sovereignty.

Motifs

Special Relationship with Indra

With its roots stretching back into the Vedic past, the Vāmana myth does not forget Viṣṇu's firm alliance with Indra (see Figure 7). It may be useful to highlight here the exchange of power that occurs between the two gods as Indra fades and Viṣṇu's importance begins to rise.

By the time of the late Brāhmaṇas the inculpability and power of the sovereign Śakra has begun to wane, and we hear of the retribution Indra receives for his sins. When Indra violated his pact of friendship with Namuci and killed him through guile, he became polluted and had to be purified with hymns (*T.B.* III.225). By the time of the epic *Mahābhārata,* Indra's sins and the losses he suffered from them serve as a basis for the divine birth of the Pāṇḍavas. He killed the sons of Tvāṣṭṛ (brahminicide) and his *tejas* diminished; he violated the pact of friendship by killing Vṛtra-Namuci and his *balam* diminished; taking the appearance of Gautama he violated Ahalyā, and for this his *rūpam* diminished.[47] Certainly by the time of the epics, if not before,[48] he is a "spent force," a nominal sovereign who is no longer immune to the ethical code of the universe and who can no longer defend the cosmos against demons nor regenerate it with his virility.

It is clear that, as Viṣṇu rises in importance, he becomes the mythological heir to Indra's legacy. The *Rāmāyaṇa* records this process at several points:

> When Indra hears of Rāvaṇa's advance he becomes flustered at the news and anxiously seeks Viṣṇu's advice and confesses his inferiority (*Rām.* VII.27.3–13). Prior to killing Vṛtra Indra acknowledged Viṣṇu's superiority and asked for his help. . . . Armed with only one-third of Viṣṇu's strength he slays Vṛtra, but immediately after is consumed with the anguish of guilt-consciousness and has to offer a horse sacrifice for atonement and purgation. (*Rām.* VII.84,85)[49]

Thus by the epic and Purāṇic myths, Indra is a virtual homme de paille, with Viṣṇu taking over his demon-conquering tasks, certainly one of the raisons d'être of the avatāras, and his ability to change shape to accomplish a task. Although Indra retains his title of king, Viṣṇu gains his wife, Śrī, the very symbol of sovereignty.[50]

Given this, and remembering the Brāhmaṇic "preforms" of the

TEXT	R.I.	C.S.	M.	A.T.	L.L.
MAHĀBHARĀTA III.13.23–25 (CE)	x	x			
III.271 (CE)	x				
XII.326.72–76	x				
note #837 (CE)					
RĀMĀYAṆA I.29	x				
HARIVAṀŚA Ch. 41	x				
Ch. 248–256	x	x		x	x
AGNI PURĀṆA Ch. 4.4–11	x	x			
Ch. 276.13–17	x			x	
BRAHMĀ PURĀṆA Ch. 213.80–105	x	x			
Ch. 73	x	x			
BRAHMĀṆḌA PURĀṆA II.73.75–87	x	x			
BHĀGAVATA PURĀṆA II.7.17–19	x			x	
V.24.17–18	x			x	
VIII.15–23	x	x			
BHAVIṢYA PURĀṆA IV.76.1–27		x			
KŪRMA PURĀṆA I.16.1–69	x	x		x	
MATSYA PURĀṆA Ch. 244–246	x	x			
NĀRADA PURĀṆA I.10–11	x	x			
PADMA PURĀṆA Sṛṣṭi.25	x	x		x	
Uttara.266–267	x	x		x	
SKANDA PURĀṆA I.1.18–19	x			x	
V.1.74	x				
VII.2.14–19	x	x		x	
VII.4.19.10–14		x			
VĀMANA PURĀṆA Saro.2–10	x	x		x	
Ch. 49–65	x	x		x	
Ch. 52	x	x		x	
VĀYU PURĀṆA II.36.74–86	x	x		x	
Ch. 98.59–88	x	x			
VIṢṆUDHARMOTTARA PURĀṆA I.55	x	x		x	

R.I. = special relationship with Indra
C.S. = cosmogonic scenario
M. = mediating power and activity
A.T. = action through trickery
L.L. = loophole in the law

Figure 7 Motif Index for Vāmanāvatāra Myths

Vāmana myth in *Ś.B.* I.2.5.1ff. and the Indra-Śalāvṛki myth, it is not surprising that twenty-eight out of the thirty Vāmana versions mention that Vāmana acts *for Indra;* that he either descends for Indra's sake (e.g., *Vām.P.* 50.45, Aditi asking Viṣṇu, "Therefore, Janārdana, do so that the lord of gods, Indra, again becomes king of the gods") or that, having put Bali in Pātāla, he restores the kingship to Indra, or both.

Further, it is often mentioned that Viṣṇu, born of Aditi, becomes Indra's younger brother (as well as that of the other ten Ādityas, which is not mentioned) and is not uncommonly called *Upendra* ("little Indra"):

> O Lord of Gods, upon becoming my son you must accomplish what is beneficial for the thirty [gods]. The three worlds have been conquered by Bali through force. Upon becoming the younger brother of Indra, famed as Upendra, having conquered Bali, in any way through māyā, give the three worlds eternally to my son Śakra. (*P.P.* Uttara 266.28–29)[51]

Although represented by Viṣṇu, who acts for his sake and often carries a symbol of his royalty, the parasol, Indra sometimes goes along to Bali's sacrifice with Vāmana, as previously mentioned (*Vdh.P.* I.21; *P.P.* Sṛṣṭi.25). In a myth interior to the *Sk.P.* I.1.18–19 version, Indra plays Vāmana in a doublet of the avatāra myth (*Sk.P.* I.1.18.121–129). To kill Virocana, Bali's father and reigning Asura king, Indra goes to his dwelling, asking for a boon:

> The Asura, son of Prahlāda, said this, smiling, "I shall give my own head if you want it now, or this kingdom, or Śrī, who does not go elsewhere. I give to you with little effort, that is no doubt." Thus spoken to by the Daitya, and having reflected, Hari [Indra] said, "Give me your head, furnished with the crown" (*Sk.P.* I.1.18.127–128)

And so he did. But what is especially significant about Indra in this myth is that he, too, goes to the demon disguised as a brahmin. This leads us to believe that, although the deed is done *for* the sovereign Śakra, it is accomplished only through the power of a brahmin. There is no longer a mighty battleground on which the valiant warrior makes his victory; we are at a sacrifice, where a skilled priest wins through an action from the Vedas, an association from the Brāhmaṇas, and a cosmological superiority in the universe of bhakti.

Cosmogonic Scenario

We need only recall the Vedic antecedents of Viṣṇu's three steps to establish a firm foundation for the cosmogonic significance of the Vāmana myth. In the Vedas, the steps are not so much of a primary cosmogonic nature, but rather an act through which the created world is made liveable. Their aim is "life." In the Vāmana myth this secondary creative function is preserved, as Viṣṇu strides to recapture, to re-create the three worlds in their proper, liveable fashion (i.e., with gods in heaven as recipients of the sacrifice).

That this early cosmogonic association of Viṣṇu and the three steps is maintained is evidenced in several versions that continue the alignment of the three steps, tentative in the *ṚgVeda*, explicit in the Brāhmaṇas, with the triple world. Although the Purāṇic universe has expanded upward from the earlier trailokya (that is, to a saptaloka system), *Mbh.* III.13.23–25,[52] *A.P.* 4.4–11; *Brmda.P.* II.73.75–87; and *V.P.* 98.59–88 preserve the earlier connection of the steps with earth, atmosphere, and heaven.

The cosmogonic nature of Vāmana is evoked through a second series of images that draws upon the Brāhmaṇic phase of Viṣṇu's development. This, of course, is Viṣṇu's and more particularly Vāmana's association with the sacrifice. First, the myth presents us with Viṣṇu as a dwarf who has come to the Asura's sacrifice. The only other place we have witnessed a similar situation was in *Ś.B.* I.2.5ff., when Viṣṇu was, as well as a dwarf, the sacrifice itself. The Paurāṇikas do not stop at this unspoken link. Often, Vāmana's own sacrificial nature is accented; in *Br.P.* 73, Śukra recognizes the dwarf's true nature: "He who has arrived at your sacrifice, the brahmin bearing the form of a dwarf, is not a brahmin, O Bali; truly he is the lord of the sacrifice, the bearer of the sacrifice" (*Br.P.* 73.32). And Bali responds joyously, that "the lord of sacrifice incarnate" has come to his dwelling.[53] *Vdh.P.* I.55.15 is even more explicit: "Having arrived at the sacrificial enclosure, the dwarf himself praised himself, the sacrifice, like the fire covered with ashes." This juncture in the myth is replete with pregnant associations and understated inversions: as was believed since the Brāhmaṇas, the sacrificer who strides thrice becomes Viṣṇu conquering the worlds;[54] Viṣṇu as the dwarf (who is the sacrifice) arrives at Bali's sacrifice, but by asking for land on which to perform his rites, becomes the thrice-stepping sacrificer himself, inverting his and Bali's positions, and winning back the worlds for the gods not through deceit, but through the sacrificial act.

Vāmana's brahminic character and sacrificial expertise are further elaborated on in *HV* 256:

> Once he had arrived at that place filled with illustrious ṛṣis, Viṣṇu began to discourse on the ceremony. He who is the eternal sacrifice, he described the rites appropriate to that sacrificial space. He notified them of their duties, and Śukra and the other priests he made mute with astonishment and confusion. In the presence of Bali and his pious audience, he explained, with varied and profound skill, the origin, motifs, and details of different rituals, as the Vedas prescribe them.

Perhaps, one could argue that the purely creative function of Vāmana as the sacrifice is left implicit, unexplored in these passages. But as we turn to examine the central manifestation of the "cosmogonic scenario," the theophany of *viśvarūpa,* the cosmogonic metaphors come fully into view.

As Vāmana accepts the pact-sealing water in his palm, he quits his dwarfish form and exhibits to us his theophany: the *viśvarūpa* or all-form. The description that ensues varies little from text to text:

> As the water fell into his hand, Vāmana became a nondwarf; instantly he exhibited the form containing all gods. And the moon and the sun were his eyes, heaven his head, the earth his foot, the Piśācas his toes and the yakṣas his fingers. And the Viśvedevas were at his knees, the Sādhyas and the best of gods his shanks, the yakṣas his nails, and united in a continuous row, the apsarases. His eyes were the seven stars and his body hairs the great ṛṣis. The intermediary regions were his arms, the cardinal points the ears of the Mahātmā, the Aśvins his earlobes, the wind the Mahātmā's nose. His grace was the moongod, in his mind dharma had come together, truth was his speech, the goddess Sarasvatī his tongue. His neck was Aditi, mother of gods, his bracelet was the Vedas, the gate of heaven was Matri, his eyebrows Tvāṣṭṛ and Puṣan. His mouth was Agni Vaisvārana, his testicles Prajāpati, his heart the supreme Brahmā, his manhood, indeed, the sage Kaśyapa. On his back were the Vasus, in all his joints the Maruts, his teeth all the Vedic hymns and the luminaries of stainless splendour. On the front of his chest was Mahādeva, on his back the mighty oceans, and in his belly originated the Gandharvas, the strong ones. Indeed his hips were Lakṣmī, Medhā, Dhṛtī, Kantī, and all knowledge. All the lights, know that they were indeed his supremacy. His breasts and abdomen were the Vedas, and his belly the great sacrifices; vegetable and animal sacrifices, the efforts of the twice-borns. (*M.P.* 246.53–65)

The theophany is markedly different from that of Kṛṣṇa in the *Bhagavad Gītā* and of Narasiṁha, both of which are basically destructive; this *viśvarūpa* evokes another, earlier one which, as we have seen, is already linked to Viṣṇu in the Brāhmaṇas: the *creative*, sacrificial theophany of the Puruṣa of RV X.90. The poets' intentionality in emphasizing Viṣṇu's identity with Puruṣa is voiced through Aditi, praising her future son:

> I praise him, who beholds higher knowledge and whose existence is beyond any proof. From whose head the brahmin was born, from both his arms the kṣatriya arose, from his thighs the vaiśya was born, from his feet the śūdra was born. From his mind the moon was born, and from his eyes the sun, from his mouth Agni and Indra, from his breath Vāyu. From his body the *Ṛg*, *Yajus*, and *Sāma Vedas*, whose soul exists in the seven musical notes, who is the form of the six Vedāṅgas, I praise him more and more. (*N.P.* I.11.32b–35)

The theophany itself does not simply duplicate the Puruṣasukta but plays on it, improvising on its theme. Both Puruṣasukta and Viṣṇu's *viśvarūpa* record the universal size of the god, measuring the worlds with his body ("the moon and sun were his eyes, heaven his head, the earth his foot" [*M.P.* 246.53]; "Forth from his navel came midair; the sky was fashioned from his head; earth from his feet" [RV X.90.14]). Both, as the sacrifice and the form containing all gods, have Agni as their mouth (*RV* X.90.13b) and, as sacrifice, create the sacrifice. But here the texts differ significantly: the Vedic Puruṣa must *be* sacrificed to create the world; but Viṣṇu-Vāmana exists on yet another level, as Supreme God in the Purāṇic universe, the god of bhakti who is creator, preserver, and destroyer, and does not die with his deed. His transcendence over the universe he creates is expressed through the new language of Purāṇic cosmology.

As mentioned earlier, in many versions, Viṣṇu strides not only over the trailokya, but over the expanded universe of seven worlds. In twelve versions[55] Viṣṇu strides up to the top of the Purāṇic universe, piercing the Brahmāṇḍa with his big toe.[56] This new interpretation of the strides depicts Viṣṇu as creator of and master over the Purāṇic universe, moving his *paramaṁ padaṁ* of the Vedas to a point that is even beyond the created world.[57]

The *viśvarūpa* theophany moves beyond the Vedic three steps and sacrificial form further by aligning itself with the Purāṇic structures of creation and destruction, the pralaya. The avatāra itself, by appearing at the beginning of the Treta Yuga, integrates itself into the interyugal period that, as shown, appears as a minipralaya. It is significant that Vāmana appears at the beginning of a new yuga, or the close of the interyuga space, aligning his manifestation with the second phase of pralaya—or more accurately, with that process which follows the pralaya (after the night of Brahma)—creation. Although the Paurāṇikas' versions of Vāmana's strides themselves may evoke earlier phases of the pralaya, as Biardeau notes,[58] we are bombarded with distinctly creative images from all levels of religious meaning and brought near to the core of this avatāra myth.

The Triad of Liminal Motifs

At first glance, the lack of emphasis on Viṣṇu's trickery is surprising in this myth, which is often chosen by scholars as an example of how crafty Viṣṇu can be through his avatāras. Although there is a kind of illusionary trick to the incongruence between Viṣṇu's dwarf form and the *viśvarūpa*, there is little mention of deceit. In fact, Bali, who clearly suffers the greatest loss through Vāmana's action, never himself cries foul. In *HV* 256, both Śukra and Prahlāda, in warning Bali not to give anything to the dwarf, tell him Viṣṇu has come to trick him, employing a deceitful appearance (see the preceding section, the subsection on the roles of Prahlāda and Śukra). In *Sk.P.* VII.2.19.9, it is Bali's brash son, Bāṇa, who objects to Viṣṇu's sudden change of stature, saying "Those who are wise do not win through deceit."

When one realizes from whose mouths such protestations issue, the role of "trickery" comes clear. Only those who lack true wisdom, that is, knowledge of Viṣṇu, cry deceit. Bāṇa, the ignorant son, Śukra, knowledgeable only in orthopraxy, and Prahlāda, only when *not* depicted as a Viṣṇu-bhakta (*HV* 256), accuse Viṣṇu of employing trickery. Those possessing knowledge recognize the *Vāmanarūpa* and the *viśvarūpa* as alternate forms of the god's power. To answer Bāṇa, those who are wise recognize all forms of the god, those who are not are "duped." It is the final Purāṇic reinterpretation of the Brāhmaṇic and epic situation in which trickery *was* the name of the game in the daivāsura struggle.[59] Bhakti here seems determined to wipe out any taint of pure treachery on Viṣṇu's part by its totally universal comprehension of Viṣṇu's power. In so doing, it cleverly integrates the Brāhmaṇic portrait of Viṣṇu as dwarf and sacrifice within the Purāṇic view of Viṣṇu as Creator of the Universe, indeed Container of the Universe, thus subsuming the incongruence of *Vāmanarūpa* and *viśvarūpa* within the totality of godhead; but at the same time it loses that particular mythical flavor found in the endless antics of the daivāsura struggle. In the final interpretation, the Asuras are not deceived, they are just dumb. And again, we are left feeling a little cheated ourselves of the punch of a good tale by the bhakti pedantry. Even Bali, who loses all to Viṣṇu, voices not even a whimper of complaint as his glory fades fast. His role as catalyst to Viṣṇu's transformation at the sacrifice (and significantly, *bali* means the sacrificial offering of a portion of the daily meal) makes him privy to a special knowledge of and acquiescence to the cosmic plan regulated by Viṣṇu; his experience is much of a conversion, and he is notably the only Asura antagonist whose life is not taken in direct confrontation with an avatāra.

Therefore, we cannot say that trickery and deception lie at the heart of this myth, although through its development they have played a part; instead the focus sharpens on the realm of meaning issuing from the cosmogonic scenario, primarily the *viśvarūpa* as well as its multiple creative metaphors; the interlocking meanings of the brahmin, the sacrifice, and the dwarf, and the classic cosmogonic act of the three steps.

Exegesis: The Dhundhu Myth

In dealing with the seemingly endless versions of a particular myth, the investigator cannot but help finding a favorite, one that combines all those elements which make the myth a vital one for the support of the analysis, elements which so often elude him or her in the majority of versions. Among the thirty Vāmana versions, such a myth has appealed to us, the myth that personifies our more naive and idealistic conceptions of what the Vāmanāvatāra is all about.

Strangely, and perhaps significantly, this favorite version is an aberration among the thirty: it is not about our familiar characters Bali and Vāmana, but about Viṣṇu who, in a bygone Mahāyuga, descended as a dwarf to outwit the demon Dhundhu, usurper of the three worlds. The myth is told within the expansive *Vām.P.* 49–65 Vāmana myth as its fifty-second chapter, to explain the existence of a Viṣṇupāda tīrtha prior to Vāmana's three steps on earth. The tale that ensues parallels the usual Vāmana versions, but highlights some points that remain largely in the shadows of the other versions.

In the fourth Kali Age, the demon Dhundhu practiced tapas and was rewarded with invulnerability by Brahmā. Usurping heaven and its throne, Dhundhu was not yet sated, still desiring Brahmā's abode, to which the gods had fled. To this wish, the demons reply to their king, "We don't have the power of going, O Protector of the World, by which we can go to the residence of Brahmā because the path is very far and extremely impossible" (*Vām.P.* 52.20).

This escalation of goals on Dhundhu's part makes nice symmetry with his tapas; that is, a demon who wins by force (Vedic strategy) desires only the triple world (Vedic universe); but he who conquers by tapas (Upaniṣadic strategy) desires true immortality—mokṣa (equated with Brahmā's residence; see Chapter 4) (Upaniṣadic goal).

Adamant in his desire, Dhundhu consults with Śukra, who suggests he perform 100 Aśvamedhas, as did Indra, thereby winning the Brahmaloka. Assembled at the riverbank, the Asuras begin the sacrifice, and the gods, smelling smoke, call to Viṣṇu for help. Viṣṇu "made up his mind to bind Dhundhu, feigning virtue" (*Vām.P.* 52.52a). Taking the form of a dwarf, he floated up river to the site of the Asuras' sacrifice and, pretending to be drowning, was hauled out by them. When questioned by them, he told a sad tale. The younger of two sons of a brahmin, named Netrabhasa and Gatibhasa, when his father died he was cheated out of his inheritance by his elder brother, who gave him this excuse: "A humpbacked, a dwarf, a lame person, a eunuch, a leper, a madman, a blindman—these people have no share in property" (*Vām.P.* 52.64). At his protestation, Gatibhasa was thrown into the river by his greedy brother.

Flattering the Asuras with compliments, they in return offered him a myriad of sumptuous gifts, which he declined, asking only for three steps of land. Granted this, he assumed his Trivikrama form and began striding, "robbing" [*jahāra*] the earth, atmosphere, and heaven with this first two steps, and squashing Dhundhu with his third.

Here the myth is unique in the instrumental role given to Viṣṇu's dwarfishness; the fact that he was cheated out of his possessions because he was a dwarf becomes the motivation for Dhundhu's giving, and his status as a brahmin, although present, clearly takes a back seat. Trickery is to the fore ("feigning virtue . . . robbed the earth") and Dhundhu is squelched with no time for repentance or conversion.

The myth excels in its ability to combine the expression of differing religious goals in a unique balance, while still preserving the impishness inherent, but largely ignored, in the figure of the dwarf. And by the very existence of the Gatibhasa-Vāmanāvatāra, a whole new realm of cosmological meaning is implied: that although the avatāras have sociocosmic relevance to the present Mahāyuga, they are a repetitive cosmological structure, constant through time. What vision had the poet who did not repress his urge to create this "aberrant" myth!

Notes

1. Such was the case for the Narasiṁha myths from these same four texts.

2. Wendy D. O'Flaherty, *The Origins of Evil in Hindu Mythology* (Berkeley: University of California Press, 1976) (henceforth *OEHM*), pp. 78–93.

3. Ibid., p. 130.

4. O'Flaherty's categorization does not fit perfectly, however; she says in this period there is an emphasis on svadharma.

5. O'Flaherty, *OEHM*, p. 82.

6. A similarly diachronic method is employed by Ganga Sagar Rai in his "Vāmana Legend—in the Vedas, Epics, and Purāṇas" (*Purāṇa* 12, no. 1 [1970]), although he chooses different elements or mythemes for discussion, and lacks any conclusion to his investigation.

7. *Rām.* I.29; *A.P.* 4.4–11; *Bh.P.* IV.76.1–27; *K.P.* I.16.1–69; *M.P.* 244–246; *N.P.* I.10–11; *P.P.* Uttara 266–267; *Sk.P.* I.1.18–19; *Sk.P.* V.1.74; *Sk.P.* VII.4.19.10–14; *Vām.P.* 49–65; *Vdh.P.* I.21; *Vdh.P.* I.55.

8. Cf. *Vdh.P.* I.55; *Vām.P.* 52; *P.P.* Sṛṣṭi 25; *HV* 248–256; *Mbh.* XII.326.72–76; and *Vām.P.* Saro. 2–10 allude to this.

9. In his careful study of Bali, Clifford Hospital sees the conflict between the Devas and Asuras in the epic and Purāṇic myths as centered on the relation between tapas and dharma, "with bhakti as an adjunct to dharma." *The Righteous Demon* (Vancouver: University of British Columbia Press, 1984), p. 41.

10. The Asura is called Bāṣkali in *P.P.* Sṛṣṭi 25 and in *Vdh.P.* I.21, and Dhundu in *Vām.P.* 52; this will be discussed later.

11. This is highly reminiscent of many accounts of Hiraṇyakaśipu's boon, which implies an attempt to overstep Viṣṇu's power as well.

12. Perhaps this is another of the *Bhāgavata* poets' efforts to "archaicize" the Purāṇa.

13. G. C. Tripathi, *Die Ursprung und Entwicklung der Vāmanalegende in der Indische-liturатur* (Wiesbaden: Otto Harrassowitz, 1968), p. 238.

14. The remaining versions, *Bhg.P.* V.24.17–18; *Bhg.P.* II.7.17–19; *Br.P.* 73; *HV* 41.79–103; *V.P.* 98.59–88; *Brmda.P.* II.73.75–87; *Br.P.* 213.80–105, do not mention how Bali became king of the trailokya, beginning the tale with his sovereignty already established. *V.P.* 98.74 notes that "These three worlds belonged to Bali in the Treta Yuga."

15. *Mbh.* III.13.23–25; *Mbh.* III.271; *Mbh.* XII.326.72–76; *Rām.* I.29; *HV* 41.79–103; *A.P.* 4.4–11; *A.P.* 276.13–17; *Br.P.* 213.80–105; *Brmda.P.* 73.75–87; *Bhg.P.* II.7.17–19; *Bhg.P.* V.24.17–18; *Bhg.P.* VIII.15–23; *M.P.* 244–246; *Sk.P.* I.1.18–19; VII.4.19.10–14; *Vām.P.* 52; *V.P.* 98.59–88; *Vdh.P.* I.21.

16. The epics, *Harivaṁśa, Vāyu Purāṇa,* and *Agni Purāṇa.*

17. See also *P.P.* Uttara 266–267 for a similar description.

18. Hospital notes the same dilemma and comments, "while at one level good order is being upheld, at another—that at which we observe the position of the Devas, and of the regular movement of the universe through its phases of ascent and decline—it is being disturbed" C. Hospital, *The Righteous Demon,* p. 107.

19. Only in *Vām.P.* 52, the Dhundhu myth, *Vdh.P.* I.21, *Sk.P.* VII.2.14, *Br.P.* 213.80–105, and *HV* 41. 79–103 does Viṣṇu become Vāmana without being born from Aditi.

20. One must then take issue with Gonda's statement that "it seems warranted to suppose the Vāmana to be the most famous Indian instance of the widespread belief in the miraculous abilities of beings who are considerably below the usual size." *Aspects of Early Viṣṇuism,* (Delhi: Motilal Barnarsidass, 1969), p. 145.

21. Biardeau, *EMH* 4:198.

22. *Vām.P.* 49–65; *Vām.P.* Saro 2–10; *M.P.* 244–246; *Bhg.P.* VIII.15–23; and *HV* 248–256.

23. Biardeau, *EMH* 4:198.

24. Ibid., p. 199.

25. *Mbh.* III.13.23–25; *HV* 248–256; *Br.P.* 213.80–105; *Bhg.P.* V.24.17–18; *Bhg.P.* VIII.15–23; *M.P.* 244–246; *P. P.* Uttara 266–267; *Sk.P.* I.1.18–19.

26. Except *Mbh.* XII.326.72–76; *A.P.* 276.13–17; *Bhg.P.* V.24.17–18—all compressed myths.

27. *HV* 248–257; *B.P.* 73; *Bhg.P.* VIII.15–23; *Sk.P.* I.1.18–19; *Sk.P.* V.1.74; *Vām.P.* 49–65; *Vām.P.* 52; *Vdh.P.* I.55.

28. As in *Vām.P.* 52 or *Sk.P.* VIII.2.14–19.

29. O'Flaherty, *OEHM,* p. 88.

30. It is significant, however, that Prahlāda recognizes Vāmana to be Narasiṁha through his divine eye [*divyaṁ cakṣuḥ*].

31. Cf. *M.P.* 244–246; *K.P.* I.16; *Vām.P.* Saro.2–10; *Vām.P.* 49–65.

32. This is not made explicit in the *K.P.* version.

33. The *K.P.* differs from the other three versions in that Bali, listening to Prahlāda's talk of Viṣṇu, decides to take refuge in the god and is spared the curse.

34. Cf. O'Flaherty, *OEHM*, pp. 118–122; Robert Goldman, *Gods, Priests, and Warriors* (New York: Columbia University Press, 1977), Chapter 3, "Śukra, the Priest of the Demons."

35. O'Flaherty, *OEHM* p. 121.

36. *A.P.* 4.4–11; *Bhg.P.* II.7.17–19; *Sk.P.* I.5.1.74—all abbreviated versions.

37. *HV* 248–257; *B.P.* 73; *Bhg.P.* VIII.15–23; *M.P.* 244–246; *N.P.* I.10–11; *P.P.* Sṛṣṭi.25; *P.P.* Uttara 266–267; *Sk.P.* I.1.18–19; *Sk.P.* VII.2.14–19; *Vām.P.* Saro.2–10; *Vām.P.* 49–65.

38. See also *N.P.* I.11.92.

39. See also *Bhg.P.* VIII.20.14.

40. *Sk.P.* VII.2.14–19; *Sk.P.* I.1.18–19; *Vdh.P.* I.21; *Vdh.P.* I.55; *Bh.P.* IV.76.1–27; *P.P.* Sṛṣṭi. 25; *Vām.P.* 49–65; *Br.P.* 73; *Bhg.P.* VIII.15–23; *Bhg.P.* II.7.17–19; *Vām.P.* 52.

41. *Vdh.P.* I.21; *Bh.P.* IV.76.1–27 do not explore the issue, simply stating that the steps were incomplete.

42. Cf. *Vdh.P.* I.55; *P.P.* Sṛṣṭi.25.

43. *Br.P.* 73; *Bhg.P.* VIII.15–23; *Bhg.P.* II.7.17–19.

44. *HV* 248–257; *M.P.* 244–246; *N.P.* I.10–11; *Vām.P.* Saro.2–10; *Vām.P.* 49–65.

45. *B.P.* 73; *Bhg.P.* VIII.15–23; *Bh.P.* IV.76.1–27; *M.P.* 244–246; *Sk.P.* VII.2.14–19; *Vām.* Saro.2–10; *Vām.P.* 49.65.

46. An important point, to which we will return.

47. George Dumézil, *The Destiny of the Warrior* (Chicago: University of Chicago Press, 1969), pp. 74–75.

48. Cf. *Taṇḍya Mahābrāhmaṇa* XX.15.6, in which Vṛtra offers his strength to Indra, and Viṣṇu receives it on Indra's behalf.

49. S. Bhattacharji, *The Indian Theogony* (Cambridge: Cambridge University Press, 1970), p. 277.

50. For the relation of Śrī to sovereignty see Alf Hiltebeitel, "Gods, Heroes, and Kṛṣṇa: A Study of Indian and Indo-European Symbolisms" (dissertation, University of Chicago, 1973), Chapter 14, "Śrī and the Sovereignty."

51. Cf. also *Bhg.P.* VIII.23.20; *V.P.* 98.84; *Brmda.P.* II.73.84; *Vām.P.* Saro.6.33;6.34; *K.P.* I.16.43; *Sk.P.* VII.2.14.26; 14.56; 14.70.

52. Understandably, as it is pre-Purāṇic.

53. See also *Vām.P.* Saro.10.10, where Bali calls Vāmana "Yajñapatiḥ."

54. Cf. TS 2.1.1ff., also TS I.7.5.4 on identification of sacrificer's steps with Viṣṇu's steps and with the three (poetic) meters. See Chapter 3, pp. 33ff.

55. *Sk.P.* V.1.74; *B.P.* 73; *Sk.P.* I.1.18–19; *K.P.* I.16; *Vdh.P.* I.21; *Bh.P.* IV.76.1–27; *P.P.* Sṛṣṭi.25; *P.P.* Uttara 266–267; *N.P.* I.10–11; *Sk.P.* VII.2.14–19; *Bhg.P.* VIII.15–23, *Vām.P.* 49–65.

56. In several myths, *Br.P.* 73, *Bhg.P.* VIII.15–23; *K.P.* I.16; *N.P.* I.10–11; *P.P.* Sṛṣṭi.25; *P.P.* Uttara 266–267; *Sk.P.* I.1.18–19; *Sk.P.* VII.2.14–19; *Vām.P.* 49–65; *Vdh.P.* I.21, this accounts for the origin of the River Gāṅgā, which until that point flowed outside the Brahmāṇḍa (presumably as the Milky Way); cf. Heinrich von Stietencron, *Gāṅgā und Yamunā* (Wiesbaden: Otto Harrassowitz, 1972), pp. 6–69.

57. Recalling Bali's defense when Viṣṇu can take only two steps, "I cannot give what you have not created."

58. Biardeau, *EMH* 4:201–202: "the steps of Viṣṇu no longer seem destined to extend space and construct the world, but on the contrary, to fill everything with his presence to the point that there is no place for Bali: a situation which evokes the state of pralaya in which Nārāyaṇa gathers in himself all creatures and leaves nothing alive outside of himself. It is at once a resorption and a promise of resurrection."

59. In contradistinction, see O'Flaherty, *Hindu Myths* (Hammondsworth, England: Penguin Books, 1975), p. 270: "The heroic measures which the Vedic gods employ came gradually to be superseded by treacherous strategems in the Epic period and finally in the Purāṇas, by outright and elaborate deceptions which had originally been categorized as 'demonic.'"

7

Conclusions

By elucidating the Purāṇic cosmological context and subjecting the avatāra myths to analysis, motific and otherwise, we hope that certain significant elements have been allowed to surface, albeit in a free-form mélange. It behooves us at this point to begin to try to fit these pieces together into a coherent whole.

Through the delineation and application of five motific categories, the "cosmogonic scenario," or in more comprehensive terms, the relationship between the myths and Purāṇic cosmological structures, appeared to be central. This was borne out in several ways, previously discussed; chief among them is the respectively destructive and creative theophanies of Narasiṁha and Vāmana that, true to the nature of theophany, are images of ultimate meaning, of revelation of the avatāras' nature. Such a conclusion concerning the centrality of these associative images to the avatāra's meaning was also reached by Biardeau, but via a different route: "the avatāra must therefore represent symbolically the analog of the pralaya and recreation."[1] Our continued study corroborated her statement that the Viṣṇu-Śiva, brahmin-kṣatriya pairs further characterize the avatāra and are particularized expressions of the basic cosmological urgrund, creation-destruction. The kṣatric-dominant nature of Narasiṁha and brahmin-dominant nature of Vāmana were revealed especially through the absence or presence of a special relationship with Indra (motif No. 1), the brahminic element present but recessant in the sacrificial associations of Narasiṁha with the *skambha* or stake,[2] the kṣatric in Vāmana symbolized by the parasol or umbrella.[3]

Given the centrality of these basic cosmological associations, the avatāras should be studied in their relationships with each of the cosmological structures that build the Purāṇic universe.

As stated in Chapter 1, of all the materials that construct the world in which the avatāra operates, the yuga system and its "glue," dharma, are most obviously linked to Viṣṇu's descents. The *Gītā* makes this plain from the start: "Whenever the dharma withers away and adharma arises, then do I send myself forth. For the protection of good, for the destruction of evil-doers, for the establishment of the dharma, do I come into being age after age [*yuge yuge*]" (*Bhg.G.* 4.7–8). The ten avatāras are traditionally set to appear throughout the course of one Mahāyuga: the fish, tortoise, boar, and man-lion in the Kṛta; dwarf, Paraśurāma, and Rāma Dāśarathi in the Treta; Buddha and Kṛṣṇa in the Dvāpara; and Kalkin, yet to descend, in the Kali. The decline of dharma, that is, its descent or deterioration from perfection, is regulated by the yuga system as well; this is expressed in a favorite Purāṇic metaphor, that of the Bull of Dharma:

> In the Kṛta Yuga, you [the bull] had all four feet—tapas, śaucha, dayā and satya. Three of these have since been destroyed. . . . Now you have only the foot of satya left, on which you somehow manage to support yourself. But Kali, encouraged by falsehood, desires to rob you of even that unsteady support. (*Bhg.P.* I.17.24–25)

Yet the simultaneous presence of the avatāra and dharma structures almost unknowingly presents an incongruence, at least a tension that, until recently, has been either unnoticed, ignored, or glossed over. Huntington brings up the issue from one point of view, but does not resolve it satisfactorily; he notes that the frequency of the appearance of avatāras per yuga is in inverse proportion to the amount of adharma present. In other words, if the purpose of the avatāras is to preserve dharma and destroy adharma, how are we to understand the fact that they get more and more scarce as adharma increases?

> Now this diminishing number of avatāras in the successive yugas is in direct relationship to diminishing lengths of those yugas. It is not that the avatāras appear at regular intervals, but rather that the restoration of dharmic balance is felt to be necessary or desirable by Viṣṇu four times in Kṛta, only once in Kali.[4]

> If the role of the avatāras is concerned with the restoration of dharma, as the Bhagavad Gītā has claimed, it would naturally be expected that those divine incarnations would increase with the decline of dharma in the later yugas.[5]

Huntington resolves the dilemma for himself by pointing to the evolutionary nature (which, to him, is spiritual as well as physical) of the daśāvatāra group; that is, that quality counteracts the lack of quantity: "progressively fuller, or increasingly differentiated revelations of the divine are made available on earth as the regression of dharma occurs in the procession of the four yugas."[6]

Biardeau, in her study on bhakti and avatāra, finally lets the incongruity come into full light. She is troubled by the fact that, for example, when Narasiṁha descends at the end of the Kṛta, the dharma is in a less perfect state at the end of his mission than it purportedly was before he appeared. In this context, the only avatāra whose presence within the yuga structure is meaningful will be Kalkin, who will appear at the end of the Kali to restore a Golden Age, a perfect dharma. She concludes, "It is, therefore, by a kind of artifice that the correspondence is made between the avatāras and the points of passage between the yugas, other than the Kali and the Kṛta. . . . There does not seem to be a rigorous correspondence between the yuga and avatāra."[7] To Biardeau the linear nature of the declining dharma and the cyclical nature of the yugas make an unhappy marriage, and she ultimately rejects the idea of a true correspondence or rapport between the appearance of Viṣṇu as avatāra and the yuga cycle.[8] But, with Kṛṣṇa's words ringing in our ears, we cannot reject the interdependence of yuga, dharma, and avatāra with such self-assuredness as does Biardeau. Nor does the issue seem to us as clear-cut.

An alternative approach lies in an exploration of the ability of the yuga cycle to evoke other temporal structures, notably the kalpa. This concept of the *yugānta* as evocative of the *kalpānta,* that is, the pralaya, has been discussed at several points throughout this study[9] and is certainly one of the few widely corroborated statements to be made about epico-Purāṇic cosmology. The pralayic tendency inherent in the yuga (especially at *yugānta*) is amply illustrated in the language surrounding the epic battles of both the *Mahābhārata* and *Rāmāyaṇa,*[10] as well as in the avatāra myths under discussion. What is often *not* understood is that the kalpic rhythm moving within the yuga structure is not limited only to *yugānta,* or to avatāras such as Narasiṁha, Rāma, and Kṛṣṇa, who appear at the close of the yuga, but that this cosmic rhythm appears at other intervals as well and is evoked by structures other than the *kalpānta-yugānta,* macrocosm-microcosm analogy. With respect to this, a parallel rhythm exists, as has been alluded to previously;[11] the oscillation regulated by the daivāsura struggle, a rhythm of inversion and reversion, of upside-down and rightside-up, which is expressed vividly in all cosmological components (spatial, temporal, and dharmic); a pendulum swing between dharma and adharma, order and chaos; a swing clearly governed by the intervention of the avatāra. Further, this alternation between daivic and asuric, creative and destructive, evoked through the respectively coinciding nature of the avatāra (i.e., Narasiṁha as destructive, Vāmana as creative) is clearly a kalpic kind of structure: the kalpa—creation and preservation of the creation inaugurated by Brahmā (or by Viṣṇu in the form of Brahmā) and preserved by the Viṣṇu—and the night of Brahmā, equal in length to a kalpa—destruction inaugurated by Śiva (or Viṣṇu in the form of Śiva) and absorbed and contained by Nārāyaṇa.[12] Therefore, within the frame of the yuga and its classic inclusion of the deteriorization of dharma, we have two structures that are clearly oscillatory and kalpic. From the classic yugic viewpoint, dharma is deteriorating, gradual; from the viewpoint of the daivāsura conflict, to which it also pertains, dharma appears as neither-nor, there or gone, like the fate of the triple world at the end of the kalpa. Conversely, as previously seen,[13] the kalpa, although a "cosmic" temporal structure, in all other ways pertains to the triple world (i.e., is sociocosmic, even "yugic"); the *kalpānta* brings the destruction of the triple world and the liberation of (some of) its inhabitants; and the pratisarga or re-creation, pertaining again to the trailokya, is dominated by images and symbols relevant mainly to that smaller universe.[14]

How, then, are we to understand the relation between yuga, avatāra, and dharma, given the last's double nature? Does the avatāra contradict the deteriorating quality of dharma and act only within the context of its presence or absence? If so, perhaps Biardeau would be correct.

To answer, several paths can be taken. Biardeau seems to rail against the very nature of dharma itself when she bemoans the fact that the avatāras do not restore a perfect dharma (excepting Kalkin). She recognizes the upside-down—rightside-up quality inherent in the daivāsura struggle and cannot understand the avatāra's relative failure to restore a perfect dharma: "The order of the world is then reversed—without seeming to have stages in this reversal. One doesn't very well understand why the avatāra, following the yuga in which he appears, restores the dharma more or less completely."[15] From an overall, general point of view, her comment seems correct; but by reading each myth, each version, an answer to this complaint begins to appear; and it is subtle, subtle perhaps as the dharma is itself. For in the actions of both the asuric antagonists and the avatāras, we see not really black and white, but varying shades of gray; not really *Adharma* vs. *Dharma,* but a conflict in which the characters are tempered by the times. Why, if there is no degree in the demons' "reversal" of world order, is Bali, in some versions, a perfectly dharmic king? How much "truth" is there in Bāṇa's protests against Vāmana's deceit? In Śukra's premonition of Viṣṇu's trickery and deception? Going beyond Narasiṁha and Vāmana, how can we judge the dharmic nature of Kṛṣṇa's council to the Pāṇḍavas during the *Mahābhārata* battle; does the incredibly "subtle" nature of Kṛṣṇa's rendering of the dharma not signal the advent of the Kali Age itself? Perhaps no one text elucidates the relationship between Dharma-Adharma and dharma as regulated by the yugas better than the *Vāmana Purāṇa,* in which the Kali Yuga complains to Brahmā:[16]

> Finding the world following the path of virtue as in the Satya Age, Kali looked up to Brahmā, following his nature. . . . "O Chief of Gods, my nature has been destroyed by Bali." To him the venerable yogin said, "It is not your nature only, but that of the entire world that has been destroyed by that mighty one." (*Vām.P.* 49.2.4–5)

The temporal structure, complete with deteriorating dharma, is an absolute. For this reason, a Narasiṁha who restores a Kṛta Yuga through his conquest of the Asura is no more mythologically permissible than a Bali who is allowed to turn the Kali Age into a Kṛta: neither can be tolerated. The descent of Viṣṇu speaks to both yuga and dharma: it maintains the partial and dynamic nature of dharma as regulated by the yugas by allowing neither Perfect Dharma (as in Bali's shortlived reign) nor total Adharma (as in the typically asuric demon, true to svadharma) prevail. The movement of dharma between these two extremes, yet tempered by its own deteriorating nature can be visualized as the ever-narrowing swing of a pendulum between two walls of opposites (Dharma and Adharma) that converge at the point of *yugānta.* Little wonder why, in the *Mahābhārata,* with the Kali Age immanent, the dharma is so subtle and so difficult to discern.

We are beginning to see that the unique nature of the avatāra lies in its ability to join cosmological structures, particularly the kalpic and yugic understanding of both pralaya (destruction and recreation) and dharma. But the avatāra does not stop at these already significant unions, it goes on to integrate into this context the central religious structure itself, soteriology. Earlier,[17] in discussing the Purāṇic cosmology, it became clear that all of the spatial and temporal constructs built a world whose own salvation lay in its destruction; that is, that the pralaya, the destruction of the triple world at the end of the kalpa, allowed for a wholesale salvation of beings, that the very reason for the pralaya was soteriological in intent: "In other words, the final perspective and the ultimate reason for the resorption of the worlds seems to be the deliverance of beings."[18] In examining such a structure, we were faced with the enigma of the incredible inaccessibility of such a moment over against the direct access to god and mokṣa offered to man through bhakti, and intimated that the avatāra might play a role in reducing the incongruence in these positions. Now, by comprehending the role of the avatāra as yoking the near and far, specifically the kalpic and yugic, we are faced with the ultimate of these unions; that is, through the evocation of a kalpic structure, especially of the pralaya, within the yuga, the avatāra brings the reality of an easy mokṣa, heretofore inaccessible by virtue of the vastness of the kalpa, into the hands of the inhabitants of the triple world. In parallel fashion, the avatāra brings the transcendent, kalpic nature of Viṣṇu (as Nārāyaṇa) within human reach through the triple-world–oriented character of the avatāra. There is little wonder why a character like Bali or even Hiraṇyakaśipu[19] wins liberation at the avatāra's hands: he brings with him, he incarnates, the total, embracing soteriology of the pralaya.[20]

The Special Case of Narasiṁha and Vāmana

We have spent a great deal of time examining the significance of the Narasiṁha and Vāmana avatāras independently and have seen that each evokes the pralaya and its eschatological and soteriological significance. Although each is able to do so alone, the impact of the Narasiṁha-Vāmana pair far exceeds the "sum total" of the two. Not only does the avatāra pair present us with rich models of the basic cosmological structure, destruction–re-creation, but together they far more dramatically illustrate Biardeau's secondary couples, Śiva-Viṣṇu, kṣatriya-brahmin, than any single avatāra. This is easily seen by recalling the basic traits of both avatāras, discussed in Chapters 5 and 6. First, the temporal setting of the descent of Narasiṁha and Vāmana, the former at the end of the Kṛta Yuga, the latter at the beginning of the Treta Yuga, displays them as a pair framing the interyugal period, the juncture in time that plainly recalls the pralaya.

Second, we have seen that although a "brahminic" element was present in the Narasiṁha myth in the pillar as sacrificial stake, the emphasis was on the avatāra's sanguinary, bellicose, kṣatric nature. Complementarily, with the exception of the royal parasol present among Vāmana's belongings in several versions of the myth, Vāmana's character was unquestionably that of a brahmin; a trait attested to directly by the text as well as through his association or identification with the sacrifice.

Third, the respectively Śivaic or Rudraic and Vaiṣṇavic characters of Narasiṁha and Vāmana hardly need reviewing; recall the terrifying images of Narasiṁha with wild mane, covered with ashes, his associations with the Mātṛkās and the land of the dead, as well as the intermingling confrontations with Śiva himself. Likewise, that the Vāmana myth incorporates a history of Viṣṇu's associations from earliest times is by now obvious; the three steps, the alliance with Indra, the dwarf of the Brāhmaṇas, the identity of Viṣṇu and the sacrifice; the Vāmana myth is almost a natural culmination of the god's growth throughout the text. And finally, we have seen clearly that Narasiṁha's theophany is a destructive one, conjuring up all those images that herald the advent of the pralaya: the winds, the burning suns, the metaphors of flood, the omens in the sky, coupled with the appearance of a wrathful, bloodthirsty avatāra, a Rudraic countenance, come to destroy the Asura at the end of an age. At the dawn of the Treta Yuga, Vāmana's theophany recalls both Nārāyaṇa, encompassing the entire universe within his body, as during the night of Brahmā (interim between pralaya and recreation) as well as the clearly creative act of the three steps, opening up space for the triple world, making it once again habitable for both gods and men.

That Narasiṁha and Vāmana together present us with a full expression of the avatāras' significance seems almost undeniable at this point. There is such a uniqueness in the pair that we must suggest a high degree of "intentionality" inherent in this coupling. We are led to such a hypothesis not only by examining their own mythical presence, but by relating it to the character and figure that seem to foretell a great deal about the mythical nature of the avatāras; that is, Kṛṣṇa in the *Bhagavad Gītā* and *Mahābhārata*.

We have seen that the central image of each avatāra brings us closest to its nature, revealing the avatāra as Viṣṇu, lord of the universe. We have noted that the basic mythological concept of avatāra appears to have its justification or inception in Chapter 4 of the *Gītā*. Further, that there may be parallels in the *Gītā* theophany and that of Narasiṁha was briefly pointed to in Chapter 5.[21] Now, through the work of Alf Hiltebeitel,[22] we can see that within the *Mahābhārata* there are not one but two theophanies of Kṛṣṇa and that they bear a distinct relation to the theophanies of the avatāras under discussion.

Although scholars are universally aware of the *Gītā's* theophany, Hiltebeitel is joined only by R. Otto in recognizing and bringing attention to Kṛṣṇa's other epic theophany, which occurs prior to the *Gītā's*, in the Kuru Court.[23] Through a juxtaposed examination of Kṛṣṇa's two theophanies with those of Narasiṁha and Vāmana, an intrinsic relationship between our two avatāras themselves and each with epic Kṛṣṇa may be brought to light.

Kṛṣṇa	*Vāmana and Narasiṁha*
1. Theophany at Kuru Court:	1. Vāmana's theophany:
Kṛṣṇa goes to the court of the Kurus as an emissary of the Pāṇḍavas to try to avert a battle and make demands on their behalf.	Vāmana goes to the Asuras' dwelling on behalf of the gods to get back what is rightfully theirs "without a battle" (*Br.P.* 73.20).
Duryodhana regards Kṛṣṇa as having come "alone."[24]	Vāmana appears (in most cases) to have come alone and in an unassuming and modest guise.
Kṛṣṇa's theophany is revealed to all present; it is public.	Vāmana's theophany is revealed to all present; it is public.
Kṛṣṇa's theophany is a creative one (e.g., described as "variegated and auspicious or increasing) [*ṛddhimat*]; cf. Hiltebeitel, *RB,* p. 126, "Duryodhana . . . is witness to a sort of creation."	Vāmana's theophany is a creative one (see Chapter 6, pp. 136–137).
Influence of the Puruṣasūkta on Kṛṣṇa's theophany ("although in matters of mode and symbol it seems quite likely that the poets have kept the Puruṣasūkta in the backs of their minds").[25]	Influence of the Puruṣasūkta on Vāmana's theophany (see Chapter 6, p. 136).

Kṛṣṇa urges the Kuru elders to bind Duryodhana as Varuṇa does the Daityas with his nooses (prior to theophany).[26]	Viṣṇu threatens to or actually does bind Bali (cf. *HV* 248–257; *Brm.P.* II.73.75–87; *Bhg.P.* VIII.15–23; *N.P.* I.10–11; *Vām.P.* 49–65; *V.P.* 98.59–88).

"The Vāmana myth thus shows how closely, in the case of Krishna, the theme of binding is linked to the theophany."[27]

Through Hiltebeitel's work[28] it is clear that Viṣṇu's three steps find their epic transposition in scenes leading up to the theophany where Kṛṣṇa's journey to the Kuru court is marked by three refusals to accept favors at three different stages of the journey, as well as Kṛṣṇa's ability to "step over three enclosures" (especially use of words *tisro vyatikramya*).	The Vāmana myth is clearly an epico-Purāṇic, mythic transposition of the ṚgVedic record of Viṣṇu's three steps; in this case, however, the steps follow, not precede, the theophany.
2. Kṛṣṇa's *Gītā* Theophany	2. Narasiṁha's Theophany
Surrounded by the troops on the battlefield, Kṛṣṇa reserves the vision of his theophany for Arjuna alone. "when he is in the midst of many, his revelation is private, reserved for his 'friend and devotee.'"[29]	In *MP* 161–163 and *HV* 228, Narasiṁha appears among all the Asuras, but none recognizes his divinity save Prahlāda.
Arjuna is able to witness the theophany through a "divine eye" (*divyaṁ cakṣuḥ*].	In the preceeding versions Prahlāda sees Narasiṁha through a "divine eye" [*divyeṇa cakṣusā*].
Whereas Kṛṣṇa's public form is beneficent, his *viśvarūpa* is	Whereas Narasiṁha's public form is destructive, evoking

terrifying, and highly evocative of the pralaya.[30]	plainly images of the pralaya, his *viśvarūpa*, as witnessed by Prahlāda, is primarily all-encompassing (but not devouring) and beneficent.
Given the preceding, we could say that whereas Kṛṣṇa's *viśvarūpa* is more Rudraic, in his "public" form he is strongly associated with Nārāyaṇa (cf. *Mbh.* 12:330, 69; *Mbh.* 1:59.1: "Indra then made a covenant with Nārāyaṇa that together with the gods they would descend from heaven to earth with a portion of themselves." And *Mbh.* 1:61.90, "The Sempiternal God of Gods Nārāyaṇa descended with a portion of himself among mankind as the majestic Vāsudeva."[31]	Given the preceding, we could say that whereas Narasiṁha's public form is Rudraic, his *viśvarūpa,* as witnessed by Prahlāda (in *MP, HV* 228, and *P.P.V.* versions) recalls Nārāyaṇa during the night of Brahmā, as the receptacle of the worlds between pralaya and recreation.

Although we would not say blanketly that the epic theophanies prefigure those of the Purāṇic avatāras (as Hiltebeitel points out, the court theophany picks up on themes already associated with Viṣṇu Trivikrama or Vāmana) nor the complete reverse (the case is most likely one of multidirectional interpenetration; also as was evident in Chapters 2 and 3, the Vāmanāvatāra [and court theophany] draws on more ancient—Vedic and even Indo-European—themes[32] and the Narasiṁha is most centrally Purāṇic, as is the *Gītā* theophany) but that the relationship of these two avatāras to the epic theophanies of Kṛṣṇa, as seen through their own theophanies and *viśvarūpas,* places them in a highly significant position, given the primary importance that epic Kṛṣṇa (and the *Mahābhārata* as a whole) plays in the development of the mythological avatāra concept.[33] This relationship, which does not exist between the epic theophanies and any other two avatāras, combined with the complementarity between Narasiṁha and Vāmana through their juxtaposed symbolisms of destruction-creation, Śiva-Viṣṇu, kṣatriya-brahmin, and the temporal frame they create around the interyugal period, all contribute to bring into full light the highly charged significance, and perhaps centrality, they possess for understanding the mythological nature of the avatāra.

Liminality, Mediation, Centrality, and Totality

The character of the avatāra that drew us naively to this study at its inception, through the application of motific checking, has eluded us. Although Viṣṇu seemed very much the trickster, liminal and mediating, especially as Vāmana and Narasiṁha, the myths, reviewed motifically, did not bear witness to this as a central feature. Yet through the revealed importance of the cosmological significance of the avatāra, joined with the complementarity of Narasiṁha and Vāmana as a pair, a new understanding of the avatāra's mediating and liminal functions is possible.

Through F. B. J. Kuiper's excellent article, "The Three Strides of Viṣṇu," early Viṣṇu's ability to represent the unity of opposing forces has been well proven. He has seen Viṣṇu's structural function as that of a connecting link, representing the unity of the upper and nether worlds; "It is accordingly the cosmic center and the nadir with which Viṣṇu is associated."[34] Likewise, his position is central between ofttimes antagonistic cosmic parties; Kuiper comments that "Viṣṇu is the typical *madhyasthaḥ*, the connecting link between the two cosmic moieties,"[35] pointing to the examples of his role in the Indra-Vṛtra fight and Kṛṣṇa's position in the epic battle as proof.

Whereas Viṣṇu's *impartiality* in scenes such as these and the two avatāra myths cloud Kuiper's point, at least for us, he nonetheless inspires us to rethink the concepts of mediation, liminality, centrality, and totality with respect to Narasiṁha and Vāmana. And with the multivalent significance we have found by looking primarily to the cosmology as a context for interpretation, it seems natural at this point to apply the previous concepts in a like manner.[36]

Again, through the pairing of the Narasiṁha and Vāmana avatāras, an expression of cosmological completeness and centrality surfaces. In his pre-avatāra form as Viṣṇu-Nārāyana, in both myths the god is said to reside at the boundaries of the horizontal universe (the northern bank of the Milk Ocean, which according to standard cosmological theory is the next-to-last ringed-ocean, but within the myths themselves is sometimes located beyond the Lokāloka Mountain[37]). Complementarily, in avatāra form, Viṣṇu embraces the zenith and nadir of the vertical universe; as Narasiṁha, as we have seen, he is associated with the underworld and land of the dead [*yamālayaṁ*][38] and, through his strides as Vāmana, associated with the *paramaṁ padaṁ* of the universe, ofttimes he breaks through the top of the Brahmāṇḍa in a display of utter transcendence. While encompassing the universe by framing it in these alternating forms (Nārāyaṇa-Narasiṁha-Nārāyaṇa-Vāmana) the avatāra myths also present us with images of centrality; in the Narasiṁha myth, the pillar cum sacrificial stake [*stambha, skambha*], from which the avatāra issues, strongly recalls a ritualistic *axis mundi:* "Traversing the parts of the universe and linking these, and especially the sun and earth, forming the mystic centre of the cosmos, being the path which leads to the upper regions, the sacrificial stake and the other objects equivalent to, or connect with, it, belong to the god, who pervades the universe."[39]

In like fashion, Vāmana, through his three strides, creates a link between all the tiers of the universe and is often joined to the image of a cosmic pillar through this act, as well as through his identity with the sacrifice: "Just as this pillar connects Heaven and Earth 'like an axle two wheels,' so Viṣṇu is the connecting link, which forms part of both worlds. As the sacrifice strode forth from (or through) the *skambha,* so Viṣṇu as the sacrifice ascends to the sky and transmits the powers of the earth to the heavenly gods."[40] Whereas these images evoke a centrality and totality based primarily on Vedic or sacrificial associations, we have seen their Purāṇic counterparts in the all-inclusive theophanies of each avatāra.

Finally, it must be said that the avatāra's special ability to mediate comes *not* from a neither-nor quality, but from an inclusivity, a nature that partakes of both. That is to say that the avatāra's genius lies in his ability to yoke together all those cosmological structures that create and divide the cosmic and sociocosmic worlds, introducing the distant former into the reach of the latter: spatially, through the joining or encompassing of the vertical and horizontal worlds and the triple world with the higher realms; temporally, through the introduction of the kalpic rhythm into the yugic structure; cosmogonically, by bringing the powers of creation and destruction into the realm of trailokic meaning; religiously, by combining the yogic and sacrificial viewpoints, ethically, by uniting a concern for the dharma with the transcendence of a supreme deity; and soteriologically, by bringing all these cosmic structures into the sociocosmic realm, to deliver the cosmological understanding of the distant and rare opportunity for liberation (i.e., at the pralaya) into the immediate universe of the devotee, through the physical presence of the avatāra. Further, we finally can see that this ability goes beyond the mythical world and sheds light on the role of the avatāra in the development of Hindu religious thought; that is, the avatāra mediates the transition from the Purāṇic understanding of liberation as governed by cosmological law and its eventual "transcendence" by the immanent character of liberation found in full bhakti. Given this, it is no wonder that Narasiṁha's role fades as the myth revolves more and more around the bhakta Prahlāda and that Vāmana's role becomes superfluous when Bali learns and accepts (or rejects and is cursed) the idea of devotion to Viṣṇu, as taught by his grandfather.

In a typically Indian paradox these avatāras, though classically considered partial manifestations (*aṁśāvatāra*) of the deity, present us with the fullest and most richly intricate expression of the totality of Viṣṇu's divinity; how close we are to the blink of the eye of the god that never blinks.

Notes

1. Biardeau, *EMH* 4:182.

2. Cf. Chapter 5, p. 97.

3. Cf. Chapter 6, p. 124.

4. R. M. Huntington, "A Study of Purāṇic Myth from the Viewpoint of Depth Psychology" (dissertation, University of Chicago, 1973). p. 130.

5. Ibid., p. 131.

6. Ibid., p. 136.

7. Biardeau, *EMH* 4:142.

8. Ibid., p. 123.

9. Cf. Chapter 4, pp. 60ff., Jacobi and Biardeau on Yugānta-kalpānta associations.

10. Alf Hiltebeitel, "The Mahābhārata and Hindu Eschatology," *HRJ* 12, no. 2 (1972).

11. Cf. Chapter 6, p. 115.

12. Cf. Chapter 4, Figure 5.

13. Cf. Chapter 4, pp. 58ff.

14. For example, the role of the Yajñavarāha.

15. Biardeau, *EMH* 4:140.

16. We reiterate, see Chapter 6, p. 121.

17. Cf. Chapter 4, p. 65.

18. Biardeau, *EMH* 3:33.

19. Cf. *Vi.P.* I.20; *Bhg.P.* VII.10.

20. It is amazing to me that Biardeau, who emphasizes the soteriological implications of the pralaya, is silent on this facet of the avatāra's relation to the pralaya and points instead to the centrality of the disorder in royal power and generally dharmic concerns as being at the heart of the avatāra.

21. Cf. Chapter 5, p. 87.

22. Hiltebeitel, *The Ritual of Battle* (Ithaca, N.Y.: Cornell University Press, 1976); hereafter *RB*.

23. Rudolph Otto, *The Original Gītā*, trans. J. E. Turner (London: Allen & Unwin, 1939); see *RB*, pp. 120–121.

24. *RB*, p. 126.

25. Ibid., p. 128; for example, the theme of the emergence of beings from the god's body; ibid., n. 34.

26. Ibid., p. 122.

27. Ibid., p. 137.

28. Ibid., pp. 128–140.

29. Ibid., p. 126.

30. Cf. Biardeau, *EMH* 3:53; Hiltebeitel, *RB*, pp. 115–118.

31. Cf. *RB*, pp. 328–329.

32. Ibid., p. 139.

33. Cf. Paul Hacker, "Zür Entwicklung der Avatara-lehre," *Weiner Zeitschrift für die Kunde Sud- und Ostasiens* 4 (1960).

34. Kuiper, "The Three Studies of Viṣṇu," in *Indological Studies in Honor of W. Norman Brown* (New Haven, Conn.: American Oriental Society, 1962), p. 144.

35. Ibid., p. 145.

36. Notably, Kuiper has examined the Vedic-Brāhmaṇic cosmology to help shape his own ideas; i.e., the association of Vedic Viṣṇu with the *dhrūva dik;* cf. ibid., pp. 143–144.

37. Cf. Chapter 4, p. 55–57.

38. Cf. especially the Matṛkā episodes of *K.P.* I.15; *M.P.* 179; and *G.P.* 241; see Chapter 5, p. 85.

39. Gonda, *Aspects of Early Viṣṇuism,* (Delhi: Motilal Banarsidass, 1969), p. 83.

40. Kuiper, "The Three Studies of Viṣṇu," p. 151. Kuiper further notes the existence of a seventh century sculpture at Mamallāpuram portraying Viṣṇu, while taking his strides, as the supporting pillar of the universe, p. 151.

Appendix I: Translations of Narasiṁha Myths

Brahmāṇḍa Purāṇa II.5.3–29

The bard spoke:

Two sons and a beautiful daughter were born to Diti, the two elder children of Kaśyapa considered the firstborn of all. Born on the day of the Soma pressing of the Atirātra part of the Aśvamedha sacrifice of Kaśyapa, one was called Hiraṇyakaśipu because, having issued forth from the womb of Diti, he sat on that [golden] seat.

The ṛṣis spoke:

The birth of the magnanimous one named Hiraṇyakaśipu, and the majesty of that Daitya, tell us that in detail, O Lord.

The bard spoke:

The Aśvamedha of Kaśyapa took place in holy Puṣkara, with ṛṣis and Devatas, and handsome Gandharvas. When all was given according to rule and tales told according to precept, five golden seats were prepared. One seat was made of gold for the Hotṛ; the infant sat there and narrated stories one after another just like the great ṛṣi Kaśyapa. Seeing him, the ṛṣis gave him an auspicious name; because of that, he is known as Hiraṇyakaśipu. His brother was Hiraṇyākṣa, and his sister, Siṁhikā, the wife of Vipracitti and mother of Rāhu.

The Daitya Hiraṇyakaśipu engaged in supreme austerities.

> Fasting head down for a thousand years, the Daitya solicited Brahmā, who was pleased, for a boon. "Immortality and inviolability from all beings. Having conquered the gods with yoga, to become the god of all and make the sovereignty full of strength and vigor. Dānavas and demons, gods together with celestial singers, all these must be my subjects, close at hand, serving me, inviolable by wet or dry, by day or by night." Thus spoken to, Brahmā gave the boon possessing interstices.

Brahmā spoke:

> This boon you have chosen is great, O Son of Diti. Come now, so be it.

And having granted him the wish, he disappeared.

Then, having pervaded the world, everything standing and moving, the Daitya lived in many forms, conquering his enemies with power. He shone in heaven, having become the moon and the sun, and having become Vāyu, he blew on the earth everywhere. He became the herdsman, the shepherd, and the cultivator, he became the knower of all the worlds, giving interpretations of the mantras, he was leader and protector, preserver, giver of sacrifice, and sacrificer. Then all the gods and demons were drinking *his* Soma. Listen further! The Daitya was of such might, all made obeisance to him, the only one worthy of worship. Praise was sung here in ancient times by the Daityas. In whatever direction king Hiraṇyakaśipu gazed, the gods together with the maharṣis made obeisance in that direction.

Indeed, formerly, Viṣṇu as the man-lion was his death. Because his birth was for humankind and because the Lord assumed the form of a human, the man-lion is praised by wise men. The body of that god, exalted with tapas on the bank of the ocean, was full of gods and was named Sudarśana, famous and mighty. Then he who was very strong, battling with his arms, tore apart the demon with his claws, because they are neither wet nor dry.

Brahmā Purāṇa 213.44–79

Long ago in the Kṛtayuga, there was an enemy of the gods made proud by his strength. The chief of Asuras performed great austerities: he sat, engaged in incantations and fasting, keeping a vow of silence for 11,500 years. Because of his tranquility, his self-restraint, and his chastity, Brahmā was pleased. Indeed, the Self-born Lord, having approached him in an aerial car the color of fire and yoked to a swan, shining brightly said, "Greetings brahmin," together with the Ādityas, Vasus, Maruts, Kiṁnaras, the directions and regions, rivers and oceans, stars, divisions of time, birds, and great planets, the ṛṣis of the gods, holy men, Gandharvas, and the host of Apsarases. Master of everything moving and unmoving, surrounded by prosperity and all the other gods, Brahmā, eminent among the knowers of Brahman, spoke these words to the Daitya: "I am pleased with your austerities, O Virtuous Devotee. Choose a boon, God bless you. You will obtain whatever you desire."

Hiraṇyakaśipu spoke:

> O Grandfather of the World, neither gods nor demons nor Gandharvas or Yakṣas, Nāgas, or Rakṣasas, nor angry ṛṣis skilled in austerities should curse me with curses. This boon is chosen by me. Not by weapons nor swords nor rocks nor trees, not by dry nor by wet, nor high or low, but with one stroke of his hand will he who is able to kill me, together with my chariots, armies, and servants, become my death. I will become the sun, the moon, the wind, the fire, water, atmosphere, ether, and the universe. I am fury, Kāma, Varuṇa, Indra, and Yama, Kubera, the overseer of the treasure, a Yakṣa, and the leader of the Kiṁpuruṣas.

Brahmā spoke:

> Child, I give you these heavenly and marvelous boons. You will obtain all your desires, no doubt!

Vyāsa spoke:

> Having thus spoken, the Blessed One, the Grandfather, went quickly to Vairāja, dwelling place of Brahmā, which is frequented by the host of Brahmarṣis.

Then the gods, Nāgas, Gandharvas, and munis, having heard about the granting of the boon, approached the Grandfather. The gods spoke:

> O Lord, the demon will oppress us with that boon! Quickly, think of his death, O Blessed One, Primal Creator of all

beings, Self-born Lord, Creator of oblations to gods and ancestors, indeed the unevolved Prakṛti.

Vyāsa spoke:

Then, having heard the speech about the welfare of the world, the god Prajāpati, the Blessed One, spoke these words to the hosts of all the gods. Brahmā spoke: "By all means, O Gods, is the fruit of tapas to be attained by him but, at the end of his tapas, Viṣṇu, the Blessed One, will become his conqueror."

Vyāsa spoke:

Having heard these words of the Lotus-born One, all the gods went to their own celestial dwellings, filled with delight.

The Daitya Hiraṇyakaśipu, arrogant from the granting of the boon, oppressed all the people as soon as the boon was obtained. He overpowered illustrious munis in hermitages, whose vows were rigid and who were attached to truth and dharma. That mighty demon, having conquered the gods dwelling in heaven, dwelt in heaven, ruling the triple world. When the Dānava, drunk with arrogance from the boon, roamed the earth, he made the Daityas worthy of the sacrifice and the gods unworthy of the sacrifice.

Vāsava, the Ādityas, Sādhyas, Viśvadevas, and Maruts, seeking refuge, approached the mighty Viṣṇu, who gives refuge. They sought refuge in him, this Brahmā among gods, the sacrifice, Brahmādeva, the eternal one, past, present, and future lord, honored by the world, Nārāyaṇa, the all-pervading god, affording shelter.

The gods spoke:

Rescue us now from the peril of Hiraṇyakaśipu, O Lord of Gods; you are our highest god, our supreme guru. You are the supreme support of Brahmā and the others, Best of Gods, whose eyes are like petals, wide open and shining; O Causer of the destruction of enemies, for the sake of the destruction of the family of Diti, be our refuge.

Vasudeva spoke:

Immortals, abandon your fear; I will give you security, and you will recover heaven soon. I will kill the Daitya, arrogant from the granting of the boon, the chief of Dānavas, who is not to be killed by those who are supreme among the gods.

Vyāsa spoke:

Thus, the Blessed One, having spoken and having dismissed the lords of the gods, went to the abode of Hiraṇyakaśipu. The Lord, having made half his body of a man and half of a lion, with the form of a man-lion, having touched hand with hand, looking like a dark cloud, glowing with the energy of a dark cloud, and swift like a dark cloud, he, whose gait was proud like a lion's, having seen the mighty Daitya who was guarded by the arrogant troops of Daityas, he killed him with one hand.

Viṣṇudharmottara Purāṇa I.54

Śaṅkara spoke:

When the Daitya Hiraṇyākṣa was slain, his brother, Hiraṇyakaśipu, performed terrible austerities. For ten thousand and ten hundred years, bent on fasting, practicing a vow of bathing and silence and muttering prayers, through quietude, self-restraint, and the vow of chastity, Sinless One, Brahmā, pleased with him, arrived in a blazing chariot the color of the sun, yoked to a swan, and joined by the Ādityas, Sādhyas, Maruts, and Aśvins, along with the Rudras and Viśvas, the Yakṣas, Rakṣases, and snakes, the regions and cardinal points, aerial beings, and constellations, along with the streams and oceans, the months, seasons, half-years, and twilights, the stars, measurements and parts of time, along with the holy ṛṣis of the gods, the siddhas, the seven ṛṣis, the holy ṛṣis of the king, the Gandharvas and hosts of Apsarases. The venerable guru of the moving and still, Brahmā, best of Brahmāknowers, surrounded by all the celestials, spoke to the Daitya.

Brahmā spoke:

I am pleased with your devoted austerities; your vow is good. Choose a boon, bless you. Whatever is desired, you shall obtain that wish.

Hiraṇyakaśipu spoke:

> Neither gods, demons, nor Gandharvas, nor Yakṣas, snakes, or Rakṣases, neither men nor Piśācas shall kill me, O Excellent God. Nor may angry ṛṣis, endowed with tapas, curse me. Grandfather of the World, that is the boon I choose. Not by weapons nor by missiles, nor by stones or trees, neither by wet nor by dry; in no way at all may death be mine. I am the sun, the moon, the wind, the fire, the air, the stars, and the ten regions. I am wrath and passion, Varuṇa, Indra, Yama, Kubera, the supervisor, a Yakṣa, and the chief Kiṁpuruṣa.

Brahmā spoke:

> Son, I grant you these heavenly boons. Therefore, you shall obtain all these desires, not doubt.

Śaṅkara spoke:

> Having said that, the Blessed One went to the ethereal Vairāja, dwelling of the god, accompanied by the host of maharṣis. Then the gods, Nāgas, Gandharvas, and munis, having heard about the granting of the boon, met with the Grandfather.

The gods spoke:

> Because of that boon, the blessed Asura will conquer us. Be kind to us, Blessed One, and think about his death. You are the Blessed One, the Lord, the Self-Born One, the Creator of all beings, Creator of oblations to gods and ancestors, the Unmanifest, the Material Nature, the Unchangeable.

Śaṅkara spoke:

> Then the god Prajāpati, having heard that speech about the welfare of all the world, the boon giver spoke to all the godly hosts. "Inevitably, he will obtain the fruit of his tapas. At the end of his tapas, Viṣṇu will kill him."
>
> Having heard the words of the Lotus-Born One, all the gods went to their own heavenly residences, filled with joy.
>
> As soon as he received the boon, the Daitya Hiraṇyakaśipu, arrogant from the granting of the boon, being invincible himself, harassed all the people and the magnanimous sages

in hermitages, whose vows were rigid, and who were intent on truth and dharma, and restrained. Having conquered the gods and the inhabitants of the three worlds, the great Asura subjugated the triple world and dwelt in heaven. When he who was drunk from the bestowal of the boon made his dwelling in heaven, he made the Daityas deserving of the sacrificial shares and the gods undeserving of them.

The Ādityas, Vasus, Rudras, Viśvedevas, and Aśvins, the Bhṛgus and Aṅgirases, the Sādhyas, and Maruts, together with Indra sought refuge in mighty Viṣṇu, giver of refuge, the god consisting of Brahman, Viṣṇu, the eternal one, absorbed in Brahman, the lord of past, present, and future, the last resort of the world; the gods sought refuge in mighty Nārāyaṇa, who gives shelter.

The gods spoke:

O Lord of Gods, save us now, from the slaughter of Hiraṇyakaśipu. You are our supreme god among Brahmā and the others, O Best of Gods. O You, whose eyes are like full-blown, lucid flower petals, O Destroyer of the enemy, be our refuge for the destruction of the family of Diti.

The Blessed One spoke:

Abandon your fear, Immortals; I give you safety. Now, O Gods, go back to heaven quickly. That mighty Daitya, arrogant from the granting of the boon, inviolable to the chiefs of immortals, I shall slay that Dānava chief!

Śaṅkara spoke:

Having thus spoken, the Blessed One dismissed the lords of heaven and created a man-lion form, having the splendour of a thousand sunbeams; high, like a golden mountain, adorned by a mass of flames, having the luster of the submarine fire to consume the great ocean of Daitya troops, resembling a cloud that is red like the twilight, dressed in dark clothes like Acyuta, covered with a forest of devadāru trees like mighty Mt. Meru; filled with crooked teeth like the parts of the moon, appearing like a golden ocean filled with white pearls, with claws looking like coral, and having two hands that were shining and that would cause the destruction of the Daitya lord as if with the blades of anger; having a mane of curled and matted hair, golden as the flaming fire, the Soul of the Universe shone like a mountain bearing a forest fire. His tongue was moving up and down, to and fro, visible and invisible, and it quivered like the lightning of the cloud at the end of the pralaya. Having a powerful body covered with thick curly hair, with hips and shoulders looking like burning coal, having flaming breath that, going in and out, sounded like the cloud at the end of a kalpa, he was difficult to look at, invincible and terrifying like the center of the thunderbolt.

Having created the form of a man-lion, he went to the assembly hall of the Dānava chief and shattered it quickly, causing the Daityas' fear to increase. Having seen the assembly hall being shattered by the great man-lion, King Hiraṇyakaśipu summoned the Dānavas. "This terrible creature who is unparalleled has come back again. Kill that invincible one, by whom my assembly hall has been destroyed."

Having heard his speech, one hundred thousand Daityas attacked Janārdana, god of gods, with various weapons. Thousands of different weapons, O Bhargava, were seen on his body, scattered like clods of earth on a mountain. Having rendered the Daityas' weapons useless, and having slain the Dānavas, fighting with one hundred and one thousand hands and feet, he quickly seized the Daitya Hiraṇyakaśipu, who was like a big cloud pouring missiles and assaulting the man-lion. And having placed him swiftly on his lap as if he were a plantain leaf, he tore open the chest of the Daitya lord, which was like a great mountain. Having caused the Daitya chief to be abandoned by his life breaths, Keśava himself, angry man-lion, killed the Daityas, having slain the Asura, who was splattered with drops of blood.

Having worshiped Narasiṁha, the gods together with Vāsava went to their own abodes, filled with joy, and that form of the god vanished.

Matsya Purāṇa Chapters 161–163

Chapter 161

The ṛṣis spoke:

We wish to hear of the destroyer of Hiraṇyakaśipu, of the man-lion, the magnanimous one who destroys evil.

Brahmins, long ago in the Kṛta Yuga, wise king Hiraṇyakaśipu, first among Daityas, practiced severe austerities. Ten thousand years and ten hundred years, living on water, he bathed in the sacred waters, observing silence according to the vow. Then, by his quiet tapas and self-restraint, and by means of chastity, Brahmā was pleased. The Self-born Lord, approaching by a resplendent aerial car the color of the sun and yoked to a swan, with the Ādityas, Vasus, Sādhyas, Maruts, Devas, Rudras accompanied by the Viśvedevas, Yakṣas, Rakṣases, and serpent demons, the cardinal points and the intermediate regions, the rivers and oceans, and stars and the periods of the day and birds and great planets, along with gods, brahmarṣis, siddhas, the seven ṛṣis, the royal ṛṣis, holy men, Gandharvas, and Apsarases, and Gaṇas, the guru of created things, the venerable one, together with all the celestials, most excellent Brahmā, best of the knowers of Brahman, spoke these words to the Daitya: "I am satisfied by your devoted tapas, Religious One. Obtain your desire, a gracious boon."

Hiraṇyakaśipu spoke:

Not Devas, Asuras, or Gandharvas, nor Yakṣas, snakes, or Rakṣases, not men or Piśācas may kill me, Best of Gods, nor may ṛṣis curse me. This boon is chosen by me, O Grandfather if you, pleased by me, grant this. Not by arrow, nor by sword, mountain, or tree, not by dry things nor wet, not by day or by night may I be killed. May I alone be sun, Soma, wind, the Oblation eater, water and air, the stars, the ten regions. And may I be anger and lust and Varuṇa and the Vasus, Yama, and Kubera, the overseer of treasure, a Yakṣa, the ruler of the attendants of Kubera.

Brahmā spoke:

Your heavenly wishes are granted by me, my son. You will attain all your desires, no doubt.

Thus speaking, the Blessed One went skyward to Vairāja, the abode of Brahmā, dwelt in by a group of Brahmārṣis. And the gods and Nāgas and Gandharvas, together with the ṛṣis, upon hearing of the bestowal of the boon, immediately approached the Grandfather. The gods spoke:

> From the bestowal of the boon, Blessed One, the Asura will vanquish us. Be gracious quickly; think about his death, too. You yourself are king of all beings, the Creator of oblations to the gods and deceased ancestors, the unmanifest prakṛti, the wise one.

The god Prajāpati, upon hearing the speech destined for all the worlds, reassured the gods with the cool water of his words:

> O Thirty gods, certainly the fruit of tapas is to be obtained. At the end of his tapas, Viṣṇu, the Blessed One, will be his vanquisher.

Hearing the words of the Lotus-born One, all the wise men, the celestials themselves, dispersed, pleased.

Having obtained the wish, no sooner was this done than he oppressed all creatures. The Daitya Hiraṇyakaśipu was made proud by the granting of the boon. The Daitya threatened sages in hermitages, whose vows were praiseworthy, fortunate ones bent upon their devotion to truth and dharma. Upon vanquishing the gods and those in the three worlds, the Dānava dwelt in heaven after leading the three worlds into his power. When he, overflowing with the intoxication of the boon and impelled by the law of time, made the gods unworthy of worship and the Daityas fit for sacrifice, then the Ādityas and Sādhyas and Viśvedevas and Vasus together with Indra, the host of gods, Yakṣas, siddhas, twice borns and ṛṣis, they went to the shelter of mighty Viṣṇu, god of gods, who contains the sacrifice, the eternal Vasudeva. The gods spoke:

> O Nārāyaṇa, great fortunate one, the gods have come to your abode. Protect us! Kill the chief of Daityas, Hiraṇyakaśipu, O King. Indeed, you are our supreme supporter. Indeed, you are our supreme teacher. Indeed, you are our supreme god, the best of gods beginning with Brahmā.

Viṣṇu spoke:

> O Immortals, abandon your fear! I give you fearlessness. Thus, go to heaven without delay. This Daitya made arrogant by the granting of a boon, I will kill this chief of Daityas, with his companions, the lords of immortality.

Upon speaking, the Blessed One, sending away the thirty lords, resolved to become the vanquisher of Hiraṇyakaśipu. Quickly the mighty armed one, with *oṁ* as companion, the imperishable Blessed Viṣṇu, Lord Hari, went to the abode of Hiraṇyakaśipu, made bright by his tejas, like another moon in its radiance, having no superior.

Thus, having made half his body man, half his body lion, by means of the man-lion form, having touched his hand with a hand, he then saw the assembly hall of Hiraṇyakaśipu, expansive, heavenly, beautiful, gratifying the mind, possessed of all objects of desire, radiant. It was huge, extending one and one half hundreds yojanas long, five yojanas wide, with special airborne deities. It was free from fatigue, sorrow, and old age, immovable, auspicious, virtuous, having chambers and terraces, beautiful like a flame with its tejas. It was furnished with interior waters by Viśvakarman, with trees made of celestial jewels, filled with fruits and flowers, with blue, yellow, black, and white, with black and red also, with canopies, with shrubs carrying hundreds of blossoms. Having the appearance of a thick white cloud, it appeared as if floating, radiant and resplendent, having a heavenly fragrance, pleasing to the mind. Very pleasant and not unpleasant, not cold and not hot; arriving there one finds neither hunger or thirst or fatigue. Adorned by various forms, shining with many colors, not supported by columns, having eternal daylight, the moon and sun and a fire beyond that, resting on the vault of heaven, blazing and shining like the sun, containing all desires heavenly and human, and abounding in foods tasty and abundant without end. And here sweet-smelling garlands, eternal flowers, fruits, and trees; in the hot season there are cold waters, and in the cold season, hot waters. Having great branches covered with blossoms, bearing young sprouts and shoots, entirely covered by a canopy of creepers, by rivers and by waterfalls, there the king of beasts saw many sorts of trees and redolent flowers and tasty fruits, and ponds that are not too cold nor hot. The king saw all the tīrthas in his assembly hall, nalinas and sweet-smelling blue lotuses, and hundred-leaf flowers, surrounded by blue and white water lilies.

He saw handsome royal swans and pleasant Dhṛtarāṣṭra geese, Kāranda ducks, Cakra birds, cranes and also ospreys. White, transparent, and pale birds, and many swans sang too, and it was noisy with cranes. Fragrant and beautiful, having abundant clusters of flowers, he saw creepers on mountain tops bearing various lotuses. Ketaki, aśoka, and sarala trees, puṁnāga and white tilaka plants, mangoes, nīpas, basil plants, kadambas, bakulas and dhavas, priyañgu and pāṭala trees, silk-cotton trees, sāla trees, palmyra trees and tamāla trees, and beautiful campakas. And even other trees in bloom glittered in the assembly hall; coral trees and even trees having splendor equal to a blazing fire. He saw many palmyra trees rising up, having many stems and good branches, species of añjana and aśoka, and many śritraka trees, varuṇa and vatsanābha trees, breadfruit trees together with candanas, nīpas, and even a sumanas, nimba trees, holy fig trees and tindukas. Also coral trees and lodhras, mallika geese and bhadradāru trees, even āmaliki plants, rose apple and breadfruit trees, śailavālukas, wild dates and coconut trees, harītaka and vibhitaka trees, turmeric trees, hingu trees, and those of the Western Vindhya range were there. Coral trees and red jasmine, insects and kutaja, and also yellow colored amaranth, together with blue agaru, kadamba flowers and beautiful pomegranate trees, filled with seeds, seven-edged leaves and wood-apple trees covered with bees, aśoka trees and tamāla trees, various shrubs of turning creepers, bees' trees and seven-edged leaves, and many kṣiraka trees, and creepers of various forms, having leaves, flowers, and fruits were there, too. These and others, and many forest trees were seen by the man-lion.

The assembly hall was endowed with various flowers and fruits, which shone forth on all sides; cakora birds and hundred-feather birds, matta birds, black cuckoos and sārika birds, mountain flowers in bloom alight on great trees. There were red and yellow and pinkish trees from the mountains, and birds. Pheasants beheld each other, thrilled with delight. In his assembly hall, the king of Daityas, Hiraṇyakaśipu, surrounded by a thousand women, covered with clothing of many-colored ornamentation, whose ring is of priceless gems, whose diamonds are lustrous, and whose crest is shining, was seated on colored cushions measuring ten furlongs long, sitting on a heavenly carpet, resembling the sun. There the wind diffused a pleasant divine fragrance, there the Daitya Hiraṇyakaśipu, his earring blazing, abides. Gandharvas served the great Daitya Hiraṇyakaśipu, and with celestial tone they sang songs. Viśvācī and Sahajañyā, and the widely celebrated Praṁlocā, the celestials Saurabeyī and Samīcī, and Puñjikasthali, Miśrakecī, and Rambhā, and Citralesvā, Śucismitā, Cārukecī, and Ghṛtacī, Menakā, and Corvacī, those and a thousand others, skilled in dance and song, served the lord, the kind Hiraṇyakaśipu. All the sons of Diti, receivers of boons, served the mighty armed king seated there, Hiraṇyakaśipu. He of the unequalled deeds was waited on by hundreds and thousands: there were Bali, Virocana, Naraka, the son of Pṛthivī, Prahlāda, and Vipracitti and the great Asura Gaviṣṭa, and the killer of gods, Sunāmā, Pramati and Sumatirvara, Ghaṭodara, Mahāparśva, Krathana, and the Pitṛs; Viśvarūpa and Surūpa and Svabala and Mahābala, and Daśagrīva and Vālī, and Meghavāsā, the great Asura, and even Kampana and the creator Indratāpana. All the Daitya Dānavas were assembled, all those who have observed a vow, having eloquent speech, wearing a garland, all those heroes who obtained a boon, all those free from death, those and many others, and the king Hiraṇyakaśipu. All those in celestial dress waited on the magnanimous one with celestial cars of various shapes, glittering like fire. Having many variegated bracelets, having the form of the great chiefs, all the sons of Diti, having decorated limbs, served him. In his celestial assembly hall were the Asuras, all of the appearance of gold, having splendor equal to the sun, having the appearance of mountains.

In the assembly hall, the king of animals saw a balcony of bright gold and silver, a terrace bearing variegated jewels, a round window adorned with heaps of godly jewels. The king of beasts saw the Daitya whose limbs were decorated with gold and white, shining brightly like the sun, to be enjoyed by one hundred thousand Daityas.

Chapter 162

The bard spoke:

> Then, as the magnanimous one arrived like the wheel of time in the form of a man-lion, like the god of fire who is covered with ashes, the mighty son of Hiraṇyakaśipu, named Prahlāda, saw the lion god through his divine eye. Seeing him resembling a mountain of gold, having no equal, having resorted to an unprecendented body, all the Dānavas and Hiraṇyakaśipu were astonished.

Prahlāda spoke:

> O Mighty-armed One, First-born, the king of Daityas has neither seen nor heard of this man-lion form. From what divine unmanifest birthplace has this form come? My mind predicts the terrible end of the Daityas. In whose body are there gods, oceans, and rivers existing, the Himalāya, the Western Vindhya range, and other chief mountain ranges, and the moon together with the stars, Ādityas, Vasus, Kubera, and even Varuṇa, Yama, Śakra, the lord of Śacī, the winds, gods, Gandharvas and ṛṣis, and great ascetics, Nāgas, Yakṣas, Piśācas, and Rakṣases of terrific prowess? The god Brahmā, Paśupati, the immovables and all moving things also roam about while remaining in his forehead. And you, accompanied by us, surrounded by all the hosts

of Daityas, and even your honor's assembly hall, covered by one hundred aerial cars are contained in his body. All the three worlds and all the laws of the world, O King, these are seen in Narasiṁha and so is this entire world, as well as Prajāpati and the magnanimous Manu, planets and constellations, the time of upheavals and persistance and wisdom and passion, truth, tapas, and self-restraint, and Sanatkumāra and the high-minded one and all the gods and ṛṣis, anger and lust and even rapture, law and delusion and all the Pitṛs."

Hearing that speech, the king Hiraṇyakaśipu, lord of hosts, spoke to all the Dānavas. "The unparalleled king of beasts, whose body is unprecedented, must be seized; even if there is any risk, this forest roamer must be killed." All the hosts of Dānavas surrounded the king of beasts, whose prowess was terrific, and rejoicing, caused him to tremble. Then the mighty Narasiṁha, letting go the roar of a lion, shattered the celestial assembly hall, open mouthed, like time itself. When the assembly hall was broken, Hiraṇyakaśipu himself took the weapons of the lion, with an eye of fury and bewilderment. He seized the best of all weapons, the stick mantra Sudāruṇa, the terrific wheel of time, the supreme discus of Viṣṇu, and the terrible great fire that consumes the three worlds, the weapon of the Grandfather, and even the many colored thunderbolt, the thunderbolt of a twofold nature, both wet and dry. Also the terrible iron spike of Rudra, a skeleton and a club, and even the bewildering arrow of Kāma Śoṣana, Saṁtāpana, and the dissolving weapon were seized, as well as the destroyer of Rudra and even that of the cranium and of the slave, the irresistible spear and the weapon of a curlew, and even the Brahmāśiras weapon and Soma's weapon and the Śiśira, the Kampana weapon and that of Tvaṣṭṛ, which is very fearful. The mighty burning, immovable, vomiting of time, the bewildering Saṁvartana weapon and the supreme weapon of māyā, the weapon of Gandharvas and the beloved sword of jewels, Nandaka, that one which causes sleep, the churning up weapon, that of Varuṇa, and the best of weapons, the Pāśupata weapon of which the flight is unimpaired, also the Hayaśiras weapon and that of Brahmā, the weapon of Nārāyaṇa and of Indra, and the supernatural weapon of snakes, the unsurpassed weapon of the Piśācas, the drying up weapon and the extinguishing one, the mighty imagination and that which is the sending off weapon and the shaking up one, all these were seized by the Daitya.

Then Hiraṇyakaśipu hurled those divine weapons at Narasiṁha, like the sacrifice of blazing fire. The best of Daityas covered the lion with flaming weapons, as the sun at the end of the hot season covers the Himālaya with its sunbeams. The ocean of Daitya troops, stirred up by the gale of anger, washed over the man-lion in an instant, like the ocean washes over Mt. Mandara, with barbed missiles and chains and scimitars, maces and clubs, even thunderbolts and lightning, and great trees on fire, as well as mallets and javelins, mountains of stone and wooden mortar, deadly missiles, and terrible blazing sticks. The Dānavas, whose hands had been seized by the noose, their great chief like a thunderbolt, having the swiftness of lightning, whose arms and bodies were upraised, they stood there like the three-headed snake noose. Limbs adorned with a number of brightly colored garlands and the flowing of yellow cloth, girth protected by a pearl row of strings, feathers broad like the wings of geese, heads strong like Vāyu's, the Daityas wore an abundance of rings and diadems, their heads shining on all sides, in splendor equal to the rays of Sūrya in the morning. Narasiṁha appeared, covered with a mass of great burning weapons, with powerful blazes, like a mountain covered with clouds which rain incessantly. Being struck by those mighty hosts of Daityas who possessed a mass of mighty weapons, the Blessed One, standing in his glory, immovable like Himālaya, by nature did not tremble in battle.

The sons of Diti were made to tremble by him who had the form of the man-lion, whose tejas was like fire. When waves were produced from the waters of the ocean, the bodies which were tossed about by the wind shook from fear.

The bard spoke:

> Donkeys and donkey heads, sea monsters and venomous snakes, those with beast heads and others, those with heads resembling boar heads, those with the face of lapis lazuli and others, and those whose countenance had smoke as a sign, those whose heads were half half-moon faces, and those whose countenance was of shining fire; those with faces like swans and cocks, open mouthed and formidable, those frequently darting out the tongue and lion-faced ones, and those with the mouths of crows and vultures; those with two tongues, those with crooked heads and those resembling fire-mouthed demons, those with the countenance of a great shark, and other Dānavas made proud by their strength, and those of the size of a mountain did not alarm the inviolable King of Beasts. The lord of Dānavas, discharging even more abundant terrible weapons, let them loose on the King of Beasts, hissing like snakes. The terrible Dānava's arrows, shot by the chief of Dānavas, were destroyed in mid-air, like flying insects to mountains. Then the

Daityas let loose divine discuses full of fury, flaming everywhere, toward the King of Beasts. With discuses flying here and there, the sky was like Rāhu, Candra, and Āditya, with their bright appearance at the end of the yuga. Then all the discuses that were thrown like flashes of fire were swallowed by the magnanimous King of Beasts. All the discuses entering his mouth indeed shone like Candra, Sūrya, and Rāhu in the opening of the belly of a cloud. Moreover, the Daitya Hiraṇyakaśipu let loose the powerful, terrible burning spear, shining like lightning, which is a white missile. Seeing the luminous spear flying toward him, the King of Beasts, the Blessed One, shattered it with the violent sound of *hum*. The spear appeared like a great meteor, shattered on the ground by the King of Beasts, burning with a spark of fire. A group of five arrows quivered, having reached the vicinity of the lion, a beautiful sight with a garland of blue lotus blossoms. Bellowing according to nature and striding according to pleasure, he drove away that army like the winds do the top of the grass. Flying, the Daitya chiefs hurled a shower of stones as big as mountains, with exceedingly brilliant peaks and broken rocks. That shower of stones fell on the powerful head of the lion. The ten regions scattered like species of flying insects. Then, the host of Daityas covered the enemy-taming lion with a flood of stones, like clouds do the mountain with showers. But this flood of the Daityas did not cause the best of the gods to tremble, like the ocean of fearful speed did Mandara, the chief of mountains. Then, while being struck by the shower of stones, a continuous shower of water with jets the size of axles became visible. Violent floods of rain streamed forth everywhere, covering the sky, the regions, and even the intermediary regions. The rains were everywhere in the sky and over the entire earth, but they did not touch the god, continually descending to the earth. It did not pour down showers on the outside of nor did it rain down from above on the hero abiding in the form of the King of Beasts by means of *māyā*.

While being struck by tumultuous stone showers and by dessicating water showers, the Dānava hurled illusion at him, carried by fire and wind. The great chief, glorious with a thousand eyes, together with great rain clouds and showers, put an end to the fire by a great rain of water. The Dānava emitted a horrible gloom on all sides that had a hideous appearance when that *māyā* had been countered in battle, and while the Daityas and their weapons were seized by the darkness that enveloped the world, filled with his own tejas he shone like the sun. The

Dānavas saw his three-pointed frown in battle, the trident mark situated on his brow, like the Ganges flowing through heaven, earth, and the lower regions. When all illusions had been countered, the pale sons of Diti sought refuge in the Daitya Hiraṇyakaśipu. Then, flaming from anger as it were, burning with his tejas, when the Daitya chief was angered, the world was covered with darkness. Āvaha and pravaha, vivaha and hyudāvaha, parāvaha and saṁvaha, strong and mighty, and venerable parivaha, all announcing a catastrophe, these seven winds blowing in the sky were shaken. The world and planets that become visible at the destruction of the universe, indeed all were seen in the sky as they roamed about at will. The moon traveled on its course without the regular conjunction of planets, with the planets, constellations, and the full moon. The Blessed Sun became pale in the sky and then vast twilight clouds appeared. The sun let loose a mouth of flames and the Blessed One was seen abiding in the sky. Seven horrible dim suns appeared in the sky and planets remained at the horns of the moon and the sky. Śukra and Bṛhaspati, situated on the left and the right, Mars and Saturn, equal in radiance to a flaming body, all the planets, rising up together to the peaks, turning by degrees slowly, the planets that come at the end of the yuga appeared. And the moon, together with stars and planets, dispersing darkness, did not greet Rohinī for the destruction of movable and immovable objects. Candra, seized by Rāhu, was beaten by meteors; burning meteors strode upon the moon as they pleased. The god of gods sent down blood; glittering meteors fell from the sky, making a loud sound. And at an unseasonable time all the trees flowered and bore fruit, and creepers bore fruit, all of which betokened the destruction of the Daityas. Fruits bore fruits; and even flowers, flowers. They opened, closed, laughed, and wept; lotuses cried out and were caused to smoke; images of all the gods conveyed great danger. Tame beasts and birds together with wild ones predicted terrible fear there as the great battle grew near. Rivers with muddy waters ran contrary to their course, and the regions, filled with red dust, were not visible. Those trees worthy of respect were not even worshiped; broken and struck by a gust of wind, they bowed down. Whenever the shadow of all beings does not turn, the afternoon sun signals the destruction of the yuga of the worlds. Then the moon settled on top of the abode of the Daitya Hiraṇyakaśipu, at the treasury and arsenal. For the annihilation of the Asuras and the victory of the gods many terrible calamities, exemplifying horrible sights were seen. These and many other terrible calamities appeared, made by time from the annihilation of the King of Daityas.

While the earth shook from the magnanimous lord of Daityas, hosts of Nāgas, supporting the earth, of unbounded energy, fell down. Serpents with four heads, five heads, and seven heads, with mouths filled with burning venom, emitting fire, Vāsuki and Takṣaka, Karkoṭaka and Dhanaṁjaya, he whose face is of cardamon and Kalīya and the highly Mahāpadma, indeed the thousand-headed snake whose mark is the gold fan, the king, the fortunate one Śeṣa, Ananta, immovable, shaking, those shining in the water and those supporting the earth, all were shaken on all sides from the great fury. Even snakes possessing tejas and also those living at the bottom of Pātāla were shaken. Then the Daitya Hiraṇyakaśipu touched the earth, having bitten his lower lip in anger, like an ancient boar. The river Gaṅges, and even the Sarayu and Karuśikī, the Yamunā, the Kāverī and the Kṛṣṇavenā, a mountain stream and the Suvenā, the illustrious river Godāvarī, the Carmaṇvatī and the Sindhu, lord of the female and male rivers and the birthplace of crimson lotuses, whose water is like jewels, the Narmadā, with splendid water, and the river Vitravatī, the Gomatī, surrounding Gokula, and the ancient Sarasvatī, the muddy Kālamahī and the dark Puṣpavāhinī, Jambudvīpa, covered with jewels, having a beautiful appearance, the Suvarṇaprakaṭa, adorned by mountains and groves, all these were shaken. People of Pattana, a mine of people, ṛṣis and heroes, the people of Magadha and those of great villages, Mundas and even the descendants of Śuṇga, those of Suhma, Malla and Videha, those of Māla, of Kāśi and Kośala, the dwelling of Vainateya, those were shaken by the Daitya chief. Having the appearance of the peak of Kailāsa, made by Viśvakarman, the ocean named Lauhitya, terrible with crimson waters, and the great mountain, rising up one hundred yojanas tall, whose altar is of gold, the venerable one attended by five clouds, shining with golden trees resembling the sun's rays, and with enclosures, palmyras, and tamalas, with karṇikara flowers and lotuses, these both were shaken. And famous Mt. Ayomukha, whose elements are decorated, the beautiful Malaya mountain, fragrant with tamala forests, the Surāṣṭra people together with the Bahlikas and even the courageous Bhiras, the Bhojas and Paṇḍyas and Vangas, Kaliṅgas, and Tamraliptikas, also the Udras and the Pauṇḍras, the Vāmacudas together with the Keralas, these together with the gods and hosts of Apsaras were shaken by the Daitya. The abode of Agastya, which was made inaccessible, and an assembly of Siddhas were thrown about the Manohara forest. Many varicolored birds, great trees having beautiful flowers, a host of Apsaras resounding with golden horns, and even Mt. Puṣpitaka, which has the beauty of Lakṣmī, rising from the ocean, that resting place of Candra and Sūrya, appeared like the sky, scratched by great peaks, upon splitting asunder. Venerable Vidyutvan mountain, stretching one hundred yojanas on all sides was enveloped by the waters of the ocean, appearing like the beams of the sun and moon. Masses of lightning were caused to strike the best of mountains, and even the venerable mountain named Ṛṣabha after the bull. Venerable Mt. Kuñjara, beautiful home of Agastya, and unconquerable Viśālākṣa, the city of the serpents, also the Bhogavatī was shaken by the Daitya chief, and also Mt. Mahāsena and the Pāryatra mountain. He shook the best of peaks, Cakrava, and even the Vārāha mountain, and also the eastern city of Pragjyotiṣa, golden and beautiful, in which dwells the evil-minded Dānava named Naraka, and Megha, the best of mountains, giving forth sound as deep as the rumbling of a cloud. Sixty thousand mountains, Best of Twice-borns, and the great peak Meru, looking like the morning sun, whose cavern is dwelt in by Yakṣas, Rakṣases, together with Gandharvas, mighty Mt. Hemagarbha and the Hemasakha peak, and even the mighty Mt. Kailasa shook from the Daitya chief. Lake Vaikhānasa, clothed in lotus flowers of gold was shaken by him, even Lake Mānasa, filled with swans and ducks, was shaken, and even the three-peaked mountain, and the Kumārī, best of rivers. And also Mt. Mandara, clothed in a covering of frost, and Uśīrabindu and the king of mountains, the peak Candraprasthas, the peak of Prajāpati and Mt. Puṣkara and even the mountain Devābhra and indeed Mt. Renuka, Krauñca and the mountain of the seven ṛṣis and the Dhūmravarṇa mountain—these and other peaks, and countries and empires were shaken. The Dānava caused the rivers together with all the oceans to shake, and Kapila, son of the earth, and even Vyāghravān shook. Birds and the sons of virtuous women dwelling at the bottom of Pātāla, and a supreme host of Rudra and Meghanāma whose weapon is an elephant hook, Bhiṁavega and Urdhvaga, all were shaken.

And dreadful Hiranyakaśipu, armed with club and spike, like a dense cloud, having the sound of a dense cloud, sounding forth like a dense cloud, violent like a cloud, the mighty son of Diti, foe of the gods, attacked the man-lion. Assailed by the sharp claws of the King of Beasts, torn apart by him whose companion is *oṃ*, he was destroyed in battle. And the earth and Kāla, the moon and ether, Rāhu and Sūrya, and all the regions, rivers, mountains, and oceans became tranquil from the destruction of the son of Diti. Then the gods and ṛṣis, rich in religious austerities, were pleased, and praised the eternal first god with divine names. "This man-lion form which was effected by you, O God, that, knowing and seeing both past and future, people will praise."

The gods spoke:

You are Brahmā and Rudra and the great Indra, best of the gods, you are creator and manifester, the imperishable king of the worlds. They call you the best bliss and the best god and the best mantra and the supreme oblation, the best dharma and the supreme universe, the foremost puruṣa of ancient times. The best body and the supreme brahman and the best yoga and the supreme speech, the best mystery and the supreme path, the foremost puruṣa of old. They call you the highest step of high and he who is the best god, the best of the best and the best element, the foremost puruṣa of old. They call you the best of the best and the best mystery, the best of the best also the best moral greatness, the best of the best, the best which is mighty, the foremost puruṣa of old. The best of the best, also the best receptable, the best of the best, also the best purifier, the best of the best, also the best giver, the foremost puruṣa of old.

But upon saying this the Blessed One, the grandfather of all the worlds, upon praising the god Nārāyaṇa, the king went to the Brahmaloka. Then, while the Apsaras were dancing and bellowing, Lord Hari went to the northern bank of the Ocean of Milk. The god set out, having put aside the form of a man-lion, shining brightly, having recourse to his old form, which has Garuḍa as its emblem. Shining, with a vehicle of eight wheels yoked to ghosts, the god, abiding in his own unmanifest nature, the king, went home.

Padma Purāṇa V (Uttara) .42

Bhīṣma spoke:

I want to hear about the slaying of Hiraṇyakaśipu, the glorification of Narasiṁha which destroys all evils.

Pulastya spoke:

Long ago in the Kṛta yuga, mighty Hiraṇyakaśipu, primal man among Daityas, performed severe austerities, O King. Living in water for eleven thousand years, he performed the vow of bathing and observing silence. Having become endowed with tranquility, self-restraint, and chastity, Brahmā was pleased with his tapas and piety. Then the Self-born One, the Blessed Lord himself, having arrived there in an aerial cart the color of the sun, yoked to swans and splendid, joined by the Ādityas, Vasus, Sādhyas, Maruts, Devatas, Rudras, Viśvadevas, Yakṣas, Rakṣases, and serpents, and by the regions, intermediate regions, the rivers and oceans, the stars and moments, planets and great planets, accompanied by the gods, Brahmarṣis, Siddhas, and seven ṛṣis, the kingly ṛṣis and the hosts of holy men, Gandharvas, and Apsarases, the guru of everything moving and unmoving, endowed with prosperity, surrounded by all the celestials, Brahmā, eminent among Brahmā knowers, spoke these words to the Daitya.

Brahmā spoke:

I am pleased by your devoted tapas, You whose vow is good; choose a boon, God bless you. Whatever is desired, that desire you will obtain.

Hiraṇyakaśipu spoke:

Neither gods or demons or Gandharvas, not Yakṣas, serpents, or Rakṣases, not men nor Piśācas may kill me, O Best of Gods. Ṛṣis and men may not curse me with curses, O Grandfather, if I have pleased you. This is the boon chosen by me. Neither by arrows nor by missiles, nor by stones or trees, neither by dry nor by wet nor by any other will I be slain. I may become the sun, the moon, the wind, or the fire, the rain, the atmosphere, the stars or the ten regions. I am anger and lust, Varuṇa, Indra and Yama, Kubera, the overseer of the treasure, a Yakṣa and chief of the Kiṁpuruṣas.

Brahmā spoke:

O Son, this marvelous divine wish is given to you by me. Yielding all desires, dear child, you will attain it, no doubt.

Pulastya spoke:

Having said this, the Blessed One went through the air to Vairāja, the abode of Brahmā, enjoyed by the host of Brahmarṣis.

Then the gods, Gandharvas, and celestial singers, together with the ṛṣis, having heard the granting of the boon, approached the Grandfather.

The gods spoke:

O Blessed One, because of the granting of the boon, the demon will kill us, and it would be his pleasure, O Lord! So think about his death, too!

Pulastya spoke:

The Blessed One, primal maker of all beings, the Lord himself, Creator of oblations to gods and ancestors, unmanifest nature supreme, the god Prajāpati, having heard that speech which was for the welfare of all the worlds, then comforted them with words like cool rain. "The fruit of tapas is by all means to be obtained by him, O Gods. At the end of his tapas, the Blessed One, Viṣṇu himself, will act."

Having heard all these words from the Lotus-born One, O Brahmin, the gods went to their own celestial abodes, filled with joy.

As soon as the boon was obtained, the Daitya Hiraṇyakaśipu, proud from the gift of that boon, harassed all the people. The Dānava dared to attack illustrious munis in hermitages, dedicated to their vows, restrained and intent upon truth and dharma. The great demon, having vanquished the gods and those residing in the three worlds, that Dānava dwelt in heaven, commanding the triple world. Then, puffed up and proud with the intoxication of the boon, and instigated by time, he made the Daityas recipients of the sacrifice and the gods unworthy of the sacrifice.

At that time the Ādityas, Sādhyas, Viśvadevas and Indra, the Rudras, troops of gods, Yakṣas, maharṣis, and brahmins of the gods went to seek shelter in mighty Viṣṇu, god of gods, container of the sacrifice, the eternal Vasudeva.

The gods spoke:

O Illustrious Nārāyaṇa, the gods have come to you for refuge. Rescue us! Kill the chief of Daityas, Hiraṇyakaśipu, O Lord. You are our supreme support, you are our supreme guru, you are our supreme god, superior to Brahmā and the others.

Viṣṇu spoke:

Abandon your fear, O Immortals, I give you safety. O Gods, return to heaven without delay. This Daitya and his host, proud from the granting of the boon, inviolable to the chiefs of immortals, *I* will kill the Daitya chief.

Pulastya spoke:

Having said this, the Blessed One, the all-protecting imperishable Viṣṇu, Lord Hari went to the abode of Hiraṇyakaśipu. Through his tejas, having the appearance of the sun and the loveliness of the moon, having no rival, having made half his form man and half his form lion, with the form of a man-lion, having grasped hand with hand, he then saw the great celestial assembly hall. That radiant assembly hall of Hiraṇyakaśipu, endowed with all enjoyments, spreading out over one hundred yojanas and one and a half hundred yojanas wide, it was suspended in the air, moving at will, five yojanas high, free from old age, sorrow, and suffering, immovable, auspicious, and beautiful, full of palaces and thrones, beautiful like a fire with its tejas, possessing water inside, fashioned by Viśvakarman, it was endowed with trees of divine colors, yielding fruits and flowers, with blue and yellow, black and dark green, white and red, with bushes of dazzling white splendor bearing raktamañjari flowers like thick white clouds. And it was seen floating, radiant by nature and pleasant, with a heavenly scent, neither prosperous or suffering, neither cold nor hot. Having reached that assembly hall, no one had hunger, thirst, or weariness. Decorated with various and manifold forms, surpassing the moon and sun and the fire, that self-shining one shined, residing in the uppermost heaven illuminating the surroundings. All the humans shined, delighted, and there were the best of hard and soft foods, plentiful and juicy. Sweet-smelling garlands, trees bearing fruit at all times, in the hot season there was cold water and in the cold season, hot. He, the mighty one, made the trees bearing young shoots and sprouts, having great branches and flowers at the top, covered with a canopy of creepers, with fragrant flowers and juicy fruits, hot and cold lakes everywhere. O Prince, the Lord saw tīrthas in his assembly hall with water lilies, lotuses, and red lotuses, sweet smelling, with red water lilies, white water lilies, and blue lotuses, with lovely, pleasant flowers, possessed of diverse wonders. With ducks and cakravaka birds, cranes and ospreys, birds with pale wings as white as crystal. Many songs of swans, together with singing cranes were there, fragrant creepers bearing clusters of lotus blossoms. The Blessed One was thrilled, having seen reeds, khadira and arjuna trees, mango, nimbā, and nāga trees, kadamba, bakula, and dhava trees, priyaṁgu creepers, roses, śālmali and haridru trees, śāla, tāla, and tamāla trees, and beautiful campaka trees. These and other flowering trees glittered in the assembly hall: Cardamon, kakubha, kaṅkola, clove and bījapūraka spices, madhuka, kovidāra, and many tāla trees growing up, añjana, aśoka, and parṅa trees, plentiful and colorful, varuṇas and palāśas, panasas together with sandal trees, nīla trees and sumanas plants, nīpa, aśvattha, and tinduka trees; pārijāta trees, mallikas, and bhadradāru, aṭarūṣa shrubs, pīluka trees and elavāluka bark, mandārakas, kurabakas, pataṇgas, and kutajas, red kurabakas together with blue ones and aguru trees; kiṁśukas and bhavyas, pomegranate trees and bījapūrakas, kālīyakas and dukūlas, hiṅgus and sesame stalks; Date and coconut trees, harītaka and madhūka trees, saptaparṇas and bilva trees, sayāvas and śarāvata trees, asana and tamāla trees, covered over with various bushes, creepers in manifold shapes, furnished with flowers and fruits. These and many other trees born in the forest there, endowed with various flowers and fruits, glittered all around. Cakora birds and woodpeckers, cuckoos, kokila, and sārika birds flew among the great trees, which were in bloom, covered with blossoms. Red and yellow-red partridges, having gone to the top of the trees, making their living on other life, observed each other, bristling with delight. The chief of Daityas, Hiraṇyakaśipu, sat on a colorful throne measuring ten furlongs in his assembly hall. That throne, which was covered with a celestial carpet, was divine and like the sun, and on that throne, the Daitya Hiraṇyakaśipu, whose earrings shone, sat. Then the great Daityas waited on Hiraṇyakaśipu and the best of Gandharvas sang songs with heavenly rhythms. Famous Viśvācī, Sahajañyā and Pramlocā, heavenly Saurabheyī, Samīcī, and Puñjikasthalā, Miśrakeśī,

Rambhā, Citrabhā, and Śrutibhramā, Cārunetrā, Ghṛtācī, Menakā and Corvaśī—these and thousands of others skilled in song and dance pleased Hiraṇyakaśipu, lord of kings. All the sons of Diti, having obtained the boon, served him: Bali, son of Virocana, and Naraka, son of Pṛthivī, Prahlāda and Vipracitti, the great demon Gaviṣṭa, Surahantā, Dukhahantā, Sumana and Sumatis, Ghaṭodara, Mahāparśva, Krathana, and Piḍara, Viśvarūpa, Surūpa, and mighty Viśvakāya, Daśagrīva, Vālī, and Meghavāsa, that great demon, Ghaṭabha and Vitarūpa, Jvalan and Indratāpana, that assemblage of Daityas and Dānavas, all with bracelets blazing, all with garlands and clad in armor and all observing a vow, having obtained the boon, all were heroic, ready for death. These and many others, all whose garments were celestial, attended the magnanimous one, lord Hiraṇyakaśipu. All the sons of Diti, whose bodies were adorned, bearing many colorful bracelets, waiting on the mighty chief on all sides, those best of demons shone like the sun in that celestial assembly hall of Hiraṇyakaśipu. Nothing was seen nor heard of like the prosperity of Hiraṇyakaśipu, lion among Daityas, magnanimous one, nothing was seen or heard of like this in the triple world.

The lord of lions saw in the assembly hall seats of silver and gold, streets surrounded by colorful jewels and adorned by radiant lattice windows. The lord of lions saw the son of Diti, whose body was adorned by gold bracelets and necklaces, radiant and shining like the sun, honored by hundreds and thousands of Diti's children.

Then, noticing the illustrious one who had arrived like the wheel of time, disguised in the form of a man-lion, covered with ashes like the god of fire, the mighty son of Hiraṇyakaśipu named Prahlāda looked at the god who had arrived with the divine leonine form. Seeing him dwelling in that form which was extraordinary and like a golden mountain, Hiraṇyakaśipu and all the Dānavas were amazed.

Prahlāda spoke:

O Great King, O Mighty One, Firstborn among Daityas, this man-lion has been neither seen nor heard of before by me. Who is this unmanifest, supreme, and celestial form who has arrived? My mind predicts that this is horrible and will cause the end of the Daityas.

The gods, oceans, and rivers are residing in his body:

Himavān and Pāriyātra, and all the other kulaparvatas. The moon with the stars, the Ādityas together with the rays of light, Kubera and Varuṇa, Yama and Śakra, lord of Śācī, Maruts, gods, and Gandharvas, ṛṣis and ascetics, Nāgas, Yakṣas and Piśācas, Rakṣases of terrific prowess, Brahmā, the gods, and Paśupati, all those standing and moving wander about on his brow. And you, accompanied by us, surrounded by all the Daitya hosts, and the assembly hall, full of hundreds of aerial carts, all the three worlds, and the eternal dharma of the world, O King, this and the entire world is seen in the man-lion. Prajāpati and magnanimous Manu, planets and asterisms, the earth and the sky, portents and time, content and intellect, enjoyment, truth, tapas, and self-restraint, high-minded Sanatkumāra, all the gods and all the ṛṣis, fury and lust, rapture and arrogance, delusion and all the manes are there.

Pulastya spoke:

The lord Hiraṇyakaśipu, leader of the troops, having heard Prahlāda's speech, spoke to all the Dānava troops. "The chief of lions dwelling in this extraordinary body must be seized. If there is any doubt at all, this forest-dweller must be killed."

Pulastya spoke:

All the Dānava troops, having surrounded the King of Beasts, whose prowess was terrible, harassed him energetically. The mighty Narasiṁha let loose a lion's roar, open mouthed like Yama, king of death. He shattered the entire assembly hall.

While that assembly hall was being shattered, Hiraṇyakaśipu himself, eyes full of wrath, hurled missiles at the lion: the best of all the weapons, the stick weapon, Sudāruṇa, then the terrible Kālacakra and other Viṣṇucakra, the terrible and great Grandfather's weapon, fashioned from the triple world, the colorful thunderbolt and the double thunderbolt, both wet and dry, and Rudra's terrible spike and the Oṁkara mace, the Brahmāśiras weapon and the Brahmā weapon, Nārāyaṇa's weapon and Indra's, fiery and cool, Vāyu's weapon and the churning stick and skulls and slaves, the indestructible Śakti and the curlew weapon, the Brahmāśiras weapon, the Soma weapon that is cool, the arrows Mohana, Śoṣana and Saṁtāpana, causing wailing, and the Kampana weapon, causing decay, and the great obstructing weapon, the mighty burning, indestructible mace of time, the bewildering Saṁvartana weapon and the excellent weapon of deceit, the Gandharvas' weapon and the beloved sword of jewels, the weapon causing sleep, the churning weapon, and the best of weapons, Varuṇa's, and the Pāśupata weapon whose course is unobstructed, Hiraṇyakaśipu hurled these celestial weapons at Narasiṁha, like an oblation into a blazing fire. The best of Daityas covered the lion with blazing weapons like the sun covers Himavān with its sunbeams during the hot season. The ocean of troops of Daityas, stirred up by the gale of anger, washed over everything instantly like the ocean does Mt. Mainaka. With barbed missiles and chains and scimitars, maces, and clubs, with thunderbolts and lightning, and great trees with many branches, with mallets and traps, and mountains of stone and wooden mortar, with rockets blazing and Sudāruna sticks, the Dānavas, whose hands held nooses, whose great chief was swift like lightning, whose arms and bodies were upraised, stood like young serpent demons with their hoods upraised. Whose limbs were adorned with a number of brightly colored garlands, whose hollow mouths were full of very sharp fangs, who were surrounded by light, and whose bodies were adorned with Chinese silk, they shone like geese. The Dānava hurled the fire of *Māyā,* stirring the wind. Thousand-eyed Indra of great splendor, together with rain clouds, subdued the fire with great torrents of water. When the *māyā* was impeded in the battle, the Dānava emitted a gloom, dark and horrible, all over. And when darkness enveloped the world as the Dānavas seized their weapons, Narasiṁha appeared like the sun, surrounded by his own tejas. And the Dānavas saw his three-pronged frown in battle, the trident mark on his brow, looking like Gaṅgā flowing through heaven, earth, and the nether worlds. Then, when all the *māyā* had been conquered, the sons of Diti, the Daityas, despondent, sought refuge in Hiraṇyakaśipu.

Then, flaming with anger as if he were burning with tejas, when the Daitya chief was angered, the world was covered with darkness. Āvaha, Prāvaha, and Vivaha winds, Parāvaha, and Saṁvaha, mighty Udvaha and venerable Parivaha, all announcing a catastrophe, those seven winds, blowing in the sky, shook. All the planets that become visible at the destruction of the world—all these were seen in the sky roaming about as they pleased. At night the moon traveled on its course without the regular conjunction of planets, but with planets, constellations, and the full moon. The Blessed Sun became pale in the sky.

Then the vast, dark twilight cloud was seen in the sky, and the sun and the fire residing in the smoke gave up the darkness. The Blessed One was seen perpetually residing in the sky. Seven horrible, dim suns appeared in the sky, planets remained at the horns of the moon and the sky, while Śukra and Bṛhaspati were situated at the left and the right. Mars and Saturn, having the luster of Mars, all the planets rose up together to the peaks, turning slowly by degrees, horrible planets that come at the end of the yuga. The moon, together with the stars and the planets, dispelling darkness, did not greet Rohinī for the destruction of everything moving and unmoving. Candra, seized by Rahu, was beaten by meteors; burning meteors strode on the moon as they pleased. The chief god of gods sent down blood. Meteors in the form of lightning fell from the sky, making a loud sound, and at an unseasonable time, all the trees flowered and bore fruit, heralding the destruction of the Daitya. Fruit born to fruit, and even flowers to flowers, they opened, closed, laughed, wept, they lamented deeply, smoked, and burned. Images of all the gods proclaimed great danger. Tame beasts together with wild ones, beasts and birds lamented horribly as the battle of the beast drew near. Rivers with muddy waters ran contrary to their course, and the regions, filled with red dust, were not visible. Those trees worthy of respect were not even worshiped; struck by a gust of wind and broken, they bowed down. And then the shadow of all beings did not revolve.

While the sun was in the afternoon for the destruction of the worlds, then, on top of the dwelling of the Daitya Hiraṇyakaśipu, the moon settled on the treasury and arsenal, for the destruction of the demons and the victory of the gods. Many calamities were seen, exemplifying horrible sights. These and many other awful forms, proclaiming the battle, appeared and were seen for the destruction of the chief of Daityas.

While the earth was shaken by the magnanimous Daitya chief, hosts of Nāgas, supporters of earth, of unbounded energy, fell down, mouths filled with burning venom, spitting fire. Snakes with four heads, five heads, and seven heads, Vāsuki and Takṣaka, Karkoṭaka and Dhanaṁjaya, Cardamon-face and Kalīya, and the mighty Mahāpadma, the thousand-headed one whose body is pure, and the mighty one whose mark is the golden fan, the great serpent Śeṣa Ananta, who is steadfast, were shaken. Those who resided in the water and those who spread out over the earth began to shine, those seven shook on all sides with the fury of the Daitya chief. Those possessing various energies and those living in the bottom of Pātāla, when Pātāla was suddenly agitated, those immovables were shaken. Then the Daitya Hiraṇyakaśipu touched the earth, having bitten his lower lip in anger, like the ancient boar. The rivers Gaṅgā, Bhagīrathī, Kauśikī, and Sarayu, Yāmunā, Kāverī, Kṛṣṇā, Venā, and Niṁnagā, the Tuṅgabhadrā, Mahāvegā, and the river Godāvarī, the Carmaṇvatī and the Sindhu, lord of the male and female rivers, and Śona, the birthplace of crimson lotuses, whose water is like jewels, the Narmadā, with splendid water, the river Vetravatī, the Gomatī, having cattle on its sides, and the ancient Sarasvatī, the mighty Kālamahī and the Tamasā, carrying flowers, Jambudvīpa, covered with jewels, all having a beautiful appearance, decorated with a treasure of gold, having great rivers, and made of copper, Pattana of the treasure-holders, Kuśi and Rajatākara, people of Magadha, that great town, Puṇḍas and Ugras, the people of Suhmā, Malla, and Videha, of Malava, Kaśi, and Kośala, the dwelling of Vainateya—all these were shaken by the Daitya chief, and that which, having the appearance of the peak of Kailāsa was fashioned by Viśvakarman, shook as well. That ocean named Lauhitya, very terrible with jeweled waters, and the great mountain Udaya, rising up one hundred yojanas tall, whose altar is of gold, that venerable one attended by a row of clouds, shining with golden trees resembling the sun's rays, and with enclosures, palmyras, karṇika flowers and lotuses, and famous Mt. Ayomukha, decorated by minerals, and the beautiful Mt. Malaya, fragrant with tamāla forests, and the Surāṣṭra people together with the Bāhlīkas, Śūdras, and Abhīras, the Bhojas and Pāṇḍyas, Vaṅgas, Kaliṅgas, and the Tāmraliptika people, and also the Pauṇḍras and Śubhras, the Vāmacudas and Keralas—these together with the gods and hosts of Apsarases were shaken by the Daitya. The abode of Agasyta, formerly made by Agastya, beautiful and inhabited by an assembly of Siddhas and minstrels, having many varied-colored birds, great trees with flowers, attended by the host of Apsarases with golden horns, and even Mt. Puṣpitaka possessing Lakṣmī, the sight of which is dear, that resting place of the sun and moon, having split the ocean asunder, it rose up and appeared as if writing on the sky with its great peaks that were like sun- and moonbeams and were enveloped by the waters of the ocean. Vidyudvāsa mountain, stretching one hundred yojanas, where masses of lightning struck that best of mountains, and even venerable Mt. Ṛṣabha, the dwelling of Ṛṣabha, venerable Mt. Kuṁjara, the beautiful home of Agastya, and that one called Vimala, and Mālāti, unconquerable city of serpents, and even the Bhogāvatī—all were shaken by the Daitya chief. Mt. Mahāsena and Mt. Pariyatra, the best of mountains Cakrava, and Mt. Varāha, the city of Prāgjyotiṣa, golden and beautiful, in which the evil-minded Dānava named Naraka dwelt, and Megha, eminent among mountains, sounding as deep as the rumbling of a cloud, were shaken—sixty thousand mountains, O King, and the great Mt. Meru, looking like the sun and Varuṇa, whose cavern is always dwelt in by Yakṣas, Rakṣases, and Gandharvas, Mt. Hemagarbha, Mahāsena, and Mt. Meghasakha, and Kailāsa, that chief of mountains, were all shaken by the Dānava chief. Lake Vaikhānasa, clothed in golden lotuses, and even Lake Mānasa, filled with ducks and swans, were shaken by him. And the eminent three-peaked mountain, and the Kumārī, best of rivers, and also Mt. Mandara, clothed in a covering of frost, Mt. Uśīrabīja and the king of mountains, Bhadrapastha, Mt. Prajāpati and Mt. Puṣkara, Mt. Devābha and Mt. Vālukā, Krauñca and the mountain of the seven ṛṣis and Mt. Dhumravarṇa—these and other mountains, and countries and empires, the rivers together with all the oceans, these the Dānava shook. Kapila, son of the earth, and even Vyāghravan, birds, and the sons of the night, dwelling in the Pātāla hell, were shaken. And a supreme host of Rudra named Megha, whose weapon is the elephant hook, and Ūrdhvaga and Bhīmavega—all these were shaken.

Dreadful Hiraṇyakaśipu, armed with club and spike, sounded forth like a dense cloud and was swift like a cloud. That proud enemy of the gods attacked the man-lion. Assailed by the sharp great claws of the King of Beasts, torn apart by him whose companion is *oṁ*, he was slain in the battle.

And the earth and time, the moon and ether, the planets and Sūrya, and all the regions, the rivers and mountains and the great oceans became clear at the destruction of the son of Diti. Then the gods and ṛṣis, rich in tapas, were pleased and praised the eternal primal god with divine names.

The gods spoke:

O God, this man-lion form that you assumed, this people who know the personal and supreme god will praise.

Brahmā spoke:

You are Brahmā and Rudra and Mahendra, O Best of Gods, you are the creator and manifester of the worlds, imperishable and mighty. You who are the most ancient supreme being, they call you the best sage and the highest truth, the ultimate mystery and the superior oblation, the highest dharma and the supreme glory.

You who are the most ancient supreme being, they call you the highest truth, the supreme tapas, the superior purifier and the highest path, the best sacrifice and the supreme offering. You who are the most ancient supreme being, they call you the best body and the supreme Brahmā, the highest yoga and the most excellent speech, the supreme mystery, and the highest path.

Pulastya spoke:

The blessed Grandfather of all the world, having thus spoken, and having praised the god Nārāyaṇa, went to Brahmaloka.

Then, while the Apsarases were dancing and while the music played, Lord Hari went to the northern bank of the Kṣiroda ocean. That god, having put aside the form of a man-lion, shining brightly, having recourse to his ancient form, he who has Garuḍa as his emblem set out. The god whose nature is unmanifest went home to his own dwelling in an eight-wheeled vehicle, shining and possessing prosperity.

Appendix II: Translations of Vāmana Myths

Bhaviṣya Purāṇa 4.76.1–27

Śri Kṛṣṇa spoke:

The ceremony called Dvādaśī, which occurs in the month of Śravana, O Yudhiṣṭhira, destroys all sins and yields all happinesses. When the Ekadaśī is accompanied by the constellation Śravana, that Lunar day is called Vijayā and brings victory to the devotees.

The mighty Daitya named Bali, strong and invincible, made all the godly troops abandon the palace of the gods. Having gone to see MahāViṣṇu, the gods made this speech: "You are the refuge of all the gods; deliver us from evil at once! Kill the Daitya Bali, O Great-armed One, Destroyer of Bali." Having heard the gods' sorrowful speech, Viṣṇu said this, knowing Time and out of a concern for the welfare of the gods. "I know the Daitya Bali, son of Virocana, thorn of the triple world. Through tapas, his soul was transformed; he is peaceful, restrained, and a lord of his senses; he is devoted to me, his life is mine, his promise is true, and he is mighty. After a long time, his tapas will end. When I know that he is no longer endowed with discipline, having stolen his cherished kingdom, then I shall give it to the gods. For Aditi, having come to me for the sake of her son, and eager for a son, I shall do something agreeable, no doubt. That is the welfare of the gods and the disadvantage of the enemies of the gods. Be calm; we must wait for some time."

Thus spoken to, the gods left, and Viṣṇu meditated on his duty. Having meditated for a long time on the descent into the womb, Aditi made a wish. "My wish shall be." After many days went by, she became pregnant, and in the ninth month, she bore Hari in the form of a dwarf who had small feet, a small body, and a great head; just a child with tiny hands, feet, and belly, Hari Nārāyaṇa himself. But having seen the dwarf born, when she began to speak the words were restrained, and she was not able to speak even a little. On the eleventh of Bhadrapada [with the conjunction of] Śravana, O Best of Men, the earth trembled when the thrice-stepping dwarf was born. Fear was born among the Daityas, and joy among the gods. Kaśyapa, the wise Prajāpati himself, performed his saṁskāras, including the jātakarma and other ceremonies.

Wearing a belt, carrying a staff, and wearing the thread, bearing kuśa grass and clear water, and adorned by a water jar, he went to the elaborate sacrifice of mighty Bali. Having seen Bali and having approached him, Vāmana spoke that instant. "O Lord of the Sacrifice, land for the purpose of study must be given to me by measuring three strides. Do you stand [to give]?"

"Given by me and received by you," Bali spoke to the best of brahmins. Then, the dwarf whose stride is endless began to grow. Resting his feet on the earth, and covering heaven and earth with his head, covering the worlds of Indra and others with his navel and the seat of Brahmā with his forehead, he did not obtain the third step. Then the gods roared, having seen that great surprise. The Siddhas, and godly ṛṣis, filled with joy, praised him, "Very good! Very good!" Then the Lord, having conquered all the Daitya hosts and the three worlds, said to Bali, "Go to Sutala, followed by your own army. There, having enjoyed the wealth you desire, and protected by my arms, at Indra's end, you shall become Indra." Thus spoken to, Bali left, having paid obeisance to the best of men. Having dismissed Bali, Viṣṇu spoke to all the gods. "Go to your own dwellings, and remain there, free from trouble." Thus spoken to, and having worshiped the dwarf, the gods left, content.

Brahmā Purāṇa 73

Nārada spoke:

The goddess who resides in the water jar and who enhances your holiness, how did she come to the land of mortals? Tell me that at length, O Lord.

Brahmā spoke:

The great Daitya named Bali, unconquerable enemy of the gods, endowed with dharma and honor, protector of the people, devoted to his guru, with his truth, strength, and might, with his gifts and tolerance, he cannot be compared in the triple world. Having seen his great prosperity, the worried gods said to each other, "How is Bali winning? He controls the sovereignty of the triple world, free from troubles; no enemies or sickness or anxieties exist at all. There is no drought nor adharma nor scarcity nor evil folk; these are not seen even in dreams while Bali is reigning."

The gods, who were torn by the arrows of his prosperity, who were split in two by the sword of his fame, whose bodies were broken by the spear of his authority, could find no refuge. Having first shown jealousy, then they took counsel. Wearied, they went to Viṣṇu, their bodies shining from the fire of his fame.

The gods spoke:

O Bearer of the Conch, Discus, and Mace, we are indeed lifeless and suffering. You always bear weapons for our sake. O World Protector, even when you are our protector, we have such suffering. One bows to you, but how does one praise a Daitya? We seek refuge in you with the mind, with acts, and with words. Having sought refuge at your feet, how could we praise a Daitya? We worship you with great sacrifices, we speak with praises, O Acyuta, our sole refuge is you; how could we praise a Daitya? The gods with Indra at their head continually receive their vigor from you, having reached that station granted by you; how could we praise a Daitya? Having taken the form of Brahmā, you are the creator; having become Viṣṇu, you protect; through the energy of Rudra, you are the destroyer; how could we praise a Daitya? Sovereignty is the most important thing in the world, but we are deprived of sovereignty; what is the use? Our sovereignty is conquered, O Lord of Gods, how can we praise a Daitya? You have no beginning and are endless, you are the support of the world, the guru of the world. How can we praise a Daitya enemy who is mortal? Having conquered the triple world with vitality, our bodies are well-nourished through your sovereignty, we are steadfast, O Lord of Gods; how could we praise a Daitya?

Brahmā spoke:

The destroyer of the Daityas, having thus heard the speech, spoke to all the immortals about the accomplishment of the purpose of the gods.

The Blessed One spoke:

The Daitya Bali is my devotee, he is inviolable to gods and demons. As you are nourished by me, so is Bali nourished by me. O Gods, having seized the sovereignty in Indra's heaven without a battle, having bound Bali and having spoken the mantra, I will give you the sovereignty.

Brahmā spoke:

Having thus spoken, the host of gods went to heaven, and the Blessed One, Lord of Gods, entered Aditi's womb. When he was born there were festivals; he was born a brahmin dwarf, lord of sacrifice, the sacrificial puruṣa.

Meanwhile, O Excellent brahmin, mighty Bali prepared for the horse-sacrifice, joined by the best of ṛṣis. While the sacrifice continued with the chief priest Śukra, knower of the Vedas and Vedāṅgas, Bali was the sacrificer. There, with the chief priest Śukra, best of ṛṣis, as the sacrificing priest, gods, Gandharvas, and Nāgas were also present for the sake of a share of the offering. "May it be given, may it be eaten, and may there be worship," one by one and again and again, and "that is enough," while such speeches were going on, quietly Vāmana approached that place, chanting a Sāma verse. Vāmana, with colorful rings, approached the sacrificial enclosure, praising that sacrifice. The Bhargava, having seen the dwarf god, destroyer of Daityas, bearing the form of a brahmin, having quickly recognized him as the donor of the fruit of sacrifice and asceticism, he hurriedly spoke to the king of great splendor, to mighty Bali, who is a conqueror by kṣatradharma, a giver of wealth through devotion, consecrated in the sacrifice with his wife, O Excellent One. Meditating on the sacrificial puruṣa, and making the oblation separately, wise Śukra, that tiger among Bhṛgus, spoke to him.

Śukra spoke:

He who has arrived at your sacrifice, the brahmin bearing the form of a dwarf, is not a brahmin, O Bali; truly he is the lord of the sacrifice, the bearer of the sacrifice. Indeed, this "child" has arrived to beg you for the welfare of the gods. Having consulted with me, O Lord, *afterwards* you should give.

Brahmā spoke:

Then Bali, conqueror of foes, spoke to his chief priest, the Bhargava. "I am fortunate; the lord of sacrifice incarnate comes to my home. He comes and he asks for something; what advice remains?"

Brahmā spoke:

Having thus spoken with his chief priest Śukra, he went with his wife to where the chief of brahmins, Vāmana, son of Aditi, was. Having joined his hands together in a reverent gesture, he said to him, "please say whatever you like." Then Vāmana said, "O Chief of Kings, give three steps of land; nothing can be accomplished with wealth." But then, saying yes to him, and letting the water go from the pitcher that was adorned with various jewels, when the chief priest Śukra and the head ṛṣis saw this, while the world guardians and the assembly of Daityas were watching, and when the shout of victory was sounded, he gave the land to Vāmana.

Slowly Vāmana spoke, "Salutations, O Prosperous King! Give me land measuring three steps so that I can go quickly." Then the Daitya lord spoke as he watched Vāmana. The Lord of sacrifice, sacrificial puruṣa, endless Acyuta, the god striding widely, bearer of the step grew until the moon and sun were in the middle of his breasts. Having seen him, the Daitya king, together with his wife, spoke modestly. "O Viṣṇu, Lord of the World, stride as far as possible, Container of the Whole World. O Lord of Gods, now my devotion is victorious, O Creator of all Things."

Brahmā spoke:

Simultaneously, Viṣṇu, the great sacrifice, spoke these words. "O Lord of Daityas, Long-Armed one, I will stride: Watch, O Daitya chief."

Brahmā spoke:

Thus speaking, Bali said, "Stride, O Viṣṇu, again and again." Having set down his foot on the tortoise shell, he planted his foot at the sacrifice of Bali. The second step reached the eternal Brahmaloka.

Bali said:

The whole world was created by *you*, O Lord of Gods, I am not the creator. By your fault it became small; what can I do, O World Receptacle? I have never said a false word before, O Keśava; my words are truthful. Place your foot on my back.

Brahmā spoke:

Then pleased, the Blessed One having the threefold form spoke, honored by the gods. "Choose a boon, God bless you, O Daitya King. I am pleased by your devotion."

Brahmā spoke:

He said to the world protector, "I do not beg you with your three steps." Viṣṇu, pleased, gave what he himself desired in his mind. Hari gave him sovereignty of Rasātala and, in the future, the abode of Indra again, sovereignty of his own soul, and indestructable glory. Thus, having given all this to Bali, Hari established Bali, enemy of the gods, in Rasātala, together with his children and accompanied by his wives. He gave the sovereignty of the gods to Śatakratu according to his birth, and that abode which is worshiped by the gods. O Great Sage, Viṣṇu, having reached my house, the second step of my father, having seen that abode, I thought: "What shall I do that will be auspicious when the step of Viṣṇu arrives?" Looking all around and thinking my jar might be the best, that holiest water which was given by Śiva, chosen as best, grants wishes, supreme, and causes peace, auspicious and yields auspiciousness eternally, grants enjoyment and freedom, like one's own mother, elixir of the worlds, healing and pure, holy, purifying, worthy of worship, most excellent and eminent, endowed with qualities, purifying the worlds by its recollection, how much more from its sight? "Having become pure, I will use such water as an offering to my father." Having thought this, and taking that water, it was used as an offering. That offering of water fell with incantations on the foot of Viṣṇu. The water, having fallen on Meru, reached the earth in four parts, on the east, south, west, and north. That water which fell on the south side, O muni, Śaṁkara seized it with his matted locks. And that which fell on the west side went into the water jar. And that which fell on the north side, Viṣṇu seized that water. And on the east side, the gods, manes, and world guardians seized that good water; and that is why it is considered superior. The waters that are the mothers of the world and that fell on the south side, they are born from the foot of Viṣṇu, and they are the mothers of the world, worthy of praise. They reside in the matted locks of Śiva and make themselves manifest at an auspicious time. And one shall obtain all desires by remembering their power.

Brahmā Purāṇa 213.80–105

The last story was the man-lion, and the next one is the dwarf, where, having formerly assumed the form of a dwarf for the destruction of the Daitya, at the sacrifice of mighty Bali, the imperturbable demons were destroyed by Viṣṇu with his three strides: Vipracitti, Śiva, Śaṅku, and Ayaḥśaṅku; Ayaḥśirā, Aśvaśirā, and the mighty Hayagrīva; swift and terrible Ketumān, the great demon Ugravyagra, Puṣkara, and Puṣkala; and Aśvapati, Prahlāda, Aśvapati, Kumbha and Saṁhrāda, whose gait is pleasing; Anuhrāda, Harihaya, Varāha and Saṁhara, his younger brother; Śarabha, Śalabha, and Kupatha; Krodhana and Kratha, Bṛhatkīrti, Mahājihva, Śaṅkukarṇa and Mahāsvana; Dīptajihva, Arkanayana, Mṛgapāda, and Mṛgapriya; Vāyu, Gariṣṭa, Namuci, Śambara, and mighty Viskara, Candrahantā, Krodhahantā, and even Krodhavardhana; Kālaka, Kālakopa, Vṛtra, Krodha, and Virocana; Gariṣṭa and Variṣṭa, Pralamba and Narakāvu, Indratāpana, Vātāpī, and Ketumān, proud of his strength; Asilomā and Pulomā, Bāṣkala, Pramada and Mada, Svamiśra, Kālavadana, Karāla and Keśi; Ekākṣa and Candrama, Rāhu, Samhrāda, Śambara, and Svana, bearing the hundred-fire weapon, discuses, and poles. Those approaching holding cattle hammers and iron bars, striking with great stones and armed with spikes, mighty ones, bearing various awful weapons, in varied dress with faces like tortoises and cocks, like rabbits and owls, with great countenances like asses and camels, like boars, cats and peacocks. Ram-faced and crocodile-faced heroes, ones with bull, sheep, and buffalo heads, Dānavas with iguana and porcupine heads, and jackal-headed ones. Awful Dānavas with rat and frog faces, ones with wolf heads, terrible demons with the faces of sea monsters and curlews. Horse-headed ones and donkey-headed ones, peacock-faced ones, and those clothed in the skin of the chief of elephants, those whose garment was of black antelope skin. Those whose limbs were surrounded by bark and those with blue garments, those wearing turbans and those wearing diadems, and demons with earrings. Those Daityas, appearing with anointed limbs and with diverse garlands, decorated with diadems, with hair hanging down, and radiant with shell-like necks, having seized their own shining weapons energetically approached the striding Hṛṣikeśa from all sides. Having harassed all the Daityas with the soles of his feet and palms of his hands, the all-pervading one, having created that terrible form, he conquered the earth quickly.

While he was striding over the earth, the moon and Ādityas were between his breasts; while he was striding across heaven, they were situated at his navel, and while he was crossing the highest regions, they appeared again at his knees; thus the twice borns speak of the immeasurable strength of Viṣṇu. He who, having seized the whole earth and having conquered the chief of demons, mighty Viṣṇu, the excellent one, gave the earth to Śakra.

This has been the manifestation of the magnanimous one called Vāmana, this glory of Viṣṇu recited by brahmins who are learned in the Vedas.

Brahmāṇḍa Purāṇa II.73.75–87

The pride of the family of Aditi, having become a twice born, went at an auspicious time to the sacrificing chief of Daityas, Bali Vairocana. "You are the king of the triple world, endowed with all things. O King, give me three steps," said the Lord. "I shall give," King Bali Vairocana said to him, and then, having recognized the dwarf, he himself gave, delighted. O Best of Brahmins, the dwarf, the Lord, strode over heaven, sky, and earth, this whole world, with three steps. He filled the world and was above it, the soul of all beings, he surpassed the sun with his own tejas. He lit up all the regions and points of the compass, that famous one. The great-armed one, lighting up all the worlds, Janārdana shone, having taken the three worlds and the prosperity of the Asuras, and sending the demon sons and grandsons to the Pātāla hell. Namuci, Śambara, and Prahlāda, wounded and shaken by Viṣṇu, ran in all directions. To Bali and his army Mādhava showed the miracle of all the mighty beings and extraordinary creatures in his body, O Brahmin. There, the whole world saw itself. There was nothing in the world which was not pervaded by the magnanimous one.

The gods, demons, and men, having seen that form of Upendra, were all stupefied, beguiled by the tejas of Viṣṇu. Bali was bound by great nooses, together with his relatives and host of friends. All the family of Virocana was made to settle in Pātāla.

Then, having given the sovereignty over all the immortals to magnanimous Indra, the great-armed Janārdana became manifest among men.

Matsya Purāṇa Chapters 244–246

Chapter 244

The ṛṣis spoke:

> O Bard, the dharma of the king was told in detail by you, and it was marvelously auspicious, like a vision in a dream. Indeed, please speak again of the greatness of Viṣṇu; how he, upon becoming a dwarf, bound the demon Bali. Of what sort was the form of Hari that inhabited the three worlds successively?

The bard spoke:

> In ancient times a great ascetic, Śaunaka, was asked this in Kurukṣetra during a pilgrimage to the abode of Vāmana. When there was a breach made by Arjuna in Draupadī's agreement with regard to the king, he then went on a pilgrimage to the sacred spot. In the land of dharma, the land of Kurus, at the abode of Vāmana, having seen the dwarf there, Arjuna spoke these words: "For what reason was the god worshiped in the form of a dwarf, and why was that Blessed One venerated in the form of a boar in ancient times, and why has this place of Vāmana become desirable?"

Śaunaka spoke:

> I will speak of the greatness of Vāmana and of the boar, dispensing with great detail, O Descendant of the Kurus. In ancient times, when Śakra was banished and the gods were defeated, the progenitors were caused to think of regeneration. And Aditi, mother of the gods, engaged herself in supreme

religious austerities, severe and difficult to perform, for a thousand years, O Lord of the Earth. To placate Kṛṣṇa, she was silent and lived on air. On seeing her sons defeated by demons, O Descendant of Kurus, she said, "My sons are in vain," and, distressed, she bowed to Hari, Hṛṣikeśa, god of gods.

Aditi spoke:

Homage to the destroyer of all suffering, homage to you who wears a lotus wreath, homage to the good among good, to the primordial creator. Homage to you, the lotus-eyed one, homage to you who has a lotus springing from your navel, to the beautiful and patient lover, to the sight of the patient one, to the discus bearer. Homage to you, the self-born one, whose birth took place in a lotus. Homage to you in whose hands are a conch shell and a sword, homage to you whose semen is gold. [Homage] to the yogi meditating on the ātman known only to yogis who have indiscreet and discreet knowledge of the ātman, to the one with no qualities or distinctions, to you in your form as Brahman. Who was not seen by the world, on whom the world was established, homage to the gross and the subtle, to you, the god who possesses the conch. Whom men do not see, looking at the whole world; by not caring for the world, the god is situated in the heart. Thus by him the whole world might be destroyed, who is the founder of the whole world, homage, homage. Who at the beginning was the chief of the Prajāpatis, the supreme lord of lords, lord of the gods. Homage to you, the pious Kṛṣṇa. To you who was worshiped in activity and in repose for your own works, bearing the fruits of heaven and liberation, homage to you who bears the club who, thinking with his mind, destroys evil immediately. Homage to you who is supremely free from vice, to the creator, Hari. All who have come to pass, on understanding the imperishable lord of the god of gods, in death they will not attain rebirth. Homage to you who was named the sacrifice at the sacrifice, who was worshiped by those whose chief occupation is sacrifice, I give homage to you, the puruṣa of the sacrifice, Viṣṇu, the mighty lord. To you, the lord of those who know, who was praised with song in all the Vedas by brahmins conversant in the Vedas, to Viṣṇu, to Jiṣṇu, homage. Wherefrom all has arisen and will be absorbed, homage to you who is the foundation of the reppearance of all, to the great soul. By means of whom all this, beginning with Brahmā and ending with a blade of grass [exists], to escape from the web of illusion, I give homage to Upendra. The lord who, being in his own form as the waters, supports everything. I give homage to Viṣṇu, lord of all, lord of creatures, who is to be worshiped by the pure mind, by action, by song, I praise him, Upendra. He who, by means of despair, joy, anger, and so on, which are born from pleasure and pain, dances, being in all creatures, him I praise, Upendra. Who, as that vanquisher, killed tamas incarnate, this Asura, as Sūrya [kills the darkness] born of night, I give homage to Upendra. Who, abiding in his own form as Kapila, and so forth, kills the ignorance and darkness by giving knowledge, to him, Upendra, I give homage. Of whom Candra and Sūrya are the eyes, who sees the good and bad karma of all people at all times, I praise him, Upendra. The Lord of All, to whom all truth and not untruth is apparent delight, I give homage to him, the leader Viṣṇu, who is both the appearance and the disappearance. And Janārdana, having spoken that truth to me and being beyond the truth, by means of that truth let all my heart's desires be fulfilled.

Śaunaka spoke:

Thus praised, the Lord Vāsudeva spoke to her. He, invisible to creatures, was standing in her vision. "O Aditi, whose heart's desires are achieved, O You who know the Law, you will attain these favors, no doubt, from me. You must listen to me, O Excellent One, ask for something that you may wish quickly—you will prosper. Indeed, sight of me will never be fruitless."

Aditi spoke:

In that case, O God, because of my devotion, O One who is kind to Worshipers, let my son be king of the three worlds, O descendant of Vasu. The stolen kingship and the shares of sacrifice stolen by the great Asuras, these my son must attain if you, O Benefactor, are gracious. The stolen kingship causes my son's suffering O Keśava. The loss of [our] heritage from rivalry did damage to us in our hearts.

The Lord of Cows spoke:

Your favor shall be done by me as you wish, O Goddess. And thus, by means of a portion of myself, I will be born in your womb from Kaśyapa. Then, having been born in your womb, I will destroy them, the enemies. Be happy, O Nandinī.

Aditi spoke:

Homage to the lord of the god of gods, to the blessed lord of all. O God, I will not be able to carry you in my womb, O Keśava. In whom all is established, who himself governs the Universe, he who is difficult to bear, I am not able to carry him in my womb.

The Blessed One spoke:

You spoke the truth to me, O Fortunate One. In me is the world established. You will not be able to carry me together with the god Indra. However, I, together with all worlds, gods, demons, humans, all moving and unmoving things, I will support you together with Kaśyapa. Good luck to you. You will not feel exhaustion nor pain in your womb because of me. O Daughter of Dakṣa, I will accomplish your favor, which is very difficult to obtain by others. While I am abiding in your womb, he who is the enemy of your sons will start to lose his tejas, and he will feel pain. Do not worry.

Śaunaka spoke:

Having thus spoken, the lord immediately disappeared. In time, she received him in her womb, O Best of Kurus. While Kṛṣna abided in her womb, the whole earth trembled. The great mountains shook and the oceans became agitated. Wherever Aditi walked, she yielded a lovely step. Here and there the earth bows from affliction, O King of the Earth. While Madhusūdana was abiding in her womb, the tejas of all the demons was abandoned, as Brahmā had spoken.

Chapter 245

Śaunaka spoke:

Seeing all the Asuras destitute of tejas, Bali, the lord of demons, questioned his grandfather Prahlāda. "O Father, Daityas without tejas are as though burned by fire. Why do they now seem as if struck violently by Brahmā's staff? How can the safety of the Dānavas be achieved? Is there a magic created by our enemies for our annihilation because of which the Asuras are destitute of tejas?"

Śaunaka spoke:

Thus the courageous lord of Daityas was asked by his grandson, O Prince. On contemplating a long time, he spoke to the chief of demons, Bali.

Prahlāda spoke:

The mountains tremble, the earth abandons her original support, all the oceans are agitated, the Daityas are without their tejas. As before to the sunrise [they went], the planets do not go. The good fortune of the gods is supposed by portents. O Great-armed One, O Lord of Daityas, this great portent should not be thought of as insignificant, O Tormentor of the Gods.

Śaunaka spoke:

Thus having spoken to the chief of the Dānavas, Prahlāda, the best of demons, the perfect devotee, went to Hari, the lord of lords, in his mind. Prahlāda, performing beautiful and profound meditation, caused his mind to wander to where Janārdana was. Prahlāda saw him, having the form of a dwarf, carried in the womb, the first Prajāpati of the seven worlds, in the midst of the Vasus, Rudras, Aśvins and Maruts, all the Sādhyas, Ādityas, Gandharvas, snakes and Rakṣases, Virocana himself, and the chief of Asuras, Bali, Jambha, Kujambha, Naraka, Bāṇa, and other Asuras, earth, atmosphere, wind, water, fire, and the oceans, trees, rivers, lakes, cattle and deer, and all human beings and creeping animals, the creator of all the world and Lord Brahmā, planets, stars, and snakes, and Dakṣas, and so forth, and Prajāpatis. Filled with amazement at seeing this, having returned to normalcy after a while, Prahlāda spoke to the chief of demons, Bali, son of Virocana.

Prahlāda spoke:

My dear child, pay attention to the cause of the loss of tejas, as I know it. The god of gods, maker of the created world, having no source, maker of the beginning of the world, himself beginningless, the most excellent benefactor, Hari, the most excellent chief of the highest and lowest, superior to the superiors and the authority of authorities, teacher of the teachers of the seven worlds, king of kings, best of the best, having no beginning or middle, the everlasting blessed one, the magnanimous one, by means of a portion, has descended from Aditi to protect the three worlds. Who neither Rudra nor Brahmā nor Indra nor the eminent Sūrya, Soma, or Prajāpati know in his own form, but Vāsudeva, who descended with a sixteenth particle. My king who, by means of a small portion, in the form of a man-lion, previously killed my father; Vāsudeva who, dwelling with the king of all yogis, descended with a sixteenth portion. Comprehending him who has been called indestructible by the Veda knowers, they who are delivered from evil by knowledge of him enter him who is not reborn. I bow to him, the eternal Vāsudeva. Wherefrom all creatures are born, as the waves of the perpetual oceans and in whom they are absorbed in the pralaya, I bow to him, the inconceivable Vāsudeva, of whom not the form, might, or strength, of whom not the appearance of the supreme soul is known. I bow to the grandfather of Śarva, Brahmā, to the eternal Vāsudeva. Fettered, the eye is given the task of seeing the form, the skin is desired for touching, the tongue is a grasper of taste, the ear is for the hearing of men, the nose is for smelling. By whom the earth is held up on the point of a single tusk, supporting mountains, and in whom all the world rests, I am bowed in reverence to him, the king, Viṣṇu. The lord of all, who is not to be known by smell, sight, sound, and so on, the undecaying soul. He who is able to be praised, so to be grasped by the mind. I bow to the god, the king, Hari. Who, by means of a portion, descended into the womb and seized the tejas of the great Asuras. I praise him, the endless god, the king of all who is like an ax to the tree of saṁsāra. He, the god, the womb of the world, the magnanimous one, he, by means of a sixteenth portion, O Chief of the great Asuras, having entered the womb of his mother, deprived us of strength.

Bali spoke:

O Father, who is this one named Hari, who causes us fear? I have hundreds of Daityas superior in strength to Vāsudeva.

Vipracitti, Śibi, Śaṅku, Ayaḥśaṅku, Śiras, Aśvaśiras, Bhaṅgakāri, and Mahāhanu. Pratāpa, Praghaśa, Śumbha, and Kukura are very difficult to conquer; these and others are my Daitya Dānavas. They are very mighty, very strong, able to remove the burden of the earth. In Kṛṣṇa there is not half the strength equal to those, one for one.

Śaunaka spoke:

On hearing the words of his grandson, Prahlāda, chief of Daityas said, "Shame, shame on Bali, whose speech is abusive to Viṣṇu. I think the Daitya Dānavas will be destroyed, of whom you are the king with a foolish mind and no judgment or discrimination. In truth, who but you of evil intention will speak thus of the god of gods, the great fortunate one, the omnipresent leader Vāsudeva? All the Daitya Dānavas, about whom you have spoken, the gods together with Brahmā, Ananta, the immovable objects, earth, you and I and this world, with its mountains, trees, male and female rivers, oceans, islands, and worlds, are not the equal of Keśava. He who is utterly praiseworthy, the pervader, the supreme ātman who, by means of one portion will enter the whole universe; who will speak of him like that apart from you, while approaching annihilation, you who are ignorant, stupid, who has not mastered his soul, who transgresses the commands of his elders? I am miserable, in whose house was born your horrible father, the vile father of whom you are such a son, capable of censuring the god of gods. Let alone devotion to Kṛṣṇa, what is capable of destroying sinful worldly existence? Why did you not pay attention to me? My body is not dearer to me than Kṛṣṇa, the great soul. The world knows this, as you do, O Vilest son of Diti. Knowing that Hari is dearer to me than my own life, you censure him, while showing no respect to me. O Bali, as Virocana is your teacher, so I am his teacher. But Nārāyaṇa, the teacher of all the worlds, is also my teacher. Inasmuch as you censure him, the teacher of the teacher of your teacher, therefore you will go to ruin from your brief sovereignty. My god Janārdana is the world-lord, O Bali: So be it. I shall be ignored by you; nevertheless my guru is dear to me. Moreover, having censured the master of the three worlds, and because you have not paid attention to this, therefore I curse you. As this speech spoken by you concerning Viṣṇu is more terrible than the cutting off of my head, therefore fall, having lost your kingship. And as there is no rescue in the ocean of worldly existence but Kṛṣṇa, so I will soon see you fallen from sovereignty.

Śaunaka spoke:

The chief of Daityas, upon hearing the disagreeable words of his master, propitiated his teacher, prostrating himself again and again.

Bali spoke:

Be kind to me, O Father, do not be angry with me who is struck by ignorance. Drunk with pride in my strength were these words uttered by me. Realizing the ignorance by which I am affected, I am evil, O Best of sons of Diti, I, whose behavior is wicked, am cursed by you, who are wise to have done so. I am not as sorry, O Father, that I will undergo a loss of sovereignty or of wealth, than I am for having done this rude act. The sovereignty of the three worlds, or other sovereignty is not hard to find. But teachers like you are scarce in this world. Be kind to me; do not be angry, O Prince of Daityas. Seeing your anger, I am suffering O Father; not from being under a curse.

Prahlāda spoke:

I was made foolish by my anger, O Son, therefore I cursed you, and my good judgment was carried off by delusion. If my conscience had not been overcome by delusion, O great Asura, how could I curse anything, knowing that Hari is omnipresent? This curse, O Chief of Daityas, indeed will be done to you, but do not despair. Beginning now you should become devoted to the king of gods, the blessed one, to Acyuta, Hari. He will become your protector. O Hero, you should call to mind my curse that is to be attained. Just as it is recollected by you, so I will take pains to unite you with bliss.

The blessed Govinda was born, having the form of a dwarf. When Viṣṇu, lord of gods, descended, all the gods were liberated from suffering, as was Aditi, mother of the gods. A wind blew, agreeable to the touch, the sky was free from dust, and in all beings there was born a mind to do dharma. There was no agitation among the chiefs of men or demons, or among all beings of the earth, sky, or heaven. Lord Brahmā, the grandfather of the world, on performing the Jātakarma, and so on, O Lord of the Earth, and seeing Kṛṣṇa just born, and listening to the ṛṣis, was pleased.

Brahmā spoke:

Long live the king; long live the invincible one, long live the one who consists of the All-Soul; long live he who overcomes birth and old age; long live Acyuta. Long live the unconquerable one; long live the immeasurable one; long live he whose place is unmanifest; long live the meaning of the supreme reason, the omniscient one, the higher knowledge to be known, he who emanated from the ātman. Long live the eyewitness of all the worlds, the agent of the world, the protector of the world. Long live the conqueror of Śeṣa, the conqueror of all; long live him who abides in the heart of everything. Long live him who is the beginning, middle, and end; long live the receptacle of the all knowledge. Undefinable by those who strive after emancipation, he who is seen by himself, long live the lord who bears the fruit of the emancipation of the yogis, whose ornament is self-control and other qualities. Long live the extremely subtle one, he who is difficult to be understood; long live the gross one, he who contains the whole world; long live he who is gross and subtle; long live he who is beyond the senses and who possesses senses. Long live him who, by his own māyā is absorbed in yoga, Viṣṇu, sleeping on the snake Śeṣa; long live him who with a single tusk lifted up the extremities of the earth. Long live the man-lion who tore asunder the breast of the enemy; long live the soul of all; long live, at present, Vāmana, Keśava. Covered by his own veil of māyā, the embodiment of the world, Janārdana, long live the inconceivable one; long live him whose natures are countless, and who yet is one, the king. Prosper, O Hari, O One from whom all the derivatives of Prakṛti have grown; on you, O King of the World, rests the way of the dharma. Not you or I, and not Śiva or the thirty deities beginning with Indra, nor the hermits Sanaka, and so on, nor yogis, O Hari, are capable of knowing you. You are concealed by your veil of māyā in this world, O Lord of the World. What man will know you, O King of All, without your kindness? He who worships you, O Lord of pleasant Aspect, he alone knows you, and no other man does. O Master of the lord of Nandī, O King, O Vāmana, prosper for the sake of the origin of this world, All-Soul, O Large-eyed One.

Śaunaka spoke:

Thus praised, Hṛṣikeśa, having the form of a dwarf, laughing heartily, spoke to the lotus-born one: "I am praised by you, by Indra, and others, and by Kaśyapa before; the three worlds of Indra were promised to you by me. Moreover, having been praised by Aditi and also having promised to her, I will give the three worlds, freed from enemies, to Śakra. As I will do it, so Indra will be the lord of the earth, the thousand-eyed one. I speak the truth."

Then Brahmā gave the black antelope skin to Hṛṣikeśa; Bṛhaspati have the blessed one the sacred thread; Marici, son of Brahmā, gave an Āṣāṭha stick; and Vasiṣṭha the water jar; Angiras, a broom of kuśa grass; and Pulaha, a rosary string; Pulastya, two pure garments and the Vedas, adorned with *oṁ* and accents, all the śāstras, and the utterances of Saṁkhyā yoga. Having matted hair, holding a stick, an umbrella, and water jar, Vāmana, comprehending in him all gods, reached the sacrifice of Bali. Wherever the mighty Viṣṇu gave his step to a portion of ground, there the earth, having been pressed down, gave way to a chasm. Vāmana, having a slow and gentle gait, shook all the earth, together with mountains, oceans, and rivers.

Chapter 246

Śaunaka spoke:

Seeing the earth together with her mountains and forests shaking, Bali asked Uśanas, the faultless one, having bowed down, joining his palms together in obeisance, "O Teacher, why is the earth together with her oceans, mountains, and forests trembling, and why do the fires not accept the shares of the Asuras?" Thus questioned by Bali, Kāvya, best of the Veda knowers, the great-minded one, having thought a long time, spoke to the king of Daityas. "Hari, the eternal soul of the world, the womb of the world, descended in the house of Kaśyapa in a dwarf from. He walks to your sacrifice, O Bull among Daityas, putting down his feet, and from this shaking the earth is tremulous, these mountains and cami trees shake and the sea is agitated. The earth is not fit to carry the lord of beings, Iśvara, together with gods, demons, Gandharvas, Yakṣas, Rākṣases and Kiṁnaras. By this one are earth, fire, wind, and atmosphere preserved. The god preserves all men, and so forth, O Great Asura. Thus, this is the *māyā* of Kṛṣṇa; for the sake of the earth the world was held having the relation of the holder and that which is to be held. From that proximity, the Asuras are not entitled to a portion, O Best of Asuras, and thus because of him the fires do not accept the shares of the Asuras."

Bali spoke:

Fortunate am I and happy; the lord of sacrifice himself has come to my sacrifice, O brahmin; I am overjoyed! What other man is superior to me? The imperishable supreme soul, who the yogis, always absorbed in meditation, strive to see, the king of gods, he hastens toward my sacrifice. The hotṛ offers his share and the chanter praises him, the lord of sacrifice, Viṣṇu. I am overjoyed! What other man is superior? When the Lord of the Lord of All, Kṛṣṇa, arrives at my sacrifice, what can I do, O Kāvya: you are able to determine that.

Śukra spoke:

The gods enjoy the shares of sacrifice, resting on the authority of the Vedas, O Asura, but by you have the Daitya Dānavas been made enjoyers of the shares of sacrifice. And this god, abiding in sattva, made permanence in the world. The king himself, having created beings, devours them. Indeed the god Viṣṇu is intent upon staying: what will you do? Knowing this, O Fortunate One, you should do this. O King of Daityas, no vows are to be made by you, indeed even in trifling subject matters; the consideratory words will be in vain and fruitless. I am not able to give the words to be spoken by you to Kṛṣṇa, who is active for the purpose of the prosperity of the gods, O Great Asura.

Bali spoke:

O brahmin, how am I to answer, if I am begged by others; "There is nothing," when asked by the god Hari, the destroyer of the sins of saṁsāra? Hari is placated by the various observances of fasting, and when Govinda says "Give," what is better? Sacrifices rich in gifts are performed by those who are endowed with the qualities of honesty and tapas, for the purpose of him, the king of gods, who will say, "Give to me." That wise and meritorious deed, the special observance given by me, will the king of kings, Hari, accept? I will say, "There is nothing, there is nothing" to the lord, when he arrives. If I cheat him when he arrives, the fruit of my birth is in vain. If, at the sacrifice, Janārdana, the lord of sacrifice, asks me, I will give my own head without any hesitation. When asked by others, "There is nothing" was not spoken by me. How will I say that to Acyuta when he arrives? Indeed commendable is the misfortune of men met with from giving. Giving that does not cause pain is remembered as unlucky. In my kingdom, there is none who is full of pain, nor a beggar, nor unhealthy, nor unadorned, nor sorrowful, nor destitute of a wreath of garlands, and so forth. Merry, pleased, sweet smelling, and satisfied—all are possessed of every happiness. O Great fortunate One, how much more than all men am I happy! I am one whose recipients are excellent. That is the fruit grown from the seed of my giving. This is understood by me, O Best of Bhṛgus, by your grace. If, O Guru, my seed of giving falls on Janārdana, the great receptacle, what, then, is not to be gained by me? If, having obtained a gift from me, the king prospers the deities, my giving is ten times more praiseworthy than enjoyment. Indeed Hari approaches, devoted to grace for me, propitiated by sacrifice, no doubt doing a favor by his sight. Or, if he approaches with anger to kill him who is obstructing the share of the gods, thus murder by Acyuta is most praiseworthy. Thus all this universe consists of him for whom nothing is unattainable. When Hari approaches to ask me, it is not without favor. The Self-born One who creates all and can destroy it with his mind, how will Hṛṣikeśa try to kill me? Knowing this, O Guru, obstructing a gift is not what should be done when Jagannātha, Govinda approaches.

Śaunaka spoke:

Thus, while he was speaking, the lord of the world arrived, comprehending all the gods and having the illusory form of a dwarf. Seeing him appear at the edge of the sacrificial enclosure, the Asuras sitting in assembly became agitated, deprived of radiance by his tejas. There, assembled at the great sacrifice, the sages whispered, and Bali believed the whole of his existence was fruitful. Then, none of the trembling spoke at all, and the lord of the god of gods greeted them with his heart. Seeing the chief of Asuras bowing, and the best of the sages, the lord of the god of gods, Viṣṇu in the form of a dwarf, praised the sacrificial fire and honored the institutor of the sacrifice, he who performed the action of the sacrifice, the superintending priest, and the wooden implements. Then with reference to Vāmana, gracious and universal, standing at the sacrificial enclosure, the chief spoke thus, "Bravo, Bravo." Having received the guest respectfully, Bali, with body hairs bristling, worshiped Govinda, and the great Asura said this: "A mass of golden jewels, countless elephants and horses, women, garments, ornaments, and many villages, all my possessions, the entire earth or whatever you desire, that I shall give you. Choose what you need, O Beloved Dwarf."

Śaunaka spoke:

Thus spoken to by the chief of Daityas with words endowed with grace, the Lord in the form of a dwarf, smilingly and rumblingly spoke.

Vāmana spoke:

For the sake of a fire hall, give me three steps, O King. Golden jewels and villages give to those who desire them.

Bali spoke:

O Excellent One, what is the purpose of three steps? You must ask for hundreds of hundred thousands of steps.

Vāmana spoke:

O Lord of Daityas, I am satisfied by that small intention of dharma. To others who ask you can give wealth as wished for.

Śaunaka spoke:

Hearing the speech of the great-souled dwarf, the great-armed one gave to Vāmana three steps. As the water fell into his hand, Vāmana became a nondwarf; in an instant he exhibited the form containing all gods. The moon and sun were his eyes, heaven his head, the earth his foot, the Piśācas his toes and the Yakṣas his fingers. And the Viśvedevas were at his knees; the Sādhyas and the best of the gods, his shanks; the Yakṣas, his nails; and united in a continuous row, the Apsaras. His eyes were the seven stars; his hair the rays of the sun; the pores of his skin were the stars; and his body hairs the great ṛṣis. The intermediary regions were his arms; the cardinal points the ears of the Great Ātman; the Aśvins his earlobes; the wind the nose of the great Ātman. His grace was the moon god; in his mind dharma had come together; his speech was truth; his tongue was the goddess Sarasvatī. His neck was Aditi, mother of the gods; his bracelet was the Vedas; the gate of heaven was Maitrī; his eyebrows were Tvaṣṭṛ and Puṣān. His mouth was Agni Vaisvarana; his testicles Prajāpati; and his heart the supreme Brahmā; his manhood indeed the sage Kaśyapa. On his back were the gods Vasus; in all his joints the Maruts; his teeth all the Vedic hymns and the luminaries of stainless splendor. On the front of his chest was Mahādeva; and on his back the mighty oceans; and in his belly originated the Gandharvas, these strong ones. Indeed his hips were Lakṣmī, Medhā, Dhṛtī, Kantī, and all knowledge. All the lights, know that they were indeed the supremeness of him. The supreme tejas of him, of the god over the gods, had arisen. His breasts and abdomen were the Vedas; and his belly the great sacrifices, the sacrifice and animal sacrifices, and efforts of the twice borns. On seeing this godly form of Viṣṇu, the mighty ones, the chiefs of Daityas approached like moths to a flame. The king, tearing apart all the Asuras hand and foot, making his large-bodied form, he immediately conquered the earth. Striding over the earth, Candra and Aditya were at the center of his chest, then at the navel of him who was striding, then both were situated at the region of his thighs, and striding, the sun and moon were at the base of his knees. Viṣṇu, O Protector of the Earth, was acting as defender of the gods. On conquering all the three worlds and killing the bull of Asuras, Viṣṇu, the far stepping, gave the three worlds to Indra, the destroyer of strongholds. Sūtala, Pātāla, below the surface of the earth, was given to Bali by the lord Viṣṇu, the radiant Viṣṇu. Then Viṣṇu, the lord of all, spoke to the lord of Daityas.

The Blessed One spoke:

Inasmuch as that water which was given by you was received by my hand, for that you will have a good life the length of a kalpa, indeed, when the Vaivasvata Manvantara has passed, O Bali. But when the Savarṇika arrives, you will become Indra. The three worlds are given by me to the king of gods for a period of more than seventy-one caturyugas. I will restrain all who stand in the way. By the best devotion I am propitiated as before, O Bali, by Indra. On reaching the beautiful hell named Pātāla, dwell there, O Asura, while guarding it according to my instruction. There, crowded with hundreds of palaces, possessed of divine forests, ponds of fullblown lotuses, the best of rivers, flowing and pure, smelling sweet with incense, flowing, decorated with ornaments, and delighting in sandal and garlands, beautiful singing and dancing, you shall enjoy divers food and drink and comforts, O Great Asura, fulfilled by hundreds of women, you will stay this space of time. And as long as you do not quarrel with the priests and gods, so long then you will obtain these great pleasures. And if you quarrel with the priests and gods, then the nooses of Varuṇa will bind you, without a doubt. Learning this as instructed by me, you shall make no conflict with the gods or priests, O Chief of Daityas.

Śaunaka spoke:

Thus spoken to by the god, the majestic Viṣṇu, Bali questioned the great king, bowing down, filled with joy. "You have made my abode in Pātāla, the Lord having commanded it. What will be the causes of enjoyment and gifts there?"

The Blessed One spoke:

Gifts given not according to the rules prescribed, Śrāddhas without a brahmin, oblations without faith, these are those that will give you fruit. Not bringing dakṣinas to the priests, sacrifices not done according to the rules, learning without vows, these will give you fruit.

Śaunaka spoke:

Thus, giving this gift to Bali, but giving heaven to Śakra, by his omnipresent form Viṣṇu became invisible. Thus, as in olden times, Indra, honored by the three worlds, reigned, and Bali, residing in Pātāla, enjoyed his highest desires. And thus was the best of Dānavas bound by the god of gods, and for the sake of the gods he remains in the world.

O Great fortunate One, your relation is situated in Dvaraka for the annihilation of the Dānavas and the removal of the earth's burden, from where Kṛṣṇa, while in the tribe of the Yadus will seize the enemies, and joined by his companion Balarāma, will do the charioteering. Thus all is related of the learned Vāmana avatāra, O Great Hero, as you wished to hear it, O Arjuna.

Arjuna spoke:

Having heard this glorification of Keśava that was asked for, give me permission, O King; I will go from here to dwell at the Door of the Ganges.

The Bard spoke:

Having thus spoken, the Partha left and Śaunaka went to the Naimiṣa. Thus this was the glorification of Viṣṇu. He who recites this tale of Vāmana is freed from all evils. The conversations of Bali and Prahlāda, the discussion of Bali and Śukra, what was told of Bali and Viṣṇu, that man who remembers, for him there will never be mental anxiety or diseases, no agitated delusion of the mind at any time. The servant will become chief among twice borns. Hearing this which I tell, the man deprived of his own sovereignty gains the desired sovereignty and the Great Fortunate one who is bereft acquires what is desired.

Nārada Purāṇa I.10–11

Chapter 10

The one called Gaṅgā produced from Viṣṇu's toe, O Brother, tell me that one's origin, if I am to be favored by you.

Listen, O Nārada, I will tell you the origin of Gaṅgā, O Innocent One, which destroys sin and gives merit to those speaking of it and listening to it.

The sage Kaśyapa was the father of the gods, headed by Indra. His wives were Diti and Aditi, daughters of Dakṣa. Aditi was the mother of the gods, Diti mother of the Daityas. The progeny of the two were seeking victory over each other, O brahmin, for which reason the elder "Devas" are always called Daityas. The first Daitya, son of Diti, was Hiraṇyakaśipu, the strong. Prahlāda was his son, a very great Daitya chief. Virocana was his son; he was devoted to brahmins. His son was the very powerful Bali, possessor of majesty.

He was prince of an army of Daityas, O Sage. Endowed with great strength, he enjoyed this earth. Having conquered all the earth, he thought to conquer heaven.

How can his excellent army be described? Elephants and chariots, of which there are as many as ten thousand lacs of koṭis, and from elephant to elephant five hundred footmen. Kumbhānda and Kūpakarṇa were his chief ministers among the koṭis of other ministers. Bāṇa, son of Bali, was the best of a hundred sons. He was like his father in prowess and power.

Bali, whose mind was on victory over the gods, joined by a great army, advanced with banners and parasols resembling lightning and waves of the sky and ocean. Having reached the city of the enemy of Vṛtra, the Asura, standing firm, blocked that city with the help of lionlike Daityas. Then the gods, whose leader was the Wielder of the Thunderbolt, set out from that city to battle. Then the terrible battle of the gods and Daityas began, sounding like the thunder at the end of a kalpa; a clamor sounding like drums. The Daityas let loose a network of arrows at the army of the gods, and the gods also (did the same) to the army of Daityas in the exceedingly terrible battle. "Kill! Rend! Destroy! Pierce! Slay! Beat!" Thus was the great battle cry of the narrators of the two armies, together with the noises of Śara and Dundubhi, the lion's roar of the Asuras, the clanking of chariots and the "kren" sounds of the arrows themselves, and also the neighing of horses and bellowing of elephants, the howling of bows—all the world was full of sounds. Viewing the whole world, from the fire born from the striking of arrows released by the gods and demons, one thought there was an unseasonable pralaya. The demon army, bearing a multitude of listening swords, became like night, covered with clouds and flashing lightning. In that battle, a mountain was thrown by the terrible demons. The gods, swift in their valor, pounded that hill with iron arrows. Some hit elephants with elephants, chariots with chariots, some with horses struck horses with clubs and sticks. Some who were hit by iron clubs fell into the mud of blood; some whose lives were exhausted resorted to aerial carts. Daityas who were killed by the gods in the battle, having become gods, attacked the Daityas.

Then the angry troops of Daityas were being struck vehemently by the gods. With many piercing swords the terrible gods struck them down. With rocks, with thunderbolts, with swords, axes and javelins, with iron clubs and knives, missiles, discuses and spikes, and with maces, nooses and clenched fists, with spikes, spears, and iron arrows, weapons made of stone for throwing, with chariots, horses, elephants, and footmen, the battle grew fiercer. And the gods hurled diverse weapons at the Daityas. Thus for thousands of years that terrible battle went on. When the mighty Daityas prospered, the celestials were defeated. Having abandoned the world of the gods, all fled, terrified. Disguised in human form, they roamed about on the surface of the earth.

Bali, wholly devoted to Nārāyaṇa, his sovereignty unimpeded, his wealth increased like a great fire, he enjoyed the three worlds. And, engaged in gratifying Viṣṇu, he sacrificed with Aśvamedha ceremonies. He became Indra in heaven and took over the duties of the Dikpālas. For the purpose of pleasing the gods, sacrifices were made by brahmins. The Daitya king partook of all the sacrifices with oblations.

Beholding her own sons, Aditi, mother of the gods, was very distressed. "In vain I live here." Thinking this, she went to the place where Himavat resides. Desiring the sovereignty for Śakra and the conquest of the Daityas, having devoted herself to the highest meditation on Hari, she underwent austerities exceedingly difficult to perform. Sitting for a short time, and then standing on one foot for a very long time, then only on one toe, living on fruit for a little while, then eating dropped leaves, having only water, then living on air without any food, meditating with the ātman on the conception of the totality of being, knowledge, and bliss, O Nārada, she practiced austerities for thousands of divine years.

The cunning Daityas, having heard about such infinite tapas of Aditi, employed a divine form, and the mighty one approached her: "O Mother, for what purpose is this drying up of the body performed? If the Daityas know, then there might be great suffering. Give up these austerities that are full of suffering and cause the body to dry up. Learned men do not approve of these righteous deeds, accomplished with great effort. The body is to be protected diligently by those who are devoted to the dharma. Those who neglect their bodies become their own killers. Please stay happy, O Fortunate One, do not distress us and your sons. A person without a mother is well-nigh dead, no doubt, O Mother. Even among cows and beasts, where cows are orphans, abandoned by their mother, they obtain no pleasure and are as if dead. The poor and the diseased, and those traveling to another country, by only the sight of mother do they obtain great happiness. Sometimes a person becomes disinterested in food, water, gifts, affection, but never in mother. One whose mother is not home, if she is intent on virtue, a virtuous woman whose husband is her life, she should go to the forest. As there is dharma without devotion to Nārāyaṇa, as there is wealth without real pleasures, as there is home without wife and family, so there is man deprived of his mother. O Goddess, save your children who are distressed by the Daityas." Even though thus addressed, Aditi did not stir from her meditation.

Thus having spoken and having viewed her, intent on meditating on Hari, all the Asuras, full of anger, made a wish to kill her. Eyes inflamed with anger, sounding like the thunder at the end of a kalpa, through sharp teeth they emitted fire, and that fire burned the forest, which was one hundred yojanas wide and filled with various living beings. The Daityas who had gone to attack were burnt by it. The Mother of the gods, whose mind had been devoted to Acyuta for a century, survived, protected by the Sudarśana cakra of Viṣṇu, who was the death of the Daityas and who was compassionate toward his own people.

Chapter 11

> Indeed, this that you told me is very marvelous. How did that fire, having left Aditi, burn them in a moment? Please speak of Aditi's great power, which causes special wonder. Sages, who are virtuous men, are always engrossed in guiding others.

Hear, O Nārada, the glorification of those whose minds are intent upon devotion to Hari. Who is able to trouble good men engaged in meditation on Hari? Wherever there is a person devoted to Hari, there are Brahmā, Śiva, and Hari. Gods, siddhas, and munis will remain there eternally. O Eminent One, Hari resides in the heart of tranquil-minded ones, not to mention those intent on meditation on the highest name of Hari. Where one is devoted to the worship of Śiva and also to the highest worship of Viṣṇu, there resides Lakṣmī and all the gods. Where there is one who is devoted to the worship of Viṣṇu, there the fire does not go out, nor does the king or robber do harm, nor are there any diseases. Pretas, Piśācas, gourd seizers, and child seizers, Dakiṇīs, and even Rākṣases do not harm the worshipper of Acyuta. Ghosts and goblins, and so on, intent upon the worst harm, perish where there is an honest devotee intent on worshiping Lakṣmī and Hari. Where one dwells with subdued senses, who is beneficent to all, devoted to dharma and ritual acts, there are all the tīrthas and gods. Where yogis reside for a twinkling of an eye, or even half a twinkling of an eye, there is all well being that becomes a tīrtha, that becomes a religious grove. From the pronunciation of whose name all misfortune disappears, what can be said about meditation, or about worship, or hymns? O brahmin, thus the forest together with the demons was burnt by his fire. Aditi was not burned, protected by Viṣṇu's cakra.

Then, that one having a bright countenance, whose eyes are wide like lotus leaves, who bears the conch, cakra, and club, he became visible in her presence. Who illumined the faces of all the directions with the luster of his teeth and his shining smile, touching her with his holy hand, he spoke to the beloved of Kaśyapa. "O Mother of the gods, I am pleased; you have pleased me with your tapas. You have been making an effort for a long time; it will be fortunate for you, no doubt. Choose a boon! I will give you whatever is in your mind. Do not be afraid, O Beautiful, Illustrious One, there will surely be welfare." Having been spoken to by the god of gods who bears a discus, having bowed down, the Mother of the gods praised him who confers pleasure on all the worlds.

> Homage to you, O Lord of the god of gods, pervader of all, Janārdana, who is the cause of the activity of the world by the differentiation of the sattva and other guṇas. Homage to him who is many forms and who is formless, who is the magnanimous one, who is formless and who is all forms, who is without qualities and whose ātman has qualities. Homage to him, who is the protector of the world, who is the embodiment of supreme knowledge, who has affection for all people who are good devotees, and who is auspicious. Homage to the god whose forms as avatāras lords of munis worship, to the primal puruṣa, for the fulfillment of my desires. Homage to him, the cause of the world, whom the Vedas do not know, or sages do not know, who is with māyā and who is without māyā. I honor him who is the world form, the world cause, who is honored by all, and whose bright gaze is the cause of all the troubles of māyā. I honor him, lord of Kamalā, by the worship of whose lotuslike feet protected sages attain their highest goal. Whose majesty even Brahmā and the other gods do not know, I praise him, associating with devotees and being always close to devotees. He, ocean of compassion, who is the god of those who have given up attachment and who are peaceful, he is attached to the soul. I give homage to that god who is free from attachments, who is the lord of sacrifice, the act of sacrifice, who is well versed in sacrifice, who is the giver of the fruits of the sacrifice, who is the awakener of the act of sacrifice. I praise him, the eyes of the universe, after the pronunciation of whose name even the evil soul, Ajāmilo, attained the highest abode. Mahādeva in the form of Hari and Janārdana in the form of Śiva, I praise him,

> the leader of this world, the guru of the world. O lord of gods, Brahmā and the others, fettered by the bonds of māyā, do not know the supreme reality. I praise him, leader of all. He appears as if very far away to those who are unfit, even though he is residing in their lotuslike heart. I praise him, who beholds higher knowledge and whose existence is beyond any proof.
>
> From whose head the brahmin was born, from both his arms the kṣatriya arose; from his thighs the vaiśya was born; from his feet the śūdra was born. From his mind the moon was born; and from his eyes the sun was born; from his mouth the fire and Indra, and from his breath the wind was born. From his body came the Ṛg, Yajus, and Sāma Vedas, whose soul exists in the seven musical notes, who is the form of the six Vedāṅgas, I praise him more and more. You are Indra, the wind, and Soma; you are the ruler, you are death. You are the fire and even destruction; you are Varuṇa and the sun. You are gods and immovables and Piśācas and even Rākṣases, mountains, Siddhas, Gandharvas, rivers, earth, and oceans. You are the master of the worlds, you are higher than the highest. O God, from you comes all form; let me always pay homage to you. Master without a master, all-knowing, who was in the body of the last chief of the gods, O Janārdana, protect my sons who are oppressed by the Daityas.

The mother of the gods, having thus praised the god, bowing down again and again, her breasts washed with tears of joy, spoke, with folded hands. "I am favored by you, O Master of the gods, Primary cause of all. Give my sons, whose dwelling is in heaven, prosperity free from foes. O form of the world soul, all-knowing, supreme lord, O lord of Lakṣmī, what is unknown to you? Why do you make me wish for something? Then I will tell you that which my heart longs for, O Master of the gods. I am tormented by the Daityas; in vain do I have sons. I do not wish to kill them because they are also my sons. O Lord of Gods, having brought no harm to them, give prosperity to my sons." Having been spoken to, the master of the god of gods, pleased again, O brahmin, spoke to the mother of the gods with respect. "I am pleased, O Goddess, fortune to you! I will become your son, since love for the sons of a fellow wife is scarce, O Goddess. Those men who read the hymn composed by you, their sons will be prosperous and never decline. Who considers his own sons and others' sons equally, will have no grief from his sons; this is the eternal dharma." "I am not able to carry you, O god; you are the highest puruṣa, innumerable as hairs and eggs, the master of all, the cause of all. How can I carry one whose strength śruti and all the gods do not know, who is master of the god of gods, O Mighty One? Unborn, smaller than an atom, higher than the highest, mighty, how can I carry you, O God, the superior puruṣa? Even one intent upon great sins is released by merely remembering you. How can such a god be born among ordinary people? As are your boar, fish, and other avatāras, O Mighty One, so also is this one. Who knows your action, O Master of the universe? Bowed to your lotus feet, devoted to the remembrance of your name, O God, I think of you; I'll do whatever you desire." Having heard those words spoken, Janārdana, god of gods, having given protection to the mother of the gods, spoke these words.

> The truth has been spoken, O Illustrious One, there is no doubt. And listen, I will tell of the most mysterious of mysteries, Fair One. My devotees who are intent upon me, free from love and hate, those who are not pretentious, their jealousy gone, they always carry me. Those engaged in devotion to Śiva, not causing anyone distress, engaged in listening to my story, they always carry me. Also, women who are loyal to their husbands, who hold their husbands as dear as life itself, who are intent on devotion to their husbands, they, O Goddess, free from selfishness, they always carry me. He always carries me who serves his mother and father, who honors his guest, who is devoted to his guru, who is a benefactor to brahmins. Those constantly devoted to sacred shrines and intent on association with good, whose nature is doing good for the world, they always carry me. Those who engage in charity, those who look away from others' property, who are like hermaphrodites toward others' women, they always carry me. Those ever intent on worshiping the Tulasī, those devoted to my name, and those engrossed in tending cattle, they carry me eternally. Those who have given up the acceptance of gifts and who turn their faces from others' food, those who give food and water, they always carry me.
>
> But you, O Goddess, who hold your husband dearer than life itself, a holy woman, intent upon the well-being of creatures, by becoming your son I will accomplish your desire.

The master of the god of gods, having spoken to Aditi, mother of the gods, having given her the garland from around his neck, disappeared. And she, daughter of Dakṣa and mother of the gods, having bowed down to the beloved of Kamalā, returned to her own home, delighted.

Then illustrious Aditi, praised by the world, gave birth in time to a son who was praised by all the worlds. Bearing the conch and discus, tranquil, in the middle of the moon disc, holding a pitcher of nectar and rice with curds, he was called Vāmana. He was Hari, looking like a thousand Ādityas, with eyes like full-blown lotuses, furnished with all ornaments, and wearing yellow clothing, praised by bands of munis, the only ruler of all the world. Kaśyapa, overjoyed upon recognizing Hari manifest, having bowed and having joined his hands together, began to praise him.

> Homage be to you, the cause of all; homage to you, the guardian of all; homage to you, the leader of the gods; homage, homage to the destroyer of the Daityas.
>
> Homage, homage to the beloved of the devotees; homage to the one who is delighted with virtuous people; homage to the destroyer of wickedness; homage be to him, the lord of the world.
>
> Glory, glory to him who has become a dwarf for some reason, to Nārāyaṇa, to him whose step is unbounded, to him who bears a club, sword, discus, and bow; glory to him, the supreme puruṣa.
>
> Glory to him residing in the ocean; glory be to the one who dwells in the hearts of the virtuous; glory be to him whose radiance is more infinite than the sun; glory, glory to him who is the object of holy tales.
>
> Glory, glory to him whose eyes are the sun and moon; glory be to him, giver of the fruit of the sacrifice; glory to him who shines through the body of the sacrifice; glory to him, beloved of the virtuous.
>
> Glory to the cause of the cause of the world; glory be to him who is free from sound; and so forth. Glory be to him, giver of heavenly pleasure; glory, glory to him who dwells in the heart of the devotee.
>
> Glory be to you, destroyer of darkness; glory be to you, pillar of Mt. Mandara; glory be to you in the form of the sacrificial boar; glory to you, who tore asunder Hiraṇyākṣa.
>
> Glory be to you, possessor of the form of a dwarf; glory be to you, the death of the kṣatriya family; glory be to you, destroyer of Rāvaṇa; glory be to you, first born of Nanda's sons.
>
> Glory to you, beloved of Kamalā, glory to you who gives pleasure, to the destroyer of misery as soon as you are remembered, to you, many, many obeisances.
>
> Master of the sacrifice, foundation of the sacrifice, destroyer of obstacles to the sacrifice, who is of the form of the sacrifice,

who is of the form of the sacrificer, body of the sacrifice, I worship you.

Thus praised, the master of the gods, the world purifier, Vāmana spoke, laughing, increasing the delight of Kaśyapa. "O Father, I am pleased; you will be fortunate, O Honored of the gods. Soon, you will attain all your heart's desires. I have become your son in two lives. In this life also will I attain the highest virtue."

Meanwhile, the Daitya Bali began a great sacrifice, lasting a long time, joined by his guru, kāvya, and muni lords. At his sacrifice was Viṣṇu together with Lakṣmī invoked by the ṛṣis, who were discoursing on sacred texts, for the sake of accepting the oblation.

Having taken leave of his parents, the boy dwarf came to that continuing sacrifice of the Daitya whose sovereignty was mighty. Bewildering the world with a smile, Vāmana, devoted to his devotees, appeared before Bali's eyes, as if he had come to eat the offering. Whether bad or dumb or friendly, whoever is intent on devotion, Hari remains close to him. The ṛṣis, having seen Vāmana finally arrive through their eyes of knowledge, having recognized the god Nārāyaṇa, they rose together with those in the assembly hall. Realizing this, the Daitya's guru spoke to Bali alone.

Bad people act without considering their own prowess. Greetings, chief of Daityas, O good sir! Viṣṇu with his dwarfish form has become the son of Aditi and will steal your wealth. Hear my opinion, Wise One; he approaches your sacrifice. O Chief of Asuras, do not give him anything. Your own thinking and especially a guru's thinking causes happiness. But acting according to what others think and according to what women think will bring ruin. But one who does a favor to his enemies should be destroyed.

Bali spoke:

O Guru, you should not say something that opposes the path of dharma. That which Viṣṇu takes on his own, what is better than that? The wise perform sacrifices for the sake of pleasing Viṣṇu; and if he himself is the eater of the oblations, who is happier on earth than me? O Guru, the little bit given to Viṣṇu by a poor man, that becomes a superior gift, and is imperishable. The supreme puruṣa purifies even if just remembered with the highest devotion. If worshiped by someone or another, he grants the highest path. Hari destroys evil if remembered

> even by an evil heart; even though unwilling, if touched, fire burns. He on the tip of whose tongue dwell the syllables *Ha-ri,* he attains the Viṣṇuloka, where rebirth is scarce. He who is always repeating "Govinda" without passions, and so on, the sages say he will go to Viṣṇu's dwelling place. O Guru, that oblation which is offered into the fire or to brahmins with devotion to Hari, Illustrious One, that pleases Viṣṇu. But for the purpose of pleasing Hari, I will perform the best of sacrifices. I will be satisfied, no doubt, if Viṣṇu himself comes.

Thus, while the Daitya chief was speaking, Viṣṇu, in the form of a dwarf, entered the place of sacrifice, beautiful with the fire into which oblations were being offered. Having seen the dwarf resembling a thousand suns and possessed of handsome limbs, quickly standing up he [Bali] received him in a respectful posture. Having granted him a seat and having washed the feet of the dwarfish one, holding him in highest honor together with his family, he obtained supreme delight. Bali, having given water to Viṣṇu, refuge of the world, according to rule, with the hair of his body bristling and with tears of joy in his eyes, he spoke.

> Today, my birth is fruitful, today my sacrifice is fruitful, today my life is fruitful; I am fulfilled, no doubt. An exceedingly rare, fruitful shower of amṛta has come to me; merely by your coming, it is easily a festival. And all the ṛṣis who previously practiced austerities are no doubt fulfilled; today those austerities are fruitful, O Mighty One. I am content; I am satisfied; I am fulfilled, no doubt. Because of that, homage to you, homage to you, homage, homage. With your permission, at your command I will do whatever you ask. Provided with great enthusiasm, command me, Lord.

Thus having been spoken to by the sacrificiant, Vāmana spoke, smilingly, "Give me land measuring three steps for the purpose of practicing austerities." Bali, having heard this, spoke: "You have not requested the sovereignty or villages or cities or even riches; what are you doing?" Having heard that, Viṣṇu, (as though creating disinterest in him) endowed with all bodies, spoke to Bali, who was nearing a fall from his sovereignty.

> Listen, O Daitya chief, I will tell the most mysterious of mysteries. What is to be accomplished by worldly prosperity, tell me? You know that I am the one who dwells inside all beings.

All this dwells inside me; what is to be accomplished by others? Tell me. Of those who have abandoned love and hate, of those who are tranquil, who have abandoned deception, of those whose own form is eternal bliss, what is to be accomplished by wealth? Of those with tranquil minds seeing all beings like oneself, for such people everything is not separate from the self; who is the giver? What is given? This earth is under the power of the kṣatriyas—thus it is decreed in the śāstras. All obtain the highest pleasure who obey that authority. O Bali, one-sixth part is to be given to kings even by munis. This earth is to be given to brahmins by all means.

The glorification of the gift of land could not be made better. The giver of land attains supreme nirvāṇa; there is no doubt. Having given even a little land to the sacrificer learned in the Vedas, one attains the Brahmaloka, where rebirth is rare. The giver of land is called *all-bestowing;* the giver of land can attain final emancipation. It is to be known as munificence, and it destroys all evils. One possessed of a great sin, even one possessing all sins, having given ten hands worth of land, he is freed from all evils. Who gives land to a worthy person, he can obtain the fruit of all gifts. No other gift equal to the gift of land is known in the world. Bali, he who gives land to twice borns whose condition is needy, the reward of his good works I could not even tell in hundreds of years. O Daitya chief, he who would give even a little land to the needy, to those engaged in devotion to gods, he is Viṣṇu, no doubt. He by whom earth is given, full of sugar cane, wheat, nuts, tuvarī, trees, and so on, he is Viṣṇu, there is no doubt. Having given even a little land to brahmins who are poor, to needy householders, he may attain union with Viṣṇu. Having given land sown with Aḍhaka seed to brahmins engaged in the worship of god, one can gain the fruit of a three-day ablution in the Ganges. And having given land yielding a droṇa of grain to a needy brahmin intent upon perpetual wandering, listen to what fruit is gained! The fruit a man obtains having performed hundreds of aśvamedha sacrifices at the holy site of the Ganges, according to rule, *that* excellent fruit is obtained. He who gives land sown with seed measuring a khārika to a needy twice born, of that I will speak further; listen to me while I speak. Having performed thousands of aśvamedha sacrifices and hundreds of vājapeya sacrifices on the banks of the Ganges, *that* fruit is surely gained. That great gift, the gift of land, proclaimed as the superior gift, yields the fruit of final emancipation, curing all evils.

Listen, Lord of the Daitya clan, I will now tell that legend which, listened to attentively, yields the fruit of the gift of land.

O Bali, once upon a time in the Brahmā kalpa, there was a great-minded brahmin who was needy and wanting, by the name of Bhadramati. By him who knew the Vedas were all the śāstras, Purāṇas, and Dharmaśāstras heard. He had six wives named Śruti, Yasovatī, Kāminī, Malinī, and even one named Śobhā. From these wives he had two hundred and forty sons. O Best of Asuras, all of his sons were always hungry. Bhadramati, utterly destitute, seeing his beloved children afflicted with hunger and himself afflicted with hunger, moaned, his senses confused. "Fie on this miserable birth! Fie on this poor birth! Woe is this life which is without dharma! Fie on this life which is ignorant! Woe is the life without prosperity for the man who has many children. Alas, qualities, kindness, wisdom, and birth in a good family, all this looks bad to one who has plunged into the ocean of poverty. Beloved sons and grandsons, relatives, and brothers, pupils, all men abandon one who is devoid of wealth. A Caṇḍāla or a brahmin, if he is lucky, is honored. A needy man in this world is looked upon by people like a corpse. One who is successful, one who is cruel, or not cruel, one who is lacking qualities or one endowed with qualities, one who is stupid or one who is wise, if he is furnished with wealth he is to be respected, no doubt.

"Alas, poverty is suffering, and hope brings much pain. Men who are overpowered with hope suffer endlessly. Those who are slaves of hope are the slaves of all the world. Of those whose slave is hope, the world becomes their slave. For the great, honor is considered endless wealth in the world. Where honor is destroyed by the enemy called hope, there is poverty. A beggar who knows the essence of all the sciences appears as a fool; who is the savior of those seized by the great crocodile of poverty? Alas, poverty is suffering, pain, and sorrow, and an abundance of wives and sons brings great suffering."

Having thus spoken, Bhadramati, fully conversant with the meaning of all the śāstras, then thought of other dharma that might bring him wealth. Having decided that the gift of land is the very best of all gifts, he did what one does who honors with a gift. Yielding the fruit of all desires, establishing the highest dharma, the gift of land is proclaimed as the best of all gifts. Having given land, a man gains whatever he seeks. Thus having decided, the intelligent and gracious Bhadramati, joined by wife and child, went to the town called Kauśambi. The chief of brahmins there, named Sughoṣa, was fully endowed with all wealth. O Bali, having gone there, he asked for land measuring five hands. Sughoṣa, devoted to the dharma, having seen the householder and having greeted him, pleased, he spoke: "I am fulfilled, O Bhadramati, and my life is fruitful. My family became pure from your kindness, O Twice born." Having said this and having greeted him, great-minded Sughoṣa, devoted to the dharma, gave him land measuring five hands. "Viṣṇu's land, pure land protected by Viṣṇu, by the gift of land may Janārdana be pleased with me." With another mantra, O Daitya Chief, Sughoṣa gave land to the best of twice borns. Having honored him by considering him Viṣṇu, he gave him as much land as the wise brahmin Bhadramati asked for. Having given to the householder who was a devotee of Hari and conversant in the Vedas, through that gift of land Sughoṣa, together with his ancestors, soared to the dwelling place of Viṣṇu where one does not suffer. And, Bali, henceforth Bhadramati achieved his desires. Residing in Viṣṇu's dwelling place with his family for unbounded yugas and remaining in Brahmā's residence for unending koṭis of yugas, having attained Indra's abode, residing there for five kalpas, then, having reached the earth, fully endowed with all prosperity, the Illustrious One, remembering previous births, enjoyed the greatest pleasure. Then, O Daitya, Bhadramati, without a desire and fully devoted to Viṣṇu, gave land to needy brahmins. Viṣṇu, whose soul is pure, who was pleased, having given unsurpassed wealth, gave supreme liberation to him and his ancestors.

Therefore, O Daitya-lord, devoted to all dharma, give me my three steps of land so that I can perform austerities for liberation.

Then Vairocani, thrilled, took the pitcher full of water to give the earth to the brahmacārin Vāmana. The omnipresent Viṣṇu, having seen the kāvya obstructing the stream of water, put the tip of the darbha grass in his hand. The tip of that grass became a powerful weapon, equal in splendor to a koṭi of suns. Hitting its mark, like the magical recital of hymns, it was desirous of destroying the eyes of the kāvya. Śukra went to the gods and Asuras with one eye and pointed out the tip of the darbha grass, which resembled a weapon.

Bali gave mighty Viṣṇu land measuring three steps. Then the universal soul rose up to Brahmā's dwelling place; with two steps, Hari, whose body is the universe, traversed the earth. Brilliant, he took these steps from the nether regions to Brahmā's abode. The tip of his big toe pierced the Brahmāṇḍa, breaking it in half, and from that opening came water in the form of many streams, joined together and flowing, which washed Visṇu's foot, purifying the world. That superior, purifying water that had its abode outside the Brahmāṇda and had the form of streams washed the gods beginning with Brahmā, and, enjoyed by the seven ṛṣis, it rushed down upon the summit of Meru.

Having seen this happen, the host of gods with Brahmā at the head, ṛṣis, and Manus, overjoyed, sang a hymn of praise.

> Homage to you, the highest lord, to the embodiment of the highest soul, to the highest of high, to him who bears the form that has no superior, to the soul of Brahmā, to him whose mind and soul are devoted to Brahmā; homage be to him whose virtuous acts are unimpeded.
>
> O Highest Lord, O Superior Soul, better than the best, Obeisance to you, the Universal Soul, the embodiment of the world, beyond measurement.
>
> Homage to him whose two eyes are everywhere, whose arms are everywhere, homage to him whose head is everywhere, and whose gait is everywhere.

Thus praised by the heavenly sky dwellers, Brahmā and the others, having offered them protection, the mighty Viṣṇu, the eternal god of gods, was pleased. He bound the Daitya, son of Virocana, for the sake of one step. Then, having acknowledged Bali, who had fallen to his feet, he gave him Rasātala, and he who is at the service of his devotees became the doorkeeper.

What did the mighty Viṣṇu arrange as food for the son of Virocana in awful Rasātala, which is full of terrifying snakes? Sacrifice unaccompanied by Vedic formula is offered into the fire, and the awful food of worship given to an unworthy recipient. The oblation offered by an impure person or the gift given by such a person or a good deed done by such a person, that becomes worthy of enjoyment there, the fruit of which has fallen.

Thus, having given Rasātala to the demon Bali, Viṣṇu gave heaven to all the gods. Propitiated by the assemblages of immortals, praised by the maharṣis, and hymned by the Gandharvas, he assumed the form of a dwarf again.

Having seen this mighty act, the munis, discoursing on sacred texts, with smiling faces bowed down before the highest being.

Creator of all beings, Viṣṇu in a dwarfish form, bewildering the entire world, set out to the forest for austerities.

This was the story of the majestic goddess Gaṅgā, who sprang from Viṣṇu's step, by merely the recollection of which one is freed from all sins. And whoever hears this recitation of the glorification of Gaṅgā, on the river bank or at the temple, he may gain the fruit of the Aśvamedha sacrifice.

Padma Purāṇa Sṛṣṭikhaṇḍa 25

Bhīṣma spoke:

O best of Brahmins, having heard that ancient tale through your kindness; knowing it, one is freed from evils, and hearing it, one partakes of merit; I want to hear of the wonderful glorification of this tīrtha. Tell at length, O Brahmin, that which frees man, having heard it.

Pulastya spoke:

There are many holy tīrthas, O Virtuous One, the telling of which might also cause the destruction of a heinous crime. The sight of tīrthas, bathing and dipping there again, the recollection of all tīrthas brings the reward of objects that are desired. Indeed, mountains, rivers, and tīrthas are told of, fields and hermitages, O Bhīṣma, Mānasa, and other lakes. For one who goes on a pilgrimage, having kept those tīrthas in mind, there is at every step the fruit of sacrifices beginning with the Aśvamedha, no doubt. Of which of them should I speak here, tell me the truth?

Bhīṣma said:

I want to hear the deed of Viṣṇu from you, O Best of Twice borns. Having reached the sacrificial mountain, those footsteps made by Viṣṇu, mighty Viṣṇu, for what purpose were they made by the god of gods, O Wise One, Great-minded One, tell me. Which Dānava was subdued here by Viṣṇu, having placed down his foot? Tell this to me, O Great Sage. The mighty one Viṣṇu, his dwelling is in the heavenly Vaikuṇṭha. How did he make his footprint in the world of men? In the world of gods, the gods accompanied by Indra are devoted eternally to that mighty god through great tapas, O brahmin. Without devotion, not a single one is able to see the lord. The mighty dwelling of the divine boar is said to be in the Maharloka, and the great dwelling of the man-lion is proclaimed in the Janaloka, the dwelling of Trivikrama is said to be in the Tapaloka. Having left these worlds, why are there a pair of footsteps on earth, on the sacrificial mountain in Puṣkara, and on the field of Brahmā? Tell me about these steps in detail, O brahmin. By listening, the annihilation of all evils will become certain.

Pulastya spoke:

Asked properly by you, dear child, listen intently to the manner in which the footprints were made by the god Viṣṇu long ago.

All this was done by Viṣṇu for the sake of the earth, O Subduer of Foes, when all heaven was overcome by the strongest of Dānavas. Having conquered the three worlds honorably, the Devas together with Indra, those stronger Dānavas were the enjoyers of the sacrifice. All this was done by Bāṣkali, the most powerful Dānava. This being the case in the triple world, that world of everything moving and unmoving, Śakra himself became depressed and without hope of life. "Bāṣkali, chief of Dānavas, is invincible in battle with me; by Brahmā's granting of the boon, he is also unslayable by the celestials. Surrounded in the world of Brahmā by all the celestials, I will seek refuge in god; there is no other way." Having thought this, the chief of gods, surrounded by all the celestials, went quickly to the Grandfather. Upon reaching the dwelling of Brahmā, surrounded by the inhabitants of heaven, Indra told him what was to be done in the world and the calamity that had befallen him.

Indra spoke:

Don't you know why our life has become like this? By your giving of boons, all has been collected by the Daityas! Thus everything has been related by me. Something must be done with evil-minded Bāṣkali immediately. You are our father, O Grandfather, you must do something. Think on the matter, O Lord of Gods, for the sake of peace in the world. With those who do not observe anything connected with Veda and Śruti, the rituals do not go on. Because of them, day by day ours is the loss.

As is said by common people whose interest is themselves,

so we, whose benefits have disappeared, speak to you, O Lord. When a benefit is done by a person, it is multiplied a thousandfold by him. The evil-minded one, who does not really do it for others, he is burned by that help. He who is shameless, who is evil-minded, who does bad deeds, there is no place for him even in hell. When one does something only out of reciprocity, that act does not make him righteous. This also does not happen to those who are of still lower minds, with self-interest, for whom there is no place in the world but suffering. His heart rent a hundredfold, he does not attain any satisfaction, wherever he may go.

Rescue us who are drowning in misery, by telling us how our might may increase, having seen the bad condition of this world, as I mentioned, where neither studying the Vedas nor calling for sacrifices exists, desisting from auspicious celebration, where the chain of study is abandoned, where livelihood and family life have been given up, deprived of justice, nothing but breath remaining, the world has attained suffering and even worse conditions. We are exhausted by this time.

Brahmā spoke:

I know that Bāṣkali, wicked and haughty from the giving of boons, is invincible to you. He will be conquered by Viṣṇu.

Pulastya spoke:

Having controlled his inner organs, Brahmā remained intent. While meditating on that god who has four arms, through Brahmā's meditation, Viṣṇu arrived shortly while all were looking on.

Viṣṇu spoke:

Greetings, Brahmā. Stop this meditation. Whatever purpose was desired by your meditation, for that I have arrived.

Brahmā spoke:

The appearance of the lord here is a great favor. Whose else would the concern of the world be? First of all, his birth has been brought about for the sake of the world. This is the world. This is its purpose. There is really no surprise. Protecting is to be done by you as Rudra is assigned to destruction. This being the case, magnanimous Śakra's sovereignty of the three worlds, everything moving and unmoving, has been seized by Bāṣkali. Assistance must be rendered to your servant through the gift of a mantra, O Keśava.

Vāsudeva spoke:

But that Dānava, presently invincible by the giving of your boon, is to be made conquerable by the mind, by fettering him. I will become a dwarf, the destroyer of the Dānavas. Together with me Indra must go to the dwelling place of Bāṣkali. Arriving there, he must ask for a wish, for my sake: "Three steps of land for the brahmin dwarf, O King. You must grant this request of mine." Spoken to by Indra, the Lord of Dānavas may give even his own life! O Grandfather, having received the gifts of the Dānava, having deceived him, then binding him and making Pātāla his dwelling place, I will employ the form of the boar for the purpose of destroying the evil-minded one, no doubt. Go quickly, Śakra.

Pulastya spoke:

Having said this to him, he disappeared. Then, after some time, when Viṣṇu had entered Aditi's womb, auspicious omens were manifested in great numbers as Viṣṇu, support of the entire earth, became an embryo. A splendid omen indicating hostility toward the Dānavas, the sweet-smelling fragrance of jasmine flowers, was diffused. Then, having reached the prescribed measure of time, sympathizing with all beings, the god of gods, whose luster was that of the rising of a sliver of the moon, became the offspring of Aditi for the sake of the welfare of the host of thirty-three gods. While Viṣṇu descended, the faces of the Siddhas, Devas, and Asuras, whose eyes do not blink, shone with happiness. And the day, with winds blowing entirely without dust, that day the birth of Viṣṇu was in a good womb. Indeed, as he entered her womb, the goddess, afflicted by fatigue and by the weight of her bent-down belly, beautiful in her slow gait, exhaustion in her pale, tired face, quite heavy, was carrying the embryo inside of her. When indeed Nārāyaṇa entered the womb for the sake of the past and future, the desires of all beings were then attained without distress. A breeze blew softly while the rain fell, springing from the mountains. Indeed, people entered into a state of truthfulness, the roads of the intermediate regions were clear, the sky was freed from dust and the darkness slowly perished.

While Viṣṇu was inside Aditi's womb, a sense of threat originated in Aditi. Hear it from me, O Chief of Kings. "How can I, by one step, traverse Indra's heaven, and how is Bāṣkali, chief of Dānavas, to be made to dwell in Pātāla? The wealth and beauty of Śakra have been given by me. Thus I alone will be born for the annihilation of the Dānavas. I can dispatch masses of arrows, innumerable flying discuses, and manifold devastating clubs for the annihilation of the Dānavas. I will make the gods dwell in heaven and the Dānavas below the earth after a while. That deed cannot be done without me." Thus he spoke briskly. He who thought this had neither been seen nor heard. "Seeing me perform the binding of the chief of Danus with fury, previously having given beauty, wealth, and a gift to Kaśyapa, what is this upheaval of mind that flies about like the winds, greatly agitated, as though my sight has been blurred? No such form has been imagined. As though possessed, I am saying words unlike anyone else." Having become doubtful, Aditi thought about it constantly, as she carried the divine lord for a thousand celestial years.

Then a dwarf was born to her, causing welfare among living beings. When the god of gods, Janārdana, was just born, by whose birth the sight of the Dānava was taken away, the rivers carried clear water, the wind blew, bearing fragrance, and Kaśyapa obtained delight through his splendid son. The minds of all those dwelling inside the tripleworld were joyful. But when Janārdana was just born, then in the Svarloka the drums sounded. Out of the delight of the triple world, delusion and suffering were destroyed, and the host of Gandharvas sang beyond measure with loud sounds, accompanied by their master. Indeed the wives of the gods, endowed with heavy breasts, danced there, as did the assemblage of Apsarases. Then an assembly of joyful Vidyādharas and Siddhas wandered about in a celestial car. They spoke the conclusion of true and false deeds, then they acted on the stage. They sang a song, having melodies which went up and down, being at one moment sad, at the next happy. Those who have gone to heaven dance, and from now on, people will attain heaven by their dharma. Thus, while depression was gone from the resplendent Jīvaloka, those whose desires were attained were freed from the mass of darkness and desirous of reaching happiness. Rejoicing, some spoke aloud,

"Victory, victory, O Blessed One." Some were very happy, having spoken continually with shouts, then others whose minds were not ceasing spoke with loud cries, "Very good, very good!" Others meditated on the secret of the cause of birth, disease, old age, death, and destruction. Thus, in all this entire world, there was rejoicing everywhere. This highest soul Viṣṇu, lord of the world, made by Brahmā to take on deformity for the sake of the world, he is Brahmā and he is Viṣṇu and Maheśvara, and he is the gods and the sacrifices and heaven, no doubt. All this world, standing and moving, is pervaded by Viṣṇu. While he is one, he is in various forms, self-born, thus reknown. Just as the crystal jewel becomes variegated in a place whose color is accordingly, by virtue of its quality, so the Self-born One has his color through contact with the guṇas. Just as yonder household fire is named differently, namely dakṣina, ahavanīya, and so on, thus he takes on all the names of Brahmā and the others. The god Vāmana will accomplish the matter of the gods in all cases.

While the celebrated gods were thinking thus, he went, accompanied by Śakra, to the abode of Bāṣkali. He saw the city from far away, which was encircled and beautiful with eminent mansions reaching the sky, decorated with all kinds of beautiful jewels, and having well-spaced roads; that city was glorious with elephants in rut, resembling mountains of mascara, hundreds of elephants born in the lineage of the elephants of the gods. The city was brilliant with horses whose limbs were lean and had tiny ears, who were as swift as thought, charming, whose necks, foreheads, and eyes were long and beautiful. There were courtesans by the thousands, skillful in conversation, who had the brilliance of the interior of lotuses and whose faces resembled the full moon. There was no virtue or knowledge or sculpture or art that did not reside there in the city of Bāṣkali. Abounding with hundreds of gardens, garlanded by meetings and feasts of merriment it was inhabited by the Danu leaders, all free from death. That city was reverberant with the sound of lutes, fifes, and drums everywhere. The Dānavas, continually rejoicing, resplendent with many jewels, were seen sporting just like the immortals on Meru. A loud sound of prayers was uttered there by hosts of brahmins. Sin vanished with the winds and the vapor of ghee of the fires, winds that were made fragrant by the discharging of sweet-smelling incense. In his city filled with fragrant Dānavas, the Dānava Bāṣkali, having established his authority, dwelled happily in the three worlds. Knowing the law and knowing what is right and speaking the truth, abiding there, the ascetic ruled the three worlds, everything moving and unmoving. Beautiful to see, familiar with good and bad policy of all living beings, sympathizing with the poor and wretched, devoted to religious knowledge and affording protection, endowed with regal power consisting in personal preeminence, good counsel according to the Veda, and energy, having the six qualities of the five senses and strength, he spoke with a smile. Knowing the essence of Veda and Vedāṅga, sacrificer of sacrifices, rejoicing in austerities, not vulgar, devoted to morality, not injuring any creature, respecting those worthy of respect, faultless and handsome, honoring those who are honorable, knowing all things, invincible, possessing good fortune, kind looking, bestowing much wealth, having much grain and giving many gifts—that Dānava, productive of the three goals, was forever the best of men in the triple world.

Thus, living eternally in his own city, destroying the pride of gods and Dānavas, he ruled all the people in the three worlds. There was no adharma whatsoever while the Dānava was king. No one was distressed nor was anyone afflicted with disease, nor short lived, nor pained, neither was anyone stupid, nor had a sluggish appearance, nor unlucky, nor despised.

Upon seeing all excellence in one body, and having rejoiced, the Magnanimous Indra, whose knowledge is distinguished, reached the chief of Danus, placating that best of Daityas. Seeing the Dānava who was endowed with tejas, who was like the shining sun, Indra, capable of supporting the three worlds, was amazed. Having gone through the king's palace, on arrival, the Dānavas, made fierce in battle, said this to the royal chief of Dānavas:

The Dānavas spoke:

Oh, a miracle! Indra approaches your city, O Mighty One. He is alone with the chief of twice borns, a dwarf! What should we do today? Please tell us that. (He spoke to all the Dānavas in his adorned city.) The honorable king of gods is to be let in. He shall be honored by me today.

Pulastya spoke:

The chief of Dānavas, having spoken and having restrained the Dānavas, went forth alone, waiting for the sight of

Śakra in the seventh enclosure of his adorned city. At that time, Vāmana and Indra arrived and were seen and approached with affection by the lord of Dānavas, who made a bow, regarding himself fulfilled. That leader of the Dānavas spoke these words. Thrilled, he thought, "Nobody is as fortunate as I. I, who am prosperity and wealth, see Śakra has arrived at my house to ask. Desirous, he will solicit me. I will surely give even my life breath to this guest; wives, sons, dwellings. So why talk only of the three worlds?" Facing his guest, he put him on his lap, showing respect. Having embraced and greeted him, he brought him into his own home. Having performed pūjā zealously with a vessel for water and food, Bāṣkali said: "Today my life is fruitful, all my heart's desires are fulfilled. Today, O Śakra, I see you, yourself, who are my houseguest. I have been made famous among the chiefs of Dānavas by you, O King of Gods. Even before, I was meritorious. That fruit which comes with the agniṣṭoma and other sacrifices performed properly, that fruit can be obtained by seeing you, O Destroyer of Strongholds. That fruit which is attained by a gift of land or a gift of cows to a priest, that fruit has become mine today, or perhaps even that fruit which belongs to the Rājasūya. By no little tapas is one provided with the sight of you, O Vāsava. Thus, you must tell me what you wish to be done. Do not hesitate in any way. Know that it shall be done, even if it might be very difficult to accomplish. I am pure, having attained purity from the sight of you, O Slayer of Foes. You who are praiseworthy by the best of gods, your two feet will be celebrated by me. Why have you come? Tell me, O Mighty One. I think the reason for your coming is miraculous."

Indra spoke:

I recognize the chief of the chief of Dānavas, O Bāṣkali. There appears no miracle in your sight, O Best of Demons. Your guests do not go away disappointed. You are the wishing tree of those who desire something, and there is no other donor like you. In splendor, you are like the sun, in depth, resembling the ocean, in patience like the earth, in prosperity like Nārāyaṇa. This dwarf is a brahmin born in the auspicious family of Kaśyapa. I have been asked by him only, "Give me three steps of land for the purpose of my sacrificial fire hut, with which I can perform sacrifice." With this as the reason, the land is requested from you, O Mighty One. O Bāṣkali, having shown your valor, the three worlds were taken away from me by you. I am without property and resourceless. What I should give is not mine, so I will ask you for another's sake as well as my own. The request is not mine but his; do what is fitting. You are also born in the family of Kaśyapa, augmenting that family. You, who are born from the womb of Diti, are a father, honored by the three worlds. Having recognized you as such, I ask you; may he be given three steps for the purpose of a fire-hut? O Dānava, the limbs of the dwarf are very small, and I am not able to give while on alien territory. Only this much is given by me, that which you are requested for by me. If wise men approve and counselor and younger brothers and relatives and others approve, then may you give three steps of land to him. Having consulted your own family with my request, do what is fitting for you when I have come to your house, O Hero, if it is pleasing to you. That should be given immediately to the dwarf, O Great-minded One.

Bāṣkali spoke:

O King of Gods, I wish you welcome! Hail to thee; be well. Consider yourself the refuge of all. Having given possession of the burden to you, the Grandfather sits comfortably, absorbed in meditation, thinking of that highest step. Having disregarded thoughts about the world, exhausted by many battles, having sought attachment to the Ocean of Milk, Keśava sleeps happily. On the best of mountains, Kailāsa, Rudra, Lord of Umā, sports with his wife, having put the burden on you. Previously, O Śakra, all other Dānavas, stronger than the strong, were destroyed by you, without any help. The twelve Ādityas, also the eleven Rudras, the Aśvins, the Vasus, and even the eternal dharma, having recourse to the power of your arms, share the sacrifices in heaven, a hundred sacrifices that were sacrificed by you, ending with excellent gifts. Vṛtra and Namuci were slain by you, O Indra. By Viṣṇu, mighty Viṣṇu, who obeys your orders, was Hiraṇyakaśipu slain here, having taken him on his lap. Having seen you on the battlefield, wielding the thunderbolt, approaching on top of Airāvaṇa, all the Dānavas perish, those powerful Dānavas who formerly were defeated by you. In no way am I equal to you in a thousandth portion, O God of Gods; you are like this; what am I? Your coming here is surely for my rescue. No doubt, I will do it; I would give even my life breath. What good is this land spoken of by you, the king of gods, to me? These wives, children, cows, and so forth, the sovereignty of the three worlds, O Indra, must be given to the priest. It will be a great favor for me and my ancestors, no doubt. Gifts have been given by Bāṣkali formerly to Śakra when he came to his house, and whoever else comes to me with a request, he is always dear to me, and you are especially so; there is by no means any doubt, Blessed One. O Lord of Gods, I am ashamed that it is only three steps of land you have requested on behalf of the brahmin. O Mighty One, I will give him the best of villages, and to you, Indra's heaven. A gift of horses, elephants, land, of women with full breasts, by the mere sight of whom an old man becomes young. Indeed, I will make women and this earth the gift of the dwarf. O Chief of Gods, be gracious to me.

Pulastya spoke:

When so many words were spoken by Bāṣkali, O Prince, the chief priest, Uśanas, said this to the chief of Dānavas.

Uśanas spoke:

No doubt the honorable king stands in eightfold sovereignty. By no means should you say what is proper or improper and what should be given and to whom! Having considered well with ministers, and having examined well right and wrong, having conquered the gods together with Vāsava you have obtained the sovereignty of the three worlds. But at the conclusion of these words, you will suffer imprisonment. This one who is a dwarf, O King, is the eternal Viṣṇu. Nothing should be given by you; he has killed your father himself. This one who has murdered your father, your mother, and other relatives, has come to you. Being the cause of the destruction of your lineage, he will be so for you, too. He knows what is suitable for the good of the gods and not the law. By him, possessing māyā, the Dānavas are conquered. Through his māyā he has appeared to you in the form of a priestly dwarf. What more can be said? In no way is something to be given. The gift of earth should be as much as the distance of the foot of a fly. By giving, you hasten toward destruction this very day. I assure you of this truth.

Pulastya spoke:

Even though spoken to by his guru, Bāṣkali once more spoke these words. "O Guru, all was promised through my desire for dharma. The keeping of vows is the eternal dharma of the virtuous. If this is the Blessed One, Viṣṇu, there is no one more blessed than me, if, having received my gifts, he prospers the gods. Again, O Guru, I have been made fortunate by this god, if he is seen by me. He, whose appearance the yogins and priests, engaged in meditation and skilled in meditation, do not see, they bestow gifts, holding kuśa grass and water in their hands, saying "May the Blessed One, Viṣṇu, who is the eternal highest soul, be pleased by one who shares in release." Having said these words, they partake of salvation. In my youth, whenever there was doubt in my mind about what was to be done, I was advised by you and you determined what was to be done and not to be done. But there is nothing that cannot be given even to enemies when they come to my house. Having reflected upon this, I will give even my life breath to Vāmana and I will bestow heaven on Śakra. The gift that does not cause any trouble, this gift is given here, and not the gift that does cause trouble. That is not auspicious.

Pulastya spoke:

Having heard that, the guru lowered his head in shame.

Bāṣkali said:

O God, this whole earth should be given by me to you, if requested. To me it is a shame that it is only three steps of land.

Indra spoke:

That which you told me is true, O Chief of Dānavas. The request of three steps of land was made by this twice born, for he is desirous of only so much. O Son of Danu, you are asked by me on his behalf. The boon must be given.

Bāṣkali spoke:

O King of Gods, on my behalf, give three steps to Vāmana. There, live happily for a long time, O Lord of Gods.

Pulastya spoke:

This being said, and with the water offering, having spoken "May Hari himself be pleased with me," the three steps were given to Vāmana by Bāṣkali.

As soon as the gift was given by the chief of Dānavas, having abandoned the form of a dwarf, Hari tread upon the worlds through his desire for the gods' welfare. When the god, having reached the sacrificial mountain, stood facing north, the dwelling of the Dānava was situated at his left foot. There the lord of the world tread his first step to the sun and the second to the celestial pole and with the third, O King, the god reached the egg of Brahmā, which was struck and pierced by the god whose deeds are wonderful with his big toe, and indeed much water issued forth. Having overflowed Brahmā's world and all the worlds in order, the site of Dhruva, the world of the sun, and having flooded the sacrificial mountain, the goddess, having reached the steps of Viṣṇu, entered the Puṣkara tīrtha, and these steps became Vaiṣṇava on the surface of the earth.

Having arrived at the hermitage, whoever thoroughly bathes in the pool, from the sight of it gains the fruit of the aśvamedha sacrifice. Accompanied by twenty-one generations of ancestors, he might gain the world of Vaikuṇṭha. Having enjoyed numerous pleasures for three hundred kalpas, at the end of that, the king becomes a universal monarch on earth. O Bhiṣma, the stream of water that sprang forth from the great toe, that is called the Vaiṣṇava river, which has her origin in Viṣṇu's step. Gaṅgā is engendered for many reasons in Viṣṇu's step, O Prince. She by whom all this is covered, the three worlds, moving and unmoving, that beautiful water which appeared from the egg broken by the big toe, that water became the divine river known as the Viṣṇupada. Brahmā's egg, both moving and unmoving, was covered by that divine river, O Illustrious One, with miraculous powers and a desire for kindness to all.

Bāṣkali was addressed by Vāmana, "Now fulfill the steps." Head turned downward, he did not know what to answer. Having seen him being silent, the priest spoke these words.

Śukra spoke:

The power of giving is natural. But he is not capable of creating. Inasmuch as this earth exists, that earth has been given by another to you, O Mighty One.

Pulastya spoke:

Thus spoken to, Bāṣkali said to Viṣṇu, "This earth, whose measure is great, formerly created by you, is not protected by me. The earth is small, you are large, and I am not capable of creation. O God, the power of the desire of gods always wins." Then Viṣṇu, having regarded him who was without an answer as truthful, said, "Tell your desire, you who are chief of the Dānavas; I will do it. The water that has fallen into my possession was given by you, O Dānava. Because of that, you, worthy of a boon, are a fortunate recipient of boons. I will give you *your* desire; ask for what you seek." Then Janārdana, god of gods, was requested by him.

Bāṣkali spoke:

O Lord of Gods, I choose devotion to you, death by your hands. I will go to the Isle of the Blest, which is difficult to attain by ascetics.

Pulastya spoke:

Having thus spoken, Viṣṇu said to him, "Remain here until the end of one yuga, at which time I, having the form of a boar, will enter the surface of the earth. Then I will vanquish you and you will be dissolved into my body." Spoken to by him, the Dānava retreated from his presence. All the worlds were stepped upon by the dwarf, wishing to seize them, those worlds which were abandoned by the Asuras, the guardians of the truth, for the sake of the gods, and Pātāla was forever overcome by the luster of Hari and by ten awful demons, O Son of Śaṅtanu. Having seized the three worlds, the god disappeared. Bāṣkali, having made Pātāla his abode, lived happily; and wise Śakra ruled the three worlds.

This manifestation of the guru of the world is called *Trivikrama* and is accompanied by the origin of Gaṅgā, which removes all stain. On hearing the single origin of Viṣṇu's steps that has been told, O Prince, man is freed from all the evils of the world: poor sleep, ill thoughts, wrongdoing, and guilt; at the sight of the three steps of Viṣṇu, these quickly approach destruction. Having seen the succession of yugas and sinful creatures, O Bhiṣma, the subtlety displayed by Viṣṇu in his showing of the steps, any man, silent, ascends to it on earth. Having made a pilgrimage to Tripuṣkara, he obtains the fruit of the Aśvamedha sacrifice, and when he journeys to the Viṣṇupada, he is freed from all evils and death.

Padma Purāṇa Uttarakhaṇḍa 266–267

Rudra spoke:

It is said, the son of Prahlāda was known by the name of Virocana, and his son was the great-armed Bali Vairocana, the mighty one. He was the best of those who know the law, a pure and faithful ascetic, the beloved bhakta of Hari, delighting eternally in virtue. Upon conquering all the gods together with Indra and the troops of Maruts, he, the mighty one, put the three worlds in his power and held sway. The earth, yielding many grains and fruits without being ploughed, cows, filled with milk, and all the trees with fruits and flowers, all men, devoted to svadharma and free of evil, praised Hṛṣikeśa, forever free from fever. Thus Bali, lord of Daityas, made the sovereignty by means of dharma, and Indra and the thirty gods became his servants. He enjoyed the sovereignty of the three worlds, made from a pride of strength.

Through desire for the welfare of others, seeing his son whose sovereignty had fallen away, Kaśyapa, along with his wife, whose virtuousness is equal to the gods, heated his tapas near Hari, observing the vow of milk. The lord of gods, Janārdana, whose navel is a lotus, was praised. Praised by him for a thousand years, Hari together with the goddess, the eternal one, became manifest. Seeing him whose eyes are lotuses, bearing the club, conch, and discus, dark blue like a sapphire, adorned with all ornaments, with glittering necklace, bracelets, rings, and diadem, the Kauṣṭubha jewel illuminating his breast, covered with a yellow robe, together with Śrī and Garuḍa, the great-souled one, his mind possessed of joy, the best of twice borns, giving homage he praised the world lord together with his wife.

Kaśyapa said:

Obseisance to you, O Lord of Lakṣmī, All Knowing One, Lord of the World, who is the All Soul, the master of all the gods, the creation and destruction.

Obeisance to you, whose form has no beginning or end, whose form is infinite, who embodies the Vedas and Vedāṅgas, whose eyes are everywhere.

Obeisance to you, the All Soul, and to you who are more

subtle than the subtle, who is abounding in excellent qualities, whose soul is to be meditated upon, Obeisance.

Obeisance to the child of youth and the king of sport, born of Śrī, to him whose single enjoyment is eternal freedom, and who is situated in the highest dwelling place.

Obeisance to you with four souls, O Four-formed One; homage to you who has five appearances; homage to you, O Fivefold One. The fivefold one was worshiped eternally by devoted yogis, abiding in the five saṁskāras, knowing the true nature of the five things. Those five elevations of Hari, always known by you, poets whose souls are filled with the four words know it thus forever. Your servants the brahmins, twice-borns whose desired acts rest on the three Vedas, protect the whole world, O Thou who are kind to worshippers. They are released from the fetters of existence merely by your look of compassion. Homage to you, creator of the three worlds, the self-born one, the soul of all.

Obeisance to you, creator and bestower, whose form is the universe, to Nārāyaṇa, Kṛṣṇa, Vāsudeva, to the archer.

Obeisance to you, Viṣṇu, the victorious one, whose nature is pure.

Mahādeva said:

Thus being praised agreeably with the hymns of the great ṛṣi, Janārdana spoke in a deep voice, delighted. "I am pleased and honored by your devotion, O Best of Twice Borns. Choose a boon, good luck to you! I will do as you desire."

Mahādeva said:

Then Kaśyapa spoke to Hṛṣikeśa together with his wife. "O Lord of gods, upon becoming my son, you must do what is beneficial for the thirty gods. The three worlds have been forcefully conquered by Bali. Becoming the younger brother of Indra, famed as Upendra, having conquered Bali by any means with māyā, give the three worlds eternally to my son, Śakra."

Mahādeva spoke:

Spoken to by the sage, Janārdana consented, and praised by the thirty gods, he disappeared then and there.

Thus, at the proper time, the Blessed One arrived in the womb of Aditi for the great-spirited Kaśyapa, causing welfare among living things. At that time Bali, practicing great penance, began the long-continued Soma sacrifice according to precept, along with eight great ṛṣis.

Śaṁkara spoke:

At the end of a thousand years, Aditi gave birth to a dwarf, to Viṣṇu Acyuta, great lord of all the world, whose chest bears the Śrīvatsa and Kauṣṭubha, whose splendor is like the full moon, handsome, lotus eyed, little and dwarfish: Hari. Having the appearance of a youth, the god, knowing all the Vedāṅgas, was marked by the emblems of belt, staff, and dress. Then the illustrious Bhagavan spoke to them, the best of the gods. "And now tell me, Best of gods, what shall I do?"

Śaṁkara said:

Bristling with delight, the thirty gods spoke to him, the Supreme Lord. "O Madhusūdana, the sacrifice of Bali has commenced at this time. Now is not the time to challenge the Lord of Daityas, O Mighty One. Making your request, you must be pleased to take heaven and earth."

Śaṁkara said:

Thus spoken to by all thirty gods, Hari approached Bali at the place of the sacrifice, where he was seated together with eight ṛṣis. Seeing the youth arrive, the Daitya quickly stood up. Viṣṇu, having arrived himself, was full of laughter. Bali propitiated him according to rule, and placed him in the lotus seat. Having bowed down and done obeisance, he spoke in a stuttering voice. "I am blessed, my every purpose is attained, my life is fruitful. Praising you, O Chief of Vipras, what favor can I do for you? That purpose for which you have come, O Best of Twice borns, that, O Veda knower, I will give to you immediately."

Śaṁkara said:

Then, with his mind delighted, he spoke to the Lord of the Earth.

Vāmana said:

Listen, O Chief of Kings, to my reason for coming. Give me land for a fire-pit, O Lord of Daityas. Please give me the land measured by my three steps, for of all gifts, land is the best gift. He who gives land, even measuring the insignificant size of a thumb, he will be lord of the earth. No means of purification is found to be like the gift of land. He who receives land and he who gives land, both are thus of virtuous karma, and are sure to go to heaven. O Great King, give me the land for my three steps. Lord of the Earth, do not hesitate to give me this small bit of land. It will indeed be by way of giving the three worlds, O Earth-Protector.

Then the Lord of the Earth assented, his face full of delight. He agreed to make the gift of land, according to rule. But seeing him, the priest of the Daitya king, Uśanas, spoke these words, "My King, let no land be given!" Śukra said:

This is Viṣṇu, the highest lord, Hari, who has come as requested by the gods to acquire the entire earth from you through deception. Land must not be given to him, Illustrious King; you must give another property. This is my advice, Lord of the Earth.

Śaṁkara said:

But laughing, the king spoke firmly to his guru. "All pious acts done by me were done to the satisfaction of Vāsudeva. I will be blessed today if Viṣṇu comes here, himself. My life will be given to him today happily; I will surely give him just the three worlds."

Śaṁkara said:

Saying this, the devoted Lord of the Earth, having cleansed his feet, gave the requested land, after having first poured the water, according to rule. Having taken the fire around him and having paid homage, on giving the precious gift, he praised the brahmin again, his inner soul delighted.

Bali said:

I am enriched and my life is fulfilled upon giving you land, O Twice born. Take this earth as you desire, O Chief of brahmins.

Śaṁkara said:

Viṣṇu spoke to the king. "In your presence I will now measure the earth with my stride." On speaking, the supreme lord abandoned the form of a brahmin boy and, taking the thrice-stepping form, laid claim to this earth, extending sixty koṭis, with oceans, mountains, seas, and islands, gods, Asuras, and men. The puruṣa Madhusūdana, striding with one foot, said to the chief of Daitya kings, "What can I do for you?" Thus that thrice-stepping form of the lord, having great power, exists indeed for the welfare of the gods and ṛṣis and the magnanimous one. That step, not capable of being seen by Brahmā or by Śiva, which treads on all the earth, O beautiful mountain-born one, that step was more than the length of one hundred yojanas. The eternal one gave the king of Daityas the divine eye, and Janārdana showed his own form to him. Bali, Lord of Daityas, seeing the universal form of the god, obtained an unequalled rapture, flooded with tears of joy. Seeing the god, and having done obeisance and praised him with hymns, he spoke with stuttering words, his inner soul full of delight. "Seeing you, the supreme lord, I am enriched and my life is fulfilled. You must take the three worlds, O Supreme Lord."

Śaṁkara said:

Then the lord of all, Viṣṇu Acyuta, extended his imperishable second step to the higher regions, to the end of the Brahmaloka. Approaching the abode of the stars, surrounded by all the gods, the step of Acyuta was not complete, O Beautiful Woman. Then the Grandfather, seeing the step of the god of gods bearing the sign of the discus, lotus, and so on, his mind possessed of joy, said, "I am blessed"; and, taking his own water jar, he was purified by him with devotion there, while Brahmā was standing in the water. By the power of Viṣṇu the water became inexhaustible and pure water fell on the peak of Meru to become a place of pilgrimage. Indeed, for the purpose of the purification of the world, running down in four directions, the Sītā, Alakanandā, and Cakṣurbhadrā were established, according to order. The Alakanandā is known as being on the south side of Meru, and with a three-part name, flowing through heaven, earth, and the lower regions, is the Triśrotā, world-purifier. In the upper part is mentioned the Mandākinā, below the Bhogavatī, in the middle the Vegavatī; the Gaṅgā is auspicious to men for the sake of purification. Seeing her flowing forth from the middle of Meru, O Beautiful One, I hold it on my head for the sake of my own purification. But holding the beautiful water of the Ganges for a thousand celestial years, I have become Śiva, O Goddess, being worshiped in all the worlds. Whoever might carry with his head the water of the Ganges, whose origin was in Viṣṇu's footstep, or who might take a sip of it, he will become honorable in the world, no doubt. Whoever could speak, O Gaṅgā, from a distance of hundreds of yojanas, is freed from all evil as he goes to the Viṣṇuloka. As the king Bhagīratha and the great ascetic Gautama, propitiating me with tapas for the sake of Gaṅgā, asked, I gave her to them, the Gaṅgā, the auspicious Vaiṣṇava Ganges, for the benefit of all worlds, out of sympathy for the goddess, the best of rivers. Brought together by Gautama and known therefore as *Gautamī,* endowed with sovereignty and known since then as *Bhagīrathī,* through devotion to you has been narrated the most excellent birth of Gaṅgā, which is incomparable.

Then Nārāyaṇa, devoted to his mighty devotee, gave to Bali, Lord of Daityas, the beautiful Rasātala world, to all the Dānavas, Nāgas, and sea monsters. And the Daitya slayer made Bali king up until the end of the world. Accepting the worlds from Bali in the guise of a small boy, the imperishable Viṣṇu, son of Kaśyapa, gladly gave the earth to Mahendra. Then the gods, together with Gandharvas and ṛṣis of great might, praised Acyuta with divine hymns and worshiped him, having shrunk from his large form for the purpose of showing himself to them. Worshiped by the thirty gods, Hari disappeared. Thus in this manner was Śakra well protected by the great lord Viṣṇu, and the lord of the thirty obtained the mighty sovereignty of the three worlds. This is known to all, the superhuman power of the dwarf, Beautiful One, and the rest of his manifestations I will tell, in due order, O Goddess.

Skanda Purāṇa I.1.18–19

Chapter 18

Lomaśa spoke:

Overpowered by that act, Mahendra spoke to the guru. "To overcome this trouble effortlessly, tell me what to do."

Bṛhaspati said, "Having left Amarāvati, all of us, together with family, shall go elsewhere, striving to overcome this." Then all the gods did so, having abandoned Amarāvati. Indra left the same day, abiding in the form of a peacock. Yama, having become a crow, and Kubera, a lizard, Agni, having become a pigeon, and Maheśvara, having become a frog, Nairṛta instantly became a dove, and then left. Varuṇa became a partridge, and Vāyu became a turtledove.

Thus bearing various forms, and having given up heaven, they went to Kaśyapa's holy hermitage, distressed from fear. They all told their mother Aditi about the Daitya's action. Aditi, desirous for her sons, and hearing about that misfortune, spoke to Kaśyapa about the great misfortune of the gods. "O Maharṣi, hear this speech, and having heard it, do something. The gods were vanquished by the Daityas, and having abandoned Amarāvati, they have arrived at your hermitage. Protect them, Prajāpati."

Having heard her words, Kaśyapa made this speech:

Through great tapas, O Delicate Woman, the Asuras are invincible, and are permitted to be so by Bhṛgu; this you know, O Passionate One. Now, Angry One, do this quickly to accomplish the gods' purpose. Through terrible tapas, conquer them. Illustrious One, I shall tell you about this vow for the accomplishment of the purpose. Do what I say zealously and according to rule, Fair One.

O Goddess, in the month of Bhadrapada, remain pure on the tenth day, eating only once, to gain Viṣṇu's grace. Hari, lord of all desires and boons, is to be asked himself with this mantra, Lovely One, by devotees: "I am your devotee, O Lord, for three days beginning with the tenth I shall perform the vow; O Viṣṇu, please give permission." The master of the world is to be requested with this mantra. Eat once, and eat only rice, and that rice should be eaten only on a banana leaf, and without salt. Make an effort to fast on the eleventh day. Stay awake at night zealously, Graceful Woman. Conclude the Dvādaśī ceremony skillfully and according to precept, performing it together with kinsmen, having fed the brahmins. This vow should be performed for twelve months, unwearied. When the eleventh of the month of Bhadrapada arrives, having worshiped Viṣṇu zealously, you should make a golden or silver image of Viṣṇu standing on a jar, according to your ability. The Dvādaśī joined by

> Śravana, which destroys all sins, on that day the ascetic maintains a fast which extinguishes all sins."

Thus spoken to by Kaśyapa and having listened, Aditi then observed the vow that lasted for a year and was endowed with restraint.

Janārdana was satisfied with the year-long vow, and then, O Brahmins, he became manifest on the twelfth of Śravana, bearing the form of a brahmin boy, Lord of Śrī, with two arms, lotus eyes, a complexion like flowers, and adorned by wild flowers. Having seen him, Aditi was filled with astonishment, and out of reverence she, whose eyes are like lotuses, praised him, joined by Kaśyapa. Aditi spoke:

> Homage to him, to the primary cause, the soul of the universe, the creator of the universe, whose soul is consciousness; to him whose form is supreme bliss, to him who is both near and far, to him whose knowledge is without obstruction, homage, homage to him.

Thus remembered by Aditi, Acyuta, lord of the gods, the Blessed One spoke, smiling, to the mother of the gods:

> Through supreme tapas I am kindly disposed to you who are sinless, and, through this form, to the accomplishment of the gods' purpose.

Having heard the words of the Blessed One, Aditi spoke to him. "O Bhagavan, the gods are vanquished by the mighty Asuras. Protect them, all the gods who have come for refuge, O Janārdana." Viṣṇu, solitary lord of Vaikuṇṭha, having heard her speech and having understood all about the gods' behavior and all about Bali and all that Bali intended to do, [thought] "What is to be done by me now, and by what means can the gods obtain the victory and the Daityas, defeat?" Having pondered everything, the great-souled Viṣṇu, the Blessed One spoke to his club. "You must go today for the purpose of killing the son of Virocana, and must slay him speedily, Illustrious One." That proud club spoke to Hṛṣikeśa as if she were laughing. "Great Bali cannot be slain by me, because he is a great worshipper of the Vedas." Then Viṣṇu spoke to his discus flatteringly. "You must go quickly to kill Bali, O Sudarśana." Sudarśana spoke to the discus-handed one quickly. "Bali cannot be killed by me, O Mighty One. O Viṣṇu, as you are devoted to the Vedas, so is he, that bull among

Daityas." He was also spoken to thus by the bow, and he who holds the Śarṅga bow was surprised. He thought a great deal, reflecting at length. Atri spoke:

Then what did all the Asuras do, tell me that?

Lomaśa spoke:

Then all the Asuras, headed by Bali, desirous of doing battle with Indra in heaven, besieged that beautiful town. All the Asuras did not know that the gods, bearing various forms, had left heaven for the hermitage of Kaśyapa. Then, having climbed the wall, the Daityas, desirous of killing the lord of gods quickly, as they entered Amarāvati, saw it was vacant, and they were delighted. Bali was coronated by Śukra on Indra's throne, according to the rules of the great coronation ceremony, and attended by the Asuras. And so the great Bali Vairocana settled into the sovereignty and shone with great prosperity, wielding the powers of Mahendra. Like Mahendra, he was honored by Nāgas and the assembly of Asuras. The wishing tree was won by him as well as Kāmadhenu and the Maṇi jewel. For all who came begging, the donor with all the gifts was great Bali, donor to the worlds. Whoever desired anything, to all those beseechers the sovereign of the Daityas fulfilled all those desires.

Śaunaka spoke:

Illustrious One, the chief of gods never donates at any time. How is it that Bali was a donor? Tell me that in detail.

Lomaśa spoke:

Whatever meritorious deed is done diligently by men, whether agreeable or disagreeable, that is to be decided by wise men. Śakra the sacrificer obtained the sovereignty of Amarāvati through one hundred Aśvamedhas. He is desirous only of pleasure. Know that this was his desired fruit, and he obtained poverty again. Having become mortal, he will lose his merit. He who is Indra would be a worm; a worm is born as Indra. Therefore, no other liberation is better than the gift. Through the gift, knowledge is obtained; and from knowledge, freedom, no doubt. And from freedom is obtained the most excellent devotion to Rudra, O Brahmins. Gracious-minded Śiva, lord of all, always gives everything. Śaṅkara is pleased even by a little water. Thus declares the ancient Itihāsa: This was done by the son of Virocana, there is no doubt.

A gambler of great sins is a scorner of gods and brahmins. Full of wickedness and desirous of others' wives, sometimes, because of evil gambling, the prize was won; flowers, betel, and sandal for a harlot. Having made the svāstika with both his hands, having taken the perfume and other things for the harlot, while running home, he stumbled and fell to the ground instantly. Because of the fall, he became unconscious for a moment. While the sinner had fainted, all at once an idea occurred to him from an act in a previous birth. The gambler, full of suffering, and having the highest misfortune, had a loathing for worldly objects! Fragrant flowers that had fallen on the ground were offered to Śiva by the gambler unintentionally. Through his meritorious deed, he obtained the abode of Yama. Yama called him *Sinner,* bringing fear to all the worlds. "You are to be cooked, Stupid One, in my great hells." Thus spoken to by the Dharmarāja, the gambler made this speech. "O Blessed One, there is nothing wicked which I have not done. But please do consider my merit also, truthfully." And it was told by Citragupta, "That which fell at the time of your death was given by you to the Supreme Soul, Śiva. And through the consequences of that act, you will obtain the abode of Indra for three hours, no doubt."

That instant, the sinner arrived, surrounded by all the gods. Mounted on Airāvata, he was brought to Śakra's palace. Śakra was awakened by his guru, whose soul was purified. "O Puraṅdara, with my own command, this gambler should be established on your throne for three hours." Hearing his guru's words, he accepted them instantly. Śakra went to another place and the gambler was sent in to the palace of the king of gods, which was filled with various marvels. He was coronated on Śakra's throne and he obtained Indra's kingdom, because of his giving of perfume to Śambhu, together with the flowers and betel. "What about those who have faith, and who always offer fragrant flowers with devotion to Śiva, the Supreme Soul?" "They have attained union with Śiva and are surrounded by Śiva's army. They obtain great delight with Śakra as their slave. And of those who are intent on devotion to Śiva, whose minds are tranquil, their happiness is difficult to obtain for Brahmā, Śakra, and the others. The wretched who are bewildered and who desire improper objects do not know that Mahādeva is to be worshiped by men who know the truth. Because of that you, a gambler, have become Indra for three hours." He was consecrated by the priest and remained on Indra's throne. Then the celebrated gambler was spoken to by Nārada. "Bring Indrāṇī, as the kingdom is well decorated." Smiling, the gambler who was dear to Śiva spoke. "I have nothing to do with Indrāṇī—such things should not be said, Honorable One." Having thus spoken, the gambler began to bestow things. He who was dear to Śiva gave Airāvata to Agastya. The wise gambler gave a horse called *Uccaiḥśravas* to Viśvāmitra and the celebrated one gave Kāmadhenu to Vasiṣṭha. Then he gave the brilliant thought gem to Gatava, and then the majestic one gave the kalpataru tree to Kauṇḍinī, and the illustrious gambler also gave away his home. Such things, and many varied jewels he gave happily to the ṛṣis for the sake of pleasing Śiva. That mighty one gave for three hours, and after three hours, the former owner came.

Indra arrived in Amarāvati, sitting down on his own throne. And then he was praised by the ṛṣis together with Śācī. The fool spoke to Śācī, "You have been enjoyed by the gambler, Beautiful One; tell the truth, Lovely One." Laughing, the Spotless One spoke to Purandara, "You see at all times by analogy to yourself, O Indra. The magnanimous one bearing the form of a gambler obtained supreme knowledge out of Śiva's kindness. Endowed with asceticism, of great might, by whom the whole delightful kingdom and other snares of māyā were abandoned, he was the conqueror of his foes." Having listened to Indrāṇī's words, O Lord of Gods, Indra became full of shame and went silently to his throne. The wise one said these words to Bṛhaspati, "I do not see Airāvata or the horse Uccaiḥśravas. All the Parijāta trees, those objects, by whom were they stolen?" The guru said this: "This great deed was done by the gambler. Today, while he was here, he gave it to the ṛṣis. While one's own authority is great, those who exercise authority on themselves and those who are always vigilant, intent on meditation on Śiva, they are dear to Śaṅkara, having relinquished the fruits of their action. And having sought this exclusive knowledge, they go to the highest abode." Having heard his speech, Indra said these words to Bṛhaspati, "Probably Yama will tell all that." Considering this for his own prosperity, and having been satisfied, Śakra, king of the gods, left together with the guru. Desirous of his own welfare, he went at that time to the town of Saṁyamanī. While he was being honored by Yama, Śakra made this speech. "My abode was given to you by the evil gambler. That horrible deed was done, and all those lovely jewels were given by him to these and to those. O Dharma! You know the truth, you are called Dharma. Why did you give them to the gambler? You did this to destroy my kingdom! Illustrious One! Bring back the elephant and other things quickly, and the other jewels that were given, from any place whatsoever."

Having listened to Śakra's words, Yama, full of wrath, spoke to the gambler. "What was done by you who are evil for pleasure? Śakra's kingdom was given by you to brahmins, and done so improperly and erroneously, Fool! Stealing another's property! With that great evil, go to hell!" Having heard Yama's words, the gambler spoke, "I shall go to hell, there's no doubt. But as long as my authority was engendered by Śakra's throne, Excellent One, then anything given to brahmins was proper."

Yama spoke:

A gift on earth is commendable, and the fruit of that act appears. A gift in heaven is not to be given by anyone to anyone anywhere. Because of that, you shall be punished, Fool. You broke the law. The guru is the ruler of the prudent one, the king is the ruler of the evil one, and I am the ruler of all the wicked ones, there is no doubt.

Having scolded the sinner, the Dharmarāja himself said to Citragupta, "Burn this one in hell." Then, smiling, Citragupta spoke to Yama.

How will the gambler become a hell goer, by whom the great elephant Airāvata was given to Agastya? And the horse born from the ocean given to magnanimous Gālava, and the shining thought gem to Viśvāmitra, if you please, and other jewels given by the gambler? Through the consequences of his actions he is to be honored in the triple world. That which is given in the name of Śiva in heaven and on earth by those who are men, that entire act is said to be without gaps and is known as *imperishable*. Because of that, there is no hell for that gambler, and those sins of the magnanimous gambler are all reduced to ashes by merely remembering them. Because of Śiva's grace, all evil acts were made good instantly.

Having listened to Citragupta's speech, the king of ghosts himself, smiling and bowing his head, said this to Śatakratu:

> You are king of the chiefs of gods, old, and greedy for the sovereignty. Through one hundred Aśvamedhas, one life is acquired by you, no doubt; that fellow has earned much more. Having requested Agastya and all the distinguished sages with an obeisance, those things should be regained by you—the elephant, jewels, and so on, by which you quickly obtain happiness.

Having consented to the words just spoken, unthoughtful Puraṅdara went to his own city and asked the ṛṣis, with neck bent, and then received the Parijāta tree. And in this way Puraṅdara obtained the kingdom, and then became king in Amarāvati.

The rebirth of the gambler was granted by Vaivasvata; through the consequences of some of his actions, he became the son of Virocana. Then Suruci became the mother of the gambler, the queen of Virocana and daughter of Vṛṣaparva. He remained in the womb of that magnanimous one. From then onward, from Prahlāda and from his son, and from Suruci, their minds were intent on giving and dharma. While he was in her womb, an excellent wish was made by the gambler, O Brahmins, a wish of high-minded people that was difficult to obtain.

Alone, Śakra went to the son of Virocana. Desirous of murder and having become a brahmin, he solicited the Daitya chief. Arriving at Virocana's dwelling, Indra made this speech. "Having become an aged brahmin, give to me, O You whose vow is Good. You are intelligent, O Daitya Chief! You are the donor in the three worlds. Illustrious One, the brahmins praise your most marvelous act and your pure fame, having stood in assemblies. I am a beggar, O Daitya Chief! Please give, O You whose vow is Good." Having heard his speech, the Daitya chief spoke these words. "What is to be given to you, Mighty One? Tell me quickly now." Indra, with a brahmin's form, spoke to Virocana. "O Daitya Chief, I ask because I am defeated. You should give to me according to your pleasure, there is no doubt." The Asura, son of Prahlāda, said this, smiling, "I shall give my own head, O Brahmin, if you want it now, or this kingdom, or Śrī, who does not go elsewhere; these I give to you, no doubt." Thus spoken to by the Daitya and having reflected, Hari said, "Give me your head, furnished with the crown."

Thus, when the words were spoken by Śakra in the form of a brahmin, having cut off his head quickly with his own hand, happily the Asura son of Prahlāda gave it to Mahendra. That which was done formerly by Prahlāda was a dharma difficult to do. Having exclusively practiced devotion to Viṣṇu, his mind intent upon Viṣṇu, he said, "There is nothing anywhere better than giving. That which is given to the afflicted, that gift is very holy. Whatever is given to the best of one's ability, that partakes of eternity. There is nothing in the three worlds more excellent than that gift." And it is said to consist of Sattvas, Rajas, and Tamas, and thus the gift given by him has the characteristic of Sattvas.

Having cut off the head, which was given to Indra in the form of a brahmin, the crown fell. The shining jewels fell all together and became the maṇḍala of the Daityas, of men, and of snakes. Virocana's gift was famous in the three worlds. And today, poets sing of the magnanimous Daitya chief. The splendid gambler became Virocana's son, born when his father passed away. His mother, faithful to her husband, having abandoned her body, then went to the world of her husband. He was coronated on his father's throne by the Bhārgava, and, called by the name *Bali,* he became famous. By him were all the mighty godly troops harassed, and they went, as was told before, to the beautiful hermitage of Kaśyapa. Then, celebrated Bali became Indra in the city of the gods. The Asura himself, having become the sun, shined with tapas. Having become the Lord himself, he protected Śiva's region. Having become Nairṛta and the Lord of the Waters, then Bali became Kubera, in the North. Thus Bali was really the enjoyer of the three worlds himself. O Brahmins, through the gambler, devoted to the praise of Śiva, Bali became intent on giving as was his previous habit. Once he stood in the middle of the assembly hall together with the Bhṛgu, surrounded by the Daitya chiefs, and spoke to Saṇḍa and Marka. "Make all the Asuras dwell here, near me. Leaving Pātāla today, do it without delay." Then having listened, the Bhargava said, smiling, "One celebrates in heaven with manifold sacrifices and with sacrificiants, O King! It is not possible to enjoy heaven otherwise, O King. What I say is true." Having understood the guru's words, the Daitya chief made this speech: "That act which was done by me, by that all the great Asuras shall go to heaven for a long time, no doubt!" Laughing, the great ascetic, Blessed One of the Bhārgavas, spoke. Śukra, best of wise men, having thought him childish, said "The speech you made, Bali, does not please me. Having arrived, O You whose vow is Good, you wish to stay. With one hundred Aśvamedhas you should sacrifice with fire. Having gone to the sphere of religious deeds, do not delay."

Having consented, magnanimous and high-souled Bali, leaving heaven at that time, joined by the Daityas, servants and the guru, together went to earth, to the Narmadā River, at whose bank was a tīrtha of great splendor called *Gurukilya*. Then the high-minded Daitya chief, having conquered the whole earth, the best of truthful ones, the son of Virocana, sacrificed, having been initiated. Illustrious Bali, joined by his guru, sacrificed with many Aśvamedhas. Having made a brahmin one of the priests, there were sixteen priests. It was completed by high-minded Bhārgava and by Bali, who was initiated. With one less than one hundred Aśvamedhas, they then tried to complete the last.

While the hundred sacrifices of the king were being completed, by the excellent vow of Aditi, previously mentioned by me, was Blessed Lord Hari pleased. Through the form of a brahmin boy, he became her son. The Lord was initiated by Kaśyapa and Aditi, and when he was initiated, Brahmā, grandfather of the world, arrived. The thread investiture was given by Brahmā, the Supreme One, and the wooden staff bestowed by high-minded Soma, the girdle was offered and the marvelous black antelope skin, and then the slippers were given to the magnanimous one by the earth. Then the alms were collected by Bhavanī for the purpose of success. Thus was it given to the Bhagavan Viṣṇu in the form of a brahmin boy.

Having saluted Aditi and Kaśyapa, Vāmana, Lord of Śrī, the Illustrious One, went to the sacrificial enclosure. The Lord himself spoke for the purpose of deceiving the sacrificer, Bali. Then the great lord went to heaven and, shaking the earth with the weight of his feet, Vāmana, bearing the form of a brahmin boy, the supreme soul Viṣṇu, was suitably praised with songs by the people, lords of sages, and troops of gods. Quickly he went to the sacrificial enclosure, and the single kinsman of the world arrived there at that time. The god, bearing the form of a brahmin boy, manifested himself, making others chant the Sāma. While the Blessed Lord, knowledgeable in Vedānta, the mighty lord Hari was being praised, he saw the great Aśvamedha sacrifice of Bali. The illustrious dwarf, bearing the form of a brahmin boy, stood on the threshold, and the space was pervaded by the great Brahmā form of the purifier, the magnanimous boy-dwarf.

Having listened, wise Bali spoke to Saṇḍa and Marka, "How many brahmins have come—go see." Having consented, O Brahmins, they stood up quickly and, going together, Saṇḍa and Marka stood at the entrance to the sacrificial tent, and saw the magnanimous lord Hari in the form of a brahmin boy. Quickly they went back to tell Bali. "A brahmacārin has arrived alone and there is no one else; he has arrived reciting in your presence, O Mahārāja. Why, we do not know; do you, Sire?" When the words were spoken by them, the great-minded one stood up instantly in order to see the brahmin boy. The great and majestic son of Virocana looked, and like a stick he fell to the ground and bowed his head to the boy. Having lead the boy in immediately, and having seated him on his own throne, he praised the boy with water for sipping and for washing his feet. Having bent his neck, he spoke with smooth words, "Where have you come from, and why? Who are you? Tell that at once, O Lord." Having heard the words of Virocana's son, Vāmana, his mind happy, began to speak.

The Blessed One spoke:

> "You are the king, lord of the triple world, and there is no other. Whoever becomes less than his family is considered an inferior man. Similarly, whoever becomes equal or superior to his family, *he* is considered a man. That act which you did was not done by your ancestors, by Hiraṇyakaśipu and others, who were the greatest of Daityas. He who was observing great austerities, by whom great austerities were done for one thousand divine years, his body was eaten by ants and surrounded by many insects. Having realized that, the chief of gods, surrounded by his great army, came previously to his town; in his presence all the Asuras were slain by the foe of the Daityas, and his queen, Vindhyā, was prevented from being carried away earlier by Nāranda, O King, who was intending to do some particular job. Because of Śambhu's grace, everything that was considered in his mind [Indra's], all that was subdued by the Daitya chief through his asceticism. And by him was her son of great luster taken to the assembly. His son, Illustrious One, was your father, who loved *his* father, and was named Virocana. By that magnanimous one was wise Indra pleased by the gift of his own head, O King. You are his son, and your highest glory is achieved. The gods were burnt like moths by the great fire of your glory and Indra was conquered by you, there is no doubt. All your deeds were heard by me, O You whose vow is Good. I am small and have come, keeping the brahmacārya vow. Give me land, O Best of Kings, for the purpose of a hut." Having heard the boy's words, Bali spoke. "O Boy! Having become a scholar, and having listened to the words spoken before, in reality I think that because of your childishness, you do not know. Tell me how much land I shall give to you; consider it quickly." Then the dwarf, smiling and with a sweet voice, spoke these words. "Brahmins who are discontent are ruined, no doubt. But those who are satisfied, they are brahmins, and not

others; they are only bearers of their dress. Devoted to svadharma, O King, and without deceit, they are free from worldly possessions. Unselfish, their anger restrained, and munificent, Great-minded One, they are the brahmins, and by them is this earth supported, Illustrious One. You are wise, and because of your abundance you are the donor in the triple world; but still you are to bestow on me land measured in three strides. I can do nothing with land in abundance, Subduer of Gods; a hermitage measuring the size of an entrance will be mine. Our three steps is enough to fill a dwelling, no doubt. O King, give to me; as long as the land shall be, for that long that amount is to be given, if you are a donor, Bali." Smiling, Bali, son of Virocana said this to him; "I will give you the whole earth with its mountains, forests, and groves; this is mine, Illustrious One! Take what is given by me. You are the solicitor, Boy! Look at the gift—you, asking the Daitya. The beggar is small, and the donor, having considered everything and having examined himself, answers those requests. He who is wise gives by analogy to himself at all times. Because of that, he is not to be requested by some solicitor who is not very fortunate. O Boy! Now I shall give to you the earth, together with rocks, forests, and groves, with her mountains and oceans; my words are not false." Again the brahmin boy spoke to the son of Virocana, "It is enough for me, O Daitya Chief, that which is given with three steps." Having heard the boy's words, then the Asura chief Bali made this speech, smiling, and thinking quickly, "Take that which was given by me, adorned by the three steps." Thus spoken to, the dwarf spoke to the Asura, smiling, "Having observed the water pouring, be pleased to give the whole world, You whose vow is Good." Having consented, Vāmana, the great son of Kaśyapa, was worshiped by Bali. At that moment, Bali was being praised intensely, together with the ṛṣis and muni chiefs. Having worshiped him, when Bali began to bestow, then that mighty son of Virocana was restrained by his guru. "The gift is not to be given by you to Viṣṇu in the form of a brahmin boy! He has come for Indra's sake, and he will impede your sacrifice today. Because of this, Viṣṇu, the light of the Supreme Soul, is not to be worshiped by you. Long ago, with the form of Mohiṇī, the amṛta was given to the gods, and by him the great Rāhu was slain, and by him, the Daityas having fled, mighty Kālanemi was slain. Thus, this great man is the lord, he is the master of everything. Having considered all this, O Wise One, you should do good or evil."

Chapter 19

Lomaśa spoke:

Thus warned by the guru Bhārgava, the smiling Daitya spoke with a deep, rumbling voice. "I have been spoken to by you with well-intended words, but I am disturbed. Whether you address me in a kind manner or scold me, your words are dear to me. I shall give whatever was requested by Viṣṇu in boy form. Being a worthy recipient, this Viṣṇu is the lord of the fruit of all action. Viṣṇu resides in the heart of those who are the best receptacles, certainly. This is Hari, lord of the universe, by whose name everything is purified, by whom the Vedas, sacrifices, mantras, tantras, and so on are all completed. Now lord Hari, soul of all, arrived with compassion to save me. There is no doubt, you truly know that." Having heard these words, he became angry and, full of rage, the Bhārgava began to curse the Daitya chief, who was devoted to dharma. "Having overstepped my words, Victorious One, you wish to give. You are wicked, fool! Because of that, you shall be destitute of wealth." And then he cursed his pupil, who possessed knowledge of the highest truth, the magnanimous one whose understanding was deep. The great poet, best of dharma knowers, went quickly to his own hermitage.

But when the Bhārgava left, Bali, son of Virocana, having praised the dwarf, resolved to grant the land. Having arrived, Vindhyāvalī, beautiful wife of Bali, washed the brahmin boy's feet, and Bali gave the land to Viṣṇu.

Then, with the previous water-pouring performed according to rule, the unborn Blessed One grew because of that great water-pouring ceremony. With the first step, the earth was pervaded by Viṣṇu, mighty Viṣṇu. With the second, all the heavens were pervaded by that magnanimous one. Viṣṇu's foot reached the Satyaloka and it was washed with water that came from the water jar of Brahmā. From the water's contact with his foot was born the Bhāgīrathī, bringing good fortune to all, by whom the triple world was made pure, and by whom all the sons of Sagara were uplifted, by whom Śambhu's braided hair was filled at that time. Having come in contact with Viṣṇu's foot, the first tīrtha of tīrthas, called *Gaṅgā,* was caused to descend by Bhāgīratha, made by Brahmā. Because of the three steps, the Supreme Soul was named Trivikrama, and the triple world was strided over by the steps of Trivikrama. With his two feet, this world, moving and still, was filled. Having abandoned his own form, the god of gods Janārdana, again in the form of a boy, sat on his own throne, and the gods together with the Gandharvas, sages, Siddhas, and Cāranas arrived at Bali's sacrifice to see the lord, master of the sacrifice. Having come there, Brahmā praised the Supreme Soul and Bali, and other Daitya chiefs came quickly. Vāmana was surrounded by all these at Bali's house. Having sat on the throne, he said to Garuḍa, "By this foolish Daitya was the land given to me with three steps, and two steps were taken. He promised, but the evil-minded one did not give one step. Because of that, the third step is to be taken by you." Thus spoken to by the magnanimous dwarf, Garuḍa, having threatened the son of Virocana, said this, "O Bali, what horrible deed you did, fool! When you did not have the means, why did you give to the Supreme Soul? With little generosity, what will you do now?" Thus spoken to, Bali sat, smiling at the lord of birds. Then to Garuḍa he spoke these words. "I am very strong, O Great-winged One, and I am not a miser. By whom all this universe was made, what can I give to him? O dear one, I was made incapable by the magnanimous one." Then the great-minded Garuḍa spoke to Bali. "O Daitya chief, knowingly prevented by the guru, you gave land to Viṣṇu. Why was this great thing forgotten by you? That third step of Viṣṇu that was promised is to be given. If you do not give, you will fall into hell, O Hero. If you do not give me the lord's third step, I will seize it forcibly, fool!" That Garuḍa, best among the victorious, having said this to the great Asura, bound the son of Virocana with Varuṇa's nooses, having become thoroughly cruel. Seeing her own husband fettered, Vindhyāvalī approached. Having raised only Bāṇa, she stood in front of Vāmana. She was questioned by the dwarf, saying, "Who is this, standing in front of me?" Then the glorious Asura chief Prahlāda spoke. "This is Bali's wife, the virtuous Vindhyāvalī, who has come to you." Having heard Prahlāda's words, Vāmana spoke, "Speak, Vindhyāvalī; what can I do for you? I shall do it." Thus spoken to by the Blessed One, Vindhyāvalī spoke. "Why was my husband bound by magnanimous Garuḍa? Tell me that quickly, Illustrious Janārdana." Glorious Hari, bearing the form of a brahmin boy, said this.

The Blessed One spoke:

"Land marked by three steps was given by me, and with the second step, the triple world was stridden over by me today.

The third step is to be given to me. Because of this, Wise Lady, your husband was fettered by me through Garuḍa.

Having heard the Blessed One's words, she made this excellent speech.

This was promised but not given to you, O Lord. And now the triple world was stridden over by your wide-stepping form. That which is ours in heaven or on earth, that you should leave alone. Little was not given, lord god of gods, master of the world.

Smiling, the Blessed One, the Lord, then spoke to Vindhyāvalī:

Where are three steps to be given now? Tell me quickly, Large-Eyed One, what you think.

And that wise woman said this, standing near the Wide-stepping One.

Why was the triple world stridden over by you, whose strides are wide, O Single king of the World? And how is he who is the single bond of the world in an unequalled form to be given all this by us? Therefore, disregarding that, O Viṣṇu, you must do something now. The three steps promised by my husband, my husband gives you now; there is no doubt. Take the step on my head, O Best of Gods. And take the second on my son's head, World Master, and take the third on my husband's head, World Protector. Thus will I bestow your three steps, Lord Keśava.

Having heard her speech, Janārdana, satisfied, spoke with smooth words to the son of Virocana:

Go to Sutala, O Daitya Chief; do not delay. Live there a long time with all the Asura assembly, and be happy. I am pleased, dear one! What is to be done? Of all donors, you are the best, O Wise One! Choose a boon, bless you. I shall grant all your wishes.

Thus spoken to by Trivikrama, the son of Virocana, skilled in speech, thus freed and embraced by the god of gods, the discus bearer, said this.

> This whole world, moving and still, was made by you. Because of that, I desire nothing from you except your lotus-like feet, O Lord. May I be devoted to your lotus-like feet, God Janārdana, and may there be devotion eternally.

Thus requested by him, the Blessed One, causing the welfare of living beings, spoke rejoicingly to the son of Virocana. The Blessed One spoke:

> O Bali, go to Sutala, surrounded by your relatives.

Then, thus spoken to by him, the Asura said this.

> What will I do in Sutala, O God of gods, tell me. I will stay near you; please do not say otherwise.

Then Hṛṣikeśa, full of pity, spoke to Bali:

> I shall be living near you always, O Prince. I shall always stay at your door. Do not be depressed, O Bali, best of demons. Listen to my excellent speech. I am your benefactor now, and I shall enjoy your dwelling along with those residing in Vaikuṇṭha.

Having heard that speech of Viṣṇu, the Daitya of unequalled splendor went to Sutala, accompanied by the Asuras. With his hundred sons, the first of whom was Bāṇa, the long-armed one dwelled there, the ultimate resort of donors. And all those in the triple world who are beggars go to Bali, and Viṣṇu, standing at his door, gives them whatever they desire. Anyone whose desires are of enjoyment, others whose desires are of liberation, and to those who are brahmins at the sacrifice he gives.

In such manner Bali became like this through Śaṅkara's grace. Long ago, by being a gambler, that was given to the Supreme Soul, having sat down on the dirty ground. Fragrance, flowers, and so on that had fallen were offered by him to Śiva, the Supreme Soul. How much more do those with great devotion offer fragrance, flowers, fruit, and water to Maheśvara; they go to Śiva's abode. There is none better than Śiva to be worshiped, O Brahmins. Those who are mute, those who are blind, those who are lame, and those who are dumb; those of low birth, Caṇḍālas and Śvapacas, and those of the lowest caste, intent on constant devotion to Śiva—they go to the highest abode. Because of this, Sadāśiva is worshiped by all sages. Sadāśiva is to be worshiped, to be greatly honored, and to be praised. Those with knowledge of the highest truth meditate on Maheśa who resides in the heart. Where life exists, there does Śiva reside. Who is without Śiva, instantly there will be inauspiciousness for him. Brahmā, Viṣṇu, and Rudra are the creators of the guṇas; Brahmā is endowed with the rajas guṇa; Viṣṇu is endowed with the sattva guṇa; and Rudra is endowed with the tamas guṇa; but Maheśvara is beyond the guṇas. Mahādeva in the liṅga form is to be praised by those striving for liberation. There is none better than Śiva, granter of enjoyment and liberation.

Skanda Purāṇa V.1.74

Vyāsa spoke:

> When did the appearance of the dwarf formerly occur, O Faultless One? I want to hear all about that from you, Best of brahmins.

Sanatkumāra spoke:

> Listen, Excellent Brahmin, to that wondrous story that destroys sin; by merely hearing it, one is freed from all sin.
>
> The chief of Daityas was said to be intent on devotion to Viṣṇu. Called Prahlāda, he was the best of all those who support the dharma; he conquered dharma with his conduct, and wealth was conquered by him with truth. The worlds were sustained by him with his courage, the earth was supported by him with his compassion, the divine oceans were conquered by him with his depth, and the enemy troops were conquered by him with his valor. Guests were conquered by that magnanimous one with respect, the sacrifice was conquered by him with his gifts, and the fire was conquered by him with oblations. His soul was purified through faultless behavior and inauspiciousness was destroyed by his tapas; brahmins were conquered by him with gifts of food, clothing, and so on. His life was conquered by saṁskāras; his soul was conquered by his endless control; breath was conquered by him with his prāṇāyāma; and Hari was conquered by him through yoga and meditation. A great yogi, he was endowed with such qualities and intent on truth and dharma. There was not nor will there ever be one whose courage was equal to Prahlāda's.

His virtuous grandson was called Bali. While he was protecting his subjects properly, while he was nourishing them properly, there was not one who was short lived or stupid, foolish, ill, wicked, or sonless, or devoid of wealth on earth. A great king, world guardian, sacrificer, and giver of great gifts, the earth, consisting of seven islands, was always protected by him.

Once, while he sat on the throne in the middle of the assembly hall, when the victory cheer was sounded, the Gandharvas sang in a lovely voice and the bands of Apsarases danced to the music of instruments. Beautiful tales were told by the clever sutas and bards, siddhas, minstrels, those versed in the traditions; and ṛṣis came together there, O Best of brahmins, as well as the Dānavas Sunda, Upasunda, Tuhuṇḍa, and others, the demon Mahīṣa and Kolbana, Śumba, Niśumba, Dhumrākṣa and Kālakeya, Kālanemi and Vikrānta, Dauhṛda, Mūṣaka, Yama, Nikumbha and Kumbha, Andhaka and Mahābala, Śaṅkha, terrible Jalandhara, Vātāpī, superior in strength, Halāyudha who was an all-conquering slayer of all and could change his form at will. These and many others, augmenting the family of Danu, attended the sinless king Bali. Siddhas and Nāgas, Kiṅnaras and Kiṁpuruṣas, aerial beings, terrestrial beings, children, and frightful Rākṣases; these and many others attended the king. That celestial assembly hall shone brightly, O Best of twice borns. Like the sky in autumn covered with bright stars, sitting in that assembly hall, king Bali looked bright. He was like Vāsava in heaven with the gods and Maruts.

Once, Nārada Devadarśana came to the assembly hall while all the Dānavas were present. Having seen him come, all those sons of Diti stood up. The best of the Kiṅnaras, along with Bali saluted him and, having honored him and given him a seat, the prince asked about his welfare. Having been shown hospitality, excellent Nārada, best of ṛṣis, spoke to Bali with words deep sounding, like a cloud.

Nārada spoke:

Listen, O Best of the sons of Diti, I have come from the hall of Viṣṇu. There in the assembly hall of the gods, which is pleasurable and heavenly, and which was built for a purpose, the gods, led by Indra, together with the Gandharvas, told each other holy tales. The gods did not tolerate the splendid tales of the Daityas I told. "The Daitya Hiraṇyakaśipu was in ancient

> times Prajāpati, conqueror of the triple world, leader by whom this earth was conquered. Having subdued all the world he enjoyed the earth. Possessed of excessive energy, he was very strong and heroic, going all places, a gallant ruler, but he was slain by the man-lion." "O Nārada, you praise Bali—how great is his strength in this world?" Having censured me, Indra, who won over the world, repeatedly delivered fierce speeches. Because of that, Best of Dānavas, you must seize the universal sovereignty, Lord of the Earth, having conquered the earth, which has come to you from your forefathers. O Best of Danu's sons, indeed the gods are supported by little strength, intent upon running away, subdued, always fearful of war. Thus, obedient to my words, you should be lord of the triple world.

Having heard Nārada's speech, Bali, son of Virocana, to conquer the triple world, was inspired with great anger. The lord of all the sons of Daityas, having consulted all the demons, battled violently with powerful Indra. And having conquered all the gods, he subjugated them together with Indra. The demon Bali Vairocana became lord of all the world.

The thirty gods, whose authority was slain, who were conquered and whose sovereignty was ruined, that troop of gods wandered about on earth like mortals. After some time spent like this, they took refuge in Brahmā. "Oh Brahmā! We have been banished from the Devaloka by Bali, O Destroyer of Foes. What can we do? Where can we go? What is the remedy for this?"

Brahmā spoke:

> Greetings, Best of Gods, listen to the best means for you. You must go to the beautiful town of Padmāvatī, O Best of Immortals. There is the excellent, most eminent among tīrthas named Uttaramānasa, where it is said eight powers are granted and the great powers of men are bestowed. O Excellent One, nine treasures reside there. In the southern part is that excellent tīrtha of Viṣṇu. Having bathed there, a man might see the goddess of the Blest, granting magical powers. And having found the highest magic and supernatural powers, one is honored in the Viṣṇuloka. Then, on the tenth day of the bright half of the month of Āśvina, one should honor Gaṇeśa in the region of the Śamī trees, which yield the eight supernatural powers. He who honors Gaṇeśa becomes victorious in all the worlds, no doubt. Always situated at the foot of the Śamī tree, yielding the best of magical and supernatural powers, a man should worship

Gaṇeśa, granter of all wishes, constantly. Having gained the best of all his desires, he becomes a rich man and has sons. Because of that, one should go with all effort to the Mahākāla forest where the Viṣṇusarastīrtha is; go there quickly! O Excellent gods, perform worship of Viṣṇu, whose tejas is unequalled. He will be your protector from all dangers, O Best of Gods.

Having heard the words of Brahmā, whose soul is praiseworthy, those gods trying to accomplish their object reached the Mahākāla forest. Having arrived there and having become pure through acts of bathing, donations, etc., those siddhas, intent on devotion to Viṣṇu, did homage. Then all the gods with Śakra at their head questioned the god Brahmā, serving him respectfully. The gods spoke:

> O Brahmā, in what way can devotion to Viṣṇu win a victory? We want to hear all that from you, O Best of Brahmā knowers.

Brahmā spoke:

> Listen, Excellent Gods, to that unsurpassed devotion to Viṣṇu. That god who wears a white garment, who is the color of the moon and who has four arms, who has a pure countenance; one should meditate on that one for the sake of removing all obstacles. Profit, victory, from whence would there be defeat for those in whose heart Janārdana resides, dark as a blue lotus, who is worshiped by the gods for the purpose of the fulfillment of their desired objects? Homage to the leader of the troop, to him who removes all obstacles.
>
> In the beginning of the kalpa I was impelled through Śauri's desire for creation. Intent on meditation on Viṣṇu, I was not able to beget progeny. The great ṛṣi Mārkaṇḍeya, lord of all the siddhas, calm, long-lived conqueror of his senses, was seen by me. Then I approached him. Having shown each other hospitality, each with sparkling eyes, O Best of Gods, having questioned each other about his health and both comfortably seated, then he, the great sage Mārkaṇḍeya, was asked by me: "Lord, by what means can one beget healthy children? I want to hear all that, O Lord, celebrated sage!" Śri Mārkaṇḍeya spoke: "Devotion to Viṣṇu, supreme, everlasting, destroying all pain and suffering, slaying all sins, holy, bestowing all happinesses, this religious practice, this great knowledge is not to be given to just anybody; not to those who are ungrateful or undeserving or

false, or to those who are unbelievers; and never to those who are envious, disagreeable, or desirous: they obstruct everything connected with the eternal dharma. That most mysterious teaching, which destroys all sins and is the purifier of purifiers and the holy of holies, the thousand names of Viṣṇu, that auspicious act of devotion to Viṣṇu, indeed producing all supernatural powers, yielding love and liberation, is auspicious. *Oṁ!* What follows is Mārkaṇḍeya's use of the mantra praising Śriviṣṇu with a thousand names, the divinity Viṣṇu, having anuṣṭubh for its meter, recited for the purpose of attaining all desires.

The gods said:

O Viṣṇu, you are a giver of boons when you grant us this wish. Become the younger brother of Śakra, born in Aditi's womb.

Thus requested by the gods lead by Brahmā and Śakra, the Lord, having consented, disappeared. Then, in some time, the Blessed One, son of Aditi, bearing the form of infinite Viṣṇu, was called Vāmana because of his dwarfishness. O Vyāsa, Bali, son of Virocana, performed a hundred horse sacrifices, desiring to rob Indra's sovereignty. O Best of those first among twice borns! Having made Kaśyapa the priest and the best of the Bhṛgus the Hotar, the grandfather himself became the brahmin priest. The best of munis, the Bhagavan Atri became the Adhvaryu, and Nārada the Udgatṛ, and Vasiṣṭha the assessor. All the lords of munis having performed in that place, O Vyāsa, then Bali, best of kings, was ready to become the sacrificer. O Best of Munis, when he was engaged in various sacrifices, "May you sacrifice! May you eat! May you give! May you meditate," those most splendid speeches were heard, O Best of brahmins.

At that auspicious time, Vāmana arrived, smiling brightly. Reciting mantras from the four Vedas, Vāmana, best of brahmins, O Chief of Kings, stood at the door. Indeed, Vyāsa, all was told to the king by the doorkeeper. And then the mighty king Bali Virocana, standing up, offering all the water, went with his own court assessors. Having worshiped Vāmana, who promotes the welfare of the world, having lead him into the middle of the assembly hall and having given him a seat at the sacrificial altar, Bali spoke: "Where did you come from, O brahmin, and what is your desire? I shall grant it." Vāmana spoke:

O King of Kings, the whole creation is made by the supreme being Brahmā; I have come to the world wishing to see the sacrifice. I have seen the sacrifice of Varuṇa, O Faultless One, and indeed I have seen Kubera's sacrifice, and the sacrifice of Dharma and, Excellent One, that one of Prajāpati. Great King, I have seen the sacrifice of Vāyu performed according to rule, and I have also seen those sacrifices of the kingly ṛṣis, Performer of great vows. O Mighty King, your sacrifice, which I am watching, is endowed with such qualities, such as there have never been before nor will there be again. Because of this, I have come, O King, for the purpose of begging from you, Sinless One.

Bali spoke:

Ask, Best of Twice borns! I will give what you desire.

Vāmana spoke:

Chief of the kingly kings! Give me three steps of land for a dwelling, if it pleases you today, Best of Princes.

Bali spoke:

O brahmin, your request is small and by no means great—elephants, war chariots, land, and manifold jewels, handsome women, female slaves of slaves, beautiful women, wealth of different kinds, riches, splendid clothes—you must ask for these, Best of brahmins. You are the deserving one; you are one who has accomplished his purpose, fully conversant with the Vedas and Vedāṅgas.

Vāmana spoke:

I have no desire on this earth, O King, Giver of Honor. Give me three steps of land now if you have faith.

Thus spoken to by the dwarf, Bali spoke these words:

Take three steps of land for a dwelling, Giver of Honor.

Having said this, that king, compelled by his fate, even though prevented by Bhṛgu, gave the land to the brahmin, O Vyāsa. And then Hari strode over the egg of Brahmā as soon as the water was offered. This whole earth, with its forests, woods, and mountains became his three steps. Then, Vyāsa, the wealth given by Bali, and all the demon troops defeated and the sovereignty given to Śatakratu, at last Viṣṇu, bearing the form of a dwarf, went to Kumudvatī.

Having made a tīrtha originating from his own self in the holy grove of prosperity and good fortune, the greatest god made his dwelling there, O Vyāsa. That tīrtha made by Vāmana is called the *Vāmana tank.* The twelfth day of the bright half of the month of Bhadra, accompanied by the constellation Śravaṇa, is called Vāmanadvādaśī, and that day is the destroyer of koṭis of murders. Having bathed on the eleventh at that tīrtha and having fasted, awake at night, a man becomes worthy of absorption into Brahmā. On the twelfth, for those who give great gifts with distinction there is nothing impossible in the three worlds.

Thus was the Vāmana tīrtha spoken of in ancient times by the great ṛṣi, the telling of which removes all evil, is holy, and bestows all desires and boons. All this is attained by it, there should be no doubt.

Skanda Purāṇa VII.2.14–19

Chapter 14

Sārasvata spoke:

Long ago in the city of Vāmana, in the region of Vastrāpatha, the blessed ṛṣi Vasiṣṭha, burning with grief for his son, came to the bank of the Svarṇarekhā river to perform tapas. In the northeast corner of the town, in the waters of the Svarṇarekha river, having bathed and meditated, he thought about the god Śiva, and Rudra, the three-eyed one who has the bull for an emblem, approached. "O Great Ṛṣi, I am pleased with you. What can I do? Tell me that."

Vasiṣṭha spoke:

Mahādeva, if you are pleased, give me a boon now. Please stay here as long as the moon and the stars do. Sinful men who bathe here, O God, their sins are always destroyed by you, and sinful men who worship the three-eyed one, Lord of Gods, you take those men to the dwelling of Śiva in aerial carts.

Sārasvata spoke:

And having said it would be so, the god Hara disappeared from there.

Having slain Hiraṇyakaśipu, mighty Narasiṁha gave the triple world to Indra and went to Kālarudra himself. In succession Bali was born, and he was exceedingly superior in strength. Mighty Bali made universal sovereignty on earth. The earth produced crops without cultivation, was possessed of good water and endowed with corn. The flowers smelled sweet and the fruits were juicy, trees bore fruit at the top, and there was honey in each lotus. All the brahmins knew the four Vedas, the kṣatriyas were skilled in battle, the vaiśyas were intent upon tending cattle, and the śūdras intent on serving. The people were good mannered, free from plague and disease, all were well fed, always happy, and always active. Their bodies were anointed with incense and saffron, they were well dressed and well ornamented, free from poverty, suffering, and death, and long lived. The earth shone with lights at night as in the daytime, and the gods roamed about in heaven as well as on earth.

The demon Bali made his sovereignty on earth as if it were heaven. The king's dwelling was always resonant with marriage music. The Daitya enjoyed the earth as does the king of gods heaven, and the chief of gods was continually pleased by Bali's sacrifices. There was no war between the gods and Dānavas; there was only one king on earth, so there was no war there. There was no war called the *quarrel of enemies*, nor was there war between lions and elephants, nor between mongooses and serpents, nor between cats and mice. All the world, standing and moving, had a friendly disposition.

Having made a tour of the triple world, Nārada went to the Nandana grove. He did not see war in the triple world, moving and unmoving, so at that time, great pain grew in his belly. "I have nothing to do with baths and such; what is the use of libations? Uttering prayers and so on, all was done by me in vain. *That* is the bath where elephants fight with biting teeth, *that* is the twilight ceremony where the earth is adorned with decapitated bodies, blood flowing from the forehead of an elephant pierced by spears and arrows; where flesh-eaters are pleased, *that* offering is dear to me. Normally invincible kṣatriyas slain in battle by elephant heads, *that* is the oblation where elephants and excellent heroes are sacrificed. This sacrifice of Nārada, in the fire of words, celebrated in the triple world, with dangling broken feet, heads, hands, hearts, and intestines, when the surface of the earth like this is worshiped, *that* is my eternal worship of gods. What have I to do with the gods in heaven, what with men on earth? What with serpents in Pātāla; they do not fight each other. I will make war on earth through the chief of gods and Upendra. Bali must go to Rasātala; my word is truth. When he pleases Hari Damodara with the sovereignty and his life, then he will become Indra. The chief of gods, slayer of Vṛtra, will fall from sovereignty. When, having gone to Vastrāpatha, the chief of gods might honor Śiva with true devotion, then, he will be free from brahminicide." By muttering this mantra, Nārada, his stomachache gone,went quickly to see the king of gods.

Having ascended the throne in Nandana, Hari [Indra] sat down. The mighty king of gods, surrounded by gods, sat gazing at the Apsaras Rambhā, who was dancing. Seeing Nārada come, that god was astonished. "Blessed Nārada seems opposed to me. Who does not dance the dance, who does not sing the song?" While Hari [Indra] was lost in thought about whether the instruments should be sounded or not, the ṛṣi came, sprinkling water. Having left the throne and risen up, Hari [Indra] stood tall. Saluting Nārada with a welcome, Hari addressed him. "O Maharṣi, welcome to you today; why have you come? In bathing, twilight worship, and offering, is everything all right with you?" Thus addressed smilingly, Nārada spoke to Hari. "If that were so, what else would I want? I do not see a place for you, who is worthy of seeing, O Lord of Heaven. As long as the sovereignty is Bali's, then I have nothing to do with you. The Ādityas and so forth, all the planets are joined by the computation of time; clouds flooded with offerings rain down, delighted, on the earth. There is no sickness or death, and Yama is afflicted by dharma. Lord of men, he enjoys the sovereignty of the earth. He is called the *Protector of the Triple World, Great Prince, Skillful in the Science of Battle;* he is praised by bards and minstrels as the lover of Lakṣmī in the triple world. He is praised by many bards and minstrels as Brahmā, Kṛṣṇa, Hari, as Indra on earth, as Sūrya, lord of riches, protector of the enemies of the gods, and as lord of gods! Without war, the Daitya hosts laugh and drink, and the elephants cry out in rut. Men mounted on chariots whirl around, and army chiefs take delight in women in their houses. Heaven is illustrious with the smoke of the sacrificial fire, the earth shines with golden form. But the world is happy, destitute of the Vedas, and the abode of Bali is resplendent with the Daitya hosts. Bali does not recognize you as the lord of gods, and all the gods are enjoying the sacrifice of Bali. You yourself must think in your heart about your enemy. I have told you what is proper.

Rambhā does not shine in the dance; Menakā does not esteem you; and Tilottamā considers King Bali lord of the gods. Urvaśī goes to him; Sukeśā speaks together with him; Mañjughoṣā, with unhappy face, does not look at you. Pulomā does not become visibly delighted without Bali; and Paulomī, having gone before Bali, praises him, as does Maṅtharā. Nārada, Parvata, Hāhā, Hūhū, and Tumburu praise Bali's kingship in front of Rudra—this I heard. Ṛṣis propitiated with offerings of butter in the dwelling of Brahmā praise *him* in front of Brahmā; I tell you this. I should not tell you what Bṛhaspati said, but Indrāṇī, having esteemed mighty Bali, gazes at his picture.

Because of this speech, the chief of gods trembled with anger. "Elephant, vajra!" he called to the charioteer, "Bring sword, armor, and chariot! Sūrya with the chariot, the Maruts with elephant, Rudra with the bull, Sauri with Mahiṣa, sound the music for me in battle today! Lords of Durgā's host, attack hastily!" Having seen the chief of gods furious, wise Bṛhaspati, having gone to the middle of the ṛṣis, said what was proper at the time. "Long ago, four policies beginning with Sāma were declared by Manu. Among those things that can be done is reconciliation. Punishment must not be imposed. Having invited Upendra, the best of gods must take counsel. The whole world, the triple world moving and unmoving is subject to him. When all other topics are finished, one should talk to him about the good and evil of this. He alone might come to earth for the accomplishment of his own purpose. Then the lord of gods, requested by the gods in the same way, did the same. "Viṣṇu came from the Satyaloka to Mt. Mandara. The ṛṣis must go there to fetch Janārdana." Having thus spoken, Nārada arrived in Mandara from heaven in order to bathe. Gautama, Atri, Bharadvāja, Viśvāmitra, and Kaśyapa, Jamadagni, and Vasiṣṭha arrived at the palace of Viṣṇu. At the mountain, Nārada made his twilight ablutions in the waters of Gaṅgā. While he was seated, the Vālakhilya maharṣis were happy. Having been saluted with courtesy, Nārada explained, "The ṛṣis have arrived at Mandara to lead Viṣṇu to heaven. O ṛṣis, it is proper for you to see him also." Having heard that speech, the maharṣis were delighted. The Vālakhilyas, dwarfs having the size of the thumb knuckle, having gone to the palace of Hari [Viṣṇu] to bathe in the waters of the Gaṅgā, in front of them did Hari [Viṣṇu] laugh at the idea of what would happen in the future. The sons of Brahmā, the Vālakhilyas, all faithful to their vows, were filled with shame and very angry and spoke to each other loudly. "By some divine command will this one become a dwarf." Having been made aware by the ṛṣis and Viṣṇu, all were reconciled, saying, "But how will Viṣṇu's release from fate occur, explain that? If Vastrāpatha becomes a superior place to Prabhāsa, then prosperity will pervade the universe, and then the field of Vastrāpatha will become a little bit better. Having seen the god Śiva, he will be freed from sin. Your power that would accomplish the impossible will always be with you. He is the only one who sees Śiva at Vastrāpatha." Indra and Upendra, having embraced, sat on the throne.

Viṣṇu spoke:

What is to be done, O King of Gods? I will certainly do it.

Indra spoke:

The mighty Daitya Bali is a member of the family of Hiraṇyakaśipu; this whole universe is pervaded by him, and the gods have been made the enjoyers of the sacrifice by him. All the earth has gone to Devaloka, O Keśava. As long as he does not change, remembering the former animosity, then Bali, fallen from kingship, should inhabit Pātāla. On earth, the king should be anyone in the family of the sun or the moon.

Sārasvata spoke:

Having heard that speech and thinking to himself, having consented, Janārdana spoke to the sages. "The ṛṣis must go there and perform a great sacrifice. Then I will come and I will control Bali."

Thus spoken to, all the sages went to the sacrificial pavilion where the great sacrifice, lasting twelve days and possessing all dakṣinas, had begun. O Prince, in the southern region of the field of Vastrāpatha, famous in Suraṣṭradeśa, lay the celebrated city of Bali. The sacrifice, in which all one's own possessions are given as an offering, commenced outside the field. All the sages were invited to the ceremony by Śukra, and Bali, very pleased, gave gifts often at the sacrifice. Much food was given to all in golden pots and the brahmin guest, versed in the Vedas, was honored with all possessions. "The sacrifice with gifts is fulfilled, the sacrifice without gifts is useless," it is said.

At that time, Viṣṇu in dwarf form arrived in Madhyadeśa. A brahmin knowing the four Vedas, a pilgrim to tīrthas, he had a big belly, dwarfish limbs, crippled feet, and a great head, a big jaw, fat calves, thick neck, and was very lustful. He was wearing white clothes, a single lock of hair, carrying a parasol and water jar, and he wandered about on the earth to see different tīrthas. The brahmin arrived in the region of Surāṣṭradeśa, in the field of Vastrāpatha. On the bank of the Svarṇarekhā River, the dwarf thought, "Having seen Bhava first, should I go to Someśvara or Śiva? Or, having worshiped Someśvara, should I go to Mandara afterwards? Thinking thus, and having reflected about what is to be done, standing here, I will worship the lord of Soma; it is decided."

(Chapters 15 and 16 deal exclusively with the pilgrimage of Vāmana to various Śaiva tīrthas.)

Chapter 17

The king spoke:

I have heard this colorful tale through your kindness. Having seen Nārāyaṇa and Śakra, Nārada went to the mountain dwelling. What did that chief of munis do then? Tell me in detail, Sage. Tortured by delusion born from the flow of saṁsāra, O Lord, make me thirstless with that story which is like amṛta in water.

Sārasvata spoke:

Then, having recognized the god who was formerly cursed by the brahmin Bhṛgu, Nārada said, "and that will not be otherwise; think about the present; what is future will definitely happen. Having become a dwarf, Viṣṇu will go to that city and later, he will bind Bali, to my pleasure. Without war, how can one endure this terrible present? All the battles between gods and demons, demons, Gandharvas, and Rākṣases, and snakes and birds have ceased. There is no war between children of rival wives; my good fortune is destroyed. First, the chief of gods was restrained by his guru; what am I to do? The welfare of man is not accomplished because of divine fortune; then the effort is to be made by a sage for man's sake, for sometimes fortune is fruitful without man's part. That speech which was spoken is in vain, because success comes without effort. Having gone, I will speak to Bali so that he will make war. If he does not listen to my speech, I will certainly curse him."

Having said this, Nārada quickly went to Bali's palace. And in only the twinkling of an eye, he stood in heaven with two disciples. The palace was like a mountain, seven stories high and of great splendor, and in addition, its assembly hall was celestial and shining, made by Viśvakarman. O Prince, Bali was seated there on the celestial throne, surrounded by all the Daityas who were laughing boldly at good stories. He was surrounded in that celestial palace by tranquil ṛṣis and brahmins, and by Uśanas himself, and by his sons, friends, and wives. The Daitya chief was being fanned with heavenly chowries held in the grasp of Devāṅganā, and he was being praised by minstrels. While they were seated there, intoxicated with pride, they chanted to each other. All those excellent Daityas and Dānavas were longing for battle. Every time they rose, they spoke and resolved to take action with the gods. "This whole triple world is ours now; with Śukra's judgment, how will the sovereignty be attained without war? And what if the Daitya chief is amiable toward the king of gods? How is it that Bali does not ask for Airāvaṇa, ever in rut. How is it that the sun does not give its clever horse? As long as greedy Kubera is not attacked on the battlefield, he will not give up wealth collected by the gods. The ocean does not show its jewels from Rasātala. As long as we do not churn the ocean, having thrown Mandara, when the shares of amṛta from the moon are enjoyed regularly by the gods, why does not the ocean give Bali his share? The wind, cold from the rivers of heaven and fragrant from the lotus stalks, as it blows softly in heaven, it does not in Bali's palace. Clouds, raised with Indra's bow, let loose rain on the earth. Shaken by Bali's sword, they go back to heaven from the earth. On our side of the earth, Yama causes people to die, but neither in heaven nor in hell is cause and effect indeed seen. Citragupta himself engraves our happiness, children, profession, and health upon our brows, unlike that of the gods. Time, like the rainy season, winter, and summer, revolves now on earth but neither in heaven nor in hell; however, on earth they roam about afraid. You, gods and demons, sister's sons, are begotten from the same seed; how is it that we reside on earth, by whom are the gods made lofty?

But, when the ocean was being churned, the Daitya chief was cheated by the gods. All the gods stood on one side and Bali on the other. When the jewels were produced, then everyone received his fate: an elephant, a horse, the tree of heaven, the moon, a herd of cattle, and a mountain. Having seized the amṛta, we were kept busy drinking by the gods. Intoxicated by the drink, you, very proud, did not know that the nectar remaining was carried to the Satyaloka by the gods. Alas! The gods are dishonest. How is it that the remainder was not given? We were cheated out of the amṛta, having realized the so-called amṛta was wine. For those without ghee, sesame oil is dear.

It is not possible to count the cunning acts of Viṣṇu; moreover that which is done is told by those who are pleased and delighted. With white body, beautiful with lovely brows, with full, plump breasts, lovely hair, a face as fair as the moon, large eyes, slender and marked by three folds of skin at a waist which is capable of being encircled by a hand, with feet like lotuses in the soil, with arms that are adorned, possessed of all ornaments and endowed with all characteristics, the goddess fascinating the triple world, born at the churning of the amṛta, rising up before the amṛta, to whomever she belongs, the amṛta becomes his. She, the lovely-eyed one, to whomever she belongs, the triple world is his subject.

All the gods, demons, and Rāksaṣes were fascinated by her, and letting go of the churning stick, they all tried to seize her. One woman, many gods, demons, Daityas, and Rākṣases—the great controversy took place. What would happen in this case? All were stopped by Viṣṇu who, having arrived, held them by the arm and said, "Alas, why are you fighting for her among yourselves? The undertaking for the purpose of amṛta will be destroyed for the sake of a woman!" Having made the first sign, she was kissed by Viṣṇu. The bearer of the celestial form, wearing a garland and adorned by forest flowers, whose form bears the blazing kauṣṭubha, bearer of the conch, discus, and mace, having placed the lovely garland in her hand, Viṣṇu stood in front of her, and having raised his arm, Hari spoke these words to everyone. "Everyone must make a circle and sit each in his own posture. Having looked to her own desire, Lakṣmī will bestow the bride's garland. That lecher who violates the svayaṁvara will be slain by everyone together as if he preyed on others' wives. For one who commits adultery, that sin equals the killing of a woman. Any other who does so, for him the same thing will be. Having recognized the universal Hari and having spoken about what was to be done, whoever she desires among the gods, Dānavas, and Daityas, among Gandharvas, snakes, and Rākṣases, he may truly be her husband."

Attracted earlier by his glance, she was fascinated by him. She observed his glance, which is the first attraction of women. Putting hand to ear and saying, "this is so," whoever a woman tortured by Kāma's arrows puts in her heart, here she may choose him, there is no doubt. Earlier, when that quarrel took place, they were stopped by Hari. When she was seized by everyone, she did not leave Hari. She spoke, "You are my husband." He replied, "Leave me and go away." Having left her at a distance, then Viṣṇu entered the gods' circle. Having left Lakṣmī, they all went to their own places. Vijayā named all the gods in order and she looked, and afterward, having deliberated, she left. "Śiva, calm and indifferent, the three-eyed husband of Gaurī, never looks at another, the three-eyed one eternally intent upon meditation." When told by her friend, "This is the Grandfather," she bowed and she moved away, and keeping silent, she did not look. "The sun has the color of the lotus, the fire's nature is that of burning, the wind blows, and Varuṇa is my father," and, saying this, she moved away. "Intent on Paulomī's face, the chief of gods does not please me. Yama Vaivasvata, pulling, punishing, splitting, cutting, binding, and murdering, does not have a mild manner." Having seen the gods, Dānavas, Gandharvas, Daityas, serpents, and Rākṣases, those terrible ones, then she moved away. Now she saw this best of men and having gotten a look at him, whose face was bewildering with large eyes, who was unsurpassed in good fortune and preeminence, lovely, bewitching even Kāma, and marked by tiny beads of sweat bristling hair, looked on by the chief of the gods, Dānavas, and Daityas with anger. The lovely one made this handsome one her husband, and then gave the garland herself.

Having seen the god's gesture, the Daityas spoke to each other. "See the share of the gods; they all went to heaven themselves. We go to the bottom of Pātāla, and men go to earth. The gods go to the three worlds; we will not be going to heaven. Let men who are kṣatriyas make the sovereignty on earth. But having left Pātāla, if the earth is protected by Daityas and Dānavas, by any one, by Rākṣases, that is not fair. Why say more about this? Bali is king in the three worlds. Having divided the jewels equally, let him rule. When the gods become arrogant, then they will see Nārada, coming from heaven like a second sun, carrying the book of war, intent on employing the staff of Brahmā, bearing the black antelope skin, tranquil with parasol, lute, and water jar, wearing a brahmin's girdle tied with a knot of three strands of muñja grass, peaceful, bearing the form of Brahmā, adorned by celestial rosaries which have drooping garlands of cord and knots made in the last kalpa." Nārada thought thus, "What is this conversation of Brahmā and Hara, proud of their own birth? What angry people are talking about this?" Having seen Nārada arrive, they all stood up in amazement. "O Lord, do us a kindness; please come in to my home. I am fortunate, I am meritorious, you have come to my house." Thus spoken to by Bali, the brahmin entered the demon's palace, and having been given a seat and water for his feet, the brahmin was honored. Having entered, all the Daityas and Dānavas were seated together. Then the Daitya Bali spoke to Nārada together with Śukra. "This is the sovereignty, these are my wives, these are my sons, and I am Bali. Tell me whatever you want; giving is my first vow."

Nārada spoke:

Brahmins who are pleased with devotion are gods of the earth. But those who are not worshiped, and zealously beg again, they are the most vile. Worshiped by you, I am pleased. What use are riches to me? I am pleased by your sovereignty, and by sacrifices, gifts, and vows. O Bali, the gods did something disagreeable to you. Being paid reverence to by you, the king of gods is not yet pleased. All the gods cannot endure your sovereignty on earth. The idea of a war between you and the gods became a troublesome matter for me in heaven. Whoever goes to enemy territories first, having prepared the army, that kṣatriya is victorious, and his sovereignty is prosperous. Your sovereignty will be destroyed; I have heard this. Realizing this, do whatever is fitting quickly.

Bali spoke:

How should the king make the sovereignty? Tell me this, Illustrious One. A gift should be given to a fit person, so tell me about him.

[Ślokas 84–204 describe the duties of a sovereign enumerated by Nārada to Bali.] Sārasvata spoke:

Having said this to the Daitya, Nārada went to Mt. Raivataka. The Daitya chief deliberated, "Now what should I do? The quarrel with the gods does not please me, O Best of Asuras."

The counselors spoke:

> It is not very proper for virtuous kṣatriyas to stay at home.
> They will see you as incompetent when they come themselves.
> Because of that, we will go together to the chief of gods.

Having heard this, he gave the first drumroll in the battle with the gods. Having gathered the army together, the Daityas set forth to Mt. Meru, where the beautiful city of the king of gods lay in the east. Having seen the army approaching Mt. Meru, the gods' army was on the march on the king of gods' command. In the eastern sector of Sumeru, the war took place. When all the gods' army joined together with the Daitya troops, their war appeared like the great pralaya. Having mounted Airāvaṇa, the king of gods approached. Mounting his chariot, the Daitya chief and others went to battle. Because the gods were the enjoyers of the sacrifice, they were not desirous of war. But seeing Bali, Airāvaṇa did not move toward the battle. Turning away from the battle, he left, surrounded by the elephants of the quarters. Bali, by whose arm the saṁkalpa was performed in sacrifice, indeed with that arm he stopped all the gods in battle. Thus impeded and turning their backs, they retreated. What did the king of gods do? The thunderbolt did not perform its function, and freed from his arm, it did not go. Then, between them, many battles took place. The mighty Daityas were not being slain in battle by the gods. In need of strength, the gods were aroused by their guru. "All the gods are immortal"; thus were the demons controlled by Śukra. Having recognized the fifth avatāra of Hari, Vāmana, the chief of gods established the sovereignty in Amarāvati, delighted. The Daitya chief danced in the war and in his own home sacrificed to the gods. The Daityas approached Pātāla, and men established the sovereignty. Then all the gods' troops took counsel with the gods. "The Daitya rules the two worlds, the lord of gods rules heaven. Until Vāmana reaches Mt. Raivataka, we should tolerate Bali. The gods should keep quiet, conquered by the Daityas."

As soon as Vāmana was born on earth, bad omens arose for the Daityas. Jackals, having entered the city, howled dissonantly in the night. Crows roamed the city day and night, crying. Snakes, dark and terrible, full of poison, crept in houses. Herons, vultures, and cranes circled about above the city. Fetuses were born upside down to women, cows, and deer. There was no butter in milk, no oil in the sesame seed. Country people were always fighting with each other. Kālī, with gaping mouth and long hair, blind, unknown, and crying, went from house to house in the city saying, "Who and what this is, is not known." An ascetic covered with ashes, a naked ascetic maintaining a vow of silence, walked ahead from house to house. He created a riot, and afterward made the sound, "Ḍāmaruḍḍāmaru." Angry clouds let loose plenty of water unseasonably; the mountains rumbled a lot, their interiors filled with hail, an earthquake occurred and a preternatural glowing of the horizons appeared after it. Having assembled, a pack of hounds, all with heads upward, howled incessantly at night in the city; and an owl imitated that sound. A comet rose in the night, indicating the destruction of the kingdom of Bali. An opening in the sun's orb made by a bolt was seen, there were dense clouds in the sky, and the moon did not shine. That opening created by Rohinī occurred in the reversal of the conjunction of planets, and the stars were counted by day by the more excellent people. A reversal of seeds occurred on earth in women, cows, and deer; horses neighed unexpectedly and elephants did not rut. The plan discussed by counselors for the destruction of the kingship did not remain secret. The fire into which an oblation was made by the brahmins with ghee did not burn. A violent wind blew, resembling a storm and shaking the trees. Banners burned in funeral mounds, and the sky became dust colored.

These and many other portents appeared at Bali's house, arising when Vāmana was born, after Nārada's coming. And another dream-vision was born that day; when the wicked Daityas are bound, they will fall into ruin.

Thus having seen the portents, he did not set out; Bali always stayed at home and maintained the sovereignty. He was not well and had a headache and pain in his body; feverish, he did not sleep, eat, or drink well; whatever he ate was not digested. All the world was perplexed.

Having seen the world inverted, Bali, his mind perplexed and distressed, took counsel with the brahmins about this. Having invited the guru Śukra and having made him sit in the assembly hall, the Daitya asked after his welfare with supreme devotion. "Everything revolves in reverse order; tell me about that. That which Nārada told me will surely come to pass. Speak a propitiatory portent together with my brahmins."

Śukra spoke:

> A sacrifice in which all one's own property is given is to be performed with brahmins and kṣatriyas, to appease the portents, and it must last for twelve years. Ṛṣis, brahmins, munis, and celibates must go to the great sacrifice, and even those who live far away. The sacrificial pavilion is to be made in the south-

ern sector of the city. Whatever pleases anyone, that is to be given by you, O Prince.

Saying, "I will do that,"he got busy with the sacrifice. Having brought together all the brahmins skillful in performing the sacrifice, they were initiated into the sacrifice, which possessed all gifts. "When asked, all my own possessions will be given by me to the brahmins. Requested, I will bestow wives, myself, sons, and friends. A gift is always to be given to brahmins by me at the sacrifice. Even if restrained, I am not to stop; it is to be given by me, surely. If I do not give when asked, then my sacrifice is in vain. Having built the celestial pavillion, which is many yojanas long, there, gifts, food, and raiment will be given." The seven ṛṣis came together to earth from heaven. All the brahmins abiding on earth assembled from every quarter, and the kṣatriyas assembled, having won all kinds of wealth. They gave various riches to the king when the sacrifice began. Dancers, singers, and reciters came from the corners of the earth, and the sound caused by the recitation of the Veda mingled with the sound of music and song. The requests of "Give, give," made the triple world deaf. The words, *give me* or *don't give* or *give me a little,* such words were not heard there at that time. Whoever asked for anything, that was given to him. Indeed, whoever asks for much is not a brahmin. Good brahmins do not accept anything for the sake of food and raiment, glittering jewels and silver, or horses, chariots, and elephants. Good brahmins do not accept homes, cows, land, or villages. Pleased by Bali's reign, what would they do with wealth?

Thus the great sacrifice in which all one's possessions are given commenced. Others danced, sang, recited, and praised the sacrifice, full of many gifts. Brahmā, Indra, Rudra, the planets, sun, and moon were worshiped with oblations and mantras. Some praised Bali and others the guru, some the Hotar and some, the followers. "Neither the region of Prajāpati nor of the chief of gods will be reached, but having given the kingdom to the chiefs of brahmins, he will certainly go to Rasātala, together with his sons and friends." The brahmins made this speech, the Daityas listened. What could they say? Assembled before Bali, they reported. Bali, thrilled, gave what was asked for.

Chapter 18

The king spoke:

When Vāmana reached the great field of Vastrāpatha, beginning then, what did he do, tell me in detail.

Sārasvata spoke:

> O Best of Princes, Vāmana made his dwelling in front of Bhava, having bathed in the water of the Svarṇarekhā and having worshiped Bhava. When he was standing alone in a quiet place free from thorns and bones, sitting on the best seat and clad in a black antelope skin, that best of brahmins, having assumed the lotus posture, became self-possessed and motionless. Having made his neck straight and concentrating on the tip of his nose, having freed his thoughts from house, fields, wife, and from wealth, and having given up the Vaiṣṇava māyā, that lord of his senses became silent. Without any food, having conquered his anger and free from the bonds of saṁsāra, having put his arms in the lotus position, he closed his eyes a little. Having realized that the mind is unsteady, the brahmin made his heart stable. In due course, with much study, he made the breaths separate as well as one, and inhaled and exhaled the breaths Vyāna, Udana, Samān, and Khyā. Having seized that breath in the quarters and having put it in his heart, he directed the breath toward Brahman.

[Ślokas 9–21 are concerned with the particulars of breath control.]

Thus, when the brahmin dwarf sat near Bhava, he saw Nārada, descended from heaven. Vāmana spoke:

> O Mahārṣi, hail to thee! Why have you come today? I bow to you, O Mahārṣi, you who are like Brahmā in the three worlds.

Nārada spoke:

> I have arrived from heaven, and I will tell you how I am. The day of Brahmā is filled with the comings and goings of the sun. The night is born at sunset, and at night the gods perish. What is to be told of the mortal world and those who die day after day? The sky has become filled with smoke; the gods have gone to Bali's dwelling. The seven ṛṣis, brahmins, and celibates have gone there, Hāhā, Hūhū, and Tumbaru have gone, Nārada and Parvata as well. The host of Apsarases and Gandharvas have arrived at Bali's palace, because the sacrifice that expiates evil portents is being performed by Bali himself. I want to go there to see the sacrifice at Bali's abode! Bali has performed one less than one thousand sacrifices. When this sacrifice is complete, the whole world will become the Daityas'. He has started

some excess at the sacrifice: "Those who ask for whatever they want, it is to be given to brahmins by me. Even if I am restrained, I am to give. My words are truthful. Myself, my wives, the kingship, my sons and dear ones, if requested and I do not give, may my sacrifice be in vain." With these words, my headache became bigger. Having promised, how will this sacrifice not be complete? I roam through the triple world, but I see no way to destroy it. Having recognized the instrument of destruction, I have come to you. As the sacrifice is not yet completed, it must be done now.

Vāmana spoke:

O Mahārṣi, hear my words; What am I to do? The gods have assembled at the sacrifice, as have all the ṛṣis and brahmins. How will it be fruitless? Again, hear my words, O Brahmārṣi, lord of brahmins. With no wife or sons, why are you like this? You have no happiness without war, nor happiness without quarreling. An argument of some kind or another is always dear to you. Bathing, twilight ceremonies, muttering prayers, oblations, libations to the manes and gods, Nārada does these and also something different, and brahmins do something else. My curiosity is born, O Mahārṣi, tell me quickly.

Nārada spoke:

Listen, Vāmana, when the end of the night of the Padma Kalpa had passed, the Brahmāṇḍa was pervaded by water, and nothing else existed. The god of gods reclined on the waters, and he is known as Nārāyaṇa. He is Brahmā, he is Śiva, there is no difference between them. When they become distinct, then they are three gods. But then the three were born distinct to make the Varāhakalpa. The gods Brahmā, Viṣṇu, and Hara possess rajas, sattva, and tamas. Brahmā fashioned the creation; Hari protects it; Hara destroys the whole triple world, moving and unmoving. Having acted thus, the lords of gods, seated on a throne on the peak of beautiful Kailāsa, consult with each other. Of the three, which god is best? Who is the greatest? Who has superior qualities? There is no fourth. Who knows? The three stand together. The light appeared from them, that became the sky. Joined by the measurement of time, it rotates as the sun's disk. "I am the greatest," "I am the best," was the argument of Hara and Brahmā. While the two quarreled, I was born from their mouths, O Lord. Why, O God, do you not know what was then spoken by Brahmā? "The ten avatāras, fish, tortoise, and so on, of long ago, are for you to sport." Those were impeded by Rudra. Having gone, saying, "The quarrel is not proper," Viṣṇu said, "Let there be ten avatāras."

At the beginning of the kalpa I was born from Brahmā's mouth, O Best of Brahmins. My birth was because of their quarrel, and therefore quarreling is dear to me.

Formerly, at the beginning of the kalpa it was thought by Brahmā himself while he was creating, "How is the creation to be performed by me, an ascetic, O Hari? The Vedas are lost. I do not know where the Vedas have gone. I do not know even whether the earth is in its place or in a dwelling below. The power to go into the middle of the waters is not mine now. The protection of the creation is to be performed by you through ten avatāras. You will become a fish in water, moving through the water in the great rivers. Having taken the Vedas swiftly, you should give them to me." And then the god who made the great form of a fish in water brought the Vedas and gave them to Brahmā long ago. "Again, having taken the form of a tortoise, you will support Mandara." So was Viṣṇu spoken to by Brahmā. "Lakṣmī will marry you." Long ago, I saw your excellent deeds at the churning, when the earth, having reached Rasātala, was not seen. In a place made for the sake of the Brahmāṇḍa, there she was not seen. Impelled by Brahmā himself, saying, "Make the form of a boar," having created the form of the great boar, he went beneath the earth. And then, having raised up the earth with the tip of his tusk, Viṣṇu led her to the appropriate place. And the third avatāra is fascinating even to Hara, by which the wide earth was supported together with the mountains.

And I will tell about the fourth, the terrible man-lion, about the gods, the sons of Aditi, and the mighty sons of Diti, the Daitya Hiraṇyakaśipu and mighty Hiraṇyākṣa.

The gods dwelt in heaven, and all the Daityas and Dānavas in Pātāla. The Daitya Hiraṇyakaśipu established the kingdom in Rasātala, and the sons of Manu were established on earth by the gods and Dānavas. O Brahmin, Hiraṇyakaśipu violated the law and established the sovereignty on earth, having vanquished the chief of gods. He seized the earth possessing seven islands, and desirous of seizing Amarāvati, he enjoyed himself, revered by his sons and grandsons. That slow-witted one tormented his sons beginning with Prahlāda. While his sons were being taught, Prahlāda also learned. While Prahlāda was being taught, he became angry: "The Daitya does not honor the gods because of his sovereignty over the two worlds." Pleased with Hiraṇyakaśipu's austerities, Lord Brahmā granted him a wish. "Immortality from the gods and men, O Best of Gods. May my death be from no one. If it must be, let it be from Viṣṇu, who may be somewhat lion, somewhat man. I will die from him, torn by his nails, but not on earth." "It will be so," but having said this, Brahmā was astonished.

With the passing of time, there was a great battle. "What will the gods do to me? What is the use of Viṣṇu? I am to be constantly worshiped with sacrifices; what can Rudra do to me?" Thus indeed, while Hiraṇyakaśipu was like this, Prahlāda praised Hari. By whom his death was to take place, he remembers only Hari. When he was being restrained, he invoked Hari, having four arms, bearing the conch, mace, and sword, dressed in yellow clothing, always decorated by the kauṣṭubha. "I call to mind Viṣṇu, single lord of the world, who bestows liberation by merely being remembered." With these words, the Daitya, disturbed, commanded the Daityas: "Slay him, that wicked one, with elephants, snakes, water, and fire."

Prahlāda spoke:

> Viṣṇu is in the elephant, and Viṣṇu is in the serpent; Viṣṇu is in the water and Viṣṇu is in the fire. O Daitya, Viṣṇu abides in you and he abides in me. Without Viṣṇu there is no Daitya host.

Even though killed, he never attained death. Hiraṇyakaśipu's breast was tortured by the fire of anger. Then, having made Prahlāda sit down in front of him, to teach his son, with these cruel words he prepared to kill his own son. "Shame on you! If you praise Nārāyaṇa, if you praise my enemy again, I will cut off your head like a flower with the best of swords. I am Viṣṇu, I am Brahmā, Rudra, and Indra; speak a wish. Having left your own father, who else do you praise, child? When the boy does not study, he does not praise his own father." Having been beaten with a stick by his guru, Prahlāda was compelled again, "Speak one word, pupil. Give me the guru's gift, so that the master is pleased, and he gives me much wealth."

Prahlāda spoke:

> Strike me first! I will make a speech, O Guru. I praise Viṣṇu, by whom the triple world, moving and unmoving, was made, raised, and pacified. May Viṣṇu be pleased with me.

> Viṣṇu is Brahmā; Viṣṇu is Hara, Indra, Vāyu, Yama, and the fire, the tattvas starting with Prakṛti, the twenty-fifth puruṣa. He resides in the body of the father, in the body of the guru, and in my body. Knowing this, how can I praise a dying wretch?

The guru spoke:

> Who is vile among men, O Pupil? In death starting with birth, O Vile One, why don't you praise your father, but instead, dying say, "Hari, Hari?"

Prahlāda spoke:

> When eating, sleeping, traveling, in fever, when spitting, in battle, the man for whom the word *Hari* does not exist, he is wretched in death. In danger, in the royal family, in war, in sickness, in intercourse, in the forest, in inability, and in the saṁnyāsi, in death, fools residing on the earth call to mind their mother, and vile men their father. There is no mother, there is no father, there are no kinsfolk for me. Without Hari there is no one; Do what you will.

With these words, the angry Daitya stood up to strike. Then Prahlāda's mother, having arrived, stood in front of her son. "Brothers, kinfolk, and sisters say, 'do not speak about Hari.' I am your mother and these are your sister, brothers, and people who are kinfolk. So it is, dear one, that we stay together for many years."

Prahlāda spoke:

> Who is my mother, who is my sister, who are my brothers, and who is my father? Listen to my kinfolk, Mother, with whom I always live; of those whose urine is drunk by me, there is much filth in their bowels. That mother is hell to me; I cannot speak further. There is no other such hell made, but made by Viśvakarman. But any being like you who does not hold Hari in her heart, for ten months she will drink urine, satisfied; I am sure of that. Brothers truly are brothers; if they fight, even in the womb, how can a wretched mother prevent them? All the kinfolk appear old; they teach wisdom to others. Why is a family called a family, whoever comes or does not come? The familial bond is meant to be a hell for us. I have another mother, another father, having known whom, those brothers, sisters, and relatives would attain liberation.

> Prakṛti is our mother, buddhi is our sister, then Ahaṁkāra is born, who is known as *I*. The tanmātras are my own five brothers who go together with me. This is my nature, the Vikāra is my kinfolk. He who is the twenty-fifth puruṣa is the bearer of these. He is my father, in my body does Hari reside as supreme soul. If he is thought of, Hari appears in the heart. Endowed with the sovereignty of the guṇas, and so on, his place is there. That sovereignty which is highly honored by you, where Viṣṇu is not worshiped along with Brahmā, Rudra, the god of wind, and the fire, is like a blade of grass to me. That one who appears before one's eyes, he roams without support. Thus, he is the Bhagavan Viṣṇu; all these reside in heaven. All the planets are joined at the pole star, and those that are stars reside there also. By Viṣṇu's command, they all do not fall to earth. At the proper time, the destruction of the universe is determined by him himself. Having reflected thus, I do not fear death by you.

At the end of his speech, having struck Prahlāda with his foot, his father spoke,

> Where is he? I will kill him first, and afterwards you, who speaks about Hari.

Prahlāda spoke:

> Blessed Hari is the elements, earth and so on; he is on the ground, in the water, what else? This whole world is Viṣṇu. Hari resides in the grass, in the wood, in the home, on the field, in the object, and in the body; he is known through jñānayoga; why is he not seen, even with the naked eye? He travels alone from Brahmā's dwelling to Rasātala and to earth in an instant. He infuses the scents, he produces everything, Viṣṇu hears everything.

Thus spoken to, and having abandoned his natural affection, Hiraṇyakaśipu rose from the throne, and having drawn his blazing sword, striking Prahlāda with the top of his hand, he said these unbearable words: "*Now* remember Viṣṇu; you, with blazing earrings, your head will fall to earth like ripe fruit from the mountain. Or else, show Viṣṇu issuing from that pillar." But Prahlāda, having abandoned his fear, sat in lotus posture on the ground. Having fixed his neck in an upward posture and having restrained his breath, meditating on the god Hari in his heart, he remained, waiting for death.

slay the Rakṣasa. Having slain Kumbhakarṇa and then Meghanada in the battle, having killed the demon Rāvaṇa while all the Rakṣases are looking, I shall give Laṅkā, built by the gods, to Vibhīṣana. And having returned to Ayodhyā, having made that kingdom free from thorns, through the pure deeds of Durvāsas and Kāla I shall go to Amarāvati with my brothers, having given the kingdom to my son.

When the Dvāpara arrives and the earth is overloaded with many kṣatriyas, when she cannot maintain herself and starts toward Pātāla, then the great Asura Kaṁsa shall be the ruler in Mathurā. Siśupāla, Jarāsaṅdha, the great Asura Kālanemi, Vasudeva, and the mighty Asura king Bāṇa, all endowed with horses and swift elephants, they shall be slain by me, O Sage. In the Kali, clouds have little water, and cows, little milk. There is no butter in the milk, and no truth among men. The worlds are afflicted by thieves and tormented by plagues; they do not have a protector, and become quarrelsome. Lowly rivers dry up in Karttika, flowing towards the west. There is no vow for the eleventh day, nor any for the dark fourteenth day. People do not know anyone courageous, even in their own homes. Everything is damaged by poverty, deprived of the twilight ablutions. In the Kali, nothing will be as it was in the previous three yugas. A child, having left his father and mother, enjoys his wife; neither his kinsfolk nor anyone else does he serve. As the Kali pervades the earth, so all the people will become of one appearance. The universe, destitute of twilight ablutions, will be infested with Mlecchas, and I shall become a brahmin, known as Kalki. Having destroyed the Mlecchas, whose priest is Yajñavalkya, I shall worship with sacrifices of gold for the purpose of expiation.

These shall be my avatāras, and when they come to pass, there shall be war. At this moment, the gods will not fight with Bali. The Daitya chief honors me; Bali shall not be slain by me. He makes a vow to give all his wealth at the great sacrifice.

Sārasvata spoke:

Having spoken to Nārada and dismissed him, the god went to see the sacrifice made by Bali, to accomplish the gods' business. Having come to the town, Vāmana looked from house to house, and arriving at the home of brahmins, he begged some food. From the house of a brahmin, intent on bathing and always engaged in the study of the Veda, did Vāmana succeed in begging food. In the beautiful temple at the crossroads he sat, surrounded by many people, moving his large waist. He shook his huge head, having large jaws and a thick neck, he danced rhythmically and sang very beautifully. Vāmana recited the four Vedas, sitting with the brahmin; the family of Daityas and all the brahmins worshiped beautiful Vāmana day and night. Then Vāmana was led by them all to the sacrificial enclosure. "Decidedly, you will ask Bali for a place for a hut. That will be a great happiness for us, for the town, and the country." Then Vāmana was requested by all the Daitya brahmin youths, "O Vāmana, you should always dwell in the town of the Daitya chief."

Sārasvata spoke:

Having said it would be so, Vāmana entered the sacrificial enclosure, and a great uproar was made by those standing at the door. He stood along with many brahmins reciting the Vedas, and the great sound of the Vedas arose in the sacrificial enclosure. First, two Daityas entered and announced to the Daitya Bali, "O Lord, the brahmin Vāmana has come to see your sacrifice, out of curiosity. As he has entered the vicinity of the door alone, Vāmana is coming toward you. O Lord, whatever he is, the dwarf is free from desires, having made the sound of the four Vedas with one mouth." Delighted, Bali spoke these words. "Let him enter! I shall worship the chief of brahmins and I will give whatever is desired. I remember the words of Smṛti which my guru spoke: 'Here is someone full of Veda who is worthy of receiving; some other worthy person would be full of austerities.' The worthy person who comes will save me. When the sacrifice begins, then the gift is to be given by me. Vāmana is not to be doubted; my words are truthful."

Having heard this, the guru Śukra restrained Bali.

Śukra spoke:

All brahmins who are miserable, blind, wretched, and so on are to be honored at the entrance, as well as those who are deaf, dwarfed, humpbacked, diseased, and cruel. The dwarf must be honored with clothes of gold and silver at the door. But the birth of four people is in vain, and sixteen types of gifts are in vain: in vain is the birth of those without sons, and those dwelling beyond dharma, and those who eat another's food, and those who desire another's wife. One should not give riches earned by unfair means, gifts to those who are not brahmins or to one who has risen and fallen, to a brahmin who does not perform the twilight sacrifice, who is lost, fallen, or a thief, to one who causes dissatisfaction or who is unkind to father and mother, to an unworthy brahmin, a husband of a Śūdra woman, to one who sells the Veda for money, as well as to an ungrateful and wanton performer of ceremonies, to one conquered by woman, or to the snake catcher, or to relatives; these are the sixteen gifts given in vain.

Sārasvata spoke:

At the end of this, Bali said, "O Guru, you should not say such things. Anyone who studies the Veda, he is Viṣṇu to me, and he has come. There should be no delay when a theologian comes to my house. By rising up and with words, and with foot washing and food, this is how one gives according to one's means as a householder. If not worshiped, the dwarf will leave the sacrificial pavilion. Then, this sacrifice in which all gifts are given becomes fruitless."

Meanwhile, Vāmana was brought near to Bali. Arriving, the Daitya saw the dwarf, having the form of Viṣṇu, shining brightly and golden like the sun. Standing up in front of him, and having made an obeisance before him, Bali said, "I am fortunate; this brahmin who is like Viṣṇu has arrived at my sacrifice." Brought to the middle of the altar, Bali gave him a seat, and having given him water to wash his feet, to sip from, and to worship with, and having worshiped him with sandal and fragrant flowers, Bali stood before him. Having immediately offered him milk and honey, and a cow, when the milk and honey were smelled by Vāmana, "Welcome," was spoken by Bali, and "Hail to thee," was said by the brahmin. "I am a beggar who has come; give!" "Tell me what, All-pervader." "Give me land, Daitya." "How much, Best of Brahmins?" "Chief of Daityas, give me three steps for my dwelling. Having made a celestial hut, I will teach pupils." "The three steps are given to you." "I accept them," said Vāmana. "Do not give," said Śukra, "this is the eternal Viṣṇu." Delighted, Bali said to his counselor Śukra, "Who would be a worthier recipient than this?" Having put the thread over his left shoulder, when the darbha grass and whole grain were put in Bali's right hand, the guru did not make the offering and did not pour the water into his hand. All the ṛṣis and hotars who were seated in the assembly hall were amazed, as were the brahmins, Daityas, lads, wives, sons, and relations. When *given* and *received* were spoken, why was the water not poured? Water is given in the hand to Vāmana for the sake of judgment. That gift which was given with words was not done in action. Having sent the sacrificer into a foul hell, there is no atonement. Uśanas spoke, "O Daitya chief, this dwarf is Hari himself. By some divine means, he has come to see you. Whether favorable or unfavorable, I do not know what he will do." The sacrificer spoke to the Bhargava, "Listen to these words, Guru: in gift-giving times, it is said by sacrificers and brahmins, too, 'I am Indra, a brahmin, Viṣṇu, wealth, and the gods.' How am I not to give to Viṣṇu, saying, 'Be pleased?' " Having spoken, Bali poured the water in Vāmana's hand. Then, having said "What is this?" he remained standing outside the sacrificial pavilion. And in the middle, the brahmin dwarf became as big as Bali. He shook hands with the Asura chief in order to accept the three steps. The sacrificer and brahmin were pleased, observed at the sacrifice by the gods and others. Vāmana grew exceedingly, having taken a four-armed form. Nārada arrived and said, "What did you do, Bali?" Pleased, he stood before them with two pupils and danced again and again. "Take the gift, O God," said Bali together with his wife. "Now, what is not gained by me when Janārdana accepts? Whatever there is, with that you should be happy. Having made his one and a half steps smaller, he asks for three steps of land." Having seen Hari growing larger, the brahmins, ṛṣis, and gods praised the Blessed One Janārdana, who was reaching the sky. The gods and ṛṣis spoke: "Victory, O God, Victory, Endless One, Victory Viṣṇu, Victory, Acyuta, Victory, O Fish. Praise to you, Victory, Tortoise, Supporter of the Earth. Obeisance to the boar, obeisance, man-lion, obeisance. Jamadagni, hail to thee, Rāma together with Lakṣmana, hail, Kṛṣṇa, world-protector, Victory to the son of Devakī. I praise the Buddha and Kṛṣṇa, I bow to Kalkin."

Sārasvata spoke:

Then Nārada sang and danced over and over, and went to heaven. Yogis beginning with Sanaka praised Janārdana. When Kṛṣṇa was growing in front of Bali, he reached the atmosphere. All stood with upturned faces, looking toward the sun. Hari, whose form was seen like an umbrella, reached the upper regions. The sun shone like a jewel on Hari's head and, appearing like a tilaka, was seen on his perfect brow by the Daityas. And while Hari grew, the sun appeared like an earring in his ear, and while growing, it appeared like the kauṣṭubha on Hari's breast. The gods beginning with Indra, the Rudras, and Vasus remained in the sky. Where there was Hari above, there was no heaven. Then, forest flowers were placed around his neck by Indra. The earth trembled, as did all those residing in the heavenly orb of the sun. "What will happen?" The Daityas, terrified, looked at the sun. The sun appeared like a lotus in his navel and like a girdle at his waist. Thus growing, Viṣṇu took his second step. There was no place for the third in the entire Brahmāṇḍa. The measuring rod of the day, creator of the universe, acted like the staff of Brahmā. This foot of Viṣṇu is worshiped and praised by the gods, demons, Gandharvas, men, snakes, and birds. He whose soul is dharma, whose staff is restrained, is sung about repeatedly by the Gandharvas. The sun, who is the staff of the axle of the wheel, is he created by Hari himself. Having conquered this earth, Gaṅgā was made as the staff of the banner by the gods, staff of the legs of Trivikrama; it certainly acts like the staff of fame. Having been struck swiftly by Hari, he reaches the top of the Brahmāṇḍa. His feet having pierced the top, he will go out quickly. This one who breaks out from the Brahmāṇḍa, called *Virāj,* his form contains all seeds and he is called the *Supreme Soul.* This universe was arranged in front of his feet. Having pierced the Brahmāṇḍa, you are not to break out of it. Thus, through him, the foot of Hari bore fruit in the Brahmāṇḍa and the Brahmāṇḍa was broken because of the foot. When it was pierced, holy water flowed toward the three worlds. Then, Gaṅgā arose from Viṣṇu's step and issued from the top. That goddess who flooded the triple world was carried by Rudra himself. The river of heaven is worshiped in heaven and is called *Gaṅgā* when she comes to earth. When she reaches Pātāla, she is known as the one who flows through heaven, earth, and the nether regions, by merely rememberance of whom, all sins may be destroyed. From the sight of her, one may obtain the fruit of a completed Aśvamedha, and by merely bathing in her, the sins made in seven births are destroyed. That man who, having bathed, worships the gods Hari and Hara, he, having surpassed the Indraloka, will go higher to the Viṣṇuloka. An ascetic, having drunken the water from Viṣṇu's step, having recognized the tattvas, and having fasted, he will go to heaven and will gain Viṣṇu's liberation.

Chapter 19

The king spoke:

Having accepted the gift from the Daitya, what did Mahāviṣṇu Janārdana do? Tell me, my interest is great!

Sārasvata spoke:

Thus praised by the gods, the god Hari, having seized the earth, banished Bali when the sacrifice was completed. At the end of the sacrifice, having obtained the gift, the sacrifice was fulfilled. But before the third step could be fulfilled, the mighty Bhagavan approached Bali and spoke, his lower lip quivering slightly: "O Daitya Chief, in debt there are fetters of frightful appearance. Deliver that step to me; if not, accept the fetters." Having heard Viṣṇu's words, Bali's son Bāṇa, having been first-born, spoke to Vāmana, whose form held the universe. "Having made the earth smaller, becoming a dwarf, and having requested three steps, how did your form come to encompass the universe? If, O Lord of the World, you ask for the third step, become a dwarf again, and Bali will grant that step. The water offering was made by Bali to the portion that appeared as a dwarf. Why is that to be given to one appearing in a universal form? Your honor, this universe was made by you. Bali dwells in this universe. Those who are wise do not win through deceit. O World Protector, this world is yours if you wish. If you know that Bali is averse to bhakti and has no limits, then he should be driven out by binding his throat; who will stop you? The master of cows makes someone else the cowherd for the sake of protection. But the first cowherd, who gives them good grass, what is he to do then?" Thus spoken to by the son of Bali, the Blessed One, Primal Creator Janārdana spoke. "Listen to my reply to the words spoken by you who are young, which is accompanied by reason. I said to your father before, Bāṇa, 'Give me three steps in proportion,' and then this was done. Why does your father Bali not know my size, Son; the three steps were made for Bali's welfare. O Bāleya, the water was given by your father, and because of that, he will dwell in Sutala for a kalpa. Bāṇa, when the Manvantara of Vaivasvata has gone and when the Savārṇika arrives, at that time Bali will become Indra." Having spoken thus to Bali's son Bāṇa, the god with three strides, approaching Bali, spoke these words sweetly. "Because the gift at the sacrifice was incomplete, you must go to that great region named Sutala, King. Dwell there in Pātāla, content."

Bali spoke:

While I dwell in Sutala, how can I see your feet? How can I worship, how can I enjoy, how can I dwell comfortably?

The Blessed One spoke:

Daitya Chief, I will dwell eternally in your heart. Henceforth, having obtained this vision, I will stay near you. There will be another holy festival after the festival of Śakra is over; there will be a great festival called Dīpapratipad. There, excellent men, delighted, well fed, and beautifully adorned, will praise you zealously with gifts of flowers and lights. That will be the holiest festival on earth, Daitya, and with that you will be happy for the whole year. Men who are firm in devotion will praise you, according to rule, and they also will become fortunate. When the sovereignty is yours, as it is now, then in the same way will there be moonlight." Having said this to the lord of the sun and moon, and having made him dwell in Sutala with his wife, having restored the earth, he went quickly to Śakra's dwelling, which was inhabited by the assembly of immortals. Having given heaven to Indra, and having made the gods the enjoyers of the sacrifice, Viṣṇu, lord of the universe, Maheśvara, disappeared while the earthly kings watched. Having seized the kingdom of Bali, it was entrusted to Manu's son, and the Daityas were sent to rule other islands by his own order. Those who had their home in Pātāla settled there. And the supreme joy of the gods was born in Bali's overthrow. Vāmana made up his mind to dwell in his own field, in his own town.

Sārasvata spoke:

O Chief of Men, this appearance of Vāmana that was told is holy and virtuous and destroys evil. When it is remembered, heard, and celebrated, may any sin be destroyed, and merit approach.

Skanda Purāṇa VII.4.19.10–14

Prahlāda spoke:

Listen, together with Durvāsas, O Best of Brahmins, to that Trivikrama form which was born on earth.

Formerly, at the end of the Kṛta yuga, Purāṅdara, having been conquered by Bali, was made to fall from his dwelling. For that reason, Madhusūdana was born from Kaśyapa as Vāmana and then became Trivikrama. And Hari, slayer of Madhu, striding over the worlds that were measured with three steps, that Blessed One made Bali the inhabitant of Pātāla. But through the Daitya's devotion to none other but Kṛṣṇa, he was pleased, and Hari himself dwelt there, bought by the devotion; and to show favor, the Blessed One became the doorkeeper.

Vāyu Purāṇa 98.59–88

The bard spoke:

Having heard from Śukra that the victory would definitely be theirs and that it would be purposeful, the Dānavas were hoping for that victory spoken of by the priest. Those Dānavas, armed with weapons and full of pride, challenged the gods. Having seen the demons approach in battle, the gods, with complete armament, fought them. That god and demon battle went on for a hundred years, and the demons conquered the gods. Broken, the gods took counsel.

The gods said:

We do not know the strength of Saṇḍa and Marka. Therefore, having performed a sacrifice with the demons, we should do what is beneficial to ourselves. Having conquered those two through that knowledge, we will conquer the demons.

Then the gods summoned Saṇḍa and Marka. "O Brahmins, abandon the demons; we will invite you to the sacrifice and, having subdued the Dānavas, we will seize the booty." So, Saṇḍa and Marka abandoned the demons, the gods attained victory, and the Dānavas perished. The gods, having overthrown the demons, captured Saṇḍa and Marka. Overcome by the curse of the priest and without any support, being bound by the gods, those two settled down in Rasātala. Thus the Dānavas were made helpless by Śakra and also by Bhṛgu's special curse.

Lord Viṣṇu was born again and again to establish the dharma and destroy adharma when the sacrifice was lax. The demons who did not obey the orders of Prahlāda were all cursed by Brahmā to be perishable at the hands of human beings.

From that dharma, Nārāyaṇa was born in the Cākṣusa Manvantara, and he began the sacrifice in the sanctuary in the Vaivasvata Manvantara. Then, in the appearance of another [Manvantara], Brahmā was the priest. But in the fourth yuga, the demons were afflicted, and he was born on earth as the destroyer of Hiraṇyakaśipu; he became the terrible Narasiṁha, messenger of the gods.

These three worlds belonged to Bali in the seventh Treta Yuga. When the triple world was possessed by the Daityas, Vāmana was born as the third incarnation. Having contracted himself in his body, causing joy to the family of Aditi, born at an auspicious time, he said to Bali, son of Virocana, who was sacrificing, "You are the king of the triple world; everything resides within you. O King, please give me three steps." "I will grant this," king Bali Vairocana said to him. And having recognized the dwarf, he himself rejoiced.

With three steps, Vāmana, the Lord, tread upon heaven, sky, and earth and, Best of brahmins, the lord seized this whole world. He who is the soul of all beings surpassed the sun with his own tejas. The glorious one illumined all the directions and regions of the sky. He, the long-armed one, looked splendid, illuminating all the worlds. Janārdana, having taken the prosperity of the demons and the three worlds, led those demons together with their sons and grandsons to Pātāla. Wicked Namuci, Śambara, and Prahlāda, beaten and driven away by Viṣṇu, scattered in all directions. Mādhava, soul of all beings, showed a miracle composed of all great creatures and all of time to the brahmins. One could see the whole world in his body; there was not even a little in the worlds that was not pervaded by the magnanimous one. Having seen that form of Upendra, gods, demons, and men, all beguiled by Viṣṇu's majesty, were stupefied.

Bali, bound by great fetters, was made to settle in Pātāla with his band of kinsfolk, all of the family of Virocana. Then, having given the imperishable sovereignty to magnanimous Indra, long-armed Janārdana became manifest among men.

Viṣṇudharmottara Purāṇa I.21

Vajra spoke:

Why in the world is Gaṅgā called *Viṣṇupadī* by the sages? Tell me that truly, O Increaser of the family of Bhṛgu.

Mārkaṇḍeya spoke:

Long ago, at the end of the Svayambhū, four troops of gods were called victorious, unconquerable, and resplendent. The chief of gods was Indra, honored in the world. The terrible Asuras were their distant brothers, and one named Bāṣkali became their king. With valor, he seized Śakra's kingdom by force. The chief of gods, his kingdom stolen, took refuge in Brahmā; and Brahmā, having taken Śakra along, sought refuge in Hari. Then Brahmā, with four beautiful faces, told the god of gods, the archer, about Bāṣkali's total victory.

The Blessed One spoke:

O Brahmā, I will recover Śatakratu's kingdom. O Soul of Dharma, retire to heaven among the gods quickly. In a dwarfish form I will go to the king Bāṣkali. Having seen me, he will be amazed, and having come, Indra must solicit him. "O Bāṣkali, having attacked, my three worlds have been seized by you. On my behalf, quickly give three steps for a fire sanctuary to the dwarf, whose legs are very short." Thus spoken to by Śakra, he will give the steps.

Mārkaṇḍeya spoke:

Spoken to by the god, Brahmā went to his own dwelling. And the god, having become a dwarf, went to Bāṣkali. Having seen Vāmana, Bāṣkali, his eyes wide open in amazement, was surrounded by many Asuras, according to his wish. At that time, Śakra arrived at his place. Bāṣkali, having honored Śakra with water for washing his feet, for sipping, and so on, spoke to him, delighted: "For what purpose have you come? I think the reason for your arrival must be a great surprise!"

Śakra spoke:

The triple world was snatched away from me through valor, O Bāṣkali. On my behalf, give three steps for a fire sanctuary to the dwarf, whose limbs are very short, O Prince. I do not wish to dwell on a piece of alien land.

Bāṣkali spoke:

King of Gods, the three steps are given happily to the dwarf. Sit here, happy and contented, Chief of Gods.

Mārkaṇḍeya spoke:

Thus spoken to by Bāṣkali, abandoning the dwarfish form, Hari strode over the worlds with a desire for the welfare of the gods. Then, having reached the Brahmaloka, the god's left foot descended into the Dānava's abode. Then the world master took his first step to the sun, the second to the pole star, and with the third that was incomplete, O Yādava, the god Keśava struck the Brahmāṇḍa. The Brahmāṇḍa, struck by him, was pierced, O Lord, and was covered with water from the outside, and filled with the water that kills sins. And through the hole made by his big toe, pure water issued forth into the egg. Having reached the gods, the river Viṣṇupadī pervaded the entire Brahmāṇḍa with prosperity and the desire to show all kindnesses, Illustrious One. All the worlds were stridden over by the dwarf, Sinless One, and then were abandoned by the Asuras, the true kinsmen of the gods. When Pātāla was not stridden over by Hari, then it was occupied by the terrible Asuras, O Son of Yadu.

Having seized the triple world, the god disappeared, and Bāṣkali resided happily in his Pātāla abode. Then wise Śakra governed the world.

This manifestation of the world guru is called *Trivikrama* and joined by the origin of Gaṅgā, which destroys all sins. This was accomplished by the same god of gods in the Vaivasvata; again were the three worlds stridden over by the feet of that saint, O Prince. For this reason, Gaṅgā is called *Viṣṇupadī,* who reached this universe and pervaded the triple world, moving and still. He who hears this origin of Gaṅgā told by me is freed from all evil, and that man who is distinguished in sin, taking a virtuous vow, O Hero, goes to the third heaven.

Viṣṇudharmottara Purāṇa I.55

Śaṅkara spoke:

When the Dānava Hiraṇyakaśipu, thorn of the gods, was slain, the surviving Daityas sought refuge in Pātāla. Among the Dānavas dwelling in Pātāla, the illustrious grandson of Prahlāda, Bali, son of Virocana, the soul of Dharma, having gained merit through terrible austerities, obtained a boon from the Grandfather; invincibility, unconquerability in battles between the gods and demons. Having realized that Bali had obtained the boon, the sons of Diti became happy again, and made Bali king of Daityas, with Prahlāda's assent. Having acquired the Daitya kingdom with four branches of the army, and having conquered the chief of gods, Śakra, he seized Amarāvati.

Removed from office, Mahendra went to Kaśyapa for shelter. Then, together with Kásyapa, he went to Brahmā for refuge. Spoken to by Brahmā, he went to the god Hari for refuge, whose immortal voice sounded like the rumbling of a cloud, and who bears the conch, discus, and club. The god, having presented Indra with the gift of safety, spoke at the time with a voice like the rumbling of a cloud.

The Blessed Lord spoke:

Go, Śakra, I shall be your protector, O Slayer of Bala. Having become the bearer of a godly form, I shall deceive Bali.

Śaṅkara spoke:

Thus spoken to, Śakra went to Kaśyapa's hermitage. He addressed the womb of Aditi with a portion, and he robbed the tejas from the Dānavas while in the womb. In time, Aditi gave birth to the figure of a dwarf at whose birth the host of gods became utterly delighted, as did the illustrious ṛṣis who see clearly the past, present, and future.

At that time, Bali, the venerable lord of Daityas, prepared for the horse sacrifice, staying on the edge of town. Bṛhaspati, having grasped the dwarf by the shoulder, led him to his sacrifice, Lion among Bhṛgus, with his māyā. Having arrived at the sacrificial enclosure, the dwarf praised himself, the sacrifice, like the fire covered with ashes. And Bali, most excellent of supporters of the Dharma, ushered him in, and he saw the illustrious and charming dwarf who was endowed with short and corpulent limbs, and was splendid with the black antelope skin, twisted locks of hair, staff, and water jar. As a tiger reclines in his own body, which will soon be jumping, so he lurked in his own body, who would soon be crossing the whole earth.

"At this time, you are ready for the horse sacrifice. Because of that, King, I ask; give me three steps of land." Thus spoken to by the god, Bali, chief of the Daitya host, offered him the water saying, "Wash," and he spoke: "And whatever else is your desire, accept that, Best of brahmins." Then Hari received the water like a whirlwind. Being watched by the best of Daityas with upturned faces, he appeared like a cloud, and Hari strode over the worlds. The Dānavas, armed with weapons, attacked quickly, bearing various heads: There were those having the head of Garuḍa, those with bird heads, and those with peacock heads, terrible Danavas with sea-monster heads and with jackal heads, mole- and frog-headed ones, and horrible wolf-headed ones, cat- and rabbit-headed ones, swan- and crow-headed ones, iguana and porcupine heads, and ram- and buffalo-headed ones, those with the heads of lions, tigers, and jackals, of leopards, monkeys, and birds, of elephants, horses, cows, donkeys, and camels, and of snakes.

Having obtained the water that was offered, then Hari grew larger, that cloudlike one being watched by the host of gods, with upturned faces.

While Hari strode over the worlds, the Dānavas watched, bearing weapons, with faces of fish and tortoises and frogs, with massive teeth, distorted eyes, large upper lips and stomachs, yellow eyes that were distorted, and bearing various and manifold heads, with thick, broad noses that were flattened, and great jaws and skulls, covered with excellent Chinese cloth; and some wearing the black antelope skin, others adorned by snakes and some decorated by a crown, some with earrings, some with bracelets, and some with helmets on their heads, some bearing bow and arrow, and others holding lances, some holding sword and shield and others bearing iron bars, some holding missile and discus and some bearing club and mace, some having stones and fetters, and some with short javelins, some holding spikes and wooden mortars, others bearing hatchets, and some carrying great trees, and warriors with great rocks.

While he was striding, Hṛṣikeśa grew on all sides. The Universal Soul destroyed the Daityas and Dānavas with those heads, like lotuses in a pool. Having churned all those Daityas like great elephants with the soles of his hands and feet, having created this terrible form, he seized the earth quickly. While he was striding on the earth, the sun and moon were between his breasts. While he was striding higher, they were situated at his navel; and while he was striding, they were situated at his knees. And then, while he was striding, they were situated at the feet of the god. Having conquered the whole earth and having killed the Asura chiefs, Viṣṇu, best of the mighty, gave the earth to Śakra. Then, having returned to his own form, he spoke to the Dānava chief.

"O Mighty Asura, at your sacrificial enclosure in Śāligrāma, the earth was measured by me, who had set foot on it. My first step reached to the top of Naurbandha, and the second to the peak of Meru, and the third was nowhere. O Daitya Chief, grant to me that which was accepted and to be obtained by me."

Bali spoke:

As long as the world is created by you, your three steps cannot be complete, O God of Gods. That which was not created by you, O God, that is mine, O Maheśvara. And, that does not exist for anyone else as well.

The Blessed One spoke:

O Chief of Dānavas, the steps are not completed by me according to the agreement. Dwell in a hell called *Pātāla,* well restrained. A town was created there by me, with a pure mind. Dwell there comfortably together with virtuous kinsmen. There you shall enjoy pleasures that are better than Indra's. You shall obtain pleasures that are free from the rules of the world, and endowed with freedom of will, you shall wander through the worlds. In two Manvantaras, you shall become Mahendra, and through my own tejas, you shall be endowed with Śakra-hood. Then, I shall slay all your enemies' troops. Agreeable and zealously performing sacrifices, you are devoted to sacred knowledge and affording shelter, an ascetic and a zealous donor, fully conversant with Veda and Vedāṅga. Because of that, you, deceived by me, are reconciled for the purpose of increasing your honor. Residing in Pātāla, you shall enjoy the pleasures of the king of gods. And there shall I make my gathering place, O

Demon Chief, and you shall sport with me, envied by the gods. And then, having become Śakra in the future Savarṇika, free from all limitations, you shall sport with me.

Śaṅkara spoke:

Having thus spoken, he who sounds like a rain cloud, whose clothes are bright and shining gold, that best of gods disappeared; and Sakra obtained the entire triple world.

Bibliography

Indian Texts and Translations

ṚgVeda-Saṁhita, ed. Lakṣman Sarup, 4 vols. Lahore: Motilal Banarsidass, 1939.

The Hymns of the ṚgVeda, trans. Ralph T. H. Griffith. Delhi: Motilal Banarsidass, 1973.

The Texts of the White Yajur Veda, trans. Ralph T. H. Griffith. Benares: E. J. Lazarus and Co., 1899.

The Veda of the Black Yajus School, entitled Taittirīya Saṅhita, trans. Arthur Berridale Keith, 2 vols. Delhi: Motilal Banarsidass, 1967; Originally published 1914.

RigVeda Brāhmaṇas: The Aitareya and Kauśītaki Brāhmaṇas of the RigVeda, trans. Arthur Berridale Keith. Delhi: Motilal Banarsidass, 1971; originally published 1920.

Śatapatha Brāhmaṇa, trans. Julius Eggeling. SBE, vols. 12, 26, 41, 43, 44. Delhi: Motilal Banarsidass, 1966; originally published 1882–1990.

The Vaiṣṇava Upaniṣads, ed. A. M. Sastri. Madras: Adyar Library, 1923.

The Vaiṣṇavopaniṣads, trans. T. R. Srinivasa Ayyangar. Madras: The Adyar Library, 1945.

The Mahābhārata, for the First Time Critically Edited, General eds. Vishnu S. Sukthankar and S. K. Balvalkar. Poona: Bhandarkar Oriental Research Institute, 1933–1966.

The Mahābhārata of Krishna Dwaipāyana Vyāsa, trans. Kisari Mohan Ganguli, publisher Pratap Chandra Roy, 12 vols. Calcutta: Bharata Press, 1889–1894.

The Mahābhārata, trans. J. A. B. van Buitenen, 2 vols. Chicago: University of Chicago Press, 1973.

The Bhagavad Gītā, trans. R. C. Zaehner. London: Oxford University Press, 1969.

Śri Harivaṁśapurāṇa, ed. Śrīrāma Sarma. Bareli: Saṁskṛti Saṁsthana, 1968.

Śriharivaṁśapurāna Bhāsha Ṭikā, ed. Pāṇḍeya Rāmateja Śāstrī. Kaśi: Paṅḍitapustakālaya, 1964.

Harivamsha, ed. Datta N. Bose, 16 parts. Bengal: Datta Bose and Co., 1935.

Harivansa ou Histoire de la famille de Hari, trans. M. A. Langlois, 2 vols. Paris: Oriental Translation Fund of Great Britain and Ireland, 1834.
The Vālmīki-Rāmāyaṇa, Critically Edited for the First Time, ed. P. L. Vaidya.
The Rāmāyaṇa, trans. Manmatha Nath Dutt. Calcutta: Girish Chandra Chakravarti, 1891–1894.
Agnipurāṇa, ed. Śrīrāma Sarma. Bareli: Saṁskṛti Saṁsthana, 1968.
Agni Purāṇam, trans. Manmatha Nath Dutt, 2 vols. Chowkhamba Sanskrit Studies vol. 54. Varanasi: Chowkhamba Sanskrit Series Office, 1967.
Śrīmadbhagavatamahāpurāṇam. Gorakhpur: Gita Press, 1964.
The Śrīmad-Bhāgavatam of Krishna-Dwaipayana Vyāsa, trans. J. M. Sanyal, 5 vols. Calcutta: Oriental Publishing Company, 1964.
Bhaviṣya Purāṇa. Bombay: Venkateśvara Steam Press, 1959.
Brahmā Purāṇa. Calcutta, 1954.
Brahmāṇda Purāṇa. Chicago: University of Chicago Microfilm Negative No. 3517.
Brahmā-Vaivarta Purāṇa, trans. Rajendra Nath Sen. The Sacred Books of the Hindus vol. 24, parts 1 and 2. Allahabad: Panini Office, Bhuvaneshwari Ashram, 1920.
Garuḍa-purāṇa, ed. Śrīrāma Sarma. Bareli: Saṁskṛti Saṁsthana, 1968.
The Garuḍa Purāṇam, trans. Manmatha Nath Dutt. Chowkhamba Sanskrit Studies vol. 67. Varanasi: Chowkhamba Sanskrit Series Office, 1968; originally published 1908.
The Kūrma Purāṇa with English Translation, ed. and trans. Anand Swarup Gupta. Varanasi: All-India Kashiraj Trust, 1972.
Liṅga-purāṇa, ed. Śrīrāma Sarma, 2 vols. Bareli: Saṁskṛti Saṁsthana, 1969.
The Liṅga Purāṇa, ed. J. L. Shastri. Ancient Indian Tradition and Mythology vol. 5, parts 1 and 2. Delhi: Motilal Banarsidass, 1973.
Mārkaṇḍeya Purāṇa, trans. F. Eden Pargiter. Delhi: Indological Book House, 1969; originally published 1904.
Mārkaṇḍeya Purāṇa, ed. Śrīrāma Sarma, 2 vols. Bareli: Saṁskṛti Saṁsthana, 1967.
Matsyapurāṇa, ed. Śrirāma Sarma, 2 vols. Bareli: Saṁskṛti Saṁsthana, 1970.
The Matsya Purāṇam, ed. Jamna Das Akhtar. The Sacred Books of the Aryans vol. 1. Delhi: Oriental Publishers, 1972.
Nāradapurāṇa, ed. Śrīrāma Sarma. Bareli: Saṁskṛti Saṁsthana, 1971.
Padma Purāṇa. Anandāśrama Sanskrit Series vol. 131. Poona, 1895.
The Śiva Purāṇa, ed. J. L. Shastri. Ancient Indian Tradition and Mythology vols. 1–4. Delhi: Motilal Banarsidass, 1969.
Skanda-purāṇam, 5 vols. Gurumandal Series no. 20. Calcutta, 1960.
The Vāmana Purāṇa with English Translation, ed. and trans. Anand Swarup Gupta. Varanasi: All-India Kashiraj Trust, 1968.
Varāhapurāṇa, ed. Śrīrāma Sarma. Bareli: Saṁskṛti Saṁsthana, 1973.
Vāyu Purāṇa. Anandāśrama Sanskrit Series 49. Poona, 1860.
The Vishnu Purāṇa: A System of Hindu Mythology and Tradition, trans. Horace Hayman Wilson. Calcutta: Punthi Pustak, 1961; Originally published 1840.
Viṣṇudharmottara Purāṇa. Bombay: Venkateśvara Steam Press (n.d.).

Other Works Consulted

Agrawala, V. S. "Purāṇa-Vidya." *Purāṇa* 1, no. 1 (1959): 89–100.

Ali, S. M. *The Geography of the Purāṇas.* New Delhi: People's Publishing House, 1966.

Badshah, B. R. *Aryan Theory of Divine Incarnations.* Lisbon: Geographical Society of Lisbon, 1892.

Bedekar, V. M. "The Legend of the Churning of the Ocean in the Epics and Purāṇas: A Comparative Study." *Purāṇa* 9, no. 1 (1967): 7–61.

Bhandarkar, R. G. *Vaiṣṇavism Śaivism and Minor Religious Systems.* Varanasi: Indological Book House, 1965.

Bhattacharji, Sukumari. *The Indian Theogony.* Cambridge: Cambridge University Press, 1970.

Biardeau, Madeleine. "Conference de Mlle. Madeleine Biardeau." *Annuaire EPHE* 72 (1964–65): 73–75.

———. "Conference de Mlle. Madeleine Biardeau." *Annuaire EPHE* 73 (1965–66): 71–75.

———. "Conference de Mlle. Madeleine Biardeau." *Annuaire EPHE* 74 (1966–67): 81–83.

———. "Conference de Mlle. Madeleine Biardeau." *Annuaire EPHE* 75 (1967–68): 72–78.

———. "Études de mythologie hindoue: cosmogonies purāṇiques." I: *BEFEO* 54 (1968): 19–45; II: *BEFEO* 55 (1969): 59–96; III: *BEFEO* 58 (1971): 17–89.

———. "Études de mythologie hindoue: bhakti et avatāra." *BEFEO* 63 (1976): 111–263.

———. "Narasiṁha, mythe et culte." In *Puruṣārtha: Récherches de Sciences sociales sur d'Asie du Sud.* Paris: Centre d'Études de l'Inde et de l'Asie du Sud, 1975.

———. "Le Sacrifice dans l'Hindouisme." In *Le Sacrifice dans l'Inde ancienne,* ed. Madeleine Biardeau and Charles Malamoud. Bibliothèque de l'École des Hautes Études, Sciences Religieuses vol. 79. Paris: Presses Universitaires de France, 1976.

Bloomfield, Maurice. "Contributions to the Interpretation of the Veda." *JAOS* 15, no. 2 (1891): 143–188.

Brown, W. Norman. "The Creation Myth in the Rig Veda." *JAOS* 62, no. 2 (1942): 85–98.

———. "The Name of the Goddess Mīnākṣī 'Fish Eye.' " *JAOS* 67 (1947): 209–214.

Chemburkar, J. "Historical and Religious Background of the Concept of Four Yugas in the Mahābhārata and the Bhāgavata Purāṇa." *Purāṇa* 16, no. 1 (1974): 67–76.

Church, Cornelia Dimmitt. "The Yuga Story: A Myth of the Four Ages of the World as Found in the Purāṇas." Dissertation, Syracuse University, 1970.

Courtright, Paul. *Gaṇeśa.* New York: Oxford University Press, 1985.

Dandekar, R. N. "Viṣṇu in the Veda." *A Volume of Studies in Indology*, pp. 95–111. Poona: Oriental Book Agency, 1941.

______. *Universe in Hindu Thought*. Bangalore: Bangalore University, 1972.

Danielou, Alain. *Hindu Polytheism*. Bollingen Series 73. New York: Pantheon Books, 1964.

Das, Bhagavan. *Krishna: A Study in the Theory of Avatāras*. Bombay: Bharatiya Vidya Bhavan, 1962.

Devasthali, G. V. *Religion and Mythology of the Brāhmaṇas*. Bhav Vishnu Ashtekar Vedic Research Series Vol. 1. Poona: University of Poona, 1965.

Dikshitar, V. R. Ramachandra. "Purāṇas—A Study." *Indian Historical Quarterly* 8 (1932).

Dimmitt, Cornelia. "Chapter One, Introduction." *Classical Hindu Mythology*, ed. Cornelia Dimmitt and J. A. B. van Buitenen. Philadelphia: Temple University Press, 1978.

Douglas, Mary. "The Meaning of Myth with Special Reference to 'La Geste d'Asdiwal.'" *The Structural Study of Myth and Totemism*, ed. Edmund Leach, pp. 49–70. A.S.A. Monographs 5. England: Tavistock Publications, 1957.

Dumézil, Georges. *The Destiny of the Warrior*, trans. Alf Hiltebeitel. Chicago: University of Chicago Press, 1969.

Eliade, Mircea. "Le temps et l'Éternite dans la Pensée indienne." *Eranos-Tagung: Mensch und Zeit* (Bd. 20): 219–252.

______. *Myth and Reality*. New York: Harper Torchbooks, 1953.

______. *Cosmos and History*. New York: Harper Torchbooks, 1959.

Eschmann, Anncharlott, Herman Kulke, and Gaya Charan Tripathi, eds. *The Cult of Jagnnath and the Regional Tradition of Orissa*. New Delhi: Manohar Publications, 1986.

Goldman, Robert. *Gods, Priests, and Warriors*. New York: Columbia University Press, 1977.

Gombrich, Richard F. "Ancient Indian Cosmology." *Ancient Cosmologies*, ed. Carmen Blacker and Michael Loewe, pp. 110–142. London: Allen & Unwin Ltd., 1975.

Gonda, Jan. *Loka: World and Heaven in the Veda*. Amsterdam; N. V. Nöord-Hollandsche Uitgevers Maatschappij, 1966.

______. "A Note on Indra in Purāṇic Literature." *Purāṇa* 9, no. 2 (1967): 222–261.

______. *Aspects of Early Viṣṇuism*. Delhi: Motilal Banarsidass, 1969.

______. *Viṣṇuism and Śivaism*. London: The Athlone Press, 1970.

Grainger, Oswald Joseph. "The Rise of the Incarnation Idea in Indian Religion." Dissertation, University of Chicago, 1927.

Gupta, Anand Swarup. "Purāṇic Theory of the Yugas and Kalpas—A Study." *Purāṇa* 11, no. 2 (1969): 304–321.

Gupta, Shakti M. *Vishnu and His Incarnations*. Bombay: Somaiya Publications Pvt. Ltd., 1974.

Hacker, Paul. *Prahlāda: Werden und Wandlungen einer Idealgestalt*. Wiesbaden: Akademie der Wissenschaften und der Literatur No. 9, 1959.

______. "Zur Entwicklung der Avatāralehre." *Weiner Zeitschrift für die Kunde Sud-und Ostasiens* 4 (1960): 47–70.

Hazra, R. C. *Studies in the Purāṇic Records on Hindu Rites and Customs*. Delhi: Motilal Banarsidass, 1940.

Herbert, Jean. *Nārada: précédé d'une étude sur Les Avatars de Vishnou*. Lyon: Author, 1949.

Hiltebeitel, Alf. "The Mahābhārata and Hindu Eschatology." *HRJ* 12, no. 2 (1972).

______. "Gods, Heroes, and Kṛṣṇa: A Study of Indian and Indo-European Symbolisms." Dissertation, University of Chicago, 1973.

______. *The Ritual of Battle*. Ithaca, N.Y.: Cornell University Press, 1976.

______. "The Indus Valley 'Proto-Śiva' Reexamined through Reflections on the Goddess, the Buffalo, and the Symbolism of Vāhanas." *Anthropos* 73(1978): 767–797.

Hospital, Clifford. *The Righteous Demon: A Study of Bali*. Vancouver: University of British Columbia Press, 1984.

Huntington, Ronald M. "A Study of Purāṇic Myth from the Viewpoint of Depth Psychology." Dissertation, University of Southern California, 1960.

______. "Avatāras and Yugas." *Purāṇa* 6 (1964): 8–39.

Jacobi, Hermann. "Ages of the World (Indian)." *ERE* 1: 207.

______. "Incarnation (Indian)." *ERE* 7: 193.

James, E. O. *Creation and Cosmology*. Leiden: E. J. Brill, 1969.

Janaki, K. S. S. "Paraśurāma." *Purāṇa* 8, no. 1 (1966): 52–82.

Karmarkar, A. P. "The Matsyāvatāra of Viṣṇu." *A Volume of Studies in Indology*, pp. 253–257. Poona: Oriental Book Agency, 1941.

Karmarkar, R. D. "The Measure of the Brahmāṇaṇḍa and the Location of the Devaloka." *ABORI* 28 (1948): 281–288.

Katre, S. D. "Avatāras of God." *Allahabad University Studies* 10 (1934): 37–130.

Keith, Arthur Berridale. "The Game of Dice." *JRAS* 1908, pp. 823–828.

Khan, Md. Abdul Waheed. *An Early Sculpture of Narasiṁha*. Hyberabad: Government of Andhra Pradesh, 1964.

Kirfel, Willibald. *Das Purāṇa Pañcalakṣaṇa*. Bonn: Kurt Schroeder, 1927.

______. *Die Kosmographie der Inder*. Hildeshelm: Georg Olms Verlagsbuchandlung, 1967.

Krishnadasa, Rai. "Purāṇic Geography: Chatur-dvīpa and Sapta-dvīpa." *PurānĽa* 1, no. 2 (1960): 202–205.

Kuiper, F. B. J. "The Three Strides of Vịsṇu." *Indological Studies in Honor of W. Norman Brown*, pp. 137–151. New Haven, Conn.: American Oriental Society, 1962.

Levi-Strauss, Claude. *The Raw and the Cooked*. New York: Harper Torchbooks, 1970.

Long, J. Bruce. "Life Out of Death: A Structural Analysis of the Myth of the 'Churning of the Ocean of Milk.'" In *Hinduism: New Essays in the History of Religions*, ed. Bardwell L. Smith, pp. 171–207. Leiden: E. J. Brill, 1976.

Macdonell, A. A. "Mythological Studies in the RigVeda. II: The Mythological Basis in the RigVeda of the Dwarf and Boar Incarnations of Viṣṇu." *JRAS* 1895: 165–190.

______. *Vedic Mythology.* Delhi: Motilal Banarsidass, 1974; originally published 1898.

Machek, V. "Origin of the God Viṣṇu." *Archiv́ Orientalní* 28 (1960).

Mankad, D. R. *Purāṇic Chronology.* Anand: Gaṅgājāḷa Prakashan, 1952.

______. "The Yugas." *Poona Orientalist* 6 (1941).

______. "The Manvantara." *IHQ* 18, no. 3 (1942).

______. "Manvantara-Caturyuga Method." *ABORI* 23 (1942): 271–290.

______. "Studies in Purāṇic History, Genealogies, and Chronology in Modern Times." *Purāṇa* 4, no. 1 (1962): 3–22.

Muir, John. *Sanskrit Texts of India,* vol. 4. London: Trubner and Co., 1863.

Narahari, H. G. "The Vedic Doctrine of the Worlds Above." *ABORI* 23 (1942): 302–313.

O'Flaherty, Wendy Doniger. "The Submarine Mare in the Mythology of Śiva," *JRAS* 1971, no. 1: 9–27.

______. *Asceticism and Eroticism in the Mythology of Śiva.* London: Oxford University Press, 1973.

______. *Hindu Myths.* Hammondsworth, England: Penguin Books, 1975.

______. *The Origins of Evil in Hindu Mythology.* Berkeley: University of California Press, 1976.

______. "Inside and Outside the Mouth of God: The Boundary between Myth and Reality." *Daedalus,* 109, no. 2 (1980): 93–125.

______. *Tales of Sex and Violence.* Chicago: University of Chicago Press, 1985.

Oldenberg, Hermann. *La Religion du Veda,* trans. Victor Henry. Paris: Felix Alcan, 1903.

Otto, Rudolph. *The Original Gītā,* trans. J. E. Turner. London: Allen & Unwin, 1939.

Pargiter, F. E. *Ancient Indian Historical Tradition.* Delhi: Motilal Banarsidass, 1962.

Parrinder, E. G. *Avatar and Incarnation.* London: Faber & Faber, 1970.

Pocock, David. "The Anthropology of Time-Reckoning." In *Myth and Cosmos,* ed. John Middleton, pp. 303–314 Garden City, N.Y.: Natural History Press, 1967.

Propp, Vladimir. *The Morphology of the Folktale.* Austin: University of Texas Press, 1968.

Pusalker, A. D. *Studies in the Epics and Purāṇas of India.* Bombay: Bharatiya Vidya Bhavan, 1963.

Rai, Ganga Sagar. "Vāmana Legend—In the Vedas, Epics and Purāṇas." *Purāṇa* 12, no. 1 (1970): 102–140.

______. "Propriety of Using Umbrella and Shoes by Vāmana as Brahmacārin." *Purāṇa* 12, no. 2 (1972): 141–146.

Riviere, J. Roger. "New Positions of Western Orientalism in Account with the Purāṇas." *Purāṇa* 7, no. 2 (1965): 300–305.

Sharma, B. N. "Vāmana and Viṣṇu." *Purāṇa* 8, no. 2 (1966): 246–258.

______. "Vāmana in Literature and Art." *Purāṇa* 12, no. 1 (1970): 54–64.

Sorensen, Soren. *An Index to the Names in the Mahābhārata*. Delhi: Motilal Banarsidass, 1963; originally published 1904.
Stietencron, Heinrich von. *Gaṅgā und Yamunā*. Wiesbaden: Otto Harrassowitz, 1972.
Swain, A. C. *A Study of the Man-Lion Myth in the Epics and Purāṇa-Texts*. Publications of the Centre of Advanced Study in Sanskrit, class A, no. 3. Poona: University of Poona, 1970.
Tarabout, Giles. "Sacrifier et Donner à Voir en pays Malabar." *Publications de l'École Française d'Extrême-Orient 147* (1986).
Thompson, Stith. "Motif." *ESS* 1: 711.
Tripathi, Gaya Charan. *Die Ursprung und Entwicklung der Vāmanalegende in der Indische-literatur*. Wiesbaden: Otto Harrassowitz, 1968.
Turner, Victor. *The Forest of Symbols*. Ithaca, N.Y.: Cornell University Press, 1967.
______. *The Ritual Process*. England: Routledge & Kegan Paul, 1969.
______. "Liminal to Liminoid in Play, Flow, and Ritual: An Essay in Comparative Symbology." *Rice University Studies* 60, no. 3 (n.d.).
Underhill, M. M. *The Hindu Religious Year*. Calcutta: Association Press, 1921.
Vaidya, M. V. "The Palace of Hiraṇyakaśipu." *ABORI* 23 (1942): 609–620.
de Vries, Jan. "Purāṇa Studies." In *Oriental Studies in Honour of Cursetji Erachji Pavryl*, ed. J. D. C. Pavry. London: Oxford University Press, 1933.
Wallis, H. W. *The Cosmology of the Rigveda*. London: Williams and Norgate, 1887.
Warren, William Fairfield. *The Earliest Cosmologies*. New York: Eaton & Mains, 1909.
Zimmer, Heinrich R. "The Hindu View of World History according to the Purāṇas." *Review of Religion* 6, no. 3 (1942): 249–269.

Index